Muslims

Their Religious Beliefs and Practices

Fourth edition

Andrew Rippin

Routledge
Taylor & Francis Group
LONDON AND NEW YORK

First published 1990
by Routledge

This edition published 2012
by Routledge
2 Park Square, Milton Park, Abingdon, Oxon OX14 4RN

Simultaneously published in the USA and Canada
by Routledge
711 Third Avenue, New York, NY 10017

Routledge is an imprint of the Taylor & Francis Group, an informa business

British Library Cataloguing in Publication Data
A catalogue record for this book is available from the British Library

Library of Congress Cataloging in Publication Data
Rippin, Andrew, 1950-
Muslims : their religious beliefs and practices / By Andrew Rippin.—4th ed.
p. cm.—(The library of religious beliefs and practices)
Includes bibliographical references and index.
1. Islam. 2. Muslims. 3. Islam—Doctrines. 4. Islam—Customs and practices. I. Title.
BP161.2.R53 2011
297—dc22
2011007688

ISBN: 978-0-415-48939-3 (hbk)
ISBN: 978-0-415-48940-9 (pbk)
ISBN: 978-0-203-80521-3 (ebk)

Typeset in Adobe Jenson Pro
by RefineCatch Limited, Bungay, Suffolk

MIX
Paper from responsible sources
FSC
www.fsc.org
FSC® C004839

Printed and bound in Great Britain by
CPI Antony Rowe, Chippenham, Wiltshire

Contents

List of Illustrations

All images are reproduced with permission.

Preface to the fourth edition

This work was originally published in two volumes, one on the "formative period" (1990) and the other on the "contemporary period" (1993). Revising this book for a fourth edition in its current one-volume format is certainly a privilege, and I take it as a great complement that the work continues to enjoy some success as a textbook and with the general reader interested in the Islamic world. The fact that the work needs updating once again emphasizes the basic theme of the book itself: Islam, like every successful social system, is a dynamic and changing entity, moving with the times and yet strongly influenced by its historical path to the present. The basic elements of the book remain unchanged in this updated version; the chapters are structured as independently as possible to allow for some flexibility in the order in which they are read and for the omission of chapters that are not of immediate relevance, especially in a classroom setting. However, while undertaking the necessary revisions, I have also been able to take advantage of the flexibility provided through creating an online presence for this book. There is now an accompanying Routledge website which will be updated regularly so that references to ongoing scholarship and new resources can be incorporated whenever it seems desirable and as readers make suggestions. One of the implications of the development of the website is that the endnotes contained in the previous editions of the book are rendered redundant; they have thus been removed from the printed text. Those who wish to learn more about a certain topic may now go to the website, which is structured to provide information for each of the sub-headings in every chapter. The website also features references to online resources and films, has ideas for research projects and essays, and provides an audio glossary in order to facilitate pronunciation of the Arabic terms found in the book. The book itself has also been restructured slightly. The former last two chapters on feminism and Islam in the twenty-first century have been consolidated into one and a new last chapter has been added that deals with perceptions of Muslims in the world at large, raising especially the topic of Islamophobia as it impacts Muslims today. This new chapter focuses more on the world in which Muslims live than it does on Muslim beliefs and practices; however, the topics that are raised there are ones that I believe no instructor in a course on Islam today can avoid and no reader interested in Muslims and Islam can possibly not want to consider. Additionally, a short "box text" has been added to each chapter to provide some supplementary information relevant to the general topic of the chapter; I hope these will inspire curiosity and serve to stimulate further research for essay writing and research projects.

Introduction

It has been almost twenty-five years since I started work on the initial edition of this book. During that interval, scholarly writing in the field of Islamic studies has proceeded at a rapid pace. In every aspect of the field—original research, new syntheses of knowledge, and general introductions to Islam—there has been a proliferation of books and articles. This is hardly surprising: the perception that we need to know more about Islam is widespread. The common statement that "Islam is misunderstood" has perhaps become more valid than ever in the wake of the demolition of the World Trade Center towers in New York on September 11, 2001, and the string of other highly destructive events that has followed (and indeed preceded) that immensely symbolic act. The impact of those events upon Muslims is especially worthy of note in a number of senses. First, Muslims have clearly felt the implications of the "war on terrorism" championed by the United States and the continued involvement of American interests in the affairs of countries in the Muslim world, culminating in the invasion of Iraq and the war in Afghanistan. But as well, Muslims have found themselves in a situation in which their religious values are being subjected to scrutiny and attack from within their own community through the actions of those who struggle for political revolution under the banner of Islam. The vast majority of Muslims wish to dissociate themselves from all acts of violence conducted under the guise of religious activism, but they do so while striving to maintain their confidence in the values of their religion. This becomes an increasingly difficult balance when they find their religion constantly the focus of critical attention, especially in the media.

In such a situation, then, there is a great thirst for more knowledge about Islam, both from Muslims and from others. How to provide the needed tools for a good understanding is the challenge that every writer of introductory books on Islam faces. Today, as in the past, there is a temptation to write a work which will avoid the tough questions in order either to simplify or to seem "sympathetic" to Islam, given all the negative publicity about the religion that circulates in the popular media and that needs to be countered. Not only is such an approach academically unsatisfactory in my view, but it has also become polemical and divisive. Certainly, avoiding scholarly analysis in order to not appear "anti-Islamic" or to make the subject "easy" is neither academically responsible nor respectful of Islam itself, which, it seems to me, simply deserves the full rigor of analysis that humanistic and social-scientific study can provide. In undertaking that scholarly examination, we are in fact saying that Islam is a subject worthy of study, something which is essentially denied when a less than rigorous approach is undertaken. However, some authors have taken this type of critique of some other less-critical efforts at writing about Islam and turned it into a condemnation of Islamic studies in general. They have made the accusation of "political correctness" or "self-censorship" against academic writers on Islam, and have said, as in the words of one of the loudest polemicists, that those who are failing in their critical responsibilities are living in "dhimmitude," or a state of subservience to Islam. Such charges are excessive and unfounded. The task that sits in front of any serious writer on Islam is one of managing the difficult balance between the goals of being honest and of being sensitive to deeply held religious values. We each take our own route and manage our writing project in a way that responds to our own personal disposition best.

In recent years, scholarly analyses of Islam certainly have broadened their methodological perspective. There has especially been a significant move towards an approach which attempts to take into account the literary character of the historical sources. This effort has resulted in a recognition of the ideological aspects of the literary texts involved. Central has been the critical appreciation of the attempts made in those texts to define and legitimize an understanding of Islam in which the religion functions as a normative system acting, in a convenient, stabilizing, and "commonsense" manner, to justify the right to rule of a certain group of people. Islam is, of course, a "religion" in the common meaning of the word; the character that the system has adopted in its tenets and practices as conveyed in the textual sources that are available to us, however, can be seen in many instances to reflect an ideological significance for its society. This insight is as true of the formative period as it is of the modern period.

Certainly the historical picture of Islam which results from this approach to research leaves a great deal of ambiguity concerning precisely what can be known in historical terms of the very early centuries of Muslim life especially. This is because of the nature of the source material in which one sees a theological/ideological back-reading of history. As a result, what one can know, and what is explored and emphasized in this book, is how Muslims from the early ninth century (when the documentation of Islam becomes fully available) down until today view the history of their own religion and how they develop that understanding into the various manifestations of normative Islam. Given the scope and length of this book, in most instances it has only been possible to sketch out the issues rather than actually argue the proof for them as fully as may be desirable. Some Islamicists may well feel that this book has glossed over too many details which are crucial in the debate over sources and their implications or that I have ignored new aspects of arguments that have arisen in the past decades. Yet it seems to me that the attempt to write a very general textbook such as this, one which paints its picture in very large brush strokes and suggests—in some places, at least—a modified view of the popular version of the emergence, development, and future directions of Islam, continues to be worthwhile and potentially fruitful for students in opening their eyes to the complexities of understanding history. While some of the scholarship involved here has produced a good deal of debate within academic circles over the last twenty years, for myself, I have not seen any reason to change my basic ideas about the formation, development, and enunciation of Islam from those which I attempted to articulate in the first edition, although the details underlying those basic ideas are certainly always subject to reconfiguration, refinement, and tempering in the mode of expression.

It should be kept in mind that this book does not attempt to provide an entire "history of Islam." Likewise, this book does not endeavor to take into its purview the expansion of Islam into the many different regions of the world. The intellectual struggles which played a vital part in the emergence of Islam as the religion we have come to know appear to have taken place in the Islamic "heartland" of the Arabo-Persian empire; it is to that region, then, that the major attention must be paid in the first parts of the book. In dealing with the modern period, the Middle East region of the Islamic world is of central interest as well, although reference is also made to people and ideas emanating from the Indian subcontinent, South-east Asia, North America, and Europe. Islam in the contemporary world does not mean the Arab region alone, although the sense in which modern Islamic nations look to the Arab world for leadership in intellectual, political, and economic spheres must be acknowledged. The Arab world also frequently provides the source of many of the challenges to any sense of the cohesiveness to which the Muslim world may aspire. Furthermore, the role of the Arabic language as the lingua franca of discussions of Islam and as the vehicle for the enunciation of the classical Islamic vision (to which some contemporary spokespeople make frequent reference, in both positive and negative ways) certainly argues for an emphasis on the Arab world in coming to an understanding of the intellectual vision of Islam in today's world.

The focus of this book, from the formative period down to today, is that there exists a religious group of people, which, like all peoples, has moved through and been influenced by (as well as being an influence upon) history (even if recapturing that history in words may well be fraught with difficulty). The study of Islam, then, is not of a single entity but rather of something which has changed over time, has moved with the historical circumstances, and has varied for reasons which are sometimes very obscure. As a religion, Islam is also a phenomenon in which people believe and which has created its own sense of historical development. But this Muslim sense of the past has varied over time according to the needs of the situation. To try to understand this picture is, once again, the task of this book. Furthermore, central to the presentation of the emergence and history of Islam is the idea of "identity": that is, how a religion functions on both a personal and social level to provide that needed stability for daily life. The role Islam has played, and continues to play, in creating and developing an understanding of the world and of the relationship between individuals is vital; yet this, too, is not an unchanging mechanism but one which has gradually and subtly changed in response to the realities and pressures of the world. To try to understand this role of the sense of Islamic identity and the ways in which this role has responded to the needs of the situation and continues to respond is also the task of this book. Looking into the future, this book also ponders, in Part VI, the various faces of Islam which are emerging around us today and where they may be headed in light of the many challenges Muslims are facing today.

Writing about modern Islam poses special problems, and the current turmoil in various parts of the world—many of them inhabited by Muslims—certainly does not make it any easier. The attempt to come to terms with what is going on in a very fluid situation has often made me long for the relative stability of the study of past history while writing about modern debates. Even then, however, the value placed upon the past by various contemporary religious positions makes the security of the anonymity of history illusory. To understand the reasons why the contemporary religious sensibility sees itself as having something at stake in the study of history, then, brings this book together in yet another way. The reflection upon manifestations of Islam in the past may be complemented by reflections upon the present, especially as the history of that "present" becomes increasingly extended.

While the material which must be dealt with in this book is fairly complex, the basic notions underlying it are straightforward. Islam, as the religion of the people known as Muslims, was revealed by God, the same God who revealed himself to the Jews and the Christians; he is known in Arabic as Allāh. He revealed his religion to a native of the Ḥijāz on the western side of the Arabian peninsula, by the name of Muḥammad ibn ʿAbd Allāh, in the beginning of the seventh century. Over a period of twenty-two years, a scripture which is called the Qurʾān (also spelled "Koran") was revealed to Muḥammad by God. A work roughly the same length as the New Testament, the book calls on polytheists along with the Jews and the Christians to declare and put into action their commitment to God's final revealed religion. Heaven awaits those who heed the call; a fiery damnation in hell, those who ignore it. Clearly this is a message which fits within the overall Judeo-Christian tradition and, at the same time, is one which sees the whole world as eventually having to respond one way or the other to its call. As the person to whom this religion was revealed, Muḥammad is considered to have had a perfect understanding of the meaning of the message. Thus, everything which he did in his life is worthy of emulation by his followers, being the perfect expression of the will of God for humanity. Those who follow (or "submit to," as the word *muslim* suggests in its root meaning) this path of Islam form the *umma*, the community of Muslims whose common bond in religion symbolically reflects the central Islamic concept of the unity of the Divine.

PART I Formative elements of classical Islam

Significant dates

570	traditional birth date of Muḥammad
622	Muḥammad's move to Medina—the *hijra*
632	death of Muḥammad
634	death of Abū Bakr, first caliph
644	death of ʿUmar, second caliph
656	death of ʿUthmān, third caliph
661	death of ʿAlī, fourth caliph and figurehead of the Shīʿa
661–750	Umayyad dynasty
750	ʿAbbāsid dynasty begins
767	death of biographer Ibn Isḥāq
819	death of historian Ibn al-Kalbī
823	death of historian al-Wāqidī
824	death of exegete/literary scholar Abū ʿUbayda
830	Christian polemicist al-Kindī active
833	death of historian/editor Ibn Hishām
845	death of historian Ibn Saʿd
870	death of *ḥadīth* collector al-Bukhārī
875	death of *ḥadīth* collector Muslim ibn al-Ḥajjāj
887	death of *ḥadīth* collector Ibn Māja
889	death of *ḥadīth* collector Abū Dāwūd
892	death of *ḥadīth* collector al-Tirmidhī
915	death of *ḥadīth* collector al-Nasāʾī
923	death of exegete/historian al-Ṭabarī
996	death of grammarian/theologian al-Rummānī
1111	death of theologian-mystic al-Ghazālī

1 *Prehistory*

Arising when Rabbinic Judaism and Christianity were still in the process of firmly establishing themselves institutionally, Islam traces its origins to Arabia of the seventh century. Revolving around a prophet named Muḥammad with a scripture called the Qurʾān, Islam became the ideology which served to unite the Arab empire that asserted itself first in the area of the Fertile Crescent and Egypt, and then across North Africa and Persia. In doing so, it displaced to a large extent the older religions of Judaism and Christianity in its multiple forms, as well as the faith of ancient Persia, Zoroastrianism. The significance of this transformation was of enormous consequence in the unfolding of world history. Arabian society became integrated within the larger framework of the Near East, and a reciprocal integration of Near Eastern peoples into the new political and religious identity took place.

The foundations of Islam

Common wisdom would suggest that in order to understand the foundation of Islam we must have some knowledge of the historical, social, political, and economic context within which the religion emerged. As a generalization, of course, this has a degree of validity. However, it is quite possible to question the value of this approach to Islam's historical contextualization because it is highly dependent upon a notion of the religion of Islam existing as a conceptually defined entity from the very beginning of its proclamation. A more stimulating model of the foundation of Islam pictures the religion as emerging gradually, coming to a fixed sense of identity (and all that entails in terms of sources of authority) over a period of some two centuries. Certainly the gradual intertwining of developing Islamic ideology and the immediate environment presents a complex and confused picture, and thus a sketch of the political and religious situation in the Near East in the sixth through the eighth centuries can definitely help to put some of the matter in focus. The provision of such information should not be taken, however, in the sense of looking for "influences upon Muḥammad" from this pre-Islamic period (as so many early studies of Islam seemed to suggest). Rather, it should be seen as an attempt to sketch the context in which Islam did eventually achieve its fully formed status and to see the combination of factors in the society that made the religion successful and made it into the religious system that it is today. While the point may seem surprising at first, the relevance of the geographical region of Central Arabia to that emergent definition of what we have come to know as the religion of Islam is highly questionable; Islam (in its clearly defined and developed form) had its formative developing period outside the Arabian context and, while the initial impetus for the religion is connected to the Ḥijāz in Arabia, the character the religion adopted was molded by more widespread Near Eastern precedents than would appear historically possible within the narrow isolation of Arabia.

The Near East before Islam

There are three foci of interest in the centuries preceding the wave of Arab conquests of the Near East region in the seventh century. The Christian Byzantines had some influence over the Red Sea, extending at times to an alliance with the Monophysite Christians of Abyssinia; the Zoroastrian Persians, with their capital in Ctesiphon in Mesopotamia, had influence which reached at times the eastern side of Arabia and along the south coast to the Yemen; and the South Arabian kingdoms whose fluctuating fortunes, last manifested in the Himyar dynasty of the sixth century, had lost virtually all semblance of vitality by the time of the rise of the Arabs. The Arabian peninsula, although having had settled centers for several millennia, did not contain a power to be reckoned with in the world at the time. The only partial qualification to this state of affairs resided in the various tribal areas which had become pawns in the hands of external kingdoms, perhaps thereby creating the human forces which would eventually expand out of the peninsula and subjugate the earlier rulers.

In the year 527 Justinian I came to the throne of the Byzantine empire at Constantinople. He was determined to restore unity with the remnants of the decaying Roman empire, the western parts of which had been lost to the Germanic tribes, especially the Vandals and the Goths. He was successful in directing the reconquest of Italy, North Africa, and part of Spain, but by his death in 565 much of this accomplishment was being nullified as the result of continual local uprisings. The Persians took advantage of the subsequent unstable situation and undertook military initiatives on their western border with Byzantium. Heavy taxes, however, provoked instability on the edges of this newly expanded area. Heraclius, the Byzantine leader who died in 641, managed to gain supremacy in Constantinople in 610, only to witness the Persians take Antioch in 613 and Jerusalem in 614, and then march into Egypt in 619. An attempt to move on Constantinople itself in the year 626 left the Persians disorganized and overstretched. Before this final move by the Persians, Heraclius had begun a counterattack and had successfully invaded Persian territory as far as Ctesiphon in 628, recapturing Jerusalem in 629, forcing a retreat on the part of the Persian empire, and eventually causing the murder of Shah Khusro II. The overconfident Byzantines relaxed and fell victim to the Arab conquest, which started most significantly with the initial capture of Damascus in 635.

The situation in the Arabian peninsula

From the point of view of Arabia, this political situation was further confused and made more unstable by two additional factors: the interaction of the Arabs with the two major world powers of the time and the religious rivalry between Jews, the various sects of Christians, and, to a lesser extent, Zoroastrians.

Through a system of states functioning as tributaries to the Byzantines and Persians, the nomads of Arabia were kept within the confines of the desert area, and thus did not pose any great danger in the frontier area between the two empires. These tributary states, Hira (whose people are also known as the Lakhmids), under the Persians in the northeast of Arabia, and Ghassan, under the Byzantines in the northwest, provided troops to their respective overlords. By the sixth century, these areas were populated by settled bedouin tribes, and Christianity especially was making its presence felt. The Arabs of this area were, however, of little practical consequence to the world powers of the time, although towards the end of the sixth century independence was seized by the Ghassanids, while the Lakhmids were forced into an even more subservient relationship with the Persians than had previously been the case. Overall, the tributary system, while it had been in operation for a number of centuries by the time of the Arab conquests, was becoming increasingly unstable at this time.

In the south of Arabia, intertribal warfare was bringing an end to the Himyar kingdom, the last in a long line of impressive states in the area of the Yemen. One of the reasons for the gradual decline in this region was the diminishing importance of the incense trade in the fourth century, in the wake of the Christian takeover of the pagan world and the weakening of the Roman economy. South Arabia, the major source of incense for the world from antiquity (at least since the seventh century BCE), had based a great deal of its economy on the production of and trade in this material, which was used in Greco-Roman religious festivals and in medicinal preparations. With the shift in the world situation, this economy suffered greatly. Some scholars have also suggested that, around the year 300, the whole area of Arabia suffered a drought, bringing about a collapse of the traditional agricultural basis of the local economy, although the evidence for this is not overwhelming.

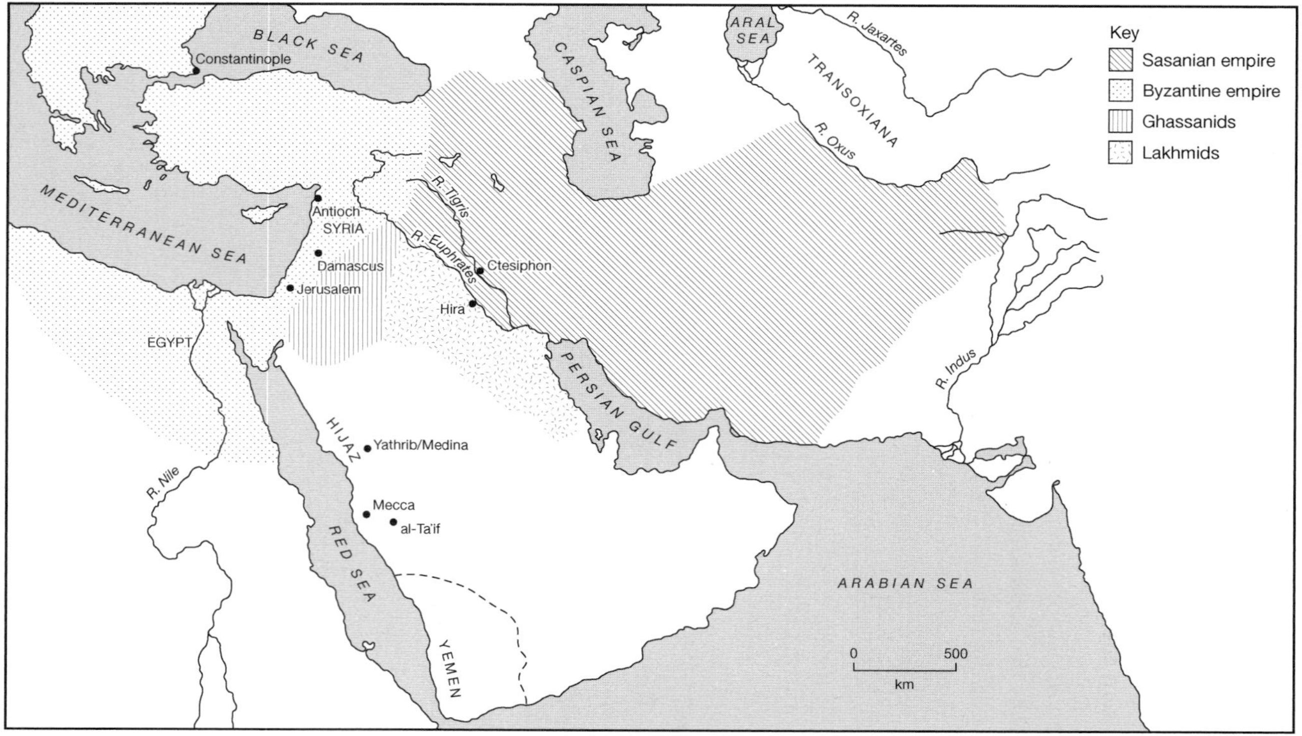

Figure 1.1 Map of the Near East, *c.* 600 CE.

Religion in the Arabian peninsula

The sedentary lifestyle of South Arabia had produced a society deeply involved in the various religious systems of the ancient Near East. Evidence, coming from inscriptions found in the area, reflects a developed stage of this religious growth; we have no information on how this religious system actually came into being. Clearly, the region was closely linked to the Mediterranean and Mesopotamian worlds. Until the fourth century, all of the evidence points to the existence of a polytheistic religion with a northern Semitic character. The worship of ʿAthtar, a male god who was the most prominent of the pantheon (he is always mentioned first in lists of gods), is often said to have been related to the Ishtar cult of the north, whose female god manifested herself in the Venus star. ʿAthtar was believed to be the bestower of blessings who could ensure good crops, many children, and success in war. There were a number of other prominent deities whose identity varied with the locality and the historical era. Keeping these different deities clear and distinct is extremely difficult, given the complexities of dealing with the inscriptional source material, but a few additional observations can be made. The moon god was variously known as Almaqah, ʿAmm, Sīn, and Wadd (the name of the latter is also known from Qurʾān 71/23), and the sun goddess was known as Shams. These gods and several others were held to be tribal patrons. As well, deities of the clan and the family also existed and these were often described simply as "the god (*ʾlh*) of so-and-so." Each level of deity was seen to govern a different sphere, each in a power relationship to the next level: first on the personal level, then on the village level, then controlling tribal land, and then controlling the world. According to the evidence of archaeological remains from various temples, sacrifices were a prominent part of religious worship. Incense offerings on stone altars and blood offerings were likely to have played a role in acquiring benefits for the person doing the sacrifice. All these activities took place within temples which were apparently attended by both men and women, with the purpose of the rituals being seen as the acquisition of the benefits which these various gods could bestow. Other features attested to by inscriptions include pilgrimage activities, ritual meals, and a code of personal purity.

Starting in the fourth or fifth century, South Arabian inscriptions speak of a monotheistic cult of "Raḥmanan, the Merciful," frequently qualified as "Lord of heaven and earth." Very little evidence is found in the inscriptions for a continuation of the earlier polytheistic cult (although since inscriptions necessarily reflect an elite and official segment of society, whether the general populace so quickly gave up its polytheistic belief is not clear). Apparently the rise of the kingdom of Himyar in about the year 380 marks this change, coming about probably as a result of, or in order to accomplish, a unification of the various South Arabian tribes. The monotheistic impetus is often seen to be a result of Jewish influence in the society, although some scholars wish to see this as a natural, independent development (based on an evolutionary picture of religion in general). Some scholars also wish to connect this development to the Quranic notion of a *ḥanīf*, the quality of being a monotheist in the face of paganism; whether this is a reference to a historical reality in terms of a movement among people or whether it refers to moral qualities of certain people is open to question. There is no independent evidence that incontrovertibly supports the existence of a native Arabian pre-Islamic monotheism. The Biblical echoes found in some of the monotheistic inscriptions, such as the phrase "the Merciful [*raḥmanan*], who is in heaven" and the use of the grammatical plural in reference to God (as in the Hebrew *elōhīm*) found in the inscriptional statement "the God(s) to whom belong the heaven and earth," suggest that Judaism is the most likely influence on the formation of this cult. Little is known of the religious character of this monotheistic trend, so additional information is not available to settle the matter definitively. It is likely that Judaism was supported by the Persians as a tool against Byzantine influence in the south of Arabia.

It is known that Judaism was present within this period of the monotheistic cult and perhaps even predated it slightly. There is clear and explicit evidence of a Jewish presence in South Arabia, attested to towards the end of the fourth century. References are found to the "community of Israel" as well as "Lord of Jewry." The presence of Jews in the Yemen continued until the mid-twentieth century, when most were removed to the newly formed State of Israel.

Christianity, meanwhile, was not in evidence in South Arabia before the sixth century, at which time it appears to have been present in a community centered in the town of Najrān. It is thought to have spread there from Abyssinia. Accounts are found of persecution of the Christians early in the sixth century by the Jewish ruler Yūsuf Asʿar, probably as a result of fears of Byzantine influence over the Christian community. Sixth-century retaliations by Abyssinian troops seem to mark the demise of Judaism as a power, with inscriptions thereafter speaking of belief in "God and His Messiah and the Holy Spirit" on the part of the rulers. There is no doubt that the Christianity which spread from Abyssinia was supported by the Byzantines against Persian influence in the area, even though it was, from the Byzantine perspective, of the heretical Monophysite persuasion. By the end of the sixth century, the Persians started to encourage Nestorian Christianity, another strain of that faith which was abhorrent to both the Byzantines and the Abyssinians, and aided the Yemenites in their removal of the Abyssinian overlords. The country was so fractured and destroyed by being subject to the manipulation of the various foreign powers that little remained by the time of the rise of the Arabs to be of any particular significance to either major empire.

The significance of Central Arabia

The area of Central Arabia remains a vast unknown territory during this historical period, of little significance to anyone in the ancient world except as a natural barrier of desert. Despite the extensive work done by scholars studying early Muslim literary texts concerned with the subject (archaeological digs have been very limited in crucial religious areas), the evidence for the role of the region as a focal point for a rich and economically explosive trade between South Arabia and the Fertile Crescent, as was once suggested, is virtually non-existent. The religious character of the region, as far as the data allow us any solid evidence, reveals a polytheistic system having basic features in common with Semitic religion in general; this includes worship of gods associated with the astral cults and beliefs in spirits inhabiting rocks, trees, and the like. The role of Mecca as a sanctuary is fairly evident, although the character of this sacred area becomes rather muddled as a result of the manipulations of the data by later historians who have overlaid what would appear to be native Arabian sanctuary traditions with Jewish ones.

Overall, given this situation, a number of things become clear in historical retrospect. Politically, the area of the Near East was unsettled at the time of the Arab conquests and was certainly in a condition which would allow for the emergence of a new configuration in political power. The interactions which did occur between the Arabs and the world at large saw the tribes being manipulated by the foreign policy of the empires, with no particular significance being given to the people themselves; this was true both in the north and in the south. The connection between the ancient empires and their religions was close, meaning that a new religious dispensation, separate from the notions connected with the old regimes, may well have found itself in a favorable position.

Prehistory in Muslim identity

There is, however, far more significance to the pre-Islamic period than the preceding interpretation of the historical data would seem to suggest. In terms of Muslim identity, the pre-Islamic period serves most emphatically as a historical, ideological, and ethical counterpoint to the Islamic ethos. It is, therefore, an era in which Muslim writers have tended to be very interested and they have provided an abundance of material purporting to portray the period. Therefore, from the standpoint of attempting to comprehend the foundation of the Islamic religion, the Muslim understanding of the period takes on a crucial and considerable role. The appreciation of this Muslim view, however, must be distinguished from reconstructing the history of the era itself; what is at issue here is the role of understanding the past and the kinds of pressures and interpretations to which such understanding becomes subject. This process, embodied within Muslim writings about the past, is one which is common to humanity: the recreation of the past embodied in the idea of "tradition," selectively formed and reshaped into a new and relevant context.

The notion of *jāhiliyya*

The pre-Islamic period is an era contrasted to the time and ethos of Islam, a contrast which is embodied in the term *jāhiliyya*. This word is found in the Qurʾān four times in reference to the idea itself and ten times in reference to people, and is also used in verbal derivations related to the word with the same sense. The term would appear to be used in the text of scripture as the opposite of "Islam," in that those who are connected to the *jāhiliyya* are those who are "ignorant of God"—at least this is the way most Muslim commentators on the Qurʾān have taken the word. For example, the Qurʾān states:

> When those who disbelieved set in their hearts fierceness, the fierceness of ignorance [*jāhiliyya*], God sent down His Shechina upon His messenger and the believers, and obliged them to the word of godfearing to which they have a better right and of which they are worthy.
>
> (Qurʾān 48/26)

The religious accomplishment of Islam, encompassed in the word "godfearing" (*taqwā*) contained in this passage, can only be judged by comparing it to what came before it. Even more significantly, the impulse to demonstrate this accomplishment of Islam appears to rest ultimately upon the desire to prove the divine status of the religious dispensation itself. What Islam has accomplished in transforming society from one of *jāhiliyya* to a "godfearing" one is, in fact, proof of the divine nature of the religion.

A consequence of this apparent impulse to illustrate the separation between *jāhiliyya* and Islam is that a large amount of material emerged which was designed to prove and provide the appropriate pre-Islamic contrast. The starting point of all this material was, of course, the Islamic position—that is, only what was needed in order to provide this counterpoint to Islamic values is presented in the texts. In no sense do the Islamic sources attempt to provide a dispassionate presentation of pre-Islamic society, politics, and religion (although some scholarly treatments of Islam certainly have attempted to employ the material to recreate that era, despite the selectivity and biases of the material itself).

Discontinuity of Islam with the past

How this approach to portraying the past functions can most easily be illustrated through an example dealing with a point of law. In legal issues the impulse to demonstrate the benefits of Islam are quite pronounced, for this often reflects very tangible elements within everyday Muslim life. Qurʾān 2/168 reads: "O people, eat anything lawful and good that exists on earth, and do not follow the steps of Satan; he is an manifest enemy of you." Common to a number of sources which deal with interpretation of the Qurʾān and which provide anecdotes about the "context" of the revelation of a verse is the following: "This verse was revealed about [the Arab tribes of] Thaqīf, Khuzāʿa and ʿĀmir ibn Ṣaʿṣaʿa who prohibited to themselves cultivated produce and grazing livestock. They also forbade the *baḥīra, sāʾiba, waṣīla* and *ḥāmī* camels" (Wāḥidī 1969: 43–4). The picture that is painted is one of various people before the revelation of the Qurʾān doing things, in this case prohibiting to themselves various foods, which were to be permitted under the Islamic dispensation. Of course, it is not possible to prove that this was not actually so, that this event did not "really happen," but that is not the point. What is of interest here is how the anecdote works within the Islamic context, for the function of such stories would seem to be the prime reason Muslim writers transmitted those accounts. The purpose of the anecdote is to provide a measure of the accomplishment of Islam and to differentiate Islam clearly from what existed previously.

In fact, it is quite possible to demonstrate in individual cases that later Muslims did not know the "facts" of the pre-Islamic period but, rather, that the anecdotes emerged for the purpose of anchoring Islam to history more firmly; there are many lucid examples of this phenomenon that are easy to locate. For example, concerning Qurʾān 2/158, "Ṣafā and Marwa are among the waymarks of God. Whoever goes on the pilgrimage to the house or performs the visitation [*ʿumra*], there is no fault on him if he circumambulates them," anecdotes are repeated which speak of the pre-Islamic practices concerning the hills of Ṣafā and Marwa but they are unclear as to whether the pre-Islamic Arabs did or did not run between them. One anecdote reads as follows:

> On Ṣafā was the image of a man called Isāf, while on Marwa was the image of a woman called Nāʾila. The people of the book [i.e. the Jews and Christians] claimed that these two had committed adultery in the Kaʿba [in Mecca], so God converted them into stone and placed them on Ṣafā and Marwa in order to act as a warning to others. . . . The people of the *jāhiliyya* stroked the idols when they circumambulated them [during their pilgrimage rituals]. When Islam came and the idols were broken, Muslims detested the circumambulation between the hills because of [their association with] the idols. So God revealed this verse.
>
> (Wāḥidī 1969: 42)

Another explanation of the verse is found in this report:

> ʿUrwa ibn al-Zubayr said to ʿĀʾisha: "I see no fault in someone who does not run between Ṣafā and Marwa, nor would it concern me if I did not run between them." ʿĀʾisha answered: "You are wrong, O son of my sister! Muḥammad ran between them and so did the Muslims. Rather it was [the pagans] who sacrificed to Manāt, the idol on the mountain of Mushallal, who did not run between them. Then God sent down this verse. If it were as you say, the verse would read, 'there is no blame on whoever does not run between them'."
>
> (Qurṭubī 1967: II, 178)

Illustrated in these anecdotes is the ambivalence of the information. Either the pre-Islamic Arabs did or did not run between the two hills. Both reports certainly provide a justification for the Muslims running between them (which, after all, is the central question for later Muslim jurists) and, at the same time, both reports provide a contrast with the pre-Islamic period. This contrast, note, can be positive or negative—either things are different from the past or they are the same. A similar phenomenon can be seen in many legal discussions, for example regarding foods being prohibited to Muslims "by virtue of not being eaten by pre-Islamic Arabs," where the evaluation as compared to the past is positive once again.

The role of the Abrahamic myth

In general, it can be said that this pre-Islamic material was recorded not with "historical" reasons in mind, if by that we mean modern principles of historical research. Rather, the accounts were transmitted and written down in order to provide the necessary information for understanding the Qurʾān within a context of Arabia, and for evaluating Islam as a whole. This may be seen in an extremely popular work that was written by Hishām ibn al-Kalbī, who died in 819, entitled *The Book of Idols*. The text gathers together poetical references to various "pre-Islamic" deities, especially those cited in the Qurʾān. Once again, however, it must be noted that the origins of this poetry are by no means obviously in the historical period before Muḥammad; it certainly is non-Islamic religiously (but not necessarily pre-Islamic historically), and that suggests the possibility at least that in the period after Muḥammad vestiges of earlier religious sentiments still remained.

Of special interest is the very beginning of Ibn al-Kalbī's book, which provides a clear theological understanding of Islamic prehistory; the example illustrates well the approach of works such as these. History is presented (indeed, as one should expect) through Islamic eyes and told according to Islamic principles, and includes in its retelling an implicit condemnation of the corruption and immorality of the pagan era which preceded Islam:

> When Ishmael, son of Abraham, may God bless them both, settled in Mecca, many children were born to him such that the number of people became so numerous that they were crowded there. They displaced the original inhabitants, the Amalekites. Later on, Mecca become so overcrowded that rivalries and strife arose among them, causing them to fight one another and as a result they spread out throughout the land seeking a livelihood. . . . No one left Mecca without carrying a stone from the sanctuary as a sign of veneration of it and of love for Mecca. Wherever they settled they would erect the stone and circumambulate it as they had done at the Kaʿba, thereby seeking blessing and affirming their attachment to the Kaʿba. They continued their veneration of the Kaʿba and Mecca despite this practice and still journeyed there on the pilgrimage

> and the visitation [*ʿumra*] according to the tradition inherited from Abraham and Ishmael, may God bless them both. In time, this led them to worship whatever they liked. They forgot their ancient beliefs and changed the religion of Abraham and Ishmael for another. They worshipped idols and returned to the practices of the nations before them. After discovering the images which the people of Noah (on him be peace!) worshipped, they adopted the worship of those which were remembered. Among the practices were some which came down from the time of Abraham and Ishmael, including the veneration and circumambulation of the temple (in Mecca), the pilgrimage, the visitation, the standing on ʿArafāt, the rituals of Muzdalifa, offering sacrifices, and uttering the ritual formulae during the pilgrimage and the visitation.
>
> (Ibn al-Kalbī 1941: 3–4)

The problem that such a passage is trying to solve for its readers is the following. Muslims know that the rituals connected to the Meccan pilgrimage were continuations of pre-Islamic rites; such rites had pagan connotations. How could God legitimate such activities? The answer is found in the figures of Abraham and Ishmael, who, having lived in Mecca and performed the pilgrimage rites there (implicitly the same ones which Muslims perform until the present time), left the heritage of the activities, but the meaning (although not the actions themselves) of them was forgotten among the pagan inhabitants of the area. While this Abrahamic background is not appealed to in every case of a positive connection between the *jāhiliyya* and Islam, it certainly is sufficiently frequent to be seen as a generalized tool for the Muslim understanding of the past. Abraham remains the "first Muslim," putting into practice the activities which would have to be revived by Muḥammad; the people in the intervening centuries are the ones who distorted the true religion which God had made available to His creation through Abraham.

The significance of prehistory

Thus we can see that the "prehistory" of Islam is a significant conceptual notion both for historians concerned with understanding the emergence of Islam and for the Muslim community itself in the understanding of its relationship to its religio-cultural heritage. For the latter, the evaluation of the accomplishment of Islam in separating its faith from the past is understood in two ways, as a radical split from the past or as a continuation of the valuable (that is, divinely sanctioned) elements. For the former, the reliance on material preserved within the framework of the evaluation of the Muslim faith means that the assessment of the rise of Islam is fraught with difficulties. In the absence of assuredly contemporaneous sources, literary or epigraphic, our knowledge of "prehistory" will remain filtered through the theologically inspired picture of the past provided by the later Muslim sources.

Frankincense in the ancient world

In the Christian Gospels, the infant Jesus is presented with gifts of "gold, frankincense and myrrh" by the kings from afar (Gospel of Matthew 2:11). These were gifts fit for a king, the symbols of wealth and status. Frankincense and myrrh were seen as exotic substances in the ancient world because they originated from the southern tip of Arabia and across the Red Sea on the Horn of Africa. For centuries, they were transported overland across the length of the Arabian peninsula and by sea to the markets of Byzantium and the Near East. What knowledge there was of Arabia at this time generally stemmed from this involvement in trade. Herodotus, in the fifth century BCE, reported that Arabia was the only country that produced frankincense, myrrh, cassia, and cinnamon.

Frankincense comes from a tree of the *Boswellia* genus. A deep incision is made in the tree, some bark is removed, and the gum-resin from the tree oozes out and hardens in the air. After about three months, the clumps are harvested to be stored and dried further. That material can then be burned as incense. It is also mixed with other aromatic substances to make perfumes, ointments, medicines, and oils.

Figure 1.2 A man cuts the bark of a frankincense tree in Oman to get the sap to flow to the surface.
Source: Tor Eigeland/*Saudi Aramco World*/SAWDIA.

Trade in frankincense likely started as early as 700 BCE. The substance was used by ancient Egyptians, Babylonians, and Persians in their temples as an offering to the gods. The Greeks and Romans used it in their households in many ways. Combined with other spices such as cinnamon and cassia, it was used to make one's clothes, hair, or beard smell pleasant. It covered up the smell of burning bodies and garbage in the street, and was employed as an insect repellent. Many medical purposes are reported, including easing headaches, pains of childbirth, stiffness in joints, ulcers, and abscesses. Pliny the Elder in the first century reports frankincense was used as an antidote for hemlock poisoning. It was also thought to be an antidote for insect bites, and it was used to stem nosebleeds, coughing and nausea, stinging eyes, and earaches. The Bible speaks of using frankincense in a number of situations, including as an offering in the holy sanctuary (Exodus 30:34; Leviticus 2; and elsewhere) and as a perfume (Song of Solomon 4:14). Burning incense was seen as a symbol of the divine name (Song of Solomon 3:6; Malachi 1:11) and an emblem of prayer (Psalms 141:2; Luke 1:10; Revelation 5:8, 8:3).

The importance of incense started to decline in the third and fourth centuries CE as the presence of the Christian church increased. The use of incense became more limited at that time as a result of the dim view taken of its "excessive" usage in non-Christian religious contexts. As well, Roman economic and political issues during that period made such valuable substances less affordable even for the wealthy.

Patricia Crone, *Meccan Trade and the Rise of Islam*, Princeton: Princeton University Press, 1987, part I, deals with the classical spice trade in the Arabian context. On the significance of, and the decline in, trade in incense see chapter 3 of Gary K. Young, *Rome's Eastern Trade: International Commerce and Imperial Policy, 31 BC–AD 305*, London: Routledge, 2001.

Suggested further reading

Patricia Crone, *Meccan Trade and the Rise of Islam*, Princeton: Princeton University Press, 1987.

Garth Fowden, *Empire to Commonwealth: Consequences of Monotheism in Late Antiquity*, Princeton: Princeton University Press, 1993.

Gerald Hawting, *The Idea of Idolatry and the Emergence of Islam: From Polemic to History*, Cambridge: Cambridge University Press, 1999.

Robert G. Hoyland, *Arabia and the Arabs from the Bronze Age to the Coming of Islam*, London: Routledge, 2001.

F. E. Peters (ed.), *Arabs and Arabia on the Eve of Islam*, Aldershot: Ashgate/Variorum, 1999.

2 *The Qur'ān*

Islam as a religion focuses on its scripture, the Qur'ān. Written in Arabic, the Qur'ān is a short book which holds a special appeal for its listeners and readers. It is relatively easy to give a brief description of the Qur'ān in terms of the book as we have it before us today. Even the Qur'ān's contents are readily summarized, as long as one does not attempt to perceive a necessarily systematic theological position within it. But accounting for how, why, and when the Qur'ān came into being as a text and why it looks and sounds the way it does is far more difficult. It will be beneficial to start with the easy tasks and then attempt the more difficult ones afterwards.

The Qur'ān as a book

The Qur'ān consists of 114 chapters, called *sūras*, arranged roughly in order of length, from the longest (some twenty-two pages of Arabic text for *sūra* 2) to the shortest (only a single line for *sūra* 108). The major exception to this principle of ordering is the first chapter, called "The Opening," *al-fātiḥa*, which is essentially a prayer and is used as such in Muslim ritual. Each chapter is divided into verses, *āyas*, the total number amounting to somewhere between 6,204 and 6,236, differing according to various schemes of counting. These verse divisions do not always correspond to the sense of the text but are generally related to the rhyme structure of the individual segments of the text. Twenty-nine chapters are preceded by disconnected letters of the Arabic alphabet, some single letters (Q—*qāf*, *sūra* 50; N—*nūn*, *sūra* 68) or up to five letters together. The significance of these so-called mysterious letters has eluded traditional Muslim and modern scholarship alike. Also prefacing each chapter, with the exception of *sūra* 9, is the *basmala*—the statement "In the name of God, the Merciful, the Compassionate" (a statement which also occurs at the beginning of a letter from Solomon to the Queen of Sheba which is cited in Qur'ān 27/30). The text as it is generally found today indicates both the Arabic consonants and the vowels according to a standard system of notation, along with a variety of other marks connected to recitation practices and verse divisions. Early manuscripts of the Qur'ān dating from the eighth and ninth centuries provide only the consonantal shapes of the Arabic script, however, and even those are often in what appears as a very rudimentary form compared to the text we know today.

Reading the Qurʾān discloses a thematic preoccupation with three major topics: law, the previous prophets, and the final judgment. The three combine to create what has been termed by some "a curious amalgam" of an assumption of Biblical knowledge on the part of the reader with another element, which would appear to be some sort of native Arabian tradition.

God as the central theme

Ruling over all of the Qurʾān, and the reference point for all the developments of the themes, is the figure of God, *Allāh* in Arabic. The all-mighty, all-powerful and all-merciful God has brought the world into being for the benefit of His creatures, has sent messages to His creatures in the past to guide them in the way of living most befitting to them and to Him, has given them the law by which they should live—and which has reached its perfection and completion in Islam—and will bring about the end of the world at a time known only to Him when all shall be judged strictly according to their deeds. The basic message is a familiar one in the Judeo-Christian tradition.

The Qurʾān declares in *sūra* 20, verses 7–8, "Be loud in your speech, yet surely He knows the secrets and what is even more hidden. God, there is no god except Him! His are the most beautiful names." This emphasis on the uniqueness of God, that He is the only god that exists, is presented in opposition to both the Jewish and the Christian traditions as well as in opposition to the polytheist idolaters. Regarding the Jews and the Christians, Qurʾān 9/30–1 has this to say:

> The Jews say, "Ezra is God's son"; the Christians say, "Christ is God's son." That is what they say with their mouths, conforming with the unbelievers before them. May God fight them off! How they are perverted! They have taken their rabbis and monks as lords apart from God, and the Messiah, the son of Mary—and they were ordered to serve God alone; there is no god except Him. Glory be to Him, above what they may associate [with Him]!
>
> (Qurʾān 9/30–1)

While the precise reference of the charge that Ezra is the son of God according to the Jews has never been made clear, the overall emphasis of the passage on the association of simple mortals alongside God is obvious enough. As far as Jesus is concerned, there is a clear denunciation of his divine sonship throughout the Qurʾān, and, while he is called al-Masīḥ, the Messiah ("the anointed one"), this is presented as his name only and not as an indication of his function or status.

As for polytheistic beliefs, Qur'ān 6/100–2 states:

> They have set up *jinn* as associates with God, even though He created them! They have imputed sons and daughters to Him without any knowledge. Glory be to Him! Exalted is He over whatever they describe! The creator of heaven and earth—how can He have a son while He has no consort, and He created everything and He has knowledge of everything? That then is God, your Lord; there is no god except Him, the Creator of everything. So serve Him for He is trustee over everything.
>
> (Qur'ān 6/100–2)

The reference to the *jinn*, or the "genies" of the Arabian Nights, is given here in such a way as to object to their being considered as having divine powers of any sort (as apparently the polytheists thought), but their existence is quite obviously accepted. Along with the angels and humanity, the *jinn* are seen as part of creation but existing in a different dimension. The creation of humanity from clay (Qur'ān 15/26, 55/14) is paralleled by the creation of the *jinn* from fire (Qur'ān 15/27, 55/15). The belief that the angels were created from light is a strong tradition in Islam but it is not actually mentioned in the Qur'ān. Overall, each part of creation has its own sphere and its own specific duties in its relationship to God. The figure of Satan (known in Arabic as *Shayṭān* and *Iblīs*) also enters here, sometimes described as one of the *jinn* but also pictured as the fallen angel. Among his many roles, Satan is the one who, in Qur'ān 7/20 and 20/120, tempts Adam and Eve in the Garden of Eden, and in Qur'ān 114/4–5 he is portrayed as the evil whisperer who finds his way into the hearts of men. In general, Satan is seen as responsible for a number of specific and more general sins related to actions which take people away from God. The force of evil, presented as the personified entity of Satan (or as a collection of "devils," *shayāṭīn*, the plural form of the word), always insinuates its way into human existence. The powerlessness of the individual before Satan's insistence as conveyed throughout the Qur'ān is illustrated by the use of the word *waswas*, meaning "whisper," a word formed through repetition of the sound of whispering and representative of the notion that Satan does not just call or speak once but comes over and over again. Satan is not, however, a rival to God in a sense that would suggest a dualistic system of deities; he is clearly a created being whose role mirrors the human experience of temptation.

The prophets of the past

The figure of God in the Qur'ān is evidently the same God who communicated to the prophets of the past. Qur'ān 20/9–14 states:

> Has Moses' story ever reached you? When he saw a fire, and told his family, "Wait here; I have glimpsed a fire. Perhaps I can bring you a brand from it, or I shall find

> some guidance at the fire." When he came to it, [a voice] called out: "Moses, I am your Lord! Take off your sandals; you are in the sacred valley, Ṭuwā. I Myself have chosen you, so listen to this revelation. Indeed I am God! There is no god except Me; therefore serve Me and perform the prayer of My remembrance."
>
> (Qurʾān 20/9–14)

This passage illustrates nicely the Quranic approach to previous revelation. The story itself is familiar from the Hebrew Bible (Exodus 3) but is presented here shorn of the extensive narrative element which seems so essential to the Judeo-Christian way of understanding scripture. In contrast, the Qurʾān simply presents a summary of the story and gets directly to the religio-moral point, each aspect of which is, in fact, central to the Islamic message. In this case, clearly, the emphasis is upon the oneness of God, but it is also on the institution of prayer and the instruction of obedience to God as the essential element of faith. To understand such passages fully in terms of a coherent overall narrative it is frequently necessary to place the Quranic accounts into the framework of the Biblical tradition. This fact emphasizes the need to consider an area far broader than Central Arabia when thinking of the original context of the message of Islam.

Twenty-eight figures other than Muḥammad are named in the Qurʾān as having been commissioned or selected by God to spread the message of the true way of obedience to Him. Only a limited number of these figures were given scriptures of some sort to share with the community. Abraham, Moses, David, and Jesus are specifically cited in this regard. Not all of the messengers are familiar from the Biblical tradition (or, at least, their identification with personages of the past is less than clear): Hūd, Ṣāliḥ, Shuʿayb, and Luqmān are generally treated as prophets of the specifically Arabian context prior to Muḥammad. Dhū ʾl-Qarnayn is identified as Alexander the Great according to the legends which have gathered around the name. Dhū ʾl-Kifl, the "lord of the portion" (mentioned in Qurʾān 21/85 and 38/48), is variously and very uncertainly identified as the Biblical Obadiah of I Kings, Ezekiel, or Elijah, but is often left as "unknown" from the perspective of history.

The stories of these prophets are recounted frequently in stereotyped passages, reflecting the general Islamic message. The prophet is commissioned by God, the prophet confronts his people, the people reject him, and the people are, as a result, destroyed, and the prophet and any persons faithful to his message are saved by the mercy of God. A *sūra* such as the eleventh, entitled "Hūd," is typical in its presentation of these stories. Here we find, joined together in narratives always similar in structure and even in wording in some instances, accounts of Noah, Hūd, Ṣāliḥ, Abraham, Lot, Shuʿayb, and Moses. The moral is always the same. God will triumph over the unbelievers and His message will always remain in the world in one form or another. A few other prophets have their stories told in more expansive form. The story of Joseph, recounted in *sūra* 12 and one of the most cohesive narratives found in the Qurʾān, is presented in an extended manner and in parts is even more elaborate than the Biblical account. This elaboration indicates that the Qurʾān is not simply a retelling of the Biblical stories but is a reflection of the popular form of the prophet stories in the Near Eastern milieu of the seventh century. Elements in the Quranic versions of these stories are sometimes found in works such as the Jewish Talmud or Midrash, for example. Thus, the context within which the Qurʾān must be read is far more than the framework provided by the text of the Bible alone; rather, the living traditions of Judaism and Christianity, and all the other faiths and folklore of the area, are reflected in the Qurʾān and provide the necessary background for its comprehension.

The famous story from Genesis 22 concerning the sacrifice of the son of Abraham is also retold in the Qurʾān, but the son is not identified by name and his identity became, for a time, subject to great debate in Islam. The context of the Quranic passage would seem to suggest that Ishmael was the one who was sacrificed, since after the discussion of the sacrifice in the Qurʾān (*sūra* 37, verses 102–9) the passage goes on in verse 112 to say, "then We gave him the good tidings of Isaac, a prophet, one of the righteous," suggesting that this was a totally separate character. The reading of Ishmael as the intended victim gained further standing through the later ideology of the Muslim community which argued that the Jews had changed the Biblical account to reflect well on their own heritage traced through Isaac; the Jews had done this rather than enhance the status of the Arabs and their descent through Ishmael (as related in the Bible, although that genealogy is nowhere echoed in the Qurʾān). Regardless, the story provides another illustration of the approach of the Qurʾān to Biblical narratives. Qurʾān 37/102–9 states:

> and when [the son] had reached the age of running with him, he said, "My son, I saw in a dream that I will sacrifice you. Consider, what do you think?" He said, "My father, do as you are ordered; you will find me, God willing, one of the steadfast." When they had surrendered and he flung him down on his brow, We called out to him, "Abraham, you have confirmed the vision! Thus We reward the good-doers. This is a manifest trial." We ransomed him by means of a mighty sacrifice and left for him among the later people, "Peace be upon Abraham!"
>
> (Qurʾān 37/102–9)

Compacted here into a few lines is a chapter of the Bible which has often been cited as one that was well crafted for its dramatic impact and for its use of narrative tension in having the young Isaac traveling to the sacrifice not knowing the fate that was in store for him. The Qurʾān, however, removes the drama but saves the message regarding the supreme faith of both Abraham and his son. This faithful attitude on the part of Isaac is also emphasized in the development of the tradition in Jewish and subsequently Christian circles, in which Abraham's son becomes the prefigurement of Jesus in his willing self-sacrifice. Also significant in the Quranic story is the emphasis on the fact that Abraham and his son "surrendered," in Arabic *aslama*, essentially "became Muslims"; even here, then (or, perhaps, especially here), the story is told with Muslim understanding and insights.

Jesus

Similar observations may be made concerning the story of Jesus, which, while it is found scattered throughout the Qur'ān rather than in one cohesive narrative, presents a picture that has often been seen to reflect varying tendencies within Christianity—Gnostic, Monophysite, and Nestorian. Born of the Virgin Mary (Qur'ān 19/16–34), Jesus spoke his first miracle from the cradle. His task on earth was to provide the "clear proofs" or "explanations" (Qur'ān 2/253 and elsewhere) and his mission was punctuated by miracles, as in Qur'ān 3/49: healing, knowing secrets, and fashioning birds out of clay into which he breathed life, the latter being a story known from the Christian apocryphal Infancy Gospel of Thomas. The crucifixion of Jesus, spoken of in Qur'ān 4/157–8, has created the greatest amount of interest, with a view to its possible reflection of sectarian Christian disputes: "[The Jews] neither killed nor crucified him, only a likeness of that was shown to them. . . . God lifted him up to Himself." The notion that Jesus did not "really" die on the cross has been seen as a continuation of Christian discussions over the nature of Jesus—was he divine and/or human? Once again, however, the Qur'ān would seem to reflect a strange amalgam, on the one hand supporting the argument for the truly divine nature of Jesus and thus denying the reality of his death, while on the other hand denying that Jesus was anything other than a human being.

The message of the judgment day

All of these prophets, and many additional figures who are not mentioned by name in the Qur'ān but who are said to have been sent (as Qur'ān 10/47 states: "Every nation has its messenger"), brought the same message of the coming judgment for those who do not repent and follow the law of God. Qur'ān 19/59–61 states:

> There followed after them [the prophets] a succession who neglected prayer and followed passions. So they shall meet error except for anyone who repents and believes and acts righteously; those—they will enter paradise and they will not be wronged in any way; the gardens of Eden which the Mercy-giving has promised His servants in the unseen.
>
> (Qur'ān 19/59–61)

The message is a simple one. All people shall die at their appointed time and then, at a point known only to God, the resurrection shall take place, at which point each person shall be judged according to the deeds they have performed on earth. "The agony of death will come in truth; that is what you have been trying to escape! The trumpet shall be blown: that is the day of the threat!" states Qur'ān 50/19–20, making reference to the eschatological trumpet, one of many Quranic elements familiar from the visions of John recorded in the Book of Revelation. The scene of the judgment is painted in graphic style. For each person, a book of deeds shall be brought forth, bearing witness to his or her good or evil state (Qur'ān 83); the image of the balance and the weighing of deeds is also employed (Qur'ān 21/47). The judgment shall determine the ultimate fate of the individual, be that either the bliss of paradise in the gardens or the burning torment of hell. Both of these places are depicted in vivid terms quite frequently in the Qur'ān, as, for example, in *sūra* 55, where the "flare of sparks and fire" and the "seething bath" of hell are contrasted to the "two gardens" of paradise, which have "every kind of fruit, flowing springs," and exotic rewards for the righteous.

The fate of the individual is described as being in the hands of God but also as up to the individual. God as the all-powerful creator can control His world fully but humanity must accept responsibility for its own actions. The tension which such statements create proved to be a major topic for theological speculation in Islam. Be that as it may, the Qur'ān is clear that each individual is expected to follow the law which God has set down in His scripture if there is to be any hope of entry into paradise in the hereafter. People are capable of sin, that being defined as an "error" in parting from the ways of God. As indicated above (p. 22), the figure of Satan is introduced to explain the presence of this potential for evil in the world.

The path to paradise

Qur'ān 4/136 proclaims:

> O you who believe, believe in God and His messenger, and the book which He has sent down on His messenger as well as the book which He sent down previously. Anyone who disbelieves in God and His angels, His books, His messengers and the last day has surely gone astray.
>
> (Qur'ān 4/136)

Here is a veritable creedal statement, bringing together all the elements considered essential for reaping the final reward in paradise. One must believe in the truth and the contents of the scripture; and what is the evidence of belief in it, if it is not putting the words into action? The previously quoted Qur'ān 19/60 emphasizes the reward "for anyone who repents and believes and acts righteously." Fulfilling the law of God—"acting righteously"—is a prerequisite for an individual to achieve salvation. The law, as proclaimed in the Qur'ān, is reminiscent of the Jewish law in matters such as its continuation of the prohibition of pork and the institution of ritual slaughter (e.g. Qur'ān 2/173, 5/1–3), some purity regulations (especially as regards women, Qur'ān 2/222, and within a ritual situation, Qur'ān 4/43, 5/6), and the emphasis on the regulation of marriage (e.g. Qur'ān 4/23), divorce (e.g. Qur'ān 4/19–22), and inheritance (e.g. Qur'ān 4/6–12). Clearly Islam sides with Judaism against Christianity in its position on the role of the law as the appropriate implementation of faith, a law given by God as a gift to humanity to provide guidance in living the proper, fully human life. As well, various emblems of Islam are mentioned in the Qur'ān, but often only in an unelaborated form. The pilgrimage (e.g. Qur'ān 2/196–200), the month of fasting (e.g. Qur'ān 2/183–7), the institution of prayer (e.g. Qur'ān 2/142–52, 2/238–9), and the idea of charity (e.g. Qur'ān 9/53–60) are all dealt with to varying degrees; regardless of the somewhat vague nature of some of the descriptions of these activities within the Qur'ān (as compared to their elaborate formulation in other Muslim sources, a topic dealt with in more detail in Chapters 7 and 15), it is clear that they are conceived as a compulsory part of Muslim life.

A dichotomy of forbidden (*ḥarām*) and permitted (*ḥalāl*) permeates the Qur'ān and provides an element of the foundation for Islamic ethics. With these words the ethical world view of the Qur'ān comes into play, providing insights into the understanding of the relationship between the sacred and the profane, of God's will for human existence, and of the moral categories by which people will be judged eligible or not for the hereafter in paradise.

The word *ḥarām* has a complex meaning structure in that the word mirrors a broader pattern known in many religious world views that brings together a basic sense of "sanctify" with the meaning of "forbid." The connotation of "sanctify" arises especially in relationship to sacred space. God is involved in establishing and maintaining the holy house (*al-bayt al-ḥarām*) in Qur'ān 5/97, a secure sanctuary (*ḥarām amīn*) in Qur'ān 28/57 and 29/67, sacred territory (*hādhihi'l-baldat alladhī ḥarramahā*) in Qur'ān 27/91, and, most of all, the sanctified mosque, *al-masjid al-ḥarām*, which is invoked on fifteen occasions and understood to be the Ka'ba in Mecca (see, for example, Qur'ān 2/144–50). The notion of the purity of these sanctified places becomes apparent when *al-masjid al-ḥarām* is spoken of in Qur'ān 9/28: "The idolaters are indeed unclean [*najas*] so let them not come near the sanctified mosque after this year of theirs." Notions of the security of the sanctified place are also strong and are linked to its inviolability (see Qur'ān 2/191, 28/57, 29/67, 48/27). Time is also sanctified in the Qur'ān in the notion of the "holy month," *al-shahr al-ḥarām*, in Qur'ān 5/2, 5/97, 9/5 and 9/36–7. The latter verses are especially noteworthy: "The month postponed [referring to the practice of calendar intercalculation] is an increase in unbelief whereby the unbelievers go astray; one year they make it profane [*yuḥillūna*] and hallow it another [*yuḥarrimūna*] to agree with the number God has hallowed [*ḥarrama*] and so profane [*yuḥillu*] what God has hallowed [*ḥarrama*]." Finally, Muslims undertaking the pilgrimage (*ḥajj*) enter a state of sanctity (*ḥurum*) by the process of *iḥrām* (Qurʾān 5/95), with an emphasis on avoiding hunting.

Ḥarām in all of these passages, then, indicates something directly connected to God and something that God dictates to, or appoints for, humanity. Obeying these proscriptions is the mark of the believer. Further, things which are *ḥarām* are free from impurity, at least in a physical sense. What is *ḥarām* is secure and inviolable, and violation of it will bring recompense, either willfully given on the part of a believer who has committed the violation or extracted by some other means from the guilty unbeliever.

It is clear that passages in which *ḥarām* has the sense of "sanctity" do not imply that the places or times are in any sense to be avoided; however, in other passages there is a clear indication of matters being forbidden and thus they are to be avoided when they are designated by the word *ḥarām*. The food laws figure prominently in this regard, as in Qurʾān 6/119, "How is it with you that you do not eat that over which God's name has been mentioned, seeing that he has distinguished for you that which he has forbidden you [*ḥarrama ʿalaykum*] unless you are constrained to it?" Meat which has not been properly slaughtered is declared *ḥarām* because it is against God's will to slaughter animals improperly. The flesh of the pig is declared *ḥarām* because it is *rijs*, an "abomination"; eating of carrion, consuming blood, and dedicating slaughtered animals to deities other than God are also declared *ḥarām* in Qurʾān 2/172–3 and 5/3, as are improper modes of slaughter (also in Qurʾān 5/3) and corrupt things (Qurʾān 7/157).

In sum, then, that which is *ḥarām* is always declared so by God alone. Things which are *ḥarām* are to be seen as simply against the will of God, or are things alienated from God, or are things connected to the sin of pagan practice. The word *ḥalāl*, on the other hand, conveys the opposite of both senses of the word *ḥarām*; that is, *ḥalāl* can mean "profane" (in opposition to the sense of *ḥarām* as "sanctify") as well as "permit" (as opposed to *ḥarām*'s "forbid"). As with *ḥarām* in the sense of "sanctify," *ḥalāl* can suggest a special relationship with God which marks its opposite off as separate. The predominant meaning of the word, however, is the assertion of the lawful character of something, or, when expressed with the negative particle "not," the equivalent of *ḥarām* in the sense of "forbidden."

Ḥalāl is employed as a legal category on seven occasions in the Qurʾān in a negative expression meaning "to be unlawful" in reference to women, marriage, and divorce; these instances appear to be specific situations in which the general permissibility of an action or circumstance is contravened, perhaps even with the sense that this is temporary, as in Qurʾān 2/230, "If he divorces her finally, she shall not be lawful [*lā tuḥillu*] to him after that until she marries another husband." *Ḥalāl* declares things permitted, especially types of food, as in Qurʾān 5/5, "The food of those who were given the book is permitted to you." *Ḥalāl* is also employed in a sense which is opposite to that of *ḥarām* in its meaning of "sanctified." One way to understand the word *ḥalāl* in these instances is that it means "ceasing ritual avoidance behavior." *Ḥalāl* is used to indicate leaving pilgrim sanctity (that is, leaving *iḥrām*) in Qurʾān 5/2, and, in the same verse, pilgrims are ordered "not to profane God's waymarks or the holy months." As noted above (pp. 27–8), the idea that the sanctified months could be altered comes in for criticism in Qurʾān 9/37, in which it is declared forbidden to make a month which is supposed to be sanctified (*ḥarām*) into one which is *ḥalāl*, thus making an inviolable month (in the sense that no fighting should take place in it) into one which can be violated.

Much of this basic moral attitude reflected in the terminology of "forbidden" and "permitted" corresponds to that found in Near Eastern religion in general and in the Bible especially. Such parallels are sometimes seen to go further. A comparison is sometimes drawn between the Biblical "ten commandments" and *sūra* 17, verses 22–39. Certainly the moral aim of many of the statements is similar: belief in only one God, showing respect to parents, not committing adultery, and so forth. In terms of its narrative structure, however, the law is quite clearly not presented in the same way in the Qurʾān as it is in the Bible. In no sense is this passage a pivotal or focal point of the text; nor is it portrayed in Muslim tradition as central within the context of Muḥammad's career. Thus, the passage does not stand parallel to the traditional understanding of the "ten commandments" in relationship to Moses and the Bible. Rather, the law in the Qurʾān is an integral part of the text with nothing to mark it off from the rest of the word of God. This presentation of the law does not preclude it being stipulated in great detail in numerous places, however, just as in the Bible, as the example of Qurʾān 4/23 shows:

> Forbidden to you [in marriage] are your mothers, your daughters, your sisters, your aunts on your father's side and on your mother's side, your brother's and your sister's daughters, your foster mothers and your foster sisters, your mothers-in-law and step-daughters who are under your guardianship being born of your wives with whom you have consummated marriage (however, if you have not consummated it with them, there is no fault on you) and the wives of your sons who are your own flesh-and-blood; nor may you take two sisters together unless this is a thing of the past. God is All-forgiving, All-merciful.
>
> (Qurʾān 4/23)

The Qurʾān also speaks of the law as it was revealed to the previous communities. Both the Torah of Moses and the Gospel of Jesus are specifically cited as previous revelations. The Qurʾān is seen as confirming both scriptures and as acting as a resolver of disputes between them: "We sent down to you the Remembrance [i.e. the Qurʾān] so you may make clear to people what was sent down to them, so perhaps they may reflect" (Qurʾān 16/44). But the Qurʾān also serves a correcting function, according to Muslim understanding, because humans have misinterpreted and tampered with the earlier revelations, infusing the word of God with human perversions (see Qurʾān 5/48). The Qurʾān provides a clear and perfect version of the will of God, the correct rendition of revelation.

The character of the Qurʾān

A summary of the contents of the Qurʾān, such as that just provided, while necessarily incomplete, glosses over an important point about the composition of the book itself—its apparent random character and seemingly arbitrary sense of organization which immediately strike most first-time readers. This unique composition is illustrated by examining the contents of any of the longer *sūras*, which are clearly a composite of many different themes and strata of thought. *Sūra* 2, for example, the longest in the Qurʾān, presents a startling picture when looked at in outline:

Verses	*Topic*
1–29	Faith and disbelief
30–39	Creation, Adam, Satan
40–86	Biblical history—Moses
87–103	Biblical history—Jews, Jesus, Moses
104–21	Polemic—Muslim, Jewish, Christian
122–41	Biblical history—Abraham
142–67	Islamic identity (direction of prayer, prayer itself, pilgrimage)
168–203	Juridical problems (food, wills, fasting, pilgrimage, etc.)
204–14	Salvation history
215–42	Juridical problems (*jihād*, marriage, divorce, etc.)
243–53	Salvation history
254–60	(mixed)
261–83	Juridical problems (charity, usury)
284–86	Faith

Such a brief outline does not do justice to the complexity of the thematic structure of the *sūra* by any means, but, even so, it does provide some material for provoking thought. How did the Qurʾān come to look the way it does, with the subject matter within individual chapters jumping from one topic to the next, with duplications and apparent inconsistencies in grammar, law, and theology abounding? Despite these apparent surface disruptions, some scholars have found a structural coherence to these compositions, noting liturgical patterning and signs of comprehensible internal development still reflected in the structure of the *sūras*. To the source critic, however, the work displays all the tendencies of rushed editing, with only the most superficial concern for the content, the editors/compilers apparently engaged only in establishing a fixed text of scripture. Within this perspective, a likely historical point for the emergence of this fixed text is provided by the rise of the Qur'ān to a status of absolute authority in matters of law and theology (as opposed to the authority of tradition, of the caliph, or of reason, as we shall see in Chapter 4). Creating a stable text of scripture, canonizing the various elements into a whole, may be seen as going hand in hand with the text being confirmed as the major source of legal and theological authority for the Muslim community.

Muslim accounts of the collection of the text

The Muslim community itself has, of course, an explanation for why the Qur'ān looks the way it does, but the contradictory nature of the accounts within the multiplicity of versions of the story has raised grave doubts on the part of many scholars as to their motivation. Generally, Muḥammad himself is excluded from any role in the collection of the text, although it is possible to find some accounts which talk of him going over the whole text with ʿAlī, his cousin, son-in-law and figurehead of the later Shīʿa. Zayd ibn Thābit, a companion of Muḥammad, is generally credited with an early collection of the scripture, and the pages of the text are said to have been entrusted to Ḥafṣa, one of Muḥammad's wives. Under the instructions of ʿUthmān, the third ruler of the empire after the death of Muḥammad, the major collection of the text "as we now have it" (as the Muslim claims put it) is said to have taken place. Working on the basis of pieces of text written "on palm leaves or flat stones or in the hearts of men," the complete text (deemed to have survived in full) was written out and distributed to the major centers of the early empire. Thus, within thirty years of the death of Muḥammad it is understood that the Qur'ān existed in its fixed, if skeletal, form; theologically, it is held that the form that the text was in at this point was an image of the "heavenly tablet," suggesting that its structure and content were precisely that which God desired for it. From this skeleton text, which indicated only the consonants of the Arabic script in a rudimentary form, the final text of the Qur'ān was developed over the next two centuries, such that all the subtleties of the language and the script were embedded within it. Most importantly from the Muslim perspective, it is held that an oral tradition preserved the full text from the time of its revelation, the written form serving only as a mnemonic device for memorization of the text. There are, in a sense, two ways of dealing with the Qur'ān within Muslim tradition: the oral, the tradition about which stems from Muḥammad, and the written, the tradition stemming from the caliph ʿUthmān.

The evidence of the manuscripts

In 1972, a treasure trove of ancient manuscripts of the Qur'ān was discovered in the Great Mosque of Sana'a during renovations. In 1979, a German team of scholars started working through some 12,000 fragments of parchment and paper, some of which (twenty-two groups of fragments) have been dated to the eighth century primarily on the basis of their use of the early Arabic script known as the *Ḥijāzī* style. This discovery has excited a good deal of scholarly and popular interest. The existence of early copies of the text of the Qurʾān might well be thought to help answer some of the riddles about its composition. So far, however, that has not been the case and only very tentative conclusions have been put forth.

Certainly, the existence of manuscripts of the Qurʾān indicates that the text (or, at the very least, substantial parts of it) existed in some sort of collected form by the eighth century. That, of course, does not tell us anything about the status of the text itself within a community of believers. Some discrepancies in the order of the *sūras* as they are found in a few manuscripts may indicate some variability in the overall form of the text. More interesting, though, is the fact that the text contains variant readings of a minor nature that suggest to some scholars that the idea of an oral tradition running parallel to the written one cannot be given historical credence. What we may have evidence of is the interpretative nature of the detailed annotations that were added to the text later: that is, that the current text is the product of reflection upon a primitive written text and not upon the parallel transmission of an oral text as the Muslim tradition has suggested.

Instances can be found, on the evidence of the early manuscripts, in which words, because of the way they were written in the primitive script of the time, were likely mispronounced as a result of a misunderstanding of the script and in the absence of a firm oral tradition. Examples include the name Ibrāhīm, more easily and better understood in a version closer to the Hebrew, Abrāhām, and Shayṭān, once again closer to the Hebrew if read Sāṭān. Both of these developed readings depend upon the misunderstanding of the early writing of the long "a" sound in the middle of the word.

A different but somewhat complex example may help to indicate what is at stake here. The very last verse (112) of *sūra* 21 starts: "He said (*qāla*), 'My Lord, judge according to the truth. Our Lord is the All-merciful.' " The reference to "My Lord" and "Our Lord" in the text indicates that the subject of "He said" cannot be God but must be the reciter of the Qurʾān, in the first place understood to be Muḥammad. Such a passage would then fall into a common form of Quranic speech found in passages normally prefaced by the imperative word "Say!" (*qul*). In the text of the Qurʾān as we now have it, the word here translated as "He said" is, in fact, more easily read as (and is written as) "Say!" due to the absence of the long "a" marker (something which commonly happens in the Qurʾān with other words, to be sure, but the word *qāla* is spelled this way only twice in the established text of scripture—here in Qurʾān 21/112 and in Qurʾān 21/4 according to some but not all traditions of the writing of the text). In the early Sanaʾa manuscripts, the absence of the long "a" in the word *qāla* is a marker of an entire set of early texts. But why should it be that this particular passage is read as "He said"? It really should read "Say!" to be parallel to the rest of the text of the Qurʾān and to fit in its own context. It would appear that in the process of editing the text most passages where this word was found were understood as "Say!" in both interpretation and writing (and thus not having a long "a"), with the unexplained exception of spelling in these two passages in *sūra* 21, which were read as if the long "a" was present. This may well have occurred because somebody was working on the basis of the written text in the absence of a parallel oral tradition, which would have maintained the "proper" reading of "Say!" if it had existed.

It is fair to say, then, that the manuscript tradition may have a significant impact upon our understanding of the early history of the text of the Qur'ān. The study of these manuscripts is still in its infancy, however, and the impact of these texts is still being assimilated by scholars. While this critical study of the history of the text of the Qur'ān has proven controversial among Muslims and has attracted a good deal of sensationalist media attention, the interest in the topic remains, at heart, a scholarly, academic one. The point of it is certainly not to displace the Qur'ān as Muslims have it but to better understand the history of how that text was transmitted in early Muslim society.

The authority of the Qur'ān

The value and the point of the stories about the collection of the Qur'ān are still in debate among scholars but, whatever the verdict in that discussion, one thing remains quite clear. The Qur'ān is, and has been from the beginning of the emergence of Islam as a firmly established religion, the primary point to which reference must always be made in order to define something as "Islamic." The Qur'ān is the defining point of Islamic identity. The emergence of the Muslim community is intimately connected with the emergence of the Qur'ān as an authoritative text in making decisions on matters of law and theology. What research has revealed is that the scripture's status and authority were debated in early times, especially between the various religious communities of the Near East and also within the newly emerging Islamic community itself. Elements of the process by which the Qur'ān emerged as the authoritative source, side by side with the emergence of the community of Islam itself, can be traced in the writing of various texts of Quranic interpretation in the early centuries of Islam, in early works of law, and in several documents of interreligious polemic. The ultimate enshrinement of the text of the Qur'ān as we now know it, understood to be literally the word of God, miraculous, inimitable, linked to an illiterate prophet, and thereby having its authority within the community, was the result of two to three centuries of vigorous debate as reflected in these texts.

Supporting the status of the authority of the Qur'ān are a number of theological dogmas connected directly to the book by which institutionalized Islam was able to argue for the Qur'ān as the prime source in law and theology. These dogmas have as their end result the skirting of issues connected to the construction of the text. They do this by seeing the very shape of the book as evidence of the divine hand at work. But it is on this point that early polemical texts reveal a great deal of discussion, and early Islamic exegetical texts dealing with the Qurʾān indicate that the argument concerning the form of the text as evidence of divine authorship took at least three centuries to reach its fully developed formulation.

The Qurʾān as the proof of Islam

It would appear that, early on, Muslims had to defend their nascent religion against Christian theological attack in the area of the Fertile Crescent, especially Iraq. The following argument was constructed: miracles prove the status of prophethood, and the Qurʾān is Muḥammad's miracle; therefore Muḥammad was truly a prophet and Islam is a true, revealed religion. All participants in the debate appear to have agreed on the first premise. What Muslims had to prove, and Christians disprove, was the validity of the second, for the conclusion, the truth of Islam, stood or fell on its credibility. Over time, the argument became one concerned to prove the "inimitability" of the Qurʾān, an argument which, its proponents were quick to point out, had a basis in the Qurʾān itself, although whether that was clear before the demands of the argument were put upon those verses is not entirely obvious. Known as the "challenge verses," the production of a text "like" the Qurʾān is encouraged but known to be impossible: "Produce a sūra like it [i.e. the Qurʾān], and call on whom you can, besides God, if you speak truthfully" (Qurʾān 10/38); "Well then bring ten chapters the like of it, forged!" (Qurʾān 11/13). God has given the Qurʾān to Muḥammad and because of its divine origin no text "like" it can, in fact, be produced. The inimitability of the text proves its divine authorship and thus its status as a miracle, confirming Muḥammad's role and the veracity of Islam.

Polemical texts from some 150 to 200 years after Muḥammad indicate the sorts of discussions that were going on; the existence of the arguments indicates that there were no clearly formulated Muslim answers to these concerns at the time. That observation suggests that the Qurʾān as a fixed text of scripture was still in the process of finding support for its authority within the community; indeed, it took at least 100 more years before the full enunciation of the doctrine of inimitability could respond cohesively to such challenges. The Christian al-Kindī, who wrote a text around the year 830, started off by demanding the following: "Show me any proof or sign of a wonderful work done by your master, Muḥammad, to certify his mission, and to prove what he did in slaughter and rapine was, like the other, by Divine command" (Kindī 1887: 64, text modified). The isolation of one of the central elements of Christian polemic against Islam—that Muḥammad's religion was spread by the sword—is combined here with the demand for proof of a miracle. Anticipating the Muslim response that the Qurʾān was that evidence, al-Kindī continues:

> The result of all of this [process by which the Qurʾān came into being] is patent to you who have read the scriptures and see how, in your book, histories are all jumbled together and intermingled; an evidence that many different hands have been at work therein, and caused discrepancies, adding or cutting out whatever they liked or disliked. Are such, now, the conditions of a revelation sent down from heaven?
>
> (Kindī 1887: 77–8, text modified)

The literary state of the Qurʾān is used against the Muslims by al-Kindī as proof of its non-divine origin.

The doctrine of inimitability

The Muslim response to these charges did not reach its full defensive literary expression until towards the end of the tenth century in the hands of the theologian-grammarian al-Rummānī (d. 996), who argued for the *iʿjāz*, "inimitability," of the Qurʾān on the basis primarily of its literary qualities, especially its easily quantifiable merits, such as its concision. At one point in his argument, al-Rummānī cites a popular Arab saying, suggests that its meaning is close to a Quranic statement, but then points out that the Qurʾān expresses the same sentiment (and even more, he claims) in fewer letters. Furthermore, what to polemical writers of earlier centuries were faults within the Qurʾān—evidence of its human production and thus non-miraculous status—become for al-Rummānī positive elements within the book. Ellipses within the text, for example, were considered positive rhetorical devices rather than evidence of rushed or careless writing. Much of this sort of argumentation became tied to an understanding of the nature of the Arabic language, a language full of rhetorical potential, of which, naturally, the Qurʾān must take full advantage. The Qurʾān, according to its own statements (Qurʾān 12/2, 26/192–5) was revealed by God "in a clear Arabic tongue" and, the argument is made, it must partake of all the features of that language. This sort of argument is difficult, if not impossible, to evaluate, due to the lack of contemporaneous profane literature by which the rhetorical accomplishment of the Qurʾān can actually be assessed. The argument remains a dogmatic one, essential to the proof of the status of the text, but one which operates (like many other religious arguments) within the presuppositions of Islam alone.

Interpretation of the Qurʾān

In fact, Muslims, in the two centuries for which there is some literary evidence before al-Rummānī, appear to have had slightly different feelings about their scripture. They appear to have been more concerned with cataloguing the peculiarities of the text itself and facing the practical job of understanding the text, rather than worrying about defending its intricacies. Therefore, the more general problem of interpretation and, hand in hand with that, the consolidation of its authority through clear enunciation of the scripture's meaning were of far greater concern.

The text of the Qurʾān presents many ambiguities, difficult words whose precise readings are uncertain, problems of textual division, and apparently incompatible statements. With the text's rise to the status of authority, or perhaps parallel to it and stimulating that very rise to authority, there emerged the discipline of interpretation, known as *tafsīr*, or, in a more general sense, the Quranic sciences called *ʿulūm al-Qurʾān*.

Fundamentally, a work of *tafsīr* provides an interpretation of the Arabic text of scripture and is defined by a number of formal characteristics: it will follow the text of the Qurʾān from beginning to end and will provide an interpretation of the text segmented into either words, phrases, or verses. While exceptions are found to these characteristics in some works which would be accepted as *tafsīrs*, the vast majority of works fit into this pattern. Early works tend to focus on certain tendencies in interpretation. Some pursue the narrative ("haggadic") aspects of the Qurʾān, developing the text into an entertaining and edifying whole, paying attention to the needs of the reader, who will approach the text of scripture with a curious and speculative mind. Thus, providing the historical background to the various pieces of revelation (in a format which later becomes known as *asbāb al-nuzūl*, the "occasions of revelation," discussed in Chapter 1) and identifying people, places, and things which are only alluded to (known later as *taʿyīn al-mubham*) became important aspects. Other works pursue the legal ("halakhic") aspects of the text, focusing on the early community's need to support legal practice by reference to the text of scripture, sometimes facilitated by organizing the Qurʾān into topics rather than following the text *ad seriatim*. Yet other works examine textual matters, including lexicographical and more narrowly "masoretic" issues. Another tendency is seen in the work of Abū ʿUbayda (who died in 824) called *Majāz al-Qurʾān*, which focuses on literary figures and expressions. It presents a listing of types of "problematic" verses in the Qurʾān and their explanation; items such as ellipses due to omission, grammatical numerical discord (e.g. plural verbs with singular subjects), and variation in the treatment of the gender of nouns are all recorded. This cataloguing of difficulties in the Qurʾān is also found in other works treating the vocabulary of the text itself as well as the text's stylistic features and variant readings. With the emergence of the doctrine of inimitability, the attitude towards these sorts of elements changed, as has already been suggested. More major works of interpretation of the Qurʾān emerged in the ninth century, and they aimed to clarify the text in light of contemporary understandings and conditions. Not only was this the result of the maturation of the Muslim community and a consolidation of opinion about the scripture but it was also the result of practical pressures. As the Islamic community expanded, it incorporated a large number of people who did not know Arabic and who were not fully acquainted with the Biblical tradition, which, as has been pointed out, seems to be an assumed basis for understanding the Quranic text. The first landmark of what became a vast library of books providing comprehensive interpretations of the Qur'ān was written by Abū Ja'far al-Ṭabarī, who died in 923. A verse-by-verse analysis provides a detailed discussion of every major interpretational trend (except sectarian tendencies, for example, Shī'ī); every idea is documented by the transmission of the opinions derived from Muḥammad's closest companions and their successors, who are pictured as having the best information regarding the understanding of the text. It is also clear that grammar along with theological perspective became the main guiding tools for constructing a mature exegesis of the Qur'ān. Grammar served to assert the scholar's status and authority within the whole discipline of *tafsīr*, such that the ability to pursue the minutiae of Arabic constructions became a focal point of argumentation over how a meaning of the text could be derived. Theology tended to play a lesser role, usually subsumed under grammatical or legal wranglings.

While a brief quotation cannot do justice to the complexities of al-Ṭabarī's text, the following short section gives some indication of his own bases for reasoning, although we do not here see his constant reference to reports from Muḥammad's companions which provide the material basis to many discussions and variations in interpretations. In the context of dealing with Qur'ān 3/7, "It is He who sent down upon you the book in which there are clear verses—they are the mother of the book—and others are ambiguous," al-Ṭabarī makes the following statement:

> Then God described these "clear verses" by saying that they are the "mother of the book," meaning that they are the source of the book which contains within it all the duties of the religion, including the responsibilities and the penalties and everything else which creation needs in the law of its religion. Also included are the responsibilities which are assigned in this world and the hereafter. These are called "the mother of the book" because they are the major portion of the book and they are a place of refuge for the people of the Qur'ān when they are in need of such. That is the practice of the Arabs in calling the gathering of a major portion of something its "mother." So they named the banner of the people under which they gathered in their fighting groups their "mother"; also the leader who handled the majority of the matters of the village or district was called its "mother." . . . "Mother of the book" is in the singular; it is not made plural as in "They are the mothers of the Book." "They" is used, however, because all of the "clear verses" are intended by "the mother of the book," but not each verse of them is the "mother of the book." If the meaning was such that each of the "clear verses" was the "mother of the book," there would be no doubt in the matter, because then it would have been said: "They are the mothers of the book." The analogous statement of God to "They are the mother of the book" as we have interpreted it in the singular sense of "mother" being the grammatical complement of "they" is in Qur'ān 23/50, "We made the son of Mary and his mother a sign." He did not say "two signs"

> because the meaning is "We made the two of them together a sign." The meaning is singular because they gave a single warning to humanity. If the intention had been that each one of them independently gave a warning to humanity, then it would have been stated, "We made the son of Mary and his mother two signs," because then in each one of them there would have been a warning. The signs are that Mary had a child not by a man and that her son spoke from the cradle as a baby. So, in each of those events there is a sign for the people.
>
> (Ṭabarī 1971: VI, 170–1)

The historicization of the text of the Qurʾān was another important element in the production of many works of exegesis. The integration of the text with the stories of the prophets of the past (primarily Biblical) in the material known as the *qiṣṣaṣ al-anbiyāʾ*, "stories of the prophets," and with the story of the life of Muḥammad as embedded in books of *Sīra* ("life story") such as that of Ibn Isḥāq (d. 767) was designed both to prove the theological fact of the reality of revelation and to provide a context for interpretation of an otherwise historically opaque text. The result was a text which was grounded in day-to-day human existence with an emphasis on the period of the formative Muslim community.

The Qurʾān as an object of faith

For the Muslim community, the Qurʾān is the word of God as revealed to Muḥammad, the focal point of the Islamic faith. As a symbol of that faith, the book has naturally garnered far more importance for the individual believer than the polemical discussions sketched above would suggest. After all, for Muslims there is no doubt about the status of their scripture; at every moment, their faith confirms for them the veracity of the book. There arose a great number of beliefs about the text of the book itself, separate from its contents, which reflect the honor and significance which is accorded to the scripture as a book. Within at most 200 years of the death of Muḥammad, traditions arose speaking of the significance of individual sections of the Qurʾān. The first chapter, *sūrat al-fātiḥa*, is argued to be not only an essential element of the ritual of prayer, but also the "greatest" of all the *sūras*, the recitation of which is recorded as curing the bite of a scorpion, for example; likewise, *sūras* 113 and 114 are seen as effective in curing illnesses. Reciting specific individual portions of the Qurʾān, the last two verses of *sūra* 2 especially, is spoken of as giving protection from Satan for the night. Recitation of *sūra* 18, *sūra* 48, or *sūra* 112 brings merit and benefits. The result of these practices has been the emergence of a complex group of medical and spiritual beliefs all connected to the book, known as *khawāṣṣ al-Qurʾān*. The history of these practices, like most popular beliefs, is not well known, but it is likely that modern practices, such as wearing a tiny copy of the Qurʾān or the name Allāh as an amulet, in the manner in which Christians wear a crucifix or Jews a star of David, has a heritage which extends well back into the early

Islamic period. The Qur'ān has been the central symbol of Islam as well as its vital source, and, as is true of Jesus in Christianity, its power and effect to move and motivate individuals has never been underestimated by Muslims.

An early manuscript of the Qur'ān

Since the early 1990s, the popular media have drawn attention to the existence of early manuscripts of the Qur'ān. Most of this coverage has taken a sensationalist approach, raising the specter of Muslim religious concerns and conspiracy theories as reasons behind the lack of progress in creating a scholarly critical text of the Qur'ān. Meanwhile, scholars have been working away, undertaking detailing analyses of the available manuscripts and trying to understand the subtle differences between the generally uniform texts.

One manuscript held in Paris (Bibliothèque nationale de France, Arabe 328) has been well known to scholars for several generations and has long been considered one of the oldest copies of the Qur'ān that we possess today. Its script (commonly referred to as *Ḥijāzī*) and readings have been studied intensively. The challenges of analyzing this copy of the Qur'ān were not fully overcome until 2006, when the Bibliothèque nationale decided to restore the manuscript by removing the blank interwoven pages from the nineteenth-century binding that, due to acidity, were harming the original parchment. This also provided an opportunity to investigate the text in conjunction with various pieces of what scholarly detective work had shown to be folios from the same original manuscript, now dispersed across Europe. Originally coming from the ancient mosque of 'Amr in Cairo, fragments of the manuscript were brought to Europe during the first part of the nineteenth century. Sections are found not only in Paris but also in St. Petersburg, along with single leaves in the Vatican library and the Khalili Collection of Islamic Art in London. A total of ninety-eight folios in reasonably good condition, covering *sūra*s 2 through 72 (with a significant number of gaps), provide about 45 percent of the overall text of scripture.

François Déroche has undertaken a detailed study of the manuscript and has suggested that a total of five copyists with widely divergent approaches to their task were involved in producing the single text. He sees the manuscript as stemming from a period before full stabilization was achieved in counting the number of verses in a *sūra* and before the variant readings were formed into their canonical sets. He has settled on a date in the third quarter of the seventh century for the original production of the manuscript. Déroche suggested that the discrepancies between the copyists are essentially the result of copying from a model which itself was hard to interpret. The manuscript provides evidence that it clearly was in use into the third *hijrī* century (ninth

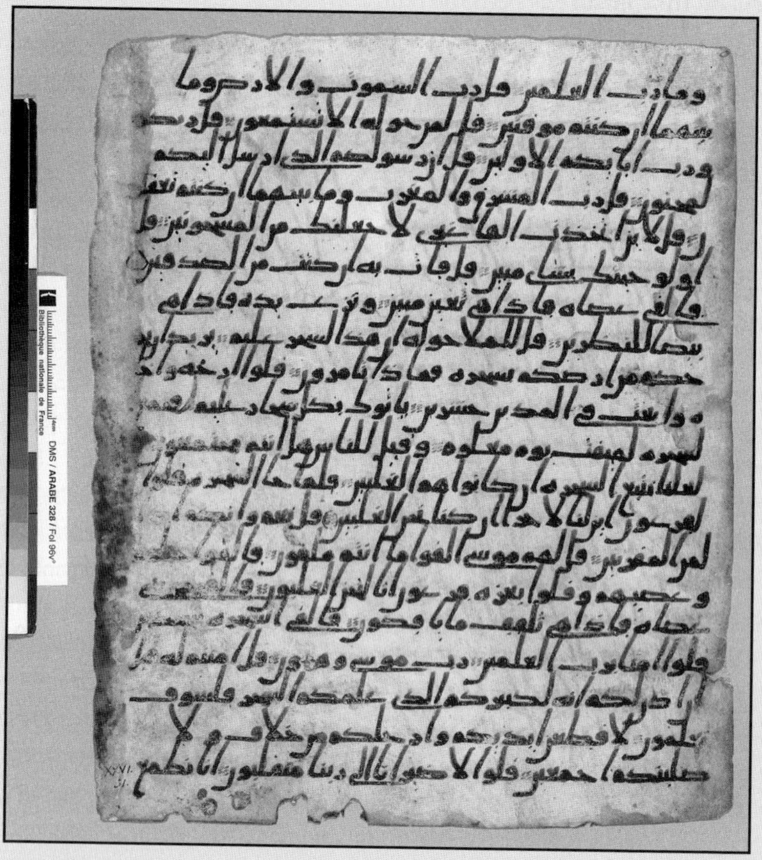

Figure 2.1 Folio 96v from a parchment manuscript (Paris Arabe 328f), using the *Hijāzī* script to write the Qur'ān. This is among the oldest copies of the Qur'ān in existence today. The text covers *sūra* 26, verses 23–51.
Source: Bibliothèque nationale de France.

century CE), given the presence of corrections provided by later users in order to bring the text into line with evolving standards, a process that took several centuries. The overall history of written transmission of the Quranic text is yet to be written by scholars and, given the evidence of this manuscript, that history will likely display a more complex picture than has commonly been assumed until now.

François Déroche, *La Transmission écrite du Coran dans les débuts de l'islam. Le Codex Parisino-petropolitanus*, Leiden: Brill, 2009, investigates the history of the manuscript. For a detailed study of the Paris portion of the manuscript, see Yasin Dutton, "An early *Muṣḥaf* according to the Reading of Ibn ʿĀmir," *Journal of Qur'anic Studies* 3 (2001): 71–89.

Suggested further reading

M. M. Al-Azami, *The History of the Qurʾānic Text from Revelation to Compilation: A Comparative Study with the Old and New Testament*, Leicester: UK Islamic Academy, 2003. (A defense of the historical integrity of the text of the Qurʾān that illustrates well the traditional Muslim position while engaging in the ongoing scholarly discussions.)

Michael Cook, *The Koran: A Very Short Introduction*, Oxford: Oxford University Press, 2000.

Jane Dammen McAuliffe (ed.), *The Cambridge Companion to the Qurʾān*, Cambridge: Cambridge University Press, 2006.

Jane Dammen McAuliffe (ed.) *Encyclopedia of the Qurʾān*, 6 vols, Leiden: Brill, 2002–6. (An essential reference work.)

Fazlur Rahman, *Major Themes of the Qur ʾan*, Minneapolis: Bibliotheca Islamica, 1980; second edition, Chicago: University of Chicago Press, 2009.

Andrew Rippin (ed.), *The Blackwell Companion to the Qurʾān*, Oxford: Blackwell, 2006.

3 *Muḥammad*

Muḥammad is the central figure in Islam. Chosen by God to receive the revelation of the Qurʾān, he has been taken by all Muslims to be the ideal man, the perfect embodiment of what it means to be a Muslim. Having lived a fairly normal existence in sixth-century Central Arabia, at the age of 40 Muḥammad revolutionized his society in ways which were both unexpected and long lasting.

Contemporary scholarship on Islam has generally not seen fit to postulate that Muḥammad did not exist. That someone named Muḥammad embodied the rallying point for the Arab conquests and provided the tag for a religious doctrine in the name of which the conquered lands were united there really is little doubt; at the very least, no profit is to be gained from denying those facts in terms of providing a cohesive historical picture. Sources external to the nascent Islamic society itself provide evidence, albeit somewhat at variance with the "accepted" portrait of the Arabian prophet, that confirms the role of the figure himself. It is important to recognize that these sources are limited in number, extremely hard to date (raising questions of Muslim influence upon the writers if the source is, in fact, much later than claimed), and questionable in their supposed "disinterested" or "objective" presentation of history.

Despite the existence of these external sources and the proliferation of documentation from within the community, the fact of the matter remains that it is very difficult to talk about Muḥammad, in either his political or religious guise, free from the perspective which later Muslim tradition has imposed upon him. The biography of Muḥammad has served a number of important functions in Islam, each of which has colored it in crucial ways. There are two major aspects which must be confronted here: (1) Muḥammad's biography must be understood as a framework for the revelation of the Qurʾān; and (2) it must be understood as a source for the normative example for Muslim behavior, the *sunna* of Muḥammad.

Muslim sources for the life of Muḥammad

Material on the life of Muḥammad is available in ample if, in fact, not excessive quantities. The earliest complete extant text stems from a version of the biography (*Sīra*) of

Figure 3.1 Dalāʾil al-khayrāt wa-shawāriq al-anwār fī dhikr al-ṣalāt ʿalā ʾl-nabī al-mukhtār ("The Guide to Blessings and Shining Lights Regarding Prayers on the Chosen Prophet"), by Abū ʿAbd Allāh Muḥammad b. Sulaymān al-Jazūlī (d. 870/1465), is one of the most famous books of prayer in Islamic literature. It features litanies in praise of Muḥammad, a description of his tomb, and a list of his names. These folios (16b and 17a from the Arabic MSS suppl. 616, copy dated 1793) present two miniatures commonly found in the text, one of them representing the Kaʿba, the other the tombs of Muḥammad, ʿUmar, and Abū Bakr in the Medina Mosque.
Source: General Collection, Beinecke Rare Book and Manuscript Library, Yale University.

Muḥammad by Ibn Isḥāq (d. 767) edited by Ibn Hishām (d. 833). This may be supplemented by other fairly early texts such as those by al-Wāqidī (d. 823) and Ibn Saʿd (d. 845). Also useful are the later *ḥadīth* collections which gather together anecdotes about Muḥammad and his life, generally organized according to legal topics and communicated by Muḥammad's closest followers, people who are deemed his "companions" in Muslim tradition. In broad outline, all these sources present the same story but matters of chronology and detail are always problematic.

The account of the events during Muḥammad's life is fairly standardized, despite the multiplicity of sources available and the numerous disagreements among scholars of Islam as to how to interpret the material in a meaningful way. Most accounts go back to the text of Ibn Isḥāq, supplemented by the various other sources. Despite valiant attempts by some scholars to elicit information, the Qurʾān has proven very opaque when it comes to Muḥammad: the name is mentioned four times—Qurʾān 3/144, 33/40, 47/2, 48/29—but without prior knowledge of the *Sīra* accounts of Ibn Isḥāq, the Quranic material provides no data beyond asserting Muḥammad's existence and a conception of his prophetic role. Furthermore, since in many places the *Sīra* may well be attempting to explain, make sense of, or clarify the elliptical and allusive text of the Qurʾān, there is the danger of going around in interpretative circles. The absence of biographical material is but one example of a general tendency in the Qurʾān not to provide any overall context. The Qurʾān simply does not provide the necessary clarifying keys by which it would be possible to extract data concerning the contemporary Arabian context, beyond the citation of a few names. It is in this vein, then, that one of the roles of the biography of Muḥammad in Islam is to be understood as providing the contextual framework for the revelation of the Qurʾān. While the details of this framework are frequently vague and contradictory, the basic theological point stands, underpinning the entire biographical corpus: God revealed the Qurʾān to Muḥammad, an ordinary man living among the Arab tribes, over a twenty-two-year period. As a result, the entire biographical account has been colored by these efforts to situate and interpret the Qurʾān.

The life of Muḥammad in the sources

Muḥammad is said to have been born around 570; this is a date fixed by a tradition which records that the "Expedition of the Elephant," the expedition by a ruler of South Arabia named Abraha, into the homeland of Muḥammad, the Ḥijāz, was in the same year. The evidence for the date of the expedition being 570 is undermined by inscriptional material found in South Arabia, which makes it more likely to have been at the end of the 540s. The significance of the date in the Muslim context is that it serves to establish Muḥammad's age as 40 when he started to receive revelations, the number forty being one of general spiritual significance in the Near East region.

Muḥammad was born into the family of Banū Hāshim in the tribe of Quraysh; his family was a prominent but not dominant group in the society at the time. He was orphaned at an early age, and lived a meager existence until he married Khadīja, an older woman with financial involvement in the camel-caravan trade. Muḥammad is thought to have been involved in the trade himself. At the age of 40 he is said to have gone on a solitary retreat in the hills near Mecca, following a religious practice of the time, at which point the angel Gabriel came to him to inform him of his commission as a prophet of the one God, Allāh. To this event is traditionally connected the Quranic passage contained in *sūra* 96: "Recite in the name of your Lord who created, created humanity from a blood clot! Recite, for your Lord is most Generous, who taught by the pen, taught humanity what it knew not." Stories of self-doubt are connected with this call to prophethood, but eventually Muḥammad followed his orders and preached the message of the Qurʾān. He had little success to begin with, perhaps converting some of the lower-class members of his society, along with his wife Khadīja and his cousin ʿAlī, his future son-in-law, fourth caliph and figurehead of the Shīʿī movement in Islam. As Muḥammad hardened his attack on the polytheistic society of Mecca, its inequalities and hypocrisies, the inhabitants became more resentful of his presence. It has been speculated that the cause of some of this resentment was his attack upon the institutions of the Meccan society, especially the town's connection to the religious shrine, the Kaʿba, which gave it a degree of prominence in Arabia at the time. Persecution of the members of this new religion is said to have increased substantially, and reports speak of a group of believers who emigrated to Abyssinia, perhaps going there to find asylum among the Christians or to attempt to make more converts among an audience who may have been thought to be sympathetic to the message of the movement. Meanwhile, Muḥammad made efforts to find a new place to live in Arabia, trying the neighboring town of al-Ṭāʾif, before being invited to Yathrib (later to be called Medina, or, fully, Madīnat al-nabī, the "City of the prophet") some 350 kilometers northeast of Mecca. Communities of Jews were living in Yathrib and these people are suggested to have been part of the attraction of the location, for a sympathetic audience for the message of Muḥammad was anticipated among these "people of the book."

The move to Yathrib is referred to as the *hijra* ("emigration" or "flight") and the year in which it happened (622) serves as the focal point of the Muslim calendar. An event to which the Qurʾān provides only ambiguous reference, it is regardless seen as the time at which the Muslim community came into being and thus the appropriate starting point for calendar dating (the notion of "community," *umma*, being a key defining element in the Islamic sense of identity). There do not appear to be any instances of the mention of the idea of a *hijrī* calendar in coins or documents from the seventh century; rather, an undefined era is employed or reference is made to an era (apparently starting in 622, however) as the "rule of the Arabs." Defining the calendar in terms of the *hijra* appears to be linked with the rise of Islam as a state religion, a notion to be explored further in Chapter 4.

It was in Yathrib/Medina that Muḥammad emerged as a forceful religious and political leader, leading the Medinan community under the terms of a type of treaty, the so-called "Constitution of Medina," within which his authority was said ultimately to derive from God: the ideal religio-political aspects of Muslim community life are embodied here. Controlled in this "constitution" were the political and civil relations of the various tribes within the Medinan federation, with all disputes to be brought before Muḥammad for arbitration. The "constitution" explicitly states:

> Whenever a dispute or controversy likely to cause trouble arises among the people of this document, it shall be referred to God and to Muḥammad, the apostle of God. God is the guarantor of the pious observance of what is in this document.
>
> (Ibn Hishām 1955: I, 504)

The actual conversion of the inhabitants of Medina to Islam was not immediate and the Jewish communities living there were accused of treachery and, eventually, all were either removed or attacked. Muḥammad's strategy in Medina, especially after his realization that the Jews were not the ready audience for his message which he had anticipated, was to return to Mecca. This aim was pursued through an attempt to curtail the trade of Mecca by random attacks on the camel caravans, producing unstable conditions for the reliable conduct of business as well as bringing the profits of such raids into Medinan hands, thus producing power and prestige for the community in the eyes of the Arabian tribes. The most important of these raids was known as the battle of Badr; taking place in 624, it started as an attack on a Meccan caravan and then became a battle with the Meccan Quraysh tribe. It provided a great victory for Muḥammad and his followers, a victory which was interpreted as a sign of divine pleasure with the strategy. In the year 625, an attack by Quraysh tribesmen resulted in a defeat for Muḥammad's followers in the Battle of Uḥud, while in 627 a Meccan army laid siege to Medina in the Battle of the Ditch. The Medinans were able to withstand the onslaught, however, and the Meccans were forced to withdraw after forty days. This success was followed by an attack directly on Mecca led by Muḥammad, which ended not with a battle but with the Treaty of Ḥudaybiyya, the terms of which allowed the Medinans to enter Mecca the next year in order to perform the pilgrimage; that treaty was honored. By that time, the power of the Medinan community had grown significantly in Arabia and by the next year, 630, Muḥammad was able to attack and take over Mecca, meeting little resistance to his efforts. The final two years of Muḥammad's life were spent in Medina, with him attempting to consolidate his position in Arabia with alliances, and at least nominal conversion to Islam, of the nomadic bedouin of Arabia.

Difficulties with the biography

This is the basic account of the life of Muḥammad as it is presented in the narrative sources available to us. Many aspects of it are debatable, especially in matters of precise dating, and, on that basis alone, the summary of the "life of Muḥammad" as presented here is fraught with difficulties and insoluble problems. Evidence of such things as the sources' tendency to "improve" over time—such that later sources are able to provide specific data where earlier ones are vague—and the overt intention of much of the material to interpret unclear passages of the Qur'ān, as mentioned above (p. 38), suggests that texts such as Ibn Isḥāq's *Sīra* are far more complex in literary terms than a historical biography might popularly be conceived today. Essentially, these texts were involved in a creative story-telling in which the raconteur's ability to elaborate, entertain, and enhance was a highly praised merit. Underlying the whole structure, however, is the attempt to provide a context for the revelation of the Qur'ān, such that ambiguous references may be made clear through the process of interpretation.

The mythic dimension of Muḥammad's biography

One other related factor acts to restrict the amount of confidence that may be placed in these accounts of Muḥammad's life, even disregarding disputes over small details. The religious importance of Muḥammad is such that it is not really feasible (nor necessarily desirable) to distinguish later religiously inspired fiction from what might be called historical "fact." The entire structure of a work such as that of Ibn Isḥāq suggests that many elements are constructed from what have been termed by one scholar "mythic *topoi*," or basic religious narrative and thematic conventions (Wansbrough 1978: 32). Such *topoi* were employed throughout the Near Eastern area in the construction of literary lives of religious figures. In addition, the *Sīra* text is composed of lists, documents, genealogies, chronologies, poetry, and formal prose. The overall effect is to create a picture of both Muḥammad and the Muslim community in its pristine form. This means that the picture which emerges, as well as the impulse behind its composition, is a normative one: it encapsulates how the Muslim community should be, projected back into the times of its founder, who has been described in mythic terms. Its intention is to portray the religion of Islam as conceptually identifiable from the time of Muḥammad.

A part of the reason for having produced such a picture of Muḥammad was to create an expression of Islam which separated it clearly from Judaism and Christianity. The role of the figurehead of a religion in producing identity for the religious community is evident in all three of the monotheistic traditions, and Muḥammad's place in this interreligious rivalry was established both through the Qur'ān (as the book given specifically to him, just as the Oral and Written Torahs were revealed to Moses in Judaism) and through the biographical material. The major concern displayed through a work such as Ibn Isḥāq's *Sīra* is the acceptance or rejection by various groups of the credentials in the hands of the messenger, that is, his scripture. At stake, then, is the authority of the person of Muḥammad, not in terms of law but as a prophet. The connection of Muḥammad to the revelation of the Qur'ān then becomes central.

The significance of the figure of Muḥammad

Another reason for the emergence of this elaborated, detailed picture of Muḥammad is far more complex and vital to the enterprise of Islam itself. In fact, regardless of how interesting the events of Muḥammad's life may be, the significance for Muslims of the person himself and the actual "facts" of the narrative (as opposed to its overall theological point) does not lie particularly in the historical narrative at all. Rather, it is the anecdotes about his life, the *aḥādīth* (singular, and frequently used in a collective sense: *ḥadīth*), and the more generalized aspects of what that behavior represents, that concern the community most of all. This is the *sunna*, the "example" provided by the life of Muḥammad which every Muslim attempts to emulate. Of course, the two aspects—the historical and the anecdotal—are intertwined and, for the historian, indistinguishable; this is, as a consequence, what has created some of the problems in trying to reconstruct the "historical Muḥammad."

The information which is found in works such as that of Ibn Isḥāq (at least in germ form), and which has been gathered together into the works of *ḥadīth* especially, is believed by Muslims to have been transmitted from the earliest generations of community members down to the collectors of these books. Such transmissions are documented by what is known as the *isnād*, the "chain" of transmitters of a report (listed backwards chronologically), while the actual text is known as the *matn*. An example is the following:

> Isḥāq told me that ʿUbayd Allāh told him on the authority of Shaybān on the authority of Yaḥyā on the authority of Muḥammad ibn ʿAbd al-Raḥmān, client of Banū Zuhra, on the authority of Abū Salama on the authority of ʿAbd Allāh ibn ʿUmar that he said, "The messenger of God (may the prayers and peace of God be upon him) said to me, 'Recite all of the Qurʾān in one month.' I said, 'But I am able to do more than that!' So (Muḥammad) said, 'Then recite it in seven days, but do not do it in less than that'."
>
> (Bukhārī 1984: VI, 517–18, tradition number 574)

Reports such as these comprise the text of a series of books devoted to the gathering together of the material, which may be arranged either according to the transmitter of the report or according to the legal topic. This latter method of organization proved the most successful, it being the principle employed in the six works which are accepted as being of major importance by the majority of Muslims. These books collect together what were considered genuine *ḥadīth* reports (and, as such, the reports serve as the theoretical basis for Islamic law). The books were each compiled by al-Bukhārī (d. 870), Muslim ibn al-Ḥajjāj (d. 875), Ibn Māja (d. 887), Abū Dāwūd (d. 889), al-Tirmidhī (d. 892), and al-Nasāʾī (d. 915).

All the reports in these books deal with what Muḥammad said and did, and what he approved or disapproved of implicitly (as indicated by his general behavior). They are classified into subjects which would appear to follow the legal discussion taking place at the time of their compilation. Al-Bukhārī, for example, has a total of ninety-three chapters with sub-headings, but in some chapters there are in fact no *ḥadīth* reports to be found under some of the sub-headings; it is clear, therefore, that he was working with a pre-arranged structure and was attempting to document the issues under discussion. The structure of his book reflects the concerns of Muslim life, ones which go beyond any narrow definition of "law" and encompass many different aspects. To take al-Bukhārī as an example again, his work starts with what might be considered "theological" topics: revelation, faith, and knowledge. He then deals with various aspects of prayer (Chapters 4–23), followed by charity, pilgrimage, and fasting (Chapters 24–32). Covered there are what have become the central symbols of Islam, enshrined in the concept of the "Five Pillars" (see Chapter 7). After that, the book covers, in Chapters 33–53, general interactions between people (with special emphasis on commerce) and then turns to certain religious concepts such as the merit of the prophets and the Qurʾān. Marriage and divorce follow, then a wide variety of topics, ranging from medicine and good manners to apostasy and dreams. The work finishes with "The Unity of God," thus bringing the sequence to closure. Muḥammad, therefore, is conceived to have had some bearing on all aspects of Muslim life, both the personal and the interpersonal, as reflected in this categorization of the *ḥadīth* material.

The problem of *ḥadīth* reports

For an individual report itself, its *isnād*, or chain of transmitters, is considered to act as a guarantor of the genuineness of the text of the report. However, the *isnād* mechanism was, according to Muslims, subject to a great deal of fraud in the early period. Muslims therefore created several methods of evaluating these *isnād*s, using criteria which dealt in particular with the life and character of the individual transmitters found in the sequence of names. The desire was to document *isnād*s which were complete in their testimony to the transmission of the text of the report from generation to generation. The citation of people of high moral integrity who conceivably could have met in their lifetimes so that the reports could have been passed on physically was the important factor in the assessment of the chains of transmitters. Not surprisingly, perhaps, such methods could really only sort out the inept *isnād* fabrications from the less inept.

The tendency to fabricate *ḥadīth* reports extended so far as to include reports which could justify the employment of *ḥadīth* reports themselves in trying to settle legal issues and others which warn against false transmission of reports. One of the most famous of all such reports is the following:

> Abū Bakr ibn abī Shayba told us that Ghundar told him on the authority of Shuʿba, and also that Muḥammad ibn al-Muthannā and Ibn Bashshār both told him that Muḥammad ibn Jaʿfar told him that Shuʿba also told him, on the authority of Manṣūr on the authority of Ribʿī ibn Ḥirāsh who heard ʿAlī, may God be pleased with him, giving a sermon in which he said that the messenger of God, may the prayers and peace of God be upon him, said, "Do not spread lies about me! Whoever spreads lies regarding me will enter the fires of hell."
>
> (Muslim 1955–6: I, 9, tradition number 1)

The forces which tried to stem the tide of extensive spreading of unreliable *ḥadīth* reports appear to have used the very practice they were trying to condemn in order to stop the practice.

We also find in the collections of *ḥadīth* reports instances which clearly are concerned with matters of interest to the community in generations after Muḥammad but which have been framed as predictions made by him. An example is the following, which raises the divisive issue of free will versus predestination as discussed by theologians several centuries into the Islamic era:

> Bundār told us that ʿAbd al-Raḥmān ibn Mahdī told him that Shuʿba told him on the authority of ʿĀṣim ibn ʿUbayd Allāh who said that he heard Sālim ibn ʿAbd Allāh reporting on the authority of his father who said that ʿUmar said: "O messenger of God, what do you think? Are the works which we do of our own creation or are they settled in advance by God?" (Muḥammad) said: "They are indeed settled in advance, O Ibn al-Khaṭṭāb, and everything has been made easy [see Qurʾān 80/20]. Whoever is of the people of happiness will do that which leads to happiness, and whoever is of the people of misery will do that which leads to misery."
>
> (Tirmidhī 1987: IV, 387–8, tradition number 2135)

Here, Muḥammad is employed as a spokesperson for the theological party which supported the doctrine of predestination; in that way, those people tried to assert the rightness of their position by citing Muḥammad as their proof. *Ḥadīth* reports may also be found which support the opposite position.

It has also been discovered by modern researchers that *isnāds* had a tendency to "grow backwards." In certain early texts a statement will be found attributed to a caliph of the Umayyad dynasty, for example, or will even be unattributed, as in the case of certain legal maxims; elsewhere, the same statements will be found in the form of *ḥadīth* reports with fully documented *isnāds* going back to Muḥammad or one of his companions. There are instances where it would have been appropriate on the basis of the arguments being conducted in texts to cite the given report from Muḥammad, had such reports been available; but, in fact, unattributed statements are found. The conclusion to be drawn from this is that at a certain point in time the *isnād* had not yet been fully developed and was not yet considered necessary by some authors to establish a report's authority. Only when the significance of a given statement was fully established did the *isnād* "grow backwards" to include Muḥammad and thus invest an opinion with the authority of the prophet of Islam.

The authority of Muḥammad

This fabrication of *ḥadīth* reports arose because of the importance which Muslims attributed to Muḥammad in the elaboration of Islam. Muḥammad's example became the legal basis for substantiation of individual items of Muslim behavior. As we shall see in Chapter 6, on the development of law, Muḥammad's practice or *sunna* became a source of law in Islam (second only to the Qurʾān) as a result of the desire to introduce both some uniformity and a sense of defined authority into the Muslim community. Because of this, the name and the authority of Muḥammad were used to substantiate legal positions; what a given group of Muslims felt was the correct or appropriate legal practice would, at the same time, sincerely be felt to be the practice of Muḥammad.

The crucial question, which is much debated in modern scholarship, is when did Muḥammad emerge as the source of authority for the community, which is clearly the position attributed to him by the ninth century? Certainly the status of the authority of Muḥammad in the early Muslim community is not clear. Coins which refer to him as *rasūl Allāh*, the "messenger of God," start appearing only in the 60s and 70s of the *hijrī* calendar and even then such citations need not be taken as necessarily invoking his authority; rather, his symbolic value as an emblem of Islam—a part of an emerging self-definition—would appear to be the point of such references, since the caliph was at the same time proclaiming himself the authority in the living community as the *khalīfat Allāh* (a matter discussed in Chapter 4). This same question also arises in the context of the discussion of the law regarding when the notion of the "local tradition" as the basis of legal practice was supplanted by the *sunna* or guided practice of Muḥammad as second in authority after the Qur'ān.

Clearly, then, the status of Muḥammad as the legal grounding for the community's actions and beliefs had an impact on the biographical material which is available to us today. Much of the material tells us more about the developments within the later Muslim community—the issues which were being elaborated, the debates which were going on—than it does about Muḥammad as a person. All the material is of great value to the historian, therefore, but it must be treated with a discerning, critical eye, always alert to the ideological value contained within any reminiscence or anecdote.

The significance of Muḥammad

In sum, then, the life of Muḥammad may be recounted on the basis of various sources and its details may be debated. The value of it as a grounding for the Qur'ān may be examined. The development of Muḥammad's role as an authority in the community can be analyzed and evidence cited. All such discussions, however, miss the essence of Muslim feelings about the significance of Muḥammad.

It has often been commented that while Muslims may think those who deny the existence of God or who utter blasphemies about Him are misguided, such discussions will not offend in the same manner in which discussions over Muḥammad will. Those who impute evil to Muḥammad or who cast aspersions on him are considered to be insulting Islam. This, upon consideration, is not surprising. The charges laid by Christians against Islam in medieval times always focused on Muḥammad and his use of "holy war," *jihād*, the permission for polygamy, and the number of marriages consummated by Muḥammad himself. "Insulting" Muḥammad in any way, therefore, always recreates the image of those times and raises the suspicion that such charges are being laid once again, even if they are in different words. But further thought reveals that "attacking" Muḥammad is, of course, attacking the way of life of individual Muslims, for their way of life is understood to rest on the example of the founder of their religion. If something is felt by Muslims to be a denigration of one aspect of the life of Muḥammad, then by implication such may be seen as an attack on the whole way of life of each and every Muslim, at least in its idealized conception.

Muḥammad, as is implied in the basis of the entire concept of the *sunna*, is the "perfect man." He is the most liberal, the best, the bravest. Most of all, Muḥammad is considered to have lived his life in a state of sinlessness (*ʿiṣma*). With such a doctrine, everything Muḥammad did is considered to be the perfect embodiment of the will of God—nothing at any point in his life would have been in contravention of that will. He is even described as being the Qurʾān itself ("He was a Qurʾān walking on earth," according to one report), so perfect was his embodiment of it. This is a doctrine which took a number of centuries to become firmly established in Islam, as evidenced by some early, divergent material which presents Muḥammad as capable of making mistakes, even on very basic religious issues. It is quite likely that the significance of the doctrine should be viewed in tandem with that of the *iʿjāz*, "inimitability," of the Qurʾān; Muḥammad's sinlessness protects not only the concept of the *sunna* but also the contents of the Qurʾān from any lack of perfection.

The picture of Muḥammad has, as a result of the notion of sinlessness, been subject to all sorts of "fantastic" elaborations, creating a mythic image of the prophet of Islam. A portrait of the "perfect man" emerges, providing details even of his physical description:

> [Muḥammad's hair was] neither lank nor short and woolly. It touched his shoulders. Muḥammad used to make four plaits with each ear exposed between two plaits. The number of white hairs did not exceed seventeen. His eyes were very wide and black. His nose was hooked. He had a broad chest. Between his navel and upper chest there was a single hair. He had three belly folds.
>
> (Ghazālī 1965: II, 381)

Descriptions such as these are not abundant in Muslim texts but they do display at least one aspect of the devotion to Muḥammad, who, although he is only ever said to have been an ordinary mortal with no supernatural attributes, inevitably became the focus for much popular speculation and devotion to his person.

The night journey of Muḥammad

More prominent in this elaboration of the picture of Muḥammad is the story of his night journey (*isrāʾ*) to Jerusalem and his ascension into heaven (*miʿrāj*). Not only is the narrative a favorite in and by itself, but the stories have been the subject of numerous artistic endeavors. The story also provides at least some of the sanction for the significance of Jerusalem in Muslim piety (this is the place from which Muḥammad ascended into heaven). As well, the account of the ascension stands as a model of Muslim spiritual devotion when interpreted on a metaphorical level as the inner journey leading to the vision of God. Issues dealing with the nature of heaven and hell, their existence, and the conditions for entrance often find themselves attached to this story. Finally, the stipulation of five prayers a day as the requirement for Muslims also finds its support in the narrative. The story functions on many different levels, therefore, and is not only a vehicle for flights of popular imagination.

Traditionally pegged to Qurʾān 17/1—"Glory be to Him, who carried His servant by night from the holy mosque to the further mosque whose surroundings We have blessed, so that We might show him some of Our signs. He is the All-hearing, the All-seeing"—the story tells of Muḥammad traveling to Jerusalem on the back of the winged horse Burāq, and from there ascending through the seven levels of heaven, meeting the great prophets of the past as he progresses: Adam, John, Jesus, Joseph, Enoch, Aaron, Moses, and Abraham. He is given a view of various aspects of hell as well. Finally he is allowed a vision of God and is given the command of fifty prayers a day for his followers. In a narrative reminiscent of the Sodom and Gomorrah account in Genesis 18, Muḥammad, at Moses's insistence, returns to God to bargain for a lower requirement; the final result is the five daily prayers. Muḥammad returns to Mecca and tells of his adventure and is able to prove the veracity of his story by knowing of the imminent arrival of a caravan in his home town which he saw when returning on Burāq. The proof of the mission provides a rousing climax to the account. When asked what proof he had for his journey to Jerusalem, Muḥammad replied that

> he had passed a certain caravan in a certain valley and the animal which he was riding on scared them and a camel ran away. [He said], "I showed them where it was while on my way to al-Shams. I carried on until I reached Ḍajanān where I passed by another caravan. The people were sleeping; they had a jar of water which was covered with something. I uncovered it, drank some water and replaced the cover as I had found it. The evidence of this is that their caravan is now approaching from al-Bayḍāʾ at the pass of al-Tanʿīm; it is led by a dark-coloured camel with two sacks on it, one black, the other multi-coloured." The people hurried to the pass and it was as Muḥammad had described.
>
> (Ibn Hishām 1955: I, 402–3)

The basic substance of the entire story of the night journey and ascension is found in Ibn Isḥāq's *Sīra* and it has continued to be elaborated up until today. Such miraculous stories are not abundant in the popular life accounts of Muḥammad (as compared to those of Jesus, for example) but they do tend to play an important role both in providing a guarantee of Muḥammad's status and in supplying a focal point for popular belief. Other instances of popular stories are frequently connected to Muḥammad's birth and youth. Very popular is the account of angels visiting him to cleanse his heart. The story exists in many renditions. One version speaks of two men in white clothes seizing the infant Muḥammad, opening his chest, and removing his heart. They then proceed to wash his heart in a golden basin with purifying water from the well of Zamzam, which was located next to the Kaʿba in Mecca. This type of story and many others like it reveal a colorful adaptation of Jewish and Christian legends regarding prophetic qualifications and initiation; the stories frequently combine this thematic borrowing with anecdotes spun around statements from the Qurʾān, as in the instance of the account of the heavenly journey.

Muḥammad as intercessor

Another aspect of the popular Muḥammad which is of great significance is that of his role as intercessor on behalf of the members of his community on the day of judgment. While not finding any explicit support within the Qurʾān (which emphasizes individual responsibility on this point), it is commonly held that Muḥammad will act as an advocate before God on behalf of his people. While this sort of idea has not developed into a notion of redemption through the prophet by his suffering on others' behalf as in Christianity, nor into an idea of Muḥammad having a store of merit which he can share, his role is clearly enunciated in the texts of classical Islam which concentrate on the events on the day of judgment. A text ascribed to the famous Ṣūfī-theologian al-Ghazālī (d. 1111) pictures Muḥammad saying in the afterlife scene, "I am the right one! I am the right one [to intercede] insofar as God allows it for whomever He wills and chooses." God then says to him, "O Muḥammad, lift your head and speak, for you will be heard; seek intercession and it will be granted" (Smith 1979: 59, 60). Once again, the popular portrait of Muḥammad constructs him as an extremely important element in the salvation of his community, someone far more significant than simply the recipient of the revelation of the Qurʾān. Islam very much revolves around its twin sources of authority, the Qurʾān and Muḥammad, with both of those entities being firmly situated in the prehistory of the community in Arabia.

Portraits of Muḥammad

On September 30, 2005, the Danish *Jyllands-Posten* newspaper published twelve editorial cartoons that depicted Muḥammad within the context of modern political and national issues. Outrage was expressed in many quarters of the Muslim world. This generated an enormous public discussion of Muslim attitudes towards the portrayal of Muḥammad in representational form. Those discussions often missed the point about the *objectionable* nature of the cartoons themselves and tended to focus on what seemed to be the apparent contradiction between the Muslim iconoclastic attitude and the existence of well-known portraits of Muḥammad that Muslims produced in medieval times. Looking at those portraits reveals how complex the attitude towards images has been in the Islamic world throughout history, and that, as with many such matters, there is no single "Islamic" position on this issue; localized understandings play a major role in setting standards and expectations.

The history of Muslim iconoclasm suggests that the position arose as a marker of distinction when Islam was viewed alongside Christianity, a reflection of the political and ideological context at the time of the flowering of the Islamic empire. This is best expressed in a positive fashion as an attempt by Muslims to find a way to have official visual symbols that were distinct. Writing took on the symbolism of Islam, even to the point of representing the power of the ruler, as is displayed on many coins from the medieval period. However, figural representation was certainly present on early coins and not unknown in later times as well. Notably, however, the mosaics of both the early Muslim architectural monuments, the Dome of the Rock and the mosque in Damascus, do not contain any animal or human representations.

The idea that the production of figural representation is forbidden in Islam is supported by *ḥadīth* reports. One such report from Muslim ibn al-Ḥajjāj's *Ṣaḥīḥ* (in the "Book on Clothes and Decorations") reads in part:

> A person came to Ibn ʿAbbās and said, "I am a person who paints pictures; give me a religious verdict about them." Ibn ʿAbbās said to him, "Come near me." He came near him such that he placed his hand upon his head and said, "I am going to narrate to you what I heard from God's messenger. I heard him say, 'All the painters who make pictures will be in the fires of Hell. A soul will be breathed into every picture prepared by him and it shall punish him in Hell!' " Ibn ʿAbbās said, "If you have to do it at all, then paint pictures of trees and lifeless things."

Painted portraits of Muḥammad started to appear around 1300 and continued to be common through the sixteenth century. The pictures especially appear in the context of treatments of the lives of the prophets and the biography of Muḥammad himself. The most famous versions are those that illustrate Muḥammad's night journey and ascension to heaven. In many portraits Muḥammad has a flaming halo surrounding him and his face is often obscured by a veil.

On the meaning of Muslim iconoclasm, see Oleg Grabar, *The Formation of Islamic Art*, New Haven, CT: Yale University Press, 1973, chapter 4. For a provocative and clear exposition of ideas about Islamic art in general, including figural representation, see Oliver Leaman, *Islamic Aesthetics: An Introduction*, Edinburgh: Edinburgh University Press, 2004.

Suggested further reading

Jonathan E. Brockopp (ed.), *The Cambridge Companion to Muḥammad*, Cambridge: Cambridge University Press, 2010.

Michael Cook, *Muhammad*, Oxford: Oxford University Press, 1983.

Tarif Khalidi, *Images of Muhammad: Narratives of the Prophet in Islam Across the Centuries*, New York: Doubleday, 2009.

Uri Rubin, *The Eye of the Beholder: The Life of Muḥammad as Viewed by the Early Muslims: A Textual Analysis*, Princeton: Darwin Press, 1995.

Annemarie Schimmel, *And Muhammad Is His Messenger: The Veneration of the Prophet in Islamic Piety*, Chapel Hill: University of North Carolina Press, 1985.

PART II Emergence of Islamic identity

Significant dates

632	death of Muḥammad
634	death of Abū Bakr, first caliph
644	death of ʿUmar, second caliph
656	death of ʿUthmān, third caliph
661	death of ʿAlī, fourth caliph and figurehead of the Shīʿa
	Muʿāwiya becomes caliph
661–750	Umayyad dynasty
680	death of Ḥusayn, son of ʿAlī
	death of caliph Muʿāwiya
685–705	rule of caliph ʿAbd al-Malik
691	Dome of the Rock built
728	death of writer al-Ḥasan al-Baṣrī
750	ʿAbbāsid dynasty begins
767	death of jurist Abū Ḥanīfa
	death of historian Ibn Isḥāq
795	death of jurist Mālik ibn Anas
798	death of jurist Abū Yūsuf
805	death of jurist al-Shaybānī
813–833	rule of caliph al-Maʾmūn
820	death of jurist al-Shāfiʿī
838	death of theologian/exegete Abū ʿUbayd
855	death of jurist Aḥmad ibn Ḥanbal
870	death of *ḥadīth* collector al-Bukhārī
875	death of *ḥadīth* collector Muslim ibn al-Ḥajjāj
884	death of jurist Dāwūd ibn Khalaf, founder of Ẓāhirī school

912	death of Mu'tazilī theologian al-Khayyāṭ
935	death of theologian al-Ash'arī
944	death of theologian al-Māturīdī
945	Buwayhids take over Baghdad
1025	death of Mu'tazilī theologian 'Abd al-Jabbār
1037	death of jurist/theologian al-Baghdādī
1055	rise of the Seljuks
1065	death of Ẓāhirī jurist/theologian Ibn Ḥazm
1096	death of jurist al-Sarakhsī
1142	death of theologian al-Nasafī
1197	death of jurist al-Marghanānī
1258	Mongol takeover of Baghdad
1453	Turkish takeover of Constantinople/Istanbul

4 *Political action and theory*

Muslim sources, frequently confirmed by the unintentional witness of contemporaneous Greek and Syriac writers, make it clear that the Arabs came surging out of the Arabian peninsula in the seventh century, with the initial attack on Damascus in 635 (the city being taken finally in 637), Ctesiphon in 637, and Jerusalem in 638. The area had been made ready for such an invasion by the political situation of the Near East, as sketched in Chapter 1. A critical matter of dispute among historians has been the extent to which religion was a motivating factor in these wars of expansion. The simple explanation that religion, in the common sense of the word, provides the underpinning of the whole phenomenon is not necessarily supported by the archaeological data available; nor is it substantiated by the historical texts, at least not when they are critically assessed in light of an understanding of the theological back-reading of history which took place well after the structures and concepts of Islam were fully established. What appears fairly plain is that in the first century of Arab rule in the Near East a religious ideology was employed both by those in power and by those struggling for power; it was by means of this ideology that authority was established in the community. Once again, then, one must be careful in speaking of the religion in the earliest period. To call it "Islam" leads easily to the glossing of the difference between what was conceived then and what the religion became by the beginning of the third Muslim century when a fixed religious system had certainly emerged (although its established normative orthodox forms were still at least a century off even at that point). Some scholars have suggested that we should refer to this early religion of the Arabs as "Hagarism," a word derived from the name used in some Greek and Syriac sources when talking about the "Muslims." Others have suggested a term such as "Muhammadanism" or even "Arab monotheism." Be that as it may, in general some of the most important evidence for making some distinction between the earlier and later roles and forms of the religion in the area comes from the political actions of the early rulers of the conquered territory, especially as the rulers affected the religious ideology and symbolism through their employment of it.

History of the Arab conquests and empire

Abū Bakr took over rule of the community in the position of "caliph" (*khalīfa*), upon the death of Muḥammad in the year 632; he was selected by a group of elders, according to traditional reports, as being the person most qualified to rule. At that time the Arabs controlled no territory outside Arabia, as far as the contemporary sources let us know. It was under Abū Bakr's leadership in the year 633 that early victories in Iraq (the city of Hira) took place. The year 634 saw the beginnings of the conquest of Syria as well as the accession of ʿUmar ibn al-Khaṭṭāb, the second caliph. Syria gradually fell into Arab hands, with the battle of Yarmuk in 636 inflicting a crushing defeat on the Byzantine army. Damascus, Antioch, Jerusalem, and finally the whole Syrian area came under Arab control by 638. Meanwhile, Iraq was falling also, with the conquest of Ctesiphon (Madāʾin) and the defeat of the Sasanian army in 637, followed by the founding of the Iraqi garrison towns of Basra and Kufa in 638. By 641, the Sasanian empire was coming close to its final end, with virtually all of Persia open to the Arabs after the battle of Nihavand. The conquest of Egypt was begun in 639 and completed by 642. With ʿUmar's death in 644, ʿUthmān ibn ʿAffān, the third caliph, took over; in his time, the armies made westward gains, coming near the Roman outreach of Carthage by 647, but the area proved much harder to subdue than the former Sasanian or Byzantine territories. Some of the islands of the Mediterranean came under Arab domination at this time, with Cyprus being taken in 649 and Rhodes and Crete occupied shortly thereafter; these conquests came as a result of the emergence of Arab sea power, which provided a means of defense for the armies against the initially superior Byzantine naval forces.

ʿUthmān was assassinated in 656, reputedly by a group of disaffected tribesmen from Egypt, and his rule was followed by that of ʿAlī ibn abī Ṭālib, cousin and son-in-law of Muḥammad. ʿAlī's position was challenged, however, by a group consisting of ʿĀʾisha, one of the widows of Muḥammad, Ṭalha and al-Zubayr, members of the group of close followers of Muḥammad. The "Battle of the Camel" was the result of this uprising, leading to the death of Ṭalha and al-Zubayr, and the removal from a position of influence of ʿĀʾisha. ʿAlī was effectively in charge until a kinsman of ʿUthmān, Muʿāwiya, revolted. Power and authority were clearly the issues at stake in this civil war once again, although rivalries between groups of Arabs, on matters both of tribal loyalties and of political and practical problems, have also been seen to be partially responsible.

ʿAlī and Muʿāwiya met in what is known as the Battle of Ṣiffīn, which was, in the end, submitted to arbitration because of the indecisive outcome of the clash. The fact of submitting the matter to this sort of resolution led to a clear erosion of ʿAlī's power, for it acted to legitimize the challenge to his authority as ruler. Probably by the year 660, Muʿāwiya had full control of his home province of Syria. In 661, ʿAlī was murdered by a rebel, creating a situation in which Muʿāwiya was able to take over Kufa, the power base of ʿAlī, and emerge as the clear leader; thus was formed what became the Umayyad dynasty, which lasted until 750. Certainly not all the people rallied behind Muʿāwiya; some supporters of ʿAlī, who gained the name the Shīʿa, or "party," of ʿAlī, remained outside the control of the new leader. Others, who are thought to have felt that the whole process was somehow illegitimate, declared themselves opposed to both sides and became known as the Khawārij, those who had "gone out" from the community. The stance of such people plays a major role in the debates over theological issues, as will be discussed in Chapter 5. It is tempting to see people such as the Khawārij as the earliest bearers of the religious impulse which became Islam; thus their rejection of the political powers of the day might be seen in religious as well as political terms. Such a reading of history remains speculative at this time, however.

Meanwhile, the expansionist wars were continuing. By 661, the armies had already arrived in Afghanistan, making their way to India, as far as the Indus river and the province of Sind. Under a succession of Umayyad rulers, the armies went into Central Asia, with Bukhara being raided in 674 and Samarqand in 676, although it took until 711 for the area to be fully settled. Sporadically from 670 onward, Constantinople was besieged, although it was never actually captured until 1453 under the Ottomans. Eastern sections of Anatolia, and Armenia, fell towards the end of the seventh century. Likewise, the conquests in the west continued, with Kairouan in present-day Tunisia being founded in 670, and Carthage finally falling into Arab hands in 693. From there, the armies went onward to the Atlantic and crossed into Spain in 710, taking over Toledo in 712. Southern France was invaded in 725 but the overstretched army was stopped from further incursions into Europe by the Battle of Tours in 732.

Muʿāwiya ruled from 661 until 680, when he died and, by previous arrangement, the leadership of the empire went to his son Yazīd. This transfer of power did not go uncontested. Almost immediately upon assuming power, Yazīd faced a rebellion by one of ʿAlī's sons, Ḥusayn, whose efforts appear to have been pitiful, although his actions had an enormous mythic power among the later Shīʿa. A more serious and lasting challenge came from ʿAbd Allāh ibn al-Zubayr, who was a member of the Quraysh tribe to which Muḥammad had belonged and a resident of Medina. Amassing power in his home base, Ibn al-Zubayr was attacked by Yazīd's Medinan governor in 680 but he was able to flee to Mecca, where he gained power, especially when Yazīd died in 683. His rebellion continued, even reaching such an extent that he was the most significant leader within the Arab empire for a certain period of time, until a strong power re-emerged within the Umayyad family, that of ʿAbd al-Malik (685–705), and he was defeated. It was also under the rule of ʿAbd al-Malik and his son al-Walīd (705–715) that the final surge of the conquests in the east and the west was accomplished. It is important to recognize the significance of these events. The view of the Umayyads as a consistent and unified dynasty governing the Islamic empire is misleading. There were major ruptures and successful declarations of independence on many occasions.

By 744 the power of the Umayyads was being challenged again and, despite a strong ruler, Marwān II (744–750), an apparently Shīʿī-inspired rebellion fomented in the eastern province of Khurasan. This eventually led to civil war and the rise of the ʿAbbāsid dynasty in 750. The Shīʿa were quickly disavowed by the new rulers, but the change in ruling families did have far-reaching consequences beyond the actual political structure of the state. A socio-economic restructuring of the empire took place, with the partial removal of the "old guard" who were entrenched in positions of power within the social system and the eventual emergence of a new and powerful class of bourgeoisie and religiously devoted scholars. The capital of the empire was moved from Syria to Baghdad and this action provided the pretext for the splintering of governance and power in various areas. For the western reaches of the empire, this eastward shift of the caliphal seat of power was cited as an example of the lack of interest exhibited by the central administration towards the more far-flung portions of the empire. A descendant of the Umayyads, ʿAbd al-Raḥmān, became the independent ruler of Spain in 756. Similar independence movements affected North Africa during the late eighth and ninth centuries. Likewise, separate dynasties emerged in the East, especially in the provinces of Khurasan and Transoxiana, in the ninth century, leading eventually to the Buwayhid family taking over political power in Baghdad itself in 945 and reducing the caliph to a person of little influence who acted only as a puppet of the real military rulers. The Mongol conquest in 1258 spelled the end of even this remnant of ʿAbbāsid caliphal prestige.

Such were the political events of the early centuries. There is little reason to harbor substantial doubts concerning the general overall chronological ordering of the conquests themselves. What is significant, however, is that during this period the gradual emergence of the classical form and character of Islam may be seen. But just what was the role of Islam in all of this political activity? Were the battles being fought religiously motivated? To what extent did this shape the structures of Islam itself? What was the role of politics in enunciating the classical form of Islam? What was the position of the caliph as the leader of the community and how did he use the idea of Islam in his ruling of the community?

The notion of *jihād*

A central image which has remained powerful in the Euro-American mind is that of the Muslim *jihād* spreading Islam by the sword across much of the known world after the time of Muḥammad. However, the religious nature of these early expansionist conquests has provided a point of considerable debate in recent decades. Medieval Muslim authors, in writing the history of the era, certainly saw the hand of God behind the spread of Islam, and the notion that this was a "struggle" in the way of God, as the word and concept *jihād* suggest, was a characteristic to be applauded. This back-projection of religious motivation has made the reconstruction of the character of this early historical period difficult.

The medieval view held that the world was divided into two arenas, *dār al-Islām*, the "house of Islam," and *dār al-ḥarb*, the "house of war." The necessity of the armed struggle against the unbelievers was clearly indicated in the Qurʾān, as in *sūra* 22, verse 39, "Permission is given to those [believers] who are fighting [the disbelievers] because they have been wronged. Surely God is able to give them victory!" Whether this was a defensive or offensive struggle mattered little because the resistance of people to Islam was often taken to be equivalent to an attack on Islam. The final goal of *jihād* must then be a world which has been brought under the control of Islam and is, by definition, peaceful.

Underlying the idea of *jihād* is a unified Muslim community, the *umma*, which has the collective duty to expand Islam; this was to be done under the leadership or commission of the caliph. Expansionist wars were the responsibility of those who were charged with the task or those who chose to engage in them as a group; defending Islam, however, was a duty which fell on everyone who was capable. An expansionist war could not be undertaken without first issuing a call for the unbelievers to join Islam; should there be resistance to that call, then the war was justified. This notion of a unified community underlying the idea of *jihād* is crucial because it emphasizes the political (as opposed to religious) significance of the doctrine, certainly as it evolved. A caliph who issued a call for *jihād* was also asserting his legitimacy in the position of caliph. (As we will see, in medieval and modern times, in the absence of the caliph, the call for *jihād* acts as an assertion of authentic Muslim identity).

Not all early wars were expansionist battles and this fact made the moral issue of war one which early Muslims had to deal with. Battles between groups, all of whom identified themselves as part of this new empire, provided a challenge which led to a terminological distinction in dealing with *ḥarb*, "war": *futūḥ*, literally "openings," were battles against unbelievers, while *fitan*, "moral disruptions," were battles between Muslims. Only the former could be a *jihād*.

The complications of the historical records, the entanglement of later Muslim theories of *jihād*, and the underlying polemical overtones of any treatment of *jihād* mean that other sources of information are needed in order to provide a clearer view of the nature of the religious and political context at the time of the rise of Islam.

The Dome of the Rock and its significance

During the rule of the Umayyad caliph ʿAbd al-Malik an event of major significance took place; the Dome of the Rock in Jerusalem was built. This is the oldest extant building of Islamic architecture and one which can be dated with significant precision due to the presence of an important inscription which is found on both sides of the outer arched octagonal colonnade within the building. The inscription was tampered with by al-Maʾmūn, the ʿAbbāsid caliph (ruled 813–833). He had ordered some repairs to the Dome in about the year 831, and he appears to have followed a general policy of attempting to obliterate signs of the accomplishments of the earlier Umayyads. Significant original information still remains in the inscription, however, apparently due to an "oversight" on the part of those who changed it. The end of the inscription, at the east end of the south face on the outer band of the colonnade, reads: "The servant of God ʿAbd Allāh the *imām* al-Maʾmūn, commander of the believers, has built this Dome in the year 72 [= 691], may God accept him." Not only is the shade of the mosaic in which the inscription has been written different when the name of the caliph is stated, but also the name is written in crowded characters. Most telling, however, is the fact that the date which is given (and is written in mosaics of the same shade as the rest of the inscription) is that of ʿAbd al-Malik, who, as all the other sources tell us, had the Dome built and who ruled from 685 to 705. A similar tampering is also witnessed on the copper inscriptions over the north and east doors, which are also held to have been written in the time of ʿAbd al-Malik, according to the evidence of the shape of the script itself.

Why was the Dome of the Rock built?

Later Muslim historians provide several reasons for ʿAbd al-Malik having built the Dome. As stated earlier, during the revolt of Ibn al-Zubayr, control of Mecca fell to the rebel leader. In order to assert his authority and independence, ʿAbd al-Malik, according to this tradition, had the Dome of the Rock built as a place of pilgrimage. This explanation attempts to account for the unique (within Islam) architectural style of the Dome, for it is not a mosque, nor is it an imitation of the Kaʿba. It is, however, clearly a place where pilgrimage-type activities—especially circumambulation—were designed to take place within the colonnaded passageways. Modern historians have objected to this interpretation, suggesting that it is doubtful that any caliph would attempt to displace Mecca as a point of pilgrimage, for this would likely entail, as a result, the total rejection of that person's legitimacy to be ruler of an "Islamic" state. Such an objection, however, is based upon a supposition that the pilgrimage to Mecca was already a central symbol of nascent Islam. It would seem just as possible to conceive that, in the era of ʿAbd al-Malik, the activity of pilgrimage was being used as a political symbol and that two pilgrimages, one in Mecca under Ibn al-Zubayr and another in Jerusalem under ʿAbd al-Malik, emerged at roughly the same time in competition with one another.

Another suggestion classically put forth to explain the existence of the Dome of the Rock is that it was a sanctuary built to commemorate the "ascension" (*miʿrāj*) of Muḥammad, as related in Chapter 3; the rock from which Muḥammad ascended into heaven is covered by the commemorative Dome. Such an interpretation is clearly late, however, for no part of the colonnade inscription of ʿAbd al-Malik found in the building makes any reference to this journey; nor do any elements of the texts which are found in the inscription and which are also found in the Qurʾān even contain an allusion to this myth. It is also worthy of note that early Muslim interpretation of Qurʾān 17/1, the key text cited as related to the *miʿrāj*, is ambiguous about the identification of *al-masjid al-aqṣā*, which is mentioned in this verse. One interpretation is that this term refers to a town near Mecca on the boundary of the sacred *ḥarām* (and, in parallel, *al-masjid al-ḥarām* refers not to a specific building but to the town of Mecca itself). Another idea is that *al-masjid al-aqṣā* is in a celestial location. Finally, the term is taken as a reference to the Temple Mount in Jerusalem as a whole, or even to Jerusalem as a whole. The association of the Muslim buildings with this term is quite late, with the so-called Mosque of ʿUmar, located on the southern end of the sanctuary platform, being identified as *al-masjid al-aqṣā* (as it is now commonly called) for the first time only in the eleventh century.

Finally, texts from various Muslim historians suggest that the Dome was built to rival the beauty of the Christian Holy Sepulcher in Jerusalem. This is an account which has echoes throughout Islamic history, for example in the accounts of Sultan Ahmet I and his commissioning the architect Mehmet Aga early in the seventeenth century to build the Blue Mosque (Sultan Ahmet Camii) in Istanbul directly opposite the Christian church of Justinian, Haghia Sophia, dedicated in 537, in order to rival its magnificence.

The interpretation of the Dome of the Rock

The latter explanation for the building of the Dome of the Rock may, in fact, contain an element which is meaningful historically when the building is interpreted as a whole in its architectural form and in light of the contents of the inscriptions. It would appear that the desire of the builder was not only to rival but to outshine all other buildings and, most importantly, to symbolize the triumph of the conquerors over the land and over the rival religions. The Dome of the Rock embodies the arrival of nascent Islam and underlines the religion's rising presence. It is a piece of work representing the ultimate propaganda of the Arab rulers over their subjects through the use of religion. That is why the building is so important to any understanding of the rise of Islam. Still, though, why the Dome should have been built over this specific rock in Jerusalem remains unclear; a suggestion that, in fact, the Muslims were completing a Christian project from an earlier time is possible but, once again, there does not seem to be an overwhelming amount of evidence for such a notion.

The evidence of the inscription on the colonnade (which people circumambulating the rock would see and perhaps be able to read, especially the one on the inner surface) also suggests significant aspects of the Arab propaganda effort. The outer face of the colonnade contains a series of passages, found today in the Qurʾān, which comprise five groups of short phrases, each emphasizing the unity and absolute unrivaled power of God, that He has had no offspring, and that Muḥammad is His messenger. The text on the inner face declares the unity of God and Muḥammad's status, and continues with verses addressed to the "people of the book," admonishing that no mistakes be made in religion, declaring the Trinity to be false, and telling of the correct view of Jesus, the spirit from God. "Do not speak of three (gods)," one of the passages warns. The polemical aspect of the inner text especially is clear. The testimony to the development of Muslim doctrine is significant also. Here we have evidence of the status of key beliefs in Islam—the non-messianic and non-divine status of Jesus, the acceptance of a multiplicity of prophets, Muḥammad's receipt of revelation, and the designation of the religion itself by the name of Islam.

The style of the architecture of the building is also significant in understanding the rise of Islam. The Dome itself is clearly modeled after Syrian Christian churches—it may be seen as the final achievement of the Byzantine architectural style—although it has also been suggested that it contains in its decorations many Sasanian traits. Certainly, the only true Arab element in the building is the inscriptional calligraphy. A close connection has been noted between the Dome and various earlier buildings of the Byzantines, including the Church of the Holy Sepulcher and the cathedral in Bosra (southern Syria) built in 512. The resemblance extends most importantly to the geometrical structure of the buildings themselves. By employing a clear tradition in Byzantine architecture, the Dome was able to provide evidence to the conquered people of the power of the new rulers. It should be noted that circumambulation appears to have been practiced by Christians who went around the tomb of Jesus in the rotunda of the Holy Sepulcher; thus, the entire rite connected to the building in early times is likely to have been one which would have reinforced this assertion of authority.

It has also been suggested that the inscription of ʿAbd al-Malik inside the Dome aimed to provide spiritual guidance to the believers and to show the fundamental difference between Christianity and Islam. That is, the Dome was built as a symbol of, and a vehicle for, the emergence of the self-definition of Islam over against Christianity. This was done through the means of a splendid building, undoubtedly built to surpass the beauty of Christian churches, but yet done in the model of a Christian edifice. It was situated in Jerusalem as a political symbol of triumph—symbolized in the very fact of its being built. Its construction served to indicate the gradual emergence of Islamic identity in a form expressive and meaningful for all to behold.

Indeed, one of the statements in the inscription refers to Islam as "the religion with God" (compare Qurʾān 3/19); from this point on, therefore, those in power are clearly arguing for their religion "Islam." The copper inscription over the north door also refers to Muslims as those who believe in God, and what He revealed to Muḥammad, and that there are no differences among the prophets, all of whom God sent (compare Qurʾān 2/136 or 3/84). Additionally, the inscription indicates the direction of early theological self-definition in the sense that the emphasis on Christianity can be seen to suggest

Islam's supersession of the Christian faith, especially in light of its doctrine of Jesus and its condemnation of notions of the Trinity. The connection of the rock over which the Dome was built to King David and the Jewish Temple may well be intended to suggest both the fulfillment of the promise of Judaism, as well as the abrogation of that dispensation—Islam has taken over the Davidic heritage in both religious and political ways.

The caliph and his authority

The Dome of the Rock represents, therefore, a conscious attempt on the part of ʿAbd al-Malik to assert the authority of the new rule and to champion the new religion of Islam. That this was very much a personal matter, one which established his own authority not only among the new subjects of the empire but also among the members of the Arab community, appears to be evidenced by the self-conception of the caliph in this early period. Thus, while the Dome of the Rock provided the symbol of the caliph's authority, the actual conception of the position provided the source of his authority.

Classical Islam displays the phenomenon of religious authority residing with a scholarly elite and ultimately, it would be claimed, with the entire community. Some evidence has been interpreted to suggest, however, that this situation was not always so. Early on, the caliph, referred to by the title *khalīfat Allāh*, the "representative (or deputy) of God," appears to have combined religious and political power, only to have the religious dimensions of the power removed in the third Muslim century (as reflected in the later theory of the caliphate), in recognition of the *de facto* change in the power structure by that time. This revamping of power appears to have occurred at the hands of the scholars after a struggle involving an explicit attempt by the caliphs to impose a specific religious system of thought which upheld their position and asserted their authority; this was put forth in opposition to the efforts and interests of scholars, who stood for their own independent authority.

Evidence for this position of the early caliph comes from the use of the title *khalīfat Allāh* as testified most significantly on coins from the reign of ʿAbd al-Malik, the builder of the Dome of the Rock. This title is used in the place of the later *khalīfat rasūl Allāh* ("deputy of the messenger of God"), which was employed by the ʿAbbāsids alongside the earlier formulation, a fact which has often (mis)led historians to believe that the two titles were directly equivalent.

Some recent scholarship has suggested that the early caliph saw himself in a mode very similar to the way in which the Shīʿa pictured their own political religious leader, the Imām (as will be discussed in Chapter 8). Obedience to the caliph was deemed to be necessary for salvation because the caliph's authority came straight from God. For the individual in the early period, therefore, the choice of whom to give one's allegiance to was a religious one, since salvation was connected to it; at least, that was the argument that those in power appear to have been suggesting.

Concomitant with the stress on his divinely approved authority, the caliph acted as judge, creating the sacred law and acting as the reference point for decisions on difficult items of law. The argument was made that his rulings were based on the Qurʾān, the practice (*sunna*)—not that of a fixed practice of the past embodied in the person of Muḥammad but the practice as found in the territory concerned—and his own (superhuman) insight.

The "inquisition" and the emergence of the scholarly elite

The early ninth-century institution of the *miḥna*, or "inquisition," unintentionally put a stop to this type of conception, although the underlying tension remained a feature of Islamic history which occasionally revealed its face. The final result of the attempt to assert caliphal control over religious dogma embodied in this "inquisition" was the emergence of an independent scholarly group of people (symbolized in the figure of Aḥmad ibn Ḥanbal, d. 855) in whom religious authority, to the extent to which that was conceived as existing, was vested. Under the ʿAbbāsid caliph al-Maʾmūn (ruled 813–833), various attempts were made to assert the power of the caliph in the community in a variety of areas concerned with religion. Significantly, beginning in 829, al-Maʾmūn declared that all government officials and religious leaders must believe in the doctrine of the "created Qurʾān"; in 833 an "inquisition," *miḥna*, was initiated, such that only those who agreed with the caliph's dogma would be allowed to hold official positions. Those who refused, including Aḥmad ibn Ḥanbal, were removed from their positions and imprisoned. This practice continued in the reigns of al-Muʿtaṣim (ruled 833–842) and al-Wāthiq (ruled 842–847) which followed. Al-Mutawakkil (ruled 847–861) put an end to the enterprise in 849, but by then it was too late.

The significance of the actual doctrine which al-Maʾmūn and his successors tried to enforce is not as important for understanding its significance as the actual act of their trying to impose it. Until this point, the authority of the caliph to enunciate and represent Islam, while not totally unchallenged, appears to have been accepted. That is, for the Umayyad and early ʿAbbāsid rulers, Islam was to a significant extent an ideological tool in the hands of the ruling powers. Al-Maʾmūn's actions in attempting to enforce a version of Islamic orthodoxy backfired and led to the increasing prominence of those who rejected the caliphal authority in favor of the authority of a scholarly elite; their authority was said to lie in their transmission and interpretation of the Qurʾān and the *sunna* of Muḥammad. It is at this point that classical Islam as we know it today began to come into existence, as is reflected in the literary sources, virtually all of which stem from a time after this period and reflect those scholarly concerns, perceptions, and interpretations of Islam.

The final implication of this change in power structure was that religion and politics in Islam became disentangled. This is reflected in the later theories of the caliphate, which recognized the fact that the two spheres were in practice separate, although mutually supportive. The institution of the caliphate was defined to have the responsibility for maintaining and implementing the ordinances of Muslim law. Beyond that, the relationship between the person of the caliph and the actual mechanism of rule in both military and religious spheres was left open, such that practical realities of the Islamic empire could be accommodated to the theory and thus legitimized.

Deciphering history through Islamic coins

Gold, silver, and copper coinage is an extremely valuable source of historical information, providing dates, names, and symbols which can provide "hard" evidence to put alongside literary sources. Such, at least, is how the situation appears. In fact, coins are far from an unambiguous source, are frustratingly difficult to put in chronological sequence, and are subject to considerable scholarly disagreement as to their interpretation. At the same time, they do have the potential to be extremely revealing about historical events.

The coinage stemming from early Islamic times has been subjected to a number of very detailed and specialized studies. The creation of a uniform coinage for the Islamic empire, implemented by the caliph ʿAbd al-Malik (ruled 685–705), was preceded by an era in which pre-existing Sasanian and Byzantine designs were used. A good deal of scholarly effort has gone into trying to sort out the historical sequence of the coins. What is illustrated by both types of coins is the gradual imposition of firm Arab rule in the early period of the empire. This is, of course, a significant historical observation and one that can be made on the basis of the coinage.

Arab-Sasanian coinage appears to have originated from mints in southern Iraq and Iran. Scholars have divided them into three phases. The earliest coins, from 651 to 661, bear the name of the Sasanian ruler—either Yazdagird or Khusraw—and have dates according to the Sasanian calendar. They show the presence of the Arabs, however, by having brief Arabic markings on them in some cases, and, in other cases, by having "In the name of God" written in Arabic. From 661 to 671, the name of an Arab governor and a date in the *hijrī* calendar begin to be found, although inconsistently and also subject to difficult interpretation because the range of dates employed on the coins can be interpreted to be either the year of the Sasanian ruler's reign or *hijrī*; the coins themselves do not indicate which calendar is being employed. During the third period, from 671 to 704, all the coins bear the name of a governor or caliph, incorporate a *hijrī* date, and provide an increasingly broad range of Arabic inscriptions. What marks all the coins, however, is the presence of the Sasanian symbols, including a fire altar, a star

(a) (b)

Figure 4.1 **(a)** The reverse side of a gold *dīnār* minted in 769 in Baghdad by the ʿAbbāsid Caliph al-Manṣūr. In the center it says "There is no god but God alone; He has no partner." Around the edge a modified version of Qurʾān 9/33 is quoted (as is common on ʿAbbāsid-era coins): "Muḥammad is the messenger of God whom He has sent with the guidance and the religion of truth to make it rise above all other religions." **(b)** The reverse side a gold *dīnār* minted around 693 in Damascus under the Umayyad Caliph ʿAbd al-Malik. This is an example of the last series in the Arab-Byzantine style, with remnants of the steps, cross, and insignia of Byzantine coins still present. Around the edge it states in Arabic, "In the name of God. There is no god but God alone; Muḥammad is the messenger of God."
Source: Michael Di Biase/*Saudi Aramco World*/SAWDIA.

and crescent, and two standing figures on the reverse, and a king's head on the obverse.

The coinage that is called Arab-Byzantine comes from the Syrian area and likewise has been divided into three phases by scholars. Highly problematic with these coins is the absence of any dates. The first series, called Pseudo-Byzantine, comes from the late 650s to the 670s and consists of loose copies of seventh-century Byzantine coins. From 670 to 690, the Umayyad "Imperial Image" series includes coins with inscriptions in Greek and/or Arabic and continues to employ Byzantine regal symbols. The last series, from the 690s, is called "Standing Caliph," with a figure being present on the coins, legends in Arabic, and the name of ʿAbd al-Malik usually being included.

Stephen Album and Tony Goodwin, *Sylloge of Islamic Coins in the Ashmolean. Volume 1: The Pre-reform Coinage of the Early Islamic Period*, Oxford: Ashmolean Museum, 2002, is the standard work on early coins. Several online sites document the coins. Good illustrations may be seen at www.grifterrec.com/coins/islam/arab_sas/arabsasanian.html and www.grifterrec.com/coins/islam/arab_byz/arabbyzantine.html.

Suggested further reading

Patricia Crone, *God's Rule: Government and Islam—Six Centuries of Medieval Islamic Political Thought*, New York: Columbia University Press, 2004.
Patricia Crone and Martin Hinds, *God's Caliph: Religious Authority in the First Centuries of Islam*, Cambridge: Cambridge University Press, 1986.
Reuven Firestone, *Jihād: The Origins of Holy War in Islam*, New York: Oxford University Press, 1999.
Wilferd Madelung, *The Succession to Muḥammad: A Study of the Early Caliphate*, Cambridge: Cambridge University Press, 1997.
Chase Robinson, *ʿAbd al-Malik*, Oxford: Oneworld, 2005.
Muhammad Qasim Zaman, *Religion and Politics under the Early ʿAbbasids: The Emergence of the Proto-Sunnī Elite*, Leiden: Brill, 1997.

5 *Theological exposition*

The role of the caliph and the learned classes in defining what Islam was to stand for, both theologically and politically, is a central theme in understanding the development of the Islamic empire itself. Both within and behind the debates which went on in the early centuries, however, lie the actual doctrines which were to emerge as the core elements of Islamic self-definition in theological terms. Certainly, no other aspect in the understanding of the formation of Islam has consumed such a great deal of intellectual effort among modern scholars as has the development of theology. Ironically, the resulting picture is one of considerable confusion, perhaps a consequence, once again, of the abundance of late source material, the variety of ways to interpret the data provided, and the absence of a substantial quantity of texts clearly traceable to the early period itself. Some relatively early works do exist, but the picture they combine to create remains disjointed.

Theological writing is the end result of an attempt at religious self-definition; it attempts to enunciate what is believed by a group of people in terms of certain tenets. Within the Near Eastern milieu, various elements emerged among the religions of Judaism, Christianity, and Islam which defined what they held in common and where they differed. Defining where Islam was to differ from the other religions and where it was to agree was what the early theological tracts attempted to accomplish. The texts do not do this in an explicit way. They do not set up interreligious comparisons. Rather, the efforts were conducted under topics which were, to a great extent, already predefined within the general religious milieu and were then enunciated from within each religious perspective.

The emergence of Islamic theological identity

The basic elements of Islamic theology find their expression within the Qurʾān and the *sunna*, and are elaborated to some extent in works such as the *Sīra* of Ibn Isḥāq (d. 767). In these contexts, the statements are not theology, of course, but rather simple creedal formulae which have been isolated as being summaries of what Islam stands for. It took

Figure 5.1 An illustration of the classical Athenian statesman, lawmaker and poet Solon (638–558 BCE), from the thirteenth-century manuscript held in Topkapi Palace Museum in Istanbul of the work by the eleventh-century Egyptian historian al-Mubashshir, *Kitāb mukhtār al-ḥikam wa-maḥāsin al-kalim* ("Choice Wise Sayings and Fine Statements").
Source: Topkapi Palace Museum/Giraudon/The Bridgeman Art Library. XIR158646 (MS Ahmed III 3206, pen & ink and gouache on paper). Turkish, out of copyright.

several centuries of scholarly reflection to mold this raw material into the mature formulations of Islamic faith. Belief in the oneness of God, in angels, in all the prophets and their scriptures, in the final judgment day, and in God's decree for humanity are often seen to be the core elements of faith for all Muslims; such simple summations arose, however, only after extensive reflection and debate concerning some very basic theological issues in the formative centuries of Islam.

The definition of a Muslim

From the available sources, one prime question emerges which seems to have been of major concern and may well have provided the stimulus toward developed theological writing. This was the issue of determining who was and who was not a Muslim. The later Muslim sources, which provide us with additional data on the origins of this dispute, picture it as first arising within the context of the history of the early Muslim community, in common with the general trend in the sources to put the origins of Islam back as far as possible. Disputes over succession within the Arab ruling groups appear to have been read and understood by later generations of Muslims in theological terms as well as political ones. At stake was whether ʿAlī, the fourth leader of the Arabs after Muḥammad, had the responsibility for avenging the death of his assassinated predecessor ʿUthmān; the clan of ʿUthmān, led by Muʿāwiya, championed the claims of its kinsman, suggesting that ʿAlī had lost rightful claim to rule because of his failure to follow up on this obligation. Civil war erupted and Muʿāwiya and the Umayyad dynasty eventually took over. From today's perspective, there seems to be little reason to dispute the basic historico-political events. Muslim theological sources, however, see far more in these events and view them as paradigms for the discussion of issues of religious self-definition; they use these earlier events for discussion of the theological disputes which were, in fact, taking place at least a century after the fact. From a historical perspective, it is worth noting that the use of military force in trying to decide the issues concerning ʿUthmān and ʿAlī indicates immediately that there certainly was a great deal at stake at this time, and the issue really was far more involved than the question concerning the death of ʿUthmān. In the later reading of these historical events, the notions of piety and the "rightful" (i.e. moral) assassination of an "unjust" ruler become the operative elements.

What emerges from the sources is a picture of a variety of groups, each going under a name which is often provided with a connection back to the times of ʿAlī and ʿUthmān, each taking its own position on what constitutes the definition of membership within the emergent Muslim community. The reasons for being concerned with this question were likely to have been of both a practical and a legal nature, over and above being the result of polemical discourse with Jews and Christians in the Near Eastern milieu.

The Khawārij

The Khawārij (or Kharijites) held a strict, activist position: all those who fall short of total adherence to the Islamic precepts are unbelievers. Any of those who might happen to slip are thus rendered targets for the Islamic *jihād* against all non-believers; membership in the community, at the very least, provided protection from such attacks. In origin the group may have been involved in even more basic discussions over the sources of authority in the community. Their slogan is said to have been *lā ḥukma illā li-llāhi*, "There is no judgment except that of God," which would suggest that they held that only God, through His expression in the Qurʾān, has made binding laws for humanity. At least in part, therefore, the Khawārij may be pictured as the scripturalist party who rejected those who attempted to supplement the single source of authority in the community with a notion of the *sunna*. For the Khawārij, this *sunna* was not a part of the divine revelation and therefore had no particular status in the framework of Islamic law; it was, in fact, like the authority of the caliph himself, part of a human endeavor which had no place alongside the divine word. It may well be, then, that they are to be identified as a pietistic group in the context of emergent Islam, facing off against the asserted power and authority of the caliph and his *sunna*. Later, however, a part of the ammunition of the Khawārij against other groups was sought in *ḥadīth* reports (that is, the *sunna* of Muḥammad), which saw certain actions, for example adultery, as taking one out of the category of "believer."

This activist position proved disruptive to the early Muslim community, although the legacy of the movement and its theological and moral position has lingered until today. The Khawārij are, in many ways, a marginal group when viewed within the overall context of Islamic history. As a group their significance faded. However, the tendency displayed in their thought has always provided a tension in Islam. Their demands for judgment of adherence to Islam—always varying in their intensity and their precise theological motivation, certainly—provided a constant threat to the unity of the community, yet those threats were enunciated under the guise of a demand for that very unity which was considered possible only with a strict implementation of a single code of Islam. Such approaches to Islam have become prominent at times of community stress. A threat from the outside to the integrity of the Muslim community has, throughout history, provided the stimulus for a retreat to a more closely defined conception of Islam and a greater call for a judgment upon fellow Muslims as to the acceptability of their practice of Islam.

The Murjiʾa

The Murjiʾa adopted a conservative position, preserving the status quo. They argued that those who appeared not to be following the outward precepts of Islam must still be accepted as Muslims; only God truly knows their religious state. A profession of faith along with an inward assent to Islam were all that was required to confirm community membership; faith (*īmān*) is "of the heart and of the tongue." The position starts with the emblem of theological identity implied by the questions concerning ʿAlī and ʿUthmān. Were these two men guilty of sin? Were their assassinations justified? The Murjiʾa are pictured in the sources as holding that the decisions on these questions must be left to God. As a theological position, this stance holds that "works"—consisting of all human actions—are not a part of faith; that is, as long as a person professes belief in Islam (through the single "act" of confession of faith), then that person is a Muslim. The actual performance of the ritual acts of Islam is not a criterion for membership in the community. This position was supported in the view of the Murjiʾa by the notion that, in the Qurʾān,

God called those who had confessed their faith (and that alone) "believers." According to Abū Ḥanīfa (d. 767), good works will be rewarded primarily in the hereafter:

> Whoever obeys God in all the laws, according to us, is of the people of paradise. Whoever leaves both faith and works is an infidel, of the people of the fire. However, whoever believes but is guilty of some breach of the law is a believing sinner, and God will do as He wishes with that person: punish the person if He wills, or forgive the person if He wills.
>
> (Abū Ḥanīfa, "Epistle to ʿUthmān al-Battī," translated in Williams 1963: 164)

In the here and now, it was frequently argued that any increase in faith as manifested in pious works was really only an increase in conviction on the part of the individual. The whole doctrine thus had a practical result in terms of the ease of conversion to Islam, as may be seen especially in the case of the spread among the Turks in Central Asia in the eleventh century of the later theological school of al-Māturīdī, which followed Abū Ḥanīfa's legal teachings.

Abū Ḥanīfa is generally pictured as the major early enunciator of the Murjiʾa position; certainly his name has become associated with documents which are seen as coming from the Murjiʾa in their details. One such document is *al-Fiqh al-Akbar*, another the *Risāla* ("letter") to ʿUthmān al-Battī. These documents, and others from the same school of thought, seem to have the preservation of the unity of the Muslim community as their central concern, as is suggested by the tolerant nature of the definition of faith according to the Murjiʾa.

The Traditionalists

A group generally termed the Traditionalists (often calling themselves, as do other groups, *ahl al-sunna*, "the people of the *sunna*"; the name "Traditionalist" refers to the use of *ḥadīth* materials in preference to the independent powers of reason) is generally connected to the figure of Aḥmad ibn Ḥanbal (d. 855) in the early period. The stance of the group represents yet another position on this question of faith, essentially arguing that there are degrees of "being Muslim." Works do count towards one's status in the community, although one can still be a believer and commit sin—there are, therefore, what may be termed "degrees of faith." This position is enunciated in works ascribed to Ibn Ḥanbal and to Abū ʿUbayd (d. 838), and is also found embodied in the books of *ḥadīth*; it becomes the position of the later theological school of al-Ashʿarī and thus of the majority form of Islam. Ibn Ḥanbal is said to have summarized his position as "faith consists in verbal assent, deeds and intention and adherence to the *sunna*. Faith increases and decreases" (creed ascribed to Ibn Ḥanbal as translated in Cragg and Speight 1980: 119).

Abū ʿUbayd was a scholar with broad intellectual interests who "contributed pioneer studies of major significance, and in all of them he displayed a degree of erudition and reached a level of achievement which won the acclaim of contemporary scholars" (Burton 1987: 46). Theologically, he argued that faith is submission to God through intention, statement of belief, and works all combined. Such faith varies by degrees, beginning with the basic confession of faith and then building from there; whoever makes the first step is entitled to be called a Muslim (and thus, in practical terms, the doctrine has the same consequences as that of the Murjiʾa) but perfection of faith is something to be reached through works. One can be termed a believer on the basis of the statement of faith but there are ranks among the believers in accordance with the extent to which such people conform to the requirements of the religious system of Islam. The Muslim who commits a grave sin, therefore, is still to be termed a believer but is not as good a believer as someone who has not committed a sin; such a person is not a believer in the full definition of that term.

The Qadariyya

A fourth position in the overall debate became associated with some people from within a group known as the Qadariyya (for example al-Ḥasan al-Baṣrī, d. 728); here, as with the Murjiʾa, a person who professes faith in Islam is considered a member of the community, but those who can be observed not following the requirements of Islam are to be considered neither believers nor unbelievers, but somewhere in between—they are hypocrites. The end result in practical terms is, once again, the same as with the Murjiʾa, but the claim is being made that it is in fact possible to have an opinion about the status of a believer's adherence to Islam. The position does not distinguish, however, between levels of faith as does that of the Traditionalists.

The problem of free will and predestination

The Qadariyya were centrally involved in another theological dispute, one which is generally understood to have provided them with their name. The Qadariyya are those who discussed the issue of *qadar*, the preordination of events in the world by God. This group held to the position of the free will of humanity and was opposed in this matter by those often said to be more closely aligned to the political powers of the day. That is, the Qadariyya were on the more revolutionary wing of the theological groupings; their espousal of free will was frequently connected to those agitating for a new political order which was opposed to the ruling Umayyad caliphs, who had appropriated both political and theological authority under the guise of having been appointed by God (and thus destined to fulfill this function). If individuals were accountable for their actions, then so were governments, according to the argument of the Qadariyya. The Murjiʾa are frequently pictured as those most supportive of the ruling powers, for their doctrine of faith as a personal concern did not facilitate judgments being made on people as to their status in the faith (beyond the actual statement of faith), whether that person be a peasant or the ruler.

The *Risāla* (often translated "Treatise" in this instance) of al-Ḥasan al-Baṣrī is generally seen as one of the earliest documents concerned with the argument for free will, although both the ascription of an early date to the text and its status as one of the earliest texts have been questioned. Al-Ḥasan argues in the treatise for the position of the individual's free will on the basis of the Qurʾān; any suggestion made in the Qurʾān that predestination is to be supported (as his opponents suggested) is to be countered by an interpretation of the passage in light of other statements. Most obvious in this regard, statements such as Qurʾān 13/27—"God sends anyone He wishes astray" (implying that the individual's fate is in the hands of God alone and there is nothing that can be done about it)—are to be interpreted in the light of other statements such as Qurʾān 14/27, "God sends wrongdoers astray," where, it is asserted, the people are *already* astray (they are already "wrongdoers," by the act of their own free will) before God confirms them in their "fate." This became the standard interpretative tool of all those who argued for the free will position in Islam. From a more positive angle, the argument also ran that God says in Qurʾān 51/56, "I have only created jinn and people so they may worship Me," meaning that all people must be free to worship God, for God would not command them to do something and then prevent them from doing it.

The Muʿtazila and the role of reason

Out of this political protest party of the Qadariyya there appears to have developed a group known as the Muʿtazila. This party adopted the theological stance of the Qadariyya. Most importantly, though, the Muʿtazila are generally credited with the perfection of the art of theological speculation in Islam in the form of *kalām*—the dialectical style of discussion where objections and then the response are put forth in the form of "If they say . . ., it is said to them . . ." While this style of discussion originated neither with the Muʿtazila nor even within Islam itself, it was through this means that the group argued their position, one which was based around the dual principle of the justice and unity of God. Working from this starting point, all the implications were systematically laid out on the basis of the use of reason in the argumentation. While the Qurʾān had its place in the discussions, it was not so much a source when used by the Muʿtazila as a testimony to the veracity of the claims which they were making. The basic assumptions of the Greek philosophical system (as understood and transmitted through Christian scholars) formed the fundamental element underlying the whole position; it was argued that reason, and not only traditional sources, could be used as a source of reliable knowledge for human beings. The Muʿtazila were the first to introduce the Greek mode of reasoning and argumentation into Islamic religious discussions, changing the face of Muslim theology for all time as a result. Greek philosophical learning remained a discipline in and by itself among Muslims (as will be explored in Chapter 10), being developed by people such as al-Kindī (d. *c.* 870), al-Farābī (d. 950) and Ibn Sīnā (d. 1037). The subject (known in Arabic as *falsafa*) was one which aroused the ire of many Traditionalists and remained, for the most part, a rival to theology as a discipline, except in the hands of the Muʿtazila, who used its tools to their advantage.

The justice of God

The notion of the justice of God, something demanded of the divinity by Greek logic, led to extensive discussions concerning the nature of God and His relationship to humanity. "Justice" for the Muʿtazila was equated with "good," such that it was not possible to conceive that God would be unjust or evil. The basic Muslim principle that God will reward the true believers after death and punish the unbelieving wrongdoers is then connected to this. God must be just in assessing this punishment or reward, and therefore humanity must have a fair chance to perform on the side of good or evil. Any sense of predestination must be removed from the Qurʾān, therefore, by reinterpretation. Al-Khayyāṭ (d. *c.* 912), the earliest author of the Muʿtazila from whom we have a complete text directly, speaks, for example, of the Quranic notion of God "sealing hearts":

> [the idea of "sealing"] is not that He prevents people from doing what He orders them to do—He is above that!—rather, it refers to the name, the judgment and the testimony [concerning an act]. Do you not notice that He said [in Qurʾān 4/155] "because of . . . their disbelief"? Thus He sealed their hearts because of what was in them of disbelief.
>
> (al-Khayyāṭ 1957: 89)

The power to act given by God to humanity carries with it the power to decide which action to undertake; individuals must therefore be fully responsible for their own fate. Evil deeds must originate in individual actions and have nothing to do with God, a problem which the doctrine of predestination seems to create. However, unjust acts do seem to occur in nature—death of young infants, death through natural disasters and so forth. This theological problem was faced in a variety of ways by members of the Muʿtazila. Some said, for example, that while God could have created a perfect world where such things did not happen, He chose not to. All this is, for the Muʿtazila, a necessary consequence of the doctrine of the justice of God.

The created Qur'ān

The Mu'tazila had their moment of political support under the 'Abbāsid caliph al-Ma'mūn (ruled 813–33), with the institution of the *miḥna* serving as an inquest body investigating the creedal stance of leading figures at the time, as discussed in Chapter 4. Here the figure of Aḥmad ibn Ḥanbal looms large for his role in resisting the creed of the Mu'tazila. A crucial issue at this time arose from the notion that the Qur'ān was the word of God; the resultant discussion concerned whether the scripture was, therefore, created "in time" or uncreated and thus existent from eternity. The argument, it is worth noting, was not a new one within the Judeo-Christian world, as may be witnessed by ideas of the "pre-existent Torah" and Jesus as the Logos who "was with God at the beginning." The Mu'tazila championed the notion of the created Qur'ān as a part of their understanding of the inherent free will of humanity, often pointing to Abū Lahab and his being condemned to hell in *sūra* 111. The Qur'ān must have been created at the time of its revelation, they argued, for otherwise the fate of Abū Lahab would have been established for all eternity, thus removing his freedom to determine his own fate. This issue was also related to the reality of God's speech. Some took God's speaking to mean that He spoke as humans speak, with the organs of speech, a point which was then rejected as impinging upon God's "otherness." For a Traditionalist such as Ibn Ḥanbal, the reality of God's actually speaking must be so, because such is stated in the Qur'ān. In the beginning, it was this element which seems to have been crucial in the development of the argument about the reality of God's speech and only later did the argument turn to one of the emergence of the Qur'ān "in time," as was the issue in the *miḥna*.

The unity of God

The debate over the created Qur'ān relates to the other important element of Mu'tazilī thought, the concept of the unity of God, *tawḥīd*. Polemic with Christianity and Manichaeism appears to have been part of the reason for the emphasis within Mu'tazilī thought on this doctrine, and the use of the Greek mode of reasoning by protagonists from these other two religions may well account for the introduction of rationalism into Islam as well, occurring initially within this polemical framework. Al-Khayyāṭ's work paints the portrait of a real threat posed by the radical dualism of the Manicheans, although it is likely that the Christian Trinity was a far more important topic of discussion. The position adopted by most of the Mu'tazila was that God can only be described in negatives. Any attempt to ascribe positive attributes to God was seen as impinging upon His unity, for such would suggest that He could be divided into a series of eternal aspects. The closest that one may come to saying something positive about God would be to say that God is "knowing," but this "knowing" occurs not by an attribute of God, but rather by and through God Himself in His essence. Once again, the parallels in these arguments to Christian discussions over the nature of Jesus in his relationship to the Father cannot be overlooked.

An implication of this position on the unity of God was the emphasis on de-anthropomorphization of the divinity, especially as He is described in the Qurʾān. Any suggestion that God might have a "face" (Qurʾān 2/272, 6/52, etc.) or be "sitting upon a throne" (Qurʾān 2/255, etc.) in reality was to be rejected and taken as a metaphorical statement by the Muʿtazila; no reference to the human form could be applied to God in its usual meaning. God's "face" was to be understood as His "essence," according to al-Khayyāṭ, for example. Thus, the discussion conducted during the *miḥna* over the status of the Qurʾān was not limited only to the matter of free will. For the Muʿtazila at least, both major aspects of their doctrine, unity and justice, were encapsulated in the idea of a created Qurʾān; an eternal Qurʾān would suggest an attribute of God (speech) which existed separately (in the concept of the "heavenly tablet") alongside God, impinging thereby on His unity, as well as suggesting predestination of events.

The fall of the Muʿtazila

The role of reason for the Muʿtazila was such that the main principles of the conduct of life—the principles of good and evil—were seen to be discoverable by any rational human. Revelation is necessary only in order to supplement what reason can discover, especially in such matters as the ritual law of Islam. For example, ʿAbd al-Jabbār (d. 1025), one of the last major medieval Muʿtazilī thinkers, suggests that the eating of meat would not be allowed in Islam if it were not for the fact that scripture supports the practice; reason cannot be seen to provide necessarily the full delineation of the law and scripture must provide the additional pointers needed. Revelation also serves to motivate people with its emphasis on the promise and the threat of the afterlife; the Muʿtazila recognized that humanity was in need of guidance and that in its "natural state" it would not follow the dictates of reason.

This view of the role of reason is significant in terms of the ultimate fate of the Muʿtazila, for it implied that the legal scholars of Islam had, in fact, no particular claim to sole possession of the right interpretation of all Muslim dogma. For the Muʿtazila, all humans are, in theory, capable of making the correct decision on issues of faith and law because of their God-given intellect. There is, therefore, implicit in this stance an anti-jurist bias that may well have proven to be a part of the cause of their ultimate downfall. Agitation by the scholarly elite whose job it was to provide the interpretation of the law is likely to have brought about the eventual political action, by the caliph al-Qādir in the years 1017 and 1041, of demanding a profession of faith which rejected the Muʿtazilī stance. This finally put a stop to the movement (at least until more recent times when it re-emerged in the guise of Modernism).

In the eleventh century, however, the Buwayhids, the rulers in Baghdad, were backing politically the remnants of the supporters of the fourth caliph, ʿAlī, known as the Shīʿa; the desire of the majority of the Muslims at the time (known as the Sunnīs) to present a united front against this pressure was probably part of the reason for this final move against the Muʿtazila (whose theology had already influenced the Shīʿa by this time and was probably perceived as a threat by the Sunnīs for that reason also). So, the eventual downfall of the Muʿtazila was undoubtedly a result of political circumstances of the time as much as their doctrine. That did not mean, however, that reason in theological thinking lost its significance, as later developments show.

Al-Ashʿarī

Abūʾl-Ḥasan al-Ashʿarī (d. 935) emerged out of the context of the Muʿtazila in the tenth century to enunciate a theological position which may be characterized as midway between the scripturalism of the Traditionalists and the audacious rationalism of the Muʿtazila; this was a position which was to last as the most significant statement of Islamic theology. In his book *al-Ibāna*, for example, al-Ashʿarī uses *kalām*-style argumentation, setting up questions to be posed to his opponents, who are stipulated to be especially the members of the Muʿtazila who "interpret the Qurʾān according to their opinions with an interpretation for which God has neither revealed authority nor shown proof" (Ashʿarī 1940: 47). To the questions which he poses in his arguments, he responds: "If they say 'yes', then it follows that . . . or if they say 'no', then it follows that . . .," with the arguments being pursued to the point of logical contradiction or contradiction with the twin sources of authority in Islam, the Qurʾān and the *ḥadīth*.

Al-Ashʿarī's method was based upon extensive use of the Qurʾān and the *ḥadīth* in order to formulate his rational arguments. He fully supported the position of predestination, God being pictured in the Qurʾān clearly as All-powerful and All-knowing; that God should not know and not be in control of what people were doing is clearly a problem if the free will position is embraced. For al-Ashʿarī, God creates the power for people to act at the moment of action (God being the only one who actually has the power to create), yet the individual is responsible for all he or she does. This responsibility is referred to as *kasb*, "acquisition"—that is, that people "acquire" the ramifications of their actions, perhaps to be thought of as similar to the workings of the "conscience" in modern terminology. Says al-Ashʿarī, "No human act can occur without His willing it, because that would imply that it occurred out of carelessness and neglect or out of weakness and inadequacy on His part to effect what He wills" (Ashʿarī 1940: 103).

God's attributes are real for al-Ashʿarī because the Qurʾān clearly states them and so it must be meaningful to speak of God's hand and God's face; de-anthropomorphization was one of the central elements of Muʿtazilī thought which al-Ashʿarī denounced, for he saw it as a symbol of rationalist excesses and willful ignorance of the sense of the Quranic text. Still, he did not wish to deny that reason indicates that speaking of these attributes of God would seem problematic when put in conjunction with an infinite God. His solution was to speak of the reality of the attributes but that these are not attributes in the same way that humans have such. God does have a hand, but we just "do not know how" this is to be conceived. The phrase *bilā kayf*, "without knowing how," became a key term in Ashʿarī theology, to be used whenever reason and the Qurʾān or *ḥadīth* met head-on in conflict.

Al-Ashʿarī saw the Qurʾān as the eternal and uncreated word of God, precisely because it was the word of God and, therefore, must partake of the character of His attributes. Those attributes (most importantly knowing, powerful, living, hearing, seeing, speech, and will) are all strongly affirmed by al-Ashʿarī, who argued that if God does not have these attributes in reality, then He is somehow deficient and that, of course, cannot be the case. For example, al-Ashʿarī states:

> one who is living, if he be not knowing, is qualified by some contrary of knowledge such as ignorance, doubt or other defects. . . . But if He had been ever qualified by some contrary of knowledge, it would have been impossible for Him ever to know. For if the contrary of knowledge had been eternal, it would have been impossible for it to cease to be; and if it had been impossible for it to cease to be, it would have been impossible for Him to have made works of wisdom. Hence, since God has made such works, and since they prove that He is knowing, it is true and certain that God has always been knowing, since it is clearly impossible for Him to have been ever qualified by some contrary of knowledge.
>
> (Ashʿarī 1953: English 14, Arabic 11)

Al-Māturīdī

Abū Manṣūr al-Māturīdī (d. 944) was another of the tenth-century theologians whose influence at the time seems to have been significant in the emergence of Sunnī Islam. Living in Transoxiana, he attacked the doctrines of the Muʿtazila and set down the foundations of his theological system. Like al-Ashʿarī, al-Māturīdī followed a middle path between traditionalism and rationalism, forging an Islam which saw the written sources of the faith dominate but which found a place for the activities of the human mind.

Only a few texts have come down to us from al-Māturīdī and his school, but one of the most important, his *Kitāb al-Tawḥīd*, is available in Arabic. The work commences by declaring that unconditional following of the teaching of another person is not valid.

God has given humanity intelligence so that all may think and that gift must be used. This, of course, is a doctrine held in common with the Muʿtazila. Reason leads to knowledge, as do the senses and transmissions from the past, either from authoritative sources or from prophets. Reason must be used to judge the information provided by the other sources of knowledge. Reason also allowed knowledge of God before prophets were sent, a position contrary to al-Ashʿarī, who held that prophets were necessary and thus belief was not incumbent upon those who had not been reached by God's messengers. Following this in al-Māturīdī's work come arguments concerning the temporality of the world, the necessary and eternal existence of God, and that God is the creator of the world. This is all demonstrated using rational proofs. Likewise, the oneness of God is proven and the matter of His attributes dealt with such that what the text of the Qurʾān says about God must be believed, although we cannot know "how" God is to be conceived of as "sitting" on His throne, for example; this suggests a greater tendency towards interpretation of such matters than in al-Ashʿarī. Al-Māturīdī supports the idea of the free will of humanity, although God is, in fact, the only creator and He creates the actions of His creation; using the same notion as al-Ashʿarī of individuals "acquiring" their actions, al-Māturīdī suggests that this acquisition is connected to the choice or intention which precedes an act. This is to be distinguished from al-Ashʿarī's sense of acquisition being the contemporaneous coming into possession of the capacity to act at the time of the action. Evil deeds, while predetermined by God, are the actions of the individual as a consequence of the choice and intention to do such acts.

Al-Māturīdī was the inheritor and perpetuator of the position of the Murjiʾa on the question of faith. Only two states exist: having faith or not having faith. The essence of faith is in the belief in one's heart, but there must be some practical consequence of this within Islam.

For a century after the death of al-Māturīdī, his teaching does not seem to have been of much importance, for some 150 years not drawing the attention of even Ashʿarī opponents. The reason for this neglect undoubtedly lies in the fact of al-Māturīdī's residency in Samarqand, and thus his being well away from the center of Islamic intellectual activity; his doctrines appear to have remained of local concern to the community in that region, with little external note taken of the development. The position of al-Māturīdī is generally presented as being a outgrowth of Abū Ḥanīfa's stance, which had already spread to Samarqand by al-Māturīdī's time. Abū Ḥanīfa's position as eponym of the Ḥanafī legal school (explored further in Chapter 6) allowed al-Māturīdī's later followers to argue for the acceptance of their theological stance in areas outside Samarqand which were already dominated by the Ḥanafī legal school; they argued this on the basis of the previous relationship between the two allegiances.

The spread and the eventual success of the school were a result of the conversion of Turks in Central Asia to Islam of this Ḥanafī–Māturīdī persuasion. The liberal theological implications that were incorporated into Ḥanafī juridical requirements—such that faith may be present in an individual even if all religious duties are ignored—is thought to have allowed for the gradual conversion of these nomadic peoples. With the expansion of the Turks, starting in the eleventh-century Seljuk period, adherence to the ideas of the Māturīdī school came to the attention of other groups in the Islamic community. The theological position of the later Māturīdī school is represented, for example, in the *ʿaqīda*, or creed, of al-Nasafī (d. 1142), which proved popular throughout the Muslim world, attracting many commentaries and elaborations even from the followers of al-Ashʿarī. In form, the creed presents what had become the classical sequence of argumentation, starting with the enumeration of the sources of knowledge and moving through discussion of God and His attributes and His nature, belief, and the communication from God via messengers, to be concluded by a discussion of life in the world. The whole theological position is thereby argued to be one cohesive whole, leading its reader from simple observations on how we know things to the compelling implication that, therefore, the Muslim way of life is the true and divinely desired one.

The role of theological writing

Theological writing became an art in Islam, although, as will become clear in Chapter 6, it never had the place of honor in the community that legal discussions held. To some extent, certainly, this is because the theological enterprise was dedicated more to the theoretical than the practical aspects of Muslim life. Islam is, to a great extent, predicated upon the idea of responding to the call from God through action; thus, the most crucial and relevant discipline to the vast majority of Muslims has been the one which guides human behavior—Islamic law—rather than theology, with its dedication to the realm of human thought. Theology did provide some of the intellectual basis for the enunciation of the distinction between Islam, on the one side, and Judaism, Christianity, and a multitude of other "lesser" religions, on the other; it was, therefore, a crucial element in the formation of Islam as an independent and individual mode of existence within which a religious way of life could be led. Theological dogma also underpinned the orientation of the legal doctrines that governed everyday Muslim life, and thus theology and law were always considered a single entity.

Early Christian theologians and Islam

During the first few centuries of the Islamic empire, Christians were a significant portion of the population in the Near East. Under Arab rule, Arabic soon became the common language for much of the population, although Syriac remained a liturgical language for many Christians.

Three Christian theologians writing in Arabic have left a considerable legacy from the early ninth century in texts they wrote arguing against Islam and defending Christianity. Each came from a different Christian Near Eastern grouping, although they all approached the subject in a similar manner. Their works are termed "apologetic," meaning that they argue in defense of Christianity against the specific attacks on Christian doctrine raised by the Qur'ān and by later Muslims, especially as those aspects became enunciated in the life story of Muḥammad. The underlying purpose of these Christian controversialists was the development of the expression of their doctrines in Arabic so that Christians could be effective in dealing with the challenge of Islam. They did this by carefully enunciating and defining a vocabulary that would properly convey Christian ideas for pastoral and practical use.

Theodore Abū Qurra lived between about 755 and 830 and was a Melkite Christian. Ḥabīb ibn Khidma Abū Rā'iṭa was a contemporary and debating partner with Theodore Abū Qurra in the early ninth century. He was a Jacobite Christian and he likely died around 850. ʿAmmār al-Baṣrī was a Nestorian Christian and perhaps died around 845. The differences between the writers in terms of the subtleties of their own Christian position do not come up for debate in their apologetic texts. They were all united in wishing to argue that Christianity alone was the true religion. In order to do so, they had to argue against the Qur'ān's claims concerning the nature of the Trinity and the incarnation of God in Jesus. Arguments were put forth on the basis of scripture, but often that ran into the Muslim charge that Jewish and Christian scriptures were not to be trusted because they had not been transmitted faithfully and were subject to corruption. As a result, reasoned arguments became the major basis for their rebuttals. To defend the Trinity, the Christian writers appealed to the nature of God's attributes as Muslims understood them, such that the divine attributes of existing, living, and speaking were argued to be the three core elements and that these were identical to the Father, Son, and Holy Spirit of the one God.

The Christian writers constructed their defense of Christianity as the true religion by arguing against Muḥammad's status as a prophet. They did this by pointing to the absence of attested miracles in the life story of Muḥammad as compared to that of Jesus and his apostles and disciples. They also devised lists of what they considered negative attributes of Islam that could be compared, they claimed, to the positive attributes of Christianity, which then supported the claim that Christianity was the true religion. They argued that people had been forced or bribed to join Islam or they had converted out of bigotry, personal preference, tribal collusion, or due to the nature of Islam's licentious laws and practices. Christians, on the other hand, became Christians despite facing persecution, because, for those with rational minds, Christianity could be shown to be the closest to the truth with its naturally intelligible claims. Since the idea of the existence of God can be known through reason—and all religions and philosophers agree there is only one God, they said—it follows, they argue, that one must also be able to discern both true and false prophethood, and true and false religion through reason.

Detailed treatment of the Christian Arabic theological texts is found in Sidney H. Griffith, *The Beginnings of Christian Theology in Arabic: Muslim—Christian Encounters in the Early Islamic Period*, Aldershot: Ashgate/Variorum, 2002, and, in more general terms, in chapter 4 of the same author's *The Church in the Shadow of the Mosque: Christians and Muslims in the World of Islam*, Princeton: Princeton University Press, 2008.

Suggested further reading

Richard Martin, Mark Woodward, and Dwi Surya Atmaja, *Defenders of Reason in Islam: Muʿtazilism from Medieval School to Modern Symbol*, Oxford: Oneworld, 1997.

Josef van Ess, *The Flowering of Muslim Theology*, Cambridge, MA: Harvard University Press, 2006.

W. Montgomery Watt, *The Formative Period of Islamic Thought*, Edinburgh: Edinburgh University Press, 1973.

A. J. Wensinck, *The Muslim Creed: Its Genesis and Historical Development*, Cambridge: Cambridge University Press, 1932.

Tim Winter (ed.), *The Cambridge Companion to Classical Islamic Theology*, Cambridge: Cambridge University Press, 2008.

6 *Legal developments*

Sunnī Islam (as compared to the Shīʿa, to be dealt with in Chapter 8) is defined not by theological allegiance but by practice grounded in theological perspectives. Following one of the four schools of law authenticated by the agreement of the community as being true implementation of the *sunna* or practice of Muḥammad makes one a member of Sunnī Islam. It is the individual believer's perspective on the law which becomes the central element of self-definition as a Muslim and which has thus evolved as the controlling element of the community's identification as a whole. Law in this sense, however, is a far broader concept than that generally perceived in the English word. Included in it are not only the details of conduct in the narrow legal sense, but also minute matters of behavior, what might even be termed "manners," as well as issues related to worship and ritual. Furthermore, the entire body of law is traditionally viewed as the "revealed will of God," subject neither to history nor to change.

The role of law in defining Islamic allegiance is emphasized by the fact that the theological schools of Islam, as discussed in Chapter 5, gained their fullest support in the guise of appendages to groups of legal scholars; this support occurred in correlation to the attitudes manifested by those theological groups towards the roles of speculative reason and tradition in human life. Theology, therefore, is not only subordinate in importance to law as a discipline but also incorporated within the whole legal framework. Since all law comes from God, law is, in fact, theology as such, for both topics deal with the contemplation of human action in relationship to the divine; because of the practical aspects of Islamic life, law requires study by Muslims in a way that theology does not.

The idea of *sunna*

The focal point of the law in Sunnī Islam is the *sunna*, the concept of the practice of Muḥammad as embodied in the *ḥadīth* and transmitted faithfully by Muḥammad's followers through the succeeding generations down to the present. The *sunna* presents, for the individual Muslim, the picture of the perfect way of life, in imitation of the precedent of Muḥammad, who was the perfect embodiment of the will of God and, in some conceptions, was the living Qur'ān quite literally. The *ḥadīth* reports are the raw material of the *sunna*, and must be sifted through by jurists in order to enunciate the details of rightful practice; the *sharīʿa* is the "way of life" for the Muslim which has been developed by the Muslim jurists on the basis of certain jurisprudential principles, the *uṣūl al-fiqh*.

The history of Islamic law indicates that the idea of the *sunna* was not always perceived in this fashion, nor indeed was the *sunna* always considered to be the authoritative body of law for members of the community. Such a position took time and much argument before it emerged. It is to Muḥammad ibn Idrīs al-Shāfiʿī (d. 820) that much of the credit must go in developing this aspect of the overall legal theory of Islam.

In contemplating that transformation, however, it must be remembered that the concept of the law of Islam was a part of the emerging ideology and symbol system which provided a sense of identity to the Muslim community. Much of Islamic law, in substantive terms, can be seen to reflect a Jewish background and concerns common to Judaism. At the same time, portions of the law appear to have developed in a pragmatic way, with the adoption of laws and practices as they were found in the lands which were conquered; this is especially evident in elements of Roman law which were adopted in the Muslim environment. These two trends—Jewish and Roman—often merged, and they were reshaped as the distinct Muslim law emerged. This process was aided by many of the legal elements being recast by Muslims such that they were seen as emerging from the historical context of the *jāhiliyya*, as was suggested in Chapter 1.

In the early community, law was employed as a tool by which unity was imposed from above and for which an authority was needed to justify the requirements of that law. In the earliest period after the conquests, it would appear that the caliphs themselves were pictured as the authorities within the community on legal matters, and it took some time before a unifying concept of the authority of Muḥammad as enunciated in the notion of the prophetic *sunna* actually emerged.

When the word *sunna* is used in texts from the early period it refers not to the *sunna* of Muḥammad but to the *sunna* of the caliphs and/or the *sunna* of a particular area, often combined with a sense of an ideal behavior which is normative. That is, as the Arab territories expanded and Islam became the emblem of that region, the law developed in a non-uniform manner under the general umbrella of "Islam." Each local area developed, in a pragmatic style, a law based upon the practice of its own region. This appears to have been supplemented to some degree by the centralized efforts of the caliph to unify his domain.

The emergence of schools of law

From the early stages of developing the law in a pragmatic and authoritative way, various "schools," *madhāhib* (*madhhab* in the singular), emerged in which people sharing common positions derived from their own personal legal deductions gathered together. The schools formed around the name of a single person, a teacher who had instructed students in the law, although it is doubtful that any of the individuals actually intended to start a "school" as such. The schools themselves did not (and do not now) demand adherence or conformity, nor did the term *madhhab* imply any particular teaching activity. What a school shared was a common interest in a specific body of legal material which, in one way or another, was connected to the eponymous founder of the school and his followers.

There can be little doubt that these schools emerged through the pious motivation and efforts of those involved in the study of law, combined with the emergence of a class of scholarly elite whose desire it was to wrest authority from the hands of the caliph. For Muslims to be sure that they were fulfilling the will of God as completely as possible, it was necessary that every detail of the law be expounded; this required that every aspect of the law must be discovered. As new situations arose, never before encountered within Muslim society, it was the jurists' responsibility to discover "the will of God" in such instances. The rules of jurisprudential theory (*uṣūl al-fiqh*) were eventually established in order to allow individual jurists to make these sorts of decisions in an orderly and "Muslim" way.

The schools of law first emerged as local centers, reflecting the geographical diversity in the law from the beginning. Basra, Kufa, Medina, and Damascus are to be distinguished as the major regions, developing their own traditions and influencing others. In Basra, the only lasting school of importance was that which became the Ibāḍī *madhhab*, a surviving relation of the theological school of the Khawārij. In Kufa, there emerged the Ḥanafiyya, under the eponym of Abū Ḥanīfa (d. 767) but developed by Abū Yūsuf (d. 798) and al-Shaybānī (d. 805) in Baghdad, as well as various Shīʿī groups, including the Imāmīs, the Zaydīs, and the Ismāʿīlīs. Al-Awzāʿī (d. 774) was associated with a school in Syria, although it did not last very long. Medina produced Mālik ibn Anas (d. 795) and provided the impetus, at the very least, for al-Shāfiʿī (d. 822). A later group, known as the Ḥanbalī school (the Ḥanābila), developed from the teachings of Ibn Ḥanbal (d. 855) with a substantial debt to Medinan practices.

The differences between these groups should not be exaggerated; the main contrast between the groups tends to be schematized best as a difference between the early groups in Iraq (who seem to have had close contact with Jewish law) and those in Medina (who had a more "liberal" attitude than their Iraqi counterparts), with the later schools following the Medinan position. The issues at stake were generally matters dealing with customary practice and local conditions rather than disputes primarily over principles or methods. This sort of differentiation between the schools actually increased over time, as the schools developed what had been the early core of the law according to their own practices. Each school developed its own practice, its own *sunna*, which, as time went on and authority was sought for individual practices, was traced back, first to prominent jurists in the past, then to companions of Muḥammad, and finally to Muḥammad himself. This "backwards growth" in authority is a tendency which has already been mentioned in Chapter 3 in terms of the growth of *isnāds*; this is the same phenomenon but on a larger, more theoretical scale. The final result was the emergence of the *sunna* of Muḥammad. The ultimate motivation behind this development was to create a structure of law which was Islamic through and through, by denying all foreign elements and justifying all the law in terms of the twin sources of Muslim life, the Qur'ān and the *sunna*.

The role of al-Shāfiʿī

It is through the person and work of al-Shāfiʿī that we can most easily see the way in which the *sunna* of Muḥammad became the authoritative source of law for all Muslims. Stimulating al-Shāfiʿī's efforts to champion this position were claims made by Traditionalists to the effect that it was not sufficient for a jurist simply to assert that such and such an item was the *sunna* of Muḥammad, using what the Traditionalists felt was independent reasoning to justify the assertion; there was, for these people, a need to prove each and every one of these statements. This is where the role of the *ḥadīth* with its *isnād* came in. The tendency to demand proof did not arise without a great deal of opposition, as evidenced most obviously within the Muʿtazilī movement, which championed the use of reason in all matters of religion. For the most part, the schools of law, to the extent to which they had emerged by this point, only accepted the arguments and the demands of the Traditionalists in so far as the latter's points would support the former's legal traditions. Where traditions from Muḥammad could be seen to agree with a legal practice, all fine and good; there was not, at this point, any support for changing the law in order to have it agree with the *ḥadīth*.

Al-Shāfiʿī systematized what appears to have been chaos by developing a procedure for legal reasoning. While other jurists prior to him and contemporary with him, people such as Abū Ḥanīfa, Abū Yūsuf and al-Shaybānī, were involved in this process also, modern scholarly research (especially that of Joseph Schacht) has shown al-Shāfiʿī to be the pivotal person in the emergence of the legal system of Islam as we know it. Al-Shāfiʿī demanded the use of systematic reasoning without arbitrary or personal deduction in formulating the law and thus he created a system that was far more cohesive on a theoretical level than had previously been the case. He argued for the authoritative *sunna* being that of Muḥammad, a *sunna* which was to be found only in traditions transmitted from Muḥammad himself; the acceptance of traditions from the companions was not to be considered sufficient. As al-Shāfiʿī states, "the enactments of the Prophet are accepted as coming from Allāh in the same way as the explicit orders of the [Qur'ān], because Allāh has made obedience to the Prophet obligatory" (al-Shāfiʿī, *Kitāb al-Umm*, as quoted in Schacht 1950: 16). Furthermore, the Qur'ān could not contradict the *sunna*; the *sunna* could only explain the Qur'ān—such had to be the hierarchy of the sources of the law. A controlled notion of *naskh*, "abrogation," was implemented in order to handle cases of apparent contradiction between and within the sources. The community of Muslims could be said never to be in contradiction of the *sunna* if they agreed on a certain practice:

> We accept the decision of the public because we follow their authority, knowing that, wherever there are *sunnas* of the Prophet, their whole body cannot be ignorant of them, although it is possible that some are, and knowing that their whole body cannot agree on something contrary to the *sunna* of the Prophet and on an error, I trust.
>
> (Shāfiʿī 1983: 204)

This, in fact, must be the case in order to guarantee the transmission of *ḥadīth* reports from Muḥammad. It is not surprising, then, to note that the books of *ḥadīth* were all compiled after the time of al-Shāfiʿī when the need for these sources was crucial.

The development of the schools of law

The major schools of law which have survived down until today have their development in the time of al-Shāfiʿī and after. The process was not one of transforming the local practice into a school as such, but of championing the doctrine of a teacher and the tradition which that teaching represented. In Kufa the Ḥanafī school, including the star pupils al-Shaybānī (who attributed his writings to Abū Ḥanīfa and thus created the literary tradition which is the school of law, *per se*) and Abū Yūsuf, became paramount and drew into their system the city of Basra. Similarly, in Medina and followed by Egypt and Mecca, Mālik ibn Anas, the person associated with the book called *al-Muwaṭṭaʾ*, one of the first written compendia of legal traditions, became central as the Mālikī school, destined to find its major development in North Africa. The book ascribed to Mālik was an attempt to provide a very limited number of traditions concerning a given topic, and then to interpret them in light of the prevailing legal system of Medina. This latter element is the controlling factor in the whole book, rather than the traditions themselves.

Al-Shāfiʿī's school appears to have been based around him personally. He considered himself a member of the school of Medina, but he ended up not following the tradition of that area. His efforts were directed towards combining the pragmatic approach and position of Medina with the demands of the Traditionalists for adherence to the *sunna* of Muḥammad. Cairo proved to be the focal point of the development of his school, an area where al-Shāfiʿī spent the last part of his life. The school emerged by the ninth century as one of the three major groupings which continued their efforts in developing the *sharī'a*, or law, of Islam and out of which eventually came the *uṣūl al-fiqh*, the principles of jurisprudence.

Principles of jurisprudence

The emergence of a fully enunciated theory of jurisprudence was not an instantaneous development of the law schools. The works of the earliest representatives of the law schools display a measure of disorder in their treatments of the law and rarely put forth the full basis of the reasoning in individual cases. It was not until the eleventh century that matters became more precise, so that definition of terms and reformulation of earlier decisions took place in works such as that of al-Sarakhsī (d. 1096) in the Ḥanafī school. This was not a simple reiteration of, or commentary upon, the earlier works, but a creative reworking of the entire structure of the *fiqh* process. The underlying drive behind the literature was a theological one in that the desire was to demonstrate the completeness of Islamic law. Since it must be possible to answer every legal question on the basis of the sources of law, these works are dedicated to demonstrating that this is so. In order to do that, cases with the most remote possibility of occurring in human interaction are dealt with, precisely to show that the law (or the skill of the jurist) was such as to cover every potentiality.

According to the developed jurisprudential theory in Sunnī Islam which has its ultimate basis in the work of al-Shāfi'ī, there are four sources from which law can be derived: the Qur'ān, the *sunna* of Muḥammad, consensus (*ijmā'*) of the community and/or the scholars, and analogy (*qiyās*). The first two provide the material basis upon which *qiyās* must operate. The vast majority of laws have, in fact, been fashioned by *qiyās* because the Qur'ān and the *sunna* provide a fairly limited set of detailed legal provisions.

In general terms, an individual jurist first had to scour the works of previous jurists to find another case under consideration that was the same, or a case with similar facts. Should he not find one, he was faced with an unprecedented instance for which he would then use *qiyās*, employing as his starting point legal information found in the Qur'ān, *sunna*, or rendered absolute law by *ijmā'*.

Qiyās works on the basis of finding the *'illa*, the common basis between a documented case and a new situation; the process depends upon the powers of deduction of the jurist and the results of his work will depend upon *ijmā'*, the consensus of opinion, in whether or not it supports his judgment. Should the decision find general support, it becomes an irrevocable law and thus may serve as the basis for further deductions by means of *qiyās*.

The operation of *ijmā'*, consensus, was a major issue in the development of the principles of jurisprudence, one which jurists took pains to prove was in fact a legitimate process substantiated by the Qur'ān and the *sunna*; only in this way, it was argued, was it possible to distinguish between jurists who delegated to themselves the right to make laws (perhaps an accusation resulting from polemical discussions with Jews and Christians) and those who worked legitimately within the Muslim framework. *Ijmāʿ* functions to confirm rulings. While, in theory, this could take place at the time of a given ruling, in practice it occurred in retrospect. If no dissenting voices were heard by the time of the following generation, then it could be taken that *ijmāʿ* had confirmed a ruling. *Ijmāʿ* is often seen to be the most crucial element of the whole legal structure, for it is through its action that all elements are confirmed, especially individual *ḥadīth* reports and even, one might say, the Qurʾān itself, which is only authoritative because all Muslims agree that it is so. This is emphasized by the fact that there is no centralized authority (in Sunnī Islam) by which such a matter can be established. Muslim theorists, however, did not view the process in this manner, since they still needed to confirm the validity of *ijmāʿ* as a concept by means of *ḥadīth* and Qurʾān. For them, the twin scriptural sources were authenticated by customary usage and their miraculous nature, rather than by consensus itself; thus no circular reasoning was involved.

Relations between the schools of law

The Traditionalist school, which had demanded a complete rejection of personal reasoning, was not totally satisfied with al-Shāfiʿī's compromise in working out the relationship between the sources of law. Ibn Ḥanbal (d. 855), who was the eponym of the Ḥanbalī school, structured his thought on the principle of adherence to *ḥadīth* in preference to personal reasoning. He manifested this attitude in his compendium of traditions, the *Musnad*. The anecdote is related that Ibn Ḥanbal never ate a watermelon because he could not find a tradition which suggested that Muḥammad had done so or that he had approved of such. Over the centuries, however, even this school, by the time it was accepted within the structures of Islamic juristic orthodoxy, came to the position of accepting the *uṣūl al-fiqh* as enunciated by the other schools, and thus embraced reasoning and consensus; watermelons were deemed acceptable.

Another school emerged in the ninth century, known as the Ẓāhirī group, founded by Dāwūd ibn Khalaf (d. 884). Claiming allegiance to the *ẓāhir* or "literal" sense of both the Qurʾān and prophetic *ḥadīth*, the school rejected all aspects of systematic reasoning employed in the application of *qiyās*. This led to peculiar combinations of stances on the part of the school in contrast to the others, appearing liberal in some instances—because it followed the letter of the law and did not extend it into the many other areas deemed analogous by other schools—and being far more strict in others. Ibn Ḥazm (d. 1065) remains the intellectual high point of this school, which, in fact, lost much of its influence after his time.

By the end of the tenth century, the four schools—Ḥanafiyya, Mālikiyya, Shāfiʿiyya, and Ḥanābila—had solidified their position to the extent that no further schools of law emerged from that point on. This did not mean that no further legal judgments were to be made, but, rather, that the principles for which the schools stood and the legal stances which they had developed were to be the points within which all further discussions were to be conducted.

The extent to which the schools disagree on points of law is of little concern to Muslims, for there is a tradition ascribed to Muḥammad (although it is not found in the canonical collections of *ḥadīth*) which addresses itself precisely to the situation: "Difference of opinion in the community is a token of divine mercy" (*Fiqh Akbar I*, as translated in Wensinck 1932: 112–13). An attitude of mutual recognition among the schools has prevailed, such that orthodoxy in matters of law is defined only by acceptance of the roots of the law; this means that the Ẓāhirī school was excluded due to its rejection of *qiyās*. Where a difference of opinion exists between the schools, it is to be taken that each opinion is an equally probable expression of God's will. On a matter seemingly as basic as the food laws, differences may be noted in whether certain animals are declared to be permissible or disapproved:

> The followers of al-Shāfiʿī disagree concerning aquatic animals. Some claim that fish are permissible but that frogs are forbidden. Others say that if the animal is in the form of a fish or of an animal ritually slaughtered in good faith, then it is permissible to eat it if it comes from the sea without being ritually slaughtered; however, if it is in the form of something which is not permitted to be eaten in good faith, then one is forbidden to eat it. This is the judgment of Abū Thawr. Others say that everything from the sea is to be judged by the law of fish, except the frog which is forbidden because the prophet forbade killing it. This is the judgment of ʿAlī ibn Khayrān.
>
> Mālik and Rabīʿa declare all aquatic animals allowable, even the tortoise and the like. This is suggested by a report from Abū Bakr who said, "There is nothing in the sea besides animals which God would slaughter for you."
>
> Abū Ḥanīfa forbids everything which does not have the form of a fish among the aquatic animals.
>
> (Baghdādī 1987: 104–5)

Thus, the Ḥanafī school allows aquatic animals to be eaten only if they have the form of a fish, while the Mālikī school considers all aquatic animals permissible. Both positions are considered equally valid and equally "orthodox" for all Muslims.

Law and morality

After considering a given legal case, a jurist is able to declare whether the resultant action itself is to be classified as falling within one aspect of a five-level categorization of acts (*al-aḥkām al-khamsa*): obligatory (*wājib*), recommended (*mandūb*), permissible (*mubāḥ*), disapproved (*makrūh*), or forbidden (*ḥarām*). Notably, in light of the Quranic data, as discussed in Chapter 2, *ḥalāl* did not become a preferred term of ethical behavior, generally (but not always) being restricted to a quality of entities and not reflective of acts themselves. As legal theory evolved, everything was deemed to be *ḥalāl* which was not specifically prohibited (and in that sense was the opposite of *ḥarām*), but in the ethical system as it developed the word *mubāḥ* became the most commonly used term for permissible. The word *ḥalāl* gained a connotation of "permitted" especially as it applied to dietary restrictions and thus referred to whatever items may be eaten by Muslims, such as ritually slaughtered food (and became a functional parallel to the way "kosher" is used in Jewish parlance).

Speaking in very broad terms, performance of obligatory actions will bring reward in the hereafter for the person concerned, while omission of the actions will bring punishment. Recommended actions bring reward but no punishment for their omission. Forbidden actions will bring punishment for being committed, but reward for being avoided, while disapproved actions bring reward for being avoided, but no punishment should they be performed. The vast majority of actions fall into the "permissible" category, the ramifications of which will not be felt in the hereafter. There are many subtleties in the application of these categories, but, in principle, they apply whether the concern is ritual, moral, or legal; all activities are considered in the same way and all are under the rule of Islam. It is in the nature of this law, however, that even an act which is declared to be disapproved can still bring about a binding result. Marriages, for example, can be dissolved in a number of ways. According to the Ḥanafī jurist al-Marghinānī (d. 1197), the most laudable way of divorce is for "the husband to repudiate his wife within a single sentence during the time she is not menstruating," and then leave her alone for the next three months. This is best because such a divorce is revocable until the end of the three-month waiting period, since it has only been pronounced once. Repeating the repudiation regularly each month over a period of three months is simply "laudable." However, "an irregular divorce is where the husband repudiates his wife with three divorces in a single statement or three (arbitrary) times during a three month period"; this is declared to be "disapproved" but, most significantly, the marriage is still considered to have been terminated in fact (Marghinānī 1975: 226–9). There is, thus, a separation between what might be considered law and morality, although it is all a part of one whole in the Muslim system, for all law ultimately has as its purpose gaining entry into paradise in the hereafter for the individual. At the same time, it is a sign of the realistic nature of Islamic law that the five moral categories of actions were adopted rather than a binary system of good versus bad (a position championed by the Muʿtazila at one point in history). The law recognizes that not all Muslims are going to be saints in every aspect of their behavior and that they will need the urging forth towards perfection that the law can provide.

Underlying this system are certain assumptions about the ethical nature of the law. In general Muslim understanding, the law has been determined by God in a manner that determines what is good and what is evil according to God's will. Reason cannot determine morality because God and His will cannot be constrained in any way. At the same time, God's will is not arbitrary: it is deemed to be purposeful. Because of this, the law is not limited to the literal statements of the Qur'ān and *sunna* as they apply to specific situations. Rather, it is reasonable for humans to extrapolate on the basis of one situation to a similar one because God's will is understood to be purposeful and thus somewhat predictable. Furthermore, because the laws found in the sources which set the dimensions of ethical action are specific in nature, they are not stated as ethical principles from which further guidance may be deduced. However, the Muslim jurists did determine three general principles which were deemed to be within the framework of Islamic law: necessity (*ḍarūra*), public welfare (*maṣlaḥa*), and equity (*istiḥṣān*). These three "are invoked to promote a good that would appear to be threatened by absolute adherence to the revealed command of God or to prevent an evil that is likely to result from such adherence" (Brown 1999: 191), although all three principles were applied very cautiously in classical juristic thinking in order to avoid permitting the law from departing from the plain meaning of scripture in too many situations.

The public role of Muslim morality—captured in the phrase "commanding right and forbidding wrong"—was a theme which, once provoked by the early disputes within the community, could hardly be avoided. However, the history of its implementation and precise dimensions displays a variation that reflects the practicalities of any given situation. At stake was the extent to which the individual Muslim and the Muslim state had responsibility for monitoring and correcting the behavior of fellow Muslims. For example, Abū Bakr al-Khallāl (d. 923) gathered together the sayings of Ibn Ḥanbal on the topic of forbidding wrong. His text provides the fullest early documentation of how the Qur'ān and the statements of Muḥammad related to this moral responsibility were implemented; an analysis shows that the doctrine was, at this time, an apolitical one which kept its distance from the political powers of the time and made no demands of, and had no expectations of, the caliph. In dealing with individuals, the approach was a non-invasive one, seizing the opportunity to speak to others when the moral occasion necessitated it and taking action only where it would not endanger oneself. Otherwise, recourse to performing the duty of commanding right and forbidding wrong "in the heart" was always sufficient. However, an activist Ḥanbalī position emerged in the tenth century, apparently as a result of the growing popularity of the legal school and the weakening of the power of the caliphate. The theory behind this stance is found in the works of Abū Ya'lā ibn al-Farrā' (d. 1066) and 'Abd al-Qādir al-Jīlānī (d. 1166). These authors present the conditions and obligations of forbidding wrong in a somewhat systematic form, emphasizing the need for knowledge of the law, the knowledge of the fact of violation and the persistence of the action, that forbidding wrong must not lead to a greater evil, that it must be likely to succeed, and that it must not involve personal risk, although even if it does it would be permissible to proceed. With Ibn Taymiyya (d. 1328), Ḥanbalī cooperation with the state reached new heights and, as such, it supported his extensive attempts to forbid wrong. In his work devoted to the topic, Ibn Taymiyya was careful to argue for respecting a balance of costs and benefits in assessing the necessity for action in any given instance. He also argues that the duty to perform the action primarily falls on those in authority; this is the purpose of state power and the administrators are the ones who have the power to be successful in accomplishing the duty (a position which obviously has moved far from Ibn Ḥanbal's own non-involvement with the state).

The role of the judge

The administration of the law in the Muslim community developed institutionally first under the Umayyads, but it arrived at its more lasting form under the ʿAbbāsids. A judge, known as a *qāḍī*, was appointed by the state to administer the *sharīʿa*. A central chief judge was also appointed by the ruling authorities, to whom all other judges as well as the ruler himself would defer on all legal issues. He became the person who recommended to the caliph the appointment of all the judges and became the major legal counselor of the ruler. The fact that all the judges (including the chief judge) were appointed by the state often led to conflicts; although in theory once a judge was appointed he was to be independent of the ruling authorities, in practice such things as implementing decisions against high government officials were extremely difficult.

One of the qualifications for being a judge was, obviously, full knowledge of the Islamic law; other requirements included having sound sight and hearing, and being free (that is, not a slave), honest, and Muslim. Such scholars were often the most strenuous upholders of Islam and they frequently saw the activities of the state as not being as fully "Islamic" as would be desirable. Their ability to criticize those who gave them their jobs, however, was tenuous. This led to a great deal of discussion over legitimacy of rule and explains why there was such a lot of debate in Islam concerning the need to follow an unjust ruler and the right of rebellion. The position of the judge and the legitimacy of the appointment to that post were never held to be affected by the nature of the ruling powers who appointed him (or her, for a woman, according to some lines of thought, could be a judge, although she certainly did not have the right to rule in the imposition of the *ḥadd* penalties—those penalties specifically prescribed in the Qurʾān for crimes such as adultery, stealing, armed robbery, drinking wine, false accusation of unchastity, and apostasy). However, many of the leading jurists found it impossible to accept a position as a *qāḍī* and made much of their refusal to do so; their principles always dictated that since, in their opinion, the ruler of the time was not fulfilling his responsibility to Islam, accepting a judicial appointment from such a person would be morally reprehensible.

The administration of justice

Judges depended upon the power of the state to put their decisions into action. This was crucial in issues of criminal justice, for example. Although the law had been structured by the jurists such that essentially there were no crimes against the state—a crime is against another person or against God—the imposition of the prescribed penalties, especially the *ḥadd* penalties found the Qurʾān, had to be enforced by some means. Eventually a police force was devised to deal with such cases. Judges were further hampered by the terms of Islamic law, which only allowed them to receive evidence that was submitted to them, rather than being able to search it out or conduct interrogations; the law was founded on the notion that blameless witnesses would always tell the truth and that oaths of innocence would always be forthcoming from all honest persons. The jurists saw themselves "in the role of spiritual advisors to the conscience of Islam rather than authoritarian directors of its practical affairs" (Coulson 1964:126). The result of this was the inevitable situation of the political powers having to assume some of the responsibility for direct administration of justice; several additional institutions emerged to deal with a variety of situations as a consequence. Among the legal officials in the community was the "investigator of complaints" (*naẓar fi ʾl-maẓālim*). This was an office originally designed to hear charges concerning the miscarriage of justice, and was thus to act as a check on judges; additional issues such as matters dealing with unjust taxes and enforcing the decisions of the *qāḍī*s were also within its purview. Later, the office emerged as a parallel system of justice, especially in matters of lawsuits; this was the result of the *maẓālim* courts having powers which the *qāḍī*s did not enjoy: the right to double-check and investigate evidence, to restrain acts of violence, and to refer people to binding arbitration.

An "inspector of the market" (*muḥtasib*, holding the office of the *ḥisba*) was also appointed, who was responsible for encouraging Islamic morality in general and thus provided the possibility of prosecutions in the general public interest. Specific duties of this office included matters relating to defective weights in the marketplace and commercial transactions where fraud or unpaid debts were suspected. Once again, the role of the judge was, to a certain extent, duplicated.

The nature of Islamic law

Overall, Muslim law is recognized to be an "ideal" system, one which will be corrupted and will suffer at the hand of corruption in the world. This is even more so because the law is, in the first instance at least, a theoretical development and an enunciation of jurists, rather than a body of law emerging from precedents, although this position is tempered to some extent by practical considerations. The theoretical nature of the law may be best described as existing in tension with its practical aspects. Islamic law is, to a degree, of a purely religious character, carrying with it only the threat of punishment by God; failure to follow the law of Islam concerning the prayer, for example, will not involve any juridical penalty in this world. An exception would be the case of a person who went so far as to deny the obligatory character of the prayer, which would then be evidence of the rejection of Islam itself. The law is flexible also to the extent that any law may be broken under duress or necessity; in such conditions, a given act previously considered forbidden becomes valid, including such things as eating pork when no other food is available or drinking wine in the absence of all other liquids. This attitude of flexibility also allowed Islamic law to spread gradually into lands distant from the central places of Islamic learning, adapting to local custom and integrating Islamic fundamentals while establishing a solid foundation to the faith.

One final implication of the character of Islamic law is to be noted in the treatment of Jewish and Christian communities living within territories controlled by Muslims. These groups, known in Islamic law as *ahl al-dhimma* or *dhimmīs*, were not subject to the specific provisions of Islamic law, precisely because it was only for those who were Muslims. Rather, these communities were allowed to be self-governing, following their own legal codes and principles, although they were considered citizens at a lower level than their Muslim neighbors, with certain restrictions on their public rights and a requirement of paying a special poll tax. Security of life, property, and religion was guaranteed by the payment of this tax, but no new religious buildings were to be erected, nor was the public display of religion to be allowed. In practice, the tolerance shown for these communities fluctuated in the Muslim world according to the political and social pressures of the time, but the theory, at the very least, echoed the character of Islamic law and its integrative religious nature.

Muslim diet and cuisine

Food laws are set out in the Qur'ān and the *sunna* and they underlie the culturally driven menus that are the feature of Muslim life. Clearly there is no such thing as "Islamic cuisine" as such, as is evidenced by the striking variety of cooking styles across the Muslim world; nationalism often expresses itself through distinctive dishes. There are, however, certain markers of Islamic identity that manifest themselves in the Muslim diet. Food has always been considered one of the greatest pleasures of Muslim life, as medieval cookbooks from the Arab world make quite clear.

The absence of pork, dog, blood, and alcohol, combined with prescribed animal slaughtering practices, are the main distinguishing characteristics of foods consumed by Muslims. The prohibition of pork appears to be an ancient Middle Eastern practice that finds justifications ranging from the uncleanliness and licentiousness of the animal itself to the dangers of disease being spread through the meat. Such interpretations have a long heritage in Jewish and Christian discussions and have been adopted in many Muslim texts as well. However, the fact of the widespread prohibition means that the absence of pork from diets generally does not act as a particular marker of Muslim identity; an exception to this may be seen in certain cultural contexts, such as in some (but not all) areas of China, where pork is commonly consumed and Muslims, as a community, are identified by the neighbors as non-pork-eaters.

The Muslim ritual slaughtering practices, such that the animal should be facing the *qibla*, the name of God is invoked, and the throat is cut cleanly across, are standard across the Muslim world and only vary in the context of hunting. In archaeological digs where camel bones that provide evidence of the Muslim butchering process are found, it is possible to take this as evidence of the presence of a Muslim population, at least in areas where the camel is found. In pre-Islamic times there is little evidence of the consumption of camel outside of Arabia itself, where camel sacrifices apparently took place. Thus, it appears that the eating of camel outside of Arabia marks the presence of Muslims and that is confirmed by the butchering practices that are evidenced by the unique markings left on the bones. Some non-Muslim communities adopted the practice of not eating camel because of its strong association with Muslims and a lingering sense of cultural resentment in places that were once dominated by Muslims. Muslims have done a similar thing with the cow in India by understanding it as a marker of being Hindu; there have been times during which Hindus living under Muslim rule were encouraged to eat beef to bring them "closer" to Islam.

Food and gender intertwine and some aspects of that may reflect Muslim social assumptions. Food preparation is associated with women in many parts of the world, and thus food becomes an area for the expression of power for females, either through limiting the supply of food or through providing poorly prepared meals. At the same time, men have an obligation to provide the materials and the ingredients required for the meals. None of this, of course, is unique to being Muslim, but such matters do intersect with issues such as divorce, given that one of the grounds on which a woman can request divorce is due to the husband's failure to provide for her properly.

A. J. Arberry, Charles Perry, and Maxime Rodinson, *Medieval Arab Cookery*, Totnes, Devon: Prospect Books, 2001, is a collection of essays on many aspects of Arab cuisine that provides useful insight into the Muslim diet. Timothy Insoll, *The Archaeology of Islam*, Oxford: Blackwell, 1999, chapter 4, is helpful for determining how to assess evidence related to food.

Figure 6.1 An illustration of the poet-mystic Ḥakīm Sanāʾī (died about 1131) leaving his shoes outside a butcher's shop, from the manuscript dated 1552 held in the Bodleian Library (Oxford) of the work dedicated to Sulṭān Ḥusayn Mīrzā (r. 1469–1506), *Majālis al-ʿushshāq* ("The Assemblies of Lovers"), which provides biographies of famous men, especially mystics.
Source: The Art Archive/Bodleian Library Oxford. MS Ouseley Add. 24, f. 44v.

Suggested further reading

Wael B. Hallaq (ed.) *The Formation of Islamic Law,* Aldershot: Ashgate/Variorum, 2004.

Marion Holmes Katz, *Body of Text: The Emergence of the Sunnī Law of Ritual Purity*, Albany: State University of New York Press, 2002.

Christopher Melchert, *The Formation of the Sunni Schools of Law, 9th and 10th Centuries C.E.*, Leiden: Brill, 1997.

Joseph Schacht, *The Origins of Muhammadan Jurisprudence*, Oxford: Clarendon Press, 1950.

Knut S. Vikør, *Between God and Sultan: A History of Islamic Law*, Oxford: Oxford University Press, 2005.

7 *Ritual practice*

To a person standing on the outside observing the presence of a religion, ritual is the most obvious sign of the character and existence of believers in that faith. Ritual activities and their attendant buildings, clothes, and assorted paraphernalia provide the emblems of a religion and become, for the members of the religion themselves, modes for the expressions of their identity. Such ritual symbols also fulfill an obvious political function for the ruler, as a way of declaring his own dedication to the values embodied in the symbols and as a way of unifying his people behind him in one common symbolic expression.

For classical Islam, the notion of the "Five Pillars" represents the epitome of the revealed law as enacted through ritual activity. The five actions—the witness to faith (*shahāda*), prayer (*ṣalāt*), charity (*zakāt*), fasting (*ṣawm*), and pilgrimage (*ḥajj*)—are duties for which each individual is responsible, separate from general ethics and rules for interpersonal relationships. They are an integral part of the belief system of Islam, being a part of the explication of theological statements of belief from at least the tenth century onwards, as illustrated by the work of al-Baghdādī (d. 1037), whose *Kitāb Uṣūl al-Dīn* includes an intertwining of theological matters with more formal legal structures.

The concept that "five pillars" were the ritual center of Islam emerged almost certainly within the second Muslim century; both the *ḥadīth* collections of al-Bukhārī (d. 870) and Muslim ibn al-Ḥajjāj (d. 875) contain early on in their books a report which states that Muḥammad said, "Islam is based upon five (principles)," followed by an enumeration of the five. While the term "pillar" is not used in these reports (that term would appear to be a tenth-century coinage), the isolation of these specific ritual activities is clear. Even earlier than the *ḥadīth* collections, al-Shāfiʿī (d. 822), in his *Risāla*, isolated prayer, charity, fasting, and pilgrimage as among the central elements of the faith; it would appear that, for him, these elements had not become the actual defining factor of Islam, but the recognition of their prominence is present. A similar observation may be made for the *Muwaṭṭaʾ* ascribed to Mālik ibn Anas (d. 795), whose work is organized such as to give prominence to the four rituals; that presentation, however, may well be the work of later editors, reflecting a more developed strain of thought than that of Mālik himself. It is equally clear that none of the individual elements of the "Five Pillars" was simply imposed upon new believers in Islam from the very beginning. Each ritual has its own history and its own significance, both aspects often being very difficult to reconstruct. None of the rituals has its requirements fully expressed in the Qurʾān.

The evidence of archaeological remains from the earliest stages of the Arab conquests, for example in the area of the Negev desert, does not provide us with any clear indication of cultic or ritual emblems in this period either. Inscriptions found in these places reveal the rise of a religious ideology by their use of various religious invocations and also exhibit the emergence of places of worship. No clues are left, however, as to the character of this worship other than the observation that it took place alongside various pagan and Christian (and probably Jewish) worship practices.

Testifying Muslim faith

The witness to faith (*shahāda*) consists of repeating the two phrases, "There is no god but God," *lā ilāha illā ʾllāh*, and "Muḥammad is the messenger of God," *Muḥammadun rasūl Allāh*. These phrases are recited in order to witness conversion to Islam. Such utterances have practical implications for the political order, therefore, entitling one to the privileges of membership in the Muslim community. The phrases must be recited in Arabic and prefaced by an honest statement of intention. Thus al-Baghdādī (1928: 186) states that the person who utters the *shahāda* must know "the truth of the statement" and must repeat it "out of understanding and with heartfelt sincerity." The *shahāda* is repeated as a part of the Muslim prayer, *ṣalāt*, and thus gains more of a sense of being an oft-repeated ritual than simply a once-in-a-lifetime statement.

The declaration of an "intention," *niyya*, which comes at the beginning not only of the utterance of the *shahāda* but of all ritual activity, is especially important in Muslim law. It is held that a statement of intention as the first step of a religious devotion declares the act is in accord with the will of God. Intention, as a discreet act in the process of ritual, brings the mind into accord with the body in any act of devotion, producing an enveloping performance for the individual. In essence, intention serves to differentiate acts of devotion—acts which are for God—from mundane acts, the difference between reading the statement of the *shahāda* in the previous paragraph and invoking it as a ritual activity.

The two basic statements of the *shahāda* are found in the Qurʾān, but they are not put together as a single statement, nor are they suggested in that book to be some sort of defining notion of what a Muslim is, as is implied within the concept of their ritual use. The refrain "There is no god but God" and variations upon it are frequent in the scripture, found, for example, in Qurʾān 47/19; "Muḥammad is the messenger of God" and statements to that effect are also found, for example in Qurʾān 48/29, but the sense is never one of a refrain, but rather of a part of an argument.

The emergence of the statement as a key part of Muslim identity is witnessed on coins from the first Muslim century and in the Dome of the Rock inscriptions, as well as in the *ḥadīth* literature. Coins from the eighth decade of the *hijrī* calendar contain phrases such as "There is no god but God alone," a statement reminiscent of Qur'ān 5/73 and similar passages, but obviously it is differentiated by the addition of the word *wāḥid*, "alone," from the first half of the *shahāda*. "Muḥammad is the messenger of God" also appears starting, it would seem, with coins from the years 77 and 78 (= 696–8). To that statement is added, "whom He sent with guidance and the religion of truth, that He might make it victorious over all religions." Such invocations continue on many coins from this point on and thus become the standard numismatic phraseology. It would appear to be an accident of history that coins continue to use a formula which does not precisely follow the *shahāda*, as might have been expected; this likely occurred because coinage was introduced before the *shahāda* reached its mature formulation. So, while the phrases of the *shahāda* themselves became stock items of the religious vocabulary, it is apparent that, by the time of the issuance of these early coins, the phrases had not yet emerged as the ritual statement which was to identify all Muslims. However, it would appear to be a short step, both historically and phraseologically, before just that occurred.

The same comments hold for the Dome of the Rock inscriptions of ʿAbd al-Malik as they do for the coins. Both phrases in reference to God and Muḥammad are found in the inscriptions, but they are found neither joined together nor distinguished as isolated elements within the texts. For example, there is the statement on the outside of the colonnade on the south side, "There is no god but God alone; He has no partner with Him," followed by "Muḥammad is the messenger of God." Over the north door, the inscription reads "Muḥammad is the servant of God and His messenger whom He sent with the guidance and the religion of truth . . .," the same as coins from Umayyad times after ʿAbd al-Malik; the lack of emphasis on the formula expressions employed in later Islamic ritual is once again notable and significant for what it reveals of the gradual development of this element of Muslim identity.

As was mentioned earlier, the idea of the "Five Pillars" is found listed in the *ḥadīth* collection of Muslim ibn al-Ḥajjāj, for example, but several of these reports indicate an instability in the matter of the *shahāda*. While all the reports confirm that testifying to faith in one way or another was the first part of the "five" elements stipulated by Muḥammad, it is expressed in a number of ways. For example, this testifying is called "declaring the oneness of God" in one instance. Furthermore, the actual form of the *shahāda* witnessed in the collection of Muslim ibn al-Ḥajjāj is specifically a testimony to faith; that is, it is prefaced by the statement *shahāda an*, "the witness to faith is that . . ." That statement is, in fact, a part of the ritual prayer (and so the traditions themselves also come within the chapter concerned with the "testimony to faith within prayer"). The fact that the material as presented by Muslim ibn al-Ḥajjāj provides a non-cohesive picture suggests two things: that the isolation of the *shahāda* as an individual part of a concept of the "Five Pillars" took place at least two centuries after Muḥammad; and that it was a formulation which received its final shape fairly late also.

Islamic prayer

Prayer, *ṣalāt*, is spoken of numerous times in the Qurʾān; the notion of regular times of prayer is stipulated on some occasions, but the text itself can only be made to support the classical Islamic practice of five prayers a day by a tenuous interpretation. Various elements of the ritual connected with the *ṣalāt* are also stipulated in the Qurʾān, including standing, bowing, prostrating, facing in a set direction known as the *qibla* (the word itself is used in the Qurʾān seven times, mainly in Qurʾān 2/142–5), and performing ablutions before prayer (Qurʾān 5/6). The Friday (noon) prayer as one for the whole community is also designated in Qurʾān 62/9. The recitation of the Qurʾān within the prayer is also sometimes seen to be supported by the text itself (Qurʾān 17/78, where reference is made to "reading at daybreak"). None of these elements, however, is presented in a systematic or detailed manner such that one could actually reconstruct a ritual on the basis of these texts alone. Rather, most are presented in a very general manner (for example, Qurʾān 25/63–4: "and the servants of the All-merciful are those . . . who spend the night bowing down to their Lord and standing"); and only later did Muslims peg upon these verses the elaborate ritual which had developed in its own way and according to many different impulses.

By the time the collections of *ḥadīth* material emerged, the ritual of the prayer had become quite explicit, although still not with total unanimity in detail. Such differences are to be found manifested in the traditions of the various schools of law, as with all the rituals in Islam, and therefore it is not possible to present a single picture of "prayer" within Islam. Basic elements are common to all schools, however, and may be summarized.

The five times of prayer (*miqāt*) are defined as daybreak (*ṣalāt al-ṣubḥ* or *fajr*), noon (*ṣalāt al-ẓuhr*), mid-afternoon (*ṣalāt al-ʿaṣr*), sunset (*ṣalāt al-maghrib*), and evening (*ṣalāt al-ʿishāʾ* or *ʿatama*), but the precise way in which these times are determined varies. Clearly, it also depends upon where in the world the individual is at a given moment, so Muslims are, in theory, praying all over the world all the time. The call to prayer (*adhān*) is given by the muezzin (*muʾadhdhin*) at each mosque (*masjid*, literally "the place of prostration" but in the Qurʾān meaning "sanctuary") but it is not necessary to go there in order to pray, except for the Friday noon prayer, for anyone may pray in any clean spot alone or in the company of others. Following the ablution, either minor (*wuḍūʾ*) or major (*ghusl*) depending on the state of ritual purity of the individual prior to the ablution, a series of recitations and body movements are undertaken in stages, many of which are liable to be supplemented by other traditional elements which vary according to the school of law. The prayer is done facing the direction of the Kaʿba in Mecca and entails recitation of sections of the Qurʾān, with a special emphasis falling on *sūra* 1. The worshipper moves from a standing position to one of bowing, half-sitting, and full prostration. The whole sequence of the ritual is repeated twice in the morning, three times at sunset, and four times in the noon, afternoon, and evening prayers.

The stipulation of these five prayer times is, according to Muslim tradition, a result of instructions given to Muḥammad while on his heavenly journey. Clearly, even on the basis of the text of the Qurʾān alone, the idea of there being five prayers took some time to emerge, but the evidence which is available to us just does not allow any insight into when the number five was decided upon or why. The suggestion that "five" is the median number between the three daily prayers of Judaism and the seven stages of the day of the Syrian Christian monastic orders fits within much of the elaboration of Muslim ritual as a conscious attempt to produce a self-definition which was midway between and yet clearly distinct from Judaism and Christianity. The number "five" is often used in Middle Eastern literature as symbolic of half a group—that is, half of "ten"—and the usage of the number itself in the Qurʾān is limited to expressions of large numbers (5,000 swooping angels in Qurʾān 3/125; one day is 50,000 years in 70/4), and simply appears to convey a significantly large quantity. The attachment of "five" to ritual matters (not only in the "five" daily prayers, but also the "five" ritual pillars, and the five "pillars" of the creed) is clearly a later development not dependent upon any symbolic or literal sense present in the Qurʾān.

Friday noon prayer

While the daily prayer may be said anywhere and may be said alone (although saying it with others is considered more meritorious), the Friday noon prayer is held in a large *jāmiʿ*, or "congregational" mosque. These buildings are generally supported by government funds, as opposed to the smaller mosques found throughout the Muslim world, which have been built with private funds and are typically used by a defined group of people for the prayer at all other times. The Friday noon prayer will always be led by an *imām*, the prayer leader (such a person may be present any time a group of Muslims prays together, however, simply to keep the group in unison), and a sermon will be given by the *khaṭīb* (who may be the same person as the *imām*). Attendance at the Friday noon prayer was declared obligatory for all Muslims who were legally capable, with the exception of "women, slaves, the sick, travellers, those tending the sick and those fleeing oppression," according to al-Baghdādī (1928: 190).

Function of prayer

Additional prayers of a non-compulsory nature, but still of the ritualized *ṣalāt* type, are also stipulated in Islam. Special prominence is given to the *witr* prayer, performed at night and to which an extra section, *rakʿa*, may be added. Additional sections may also be added to the five daily prayers. As well, there is the *wird*, the ritualized private prayer which concentrates on the recitation of the Qurʾān. Another prayer is the *duʿāʾ*, a non-ritualized individual address to God. Prayer is not therefore restricted to the daily five prayers alone but may be performed on other occasions as the need and desire arise within the individual Muslim. Thus, prayer as a phenomenon in Islam does not function simply to bring the community together at regular times of the day and the week; neither is it just a matter of providing structured time periods within the day to Muslim society, nor a way of simply producing a constant reminder of the presence of Islam in the world. Certainly it is all those things, but it also does seem to be conceived as a personal communication with God, providing the opportunity for expressions of thankfulness and worship in the full sense of those words.

The mosque

Even though it is not actually necessary for the ritual of prayer, the mosque has become the central element manifesting the physical presence of Muslims in a given place in the world, a source of identity for individual believers and a symbol and center of purity for the Muslim community. The central elements of this physical manifestation of Muslim identity as connected to the mosque may be isolated and, as such, may well provide a statement about the symbols that Muslims consider to be essential to their self-definition and self-understanding as Muslims. The phenomenon of churches turned into mosques provides an interesting illustration of such elements. The most obvious examples which allow an insight into this conversion are those found in Istanbul, which, while their transformation dates from a late period (the Turkish conquest of Constantinople was in 1453 and thus all such examples are necessarily after that date), include features which are fully representative of classical Muslim self-understanding.

Although overgrown and derelict in the 1980s and suffering from the effects of a partially completed restoration in 1964–5, the church identified as the Myrelaion and known as the Bodrum Camii or the Mesih Ali Paşa mosque in Istanbul provides a splendid example. Built in about 922, the church building is fascinating in its own right for its architectural design and the presence of a crypt underneath the building. In the late fifteenth or early sixteenth century, the church was converted into a mosque. The most obvious evidence of the conversion is the presence of the minaret, built into the southwest corner. The history of the minaret as a form of Muslim architecture is intriguing and, while its practical function of providing a place for the call to prayer is well known and often suggested to be the origin of the edifice, it seems more likely that the form was taken over from earlier buildings. The earliest examples of minarets are those found on the Mosque of al-Walīd in Damascus, constructed between 706 and

715; this mosque was built on the base of a Roman temple and incorporated the three original corner towers as minarets. (The absence of a minaret on the Dome of the Rock should be noted.) The generalized symbolism of the minaret in the early period is not hard to comprehend: towering over the inhabitants is the pillar of the conquerors. It is clear, however, that, regardless of its early function, in classical Islam a minaret became the central symbol of both the Muslim faith and the place of worship as illustrated in the conversion process of churches into mosques. (It should be noted, however, that it is quite possible for a building to be a mosque without it having a minaret.) In the Myrelaion, no other major architectural modifications were required to make the church function as a mosque. A small window appears to have been installed on the ground level to allow sufficient light for Qurʾān reading. The other changes were all internal and to do with furnishings. A *miḥrāb*, or niche, indicating the direction of prayer, was provided. This indicator would appear to be a necessary feature of converted buildings but a purpose-built mosque would, of course, be properly aligned anyway and thus it appears redundant in such instances. Yet the niche is found in all mosques. It may be that the feature was copied from the design of ancient religious buildings, being the place designated for the presence of the honored image in Roman temples, for example. A *minbar*, or pulpit, was required for the sermon (*khuṭba*) of the preacher (*khaṭīb*). A women's gallery had to be installed to keep the sexes separate. All these items had to be aligned in the correct Muslim direction, facing Mecca, within the former church structure. Ancillary chambers appear to have been constructed for the *imām* and the muezzin, and a vestibule created for latecomers. No evidence of a place for ablutions appears to exist, although the presence of a cistern within the original building complex may have provided a source for the necessary flowing water.

This pattern of conversion may be witnessed many times in Istanbul and in other parts of the Islamic world. Istanbul provides a further vivid example in the church of Saints Sergius and Bacchus, built in the year 527 for Justinian and thus older than Haghia Sophia, which with its four minarets provides another instance of a conversion. Some churches proved more problematic, as in what is believed to be the Church of St. Andrew in Krisei, now known as the Koca Mustafa Paşa Camii, which required a complete reorientation for its successful use as a mosque.

Muslim charity

Alms tax, *zakāt* (the term *ṣadaqa* is often synonymous but can also mean "freewill offerings"), like prayer, with which it is often mentioned in tandem, is demanded in the Qurʾān in statements which provide exhortations to believers to give ("You will never attain piety until you spend something of what you love," says Qurʾān 3/92), but few details are actually provided as to what to give and when. The Qurʾān responds to a

Figure 7.1 Haghia Sophia, built as a church by the Byzantine Emperor Justinian between 532 and 537. It was converted into the Ayasofya mosque in 1453 by removing the obvious Christian symbols (bells, altar, etc.), plastering over the interior mosaics, and, over a period of 150 years, adding the four minarets. The building was changed to a museum in 1934. Source: iStockphoto.

demand to know how much to give in *sūra* 2, verse 219, with the statement, "As much as you can spare!" An explicit statement is made about the recipients of the alms, with the result that Qurʾān 9/60 has served as the peg for all legal discussions on the issue: "Charity is for the poor, the needy, those working at collecting it, those whose hearts are being reconciled [to yours], for freeing of captives and debtors, and in striving along God's way, and for the wayfarer, as a duty imposed by God." A general emphasis throughout the Qurʾān falls on helping the poor, orphans, and widows, and it is also suggested that all such payments should be made discreetly, without drawing attention to the one who is giving. The alms tax given should come out of the money or produce which one possesses.

It was up to the jurists of the later centuries to develop a precise system of donation and payment. This development can be seen in the books of *ḥadīth*, and the institution of charity provided endless opportunity for the jurists to work out subtle details and theoretical considerations.

Early *ḥadīth* reports appear to be ignorant of precisely how much should be given as *zakāt* and from precisely what sorts of things it should be paid; such reports simply say that possessing "wealth" is forbidden and thus everything which is in excess should be given away. Within the developed schools of law, however, full rules emerged which, while they vary in their precise detail from school to school, can be summarized fairly accurately. Crops of the field, grapes, and dates are liable to *zakāt* on each crop, as an amount stipulated as 10 percent of the crop, paid at harvest time. Camels, oxen, and other small domestic animals which are freely grazing are also liable, the amount paid being a portion of the excess over certain stipulated amounts. Of gold, silver, and merchandise, 2.5 percent of the amount held each year is also payable. The amount may be paid directly to the recipient, but it is preferred that the tax be paid to the authorities in charge of its distribution (a notion seen to be supported by the fact that the Qur'ān refers to those involved in collecting *zakāt* as one of the groups eligible to receive it). In practice, *zakāt* became difficult to collect, especially in times of high general taxation. At various times during Muslim history, however, governments were inspired by pious scholars and attempted to return to a system of collecting *zakāt* as the only legitimate form of taxation. However, the amount collected often proved insufficient and eventually there occurred a reversion to other forms of tax on items more profitable to the government which were not covered in the traditional working out of the *zakāt* laws (for example by the imposition of import duties).

Zakāt has shown great flexibility over time in adapting to and being adapted by social and political realities. For example, variation in whether the tax was a voluntary one or a required contribution to the state frequently reflected the conditions at the time in terms of the state's prosperity. Also, the imposition of *zakāt* was seen, starting in about the eleventh century, as the central symbol of the revival of Islamic rule; the "proper" (that is, the juridical) implementation of the tax was urged by reformers and initiated by rulers at various points in history in order to bolster Islamic ideological claims. For example, al-Malik al-Kāmil (d. 1238), a ruler during the Ayyubid dynasty centered in Egypt, invoked the Islamic ideal of voluntary payment of taxes under the term *zakāt*, but the program quickly crumbled under the impact of the revenue lost by the central government.

The Muslim fast

During the ninth month of the *hijrī* calendar, Ramaḍān, a fast called *ṣawm* or *ṣiyām* is enjoined upon Muslims. From sunrise to just after sunset for the thirty days of this month of the lunar calendar, adults are ordered to abstain from all food and drink (the regulation being not to allow any material substance to enter the body in so far as that is possible), from deliberate vomiting, and from having sexual intercourse or emission of semen if that is a result of conscious desire. Menstruation, bleeding after child birth, an unsound mind, and intoxication all produce an invalid fast. Numerous legal qualifications surround the fast, including what to do if the fast is violated and what sorts of behavior in general are permissible during the month; the various schools of law see different implications arising from many of the situations. Because the lunar calendar is followed, the fast moves through the seasons, occurring some eleven days earlier each solar year.

It is considered especially meritorious to read the whole of the Qurʾān during the month of Ramaḍān. To facilitate this, the text has been divided into thirty equal sections, one for each day of the month. When the fasting month is over, the *ʿīd al-fiṭr* celebration is held; this is the major festival of the Muslim year. The day itself sees a special public prayer for the whole community and, following that, a vast feast is put on, with celebration, visiting, and giving of gifts (called the *zakāt al-fiṭr*) being special features. The Qurʾān contains several fairly detailed explanations of the fast of Ramaḍān, indicating that it was a practice which came into existence early in Islamic times, being recognized as a symbol of the religion or at least indicating Islam's comparability to Judaism and Christianity. The Qurʾān itself declares in *sūra* 2, verse 183, "O you who believe, fasting has been prescribed for you just as it was prescribed for those before you, so that you will be godfearing." The sense is, therefore, that Islam has a practice equivalent to that of Judaism and Christianity, although it is distinct in its calendar situation and length: "The month of Ramaḍān in which the Qurʾān was sent down as a guidance to the people, and as clear signs of the guidance and the salvation—so let any of you who are present during the month, fast in it" (Qurʾān 2/185). Here we have a case of a ritual which is adopted and adapted from the earlier religions but which is given a distinctly Islamic flavor and mythological significance with the month's connection to the revelation of the Qurʾān.

Stories abound in the *ḥadīth* material concerning an "earlier" fast which Muḥammad instituted on the Jewish Day of Atonement (Yom Kippur). Suggested to have been a one-day, twenty-four-hour fast, the reports of it are often seen to be an explanation of the Quranic phrase intimating that early on there had been a different fast (that is, Qurʾān 2/183, quoted above); as such, the historical value of the reports is certainly questionable. Most notable, however, is the understanding that these reports provide for the significance of Ramaḍān; the month-long fast is to be understood as the truly Islamic version of the institution of fasting.

Fasting at times other than Ramaḍān

Fasting in Islam is undertaken more often than simply during Ramaḍān. The notion of *kaffāra*, atonement for sin or for duties which have been omitted, is stipulated in the Qurʾān on a number of occasions. In *sūra* 2, verse 196, fasting is to replace the pilgrimage for those unable to go to Mecca under certain conditions; in Qurʾān 4/92, fasting is an atonement for killing a believer by mistake; in Qurʾān 5/89, fasting is prescribed for breaking an oath; in Qurʾān 5/95, fasting is the penalty for killing an animal while on the *ḥajj*; and in Qurʾān 58/4, one may fast in order to retract a divorce. In each of these situations, fasting is seen as a replacement for or another possibility in the suggested ways of making amends for one's moral or ritual errors. All these indicate that fasting as an activity in general is understood to have a certain redemptive effect within Islam; this redemption is sometimes thought to be applicable to the fasting which takes place in the month of Ramaḍān as well, at least in a limited way.

The Muslim pilgrimage

The *ḥajj* to Mecca and its surrounding area is an annual ritual lasting up to seven days which contains within it a fully detailed sequence of events enjoined upon all those who are physically able to come to the city. Performed during the first half of the last month of the year, Dhū ʾl-Ḥijja, the *ḥajj* requires a state of ritual sanctity for the activities. Prior to the *ḥajj* itself, ritual purification is undertaken, and the Kaʿba is circumambulated and a run is performed between al-Ṣafā and al-Marwa, two hillocks near the Kaʿba (today joined to the central Meccan mosque by a covered arcade); both activities are performed seven times, interspersed with prayers and invocations. On the seventh of Dhū ʾl-Ḥijja, the pilgrims participate in a prayer service at the mosque around the Kaʿba. On the following morning, the pilgrimage itself starts, and over the next three days the following activities take place.

The pilgrims assemble in Minā, just outside Mecca, and stay there for the night. The next morning, they depart for the plain of ʿArafāt, 15 kilometers east, and assemble on and around the Mount of Mercy, where a prayer ritual is performed and a ceremony entitled "the standing" is undertaken, lasting from the time the sun passes the meridian until sunset. That evening, the pilgrims return to Muzdalifa, about halfway back to

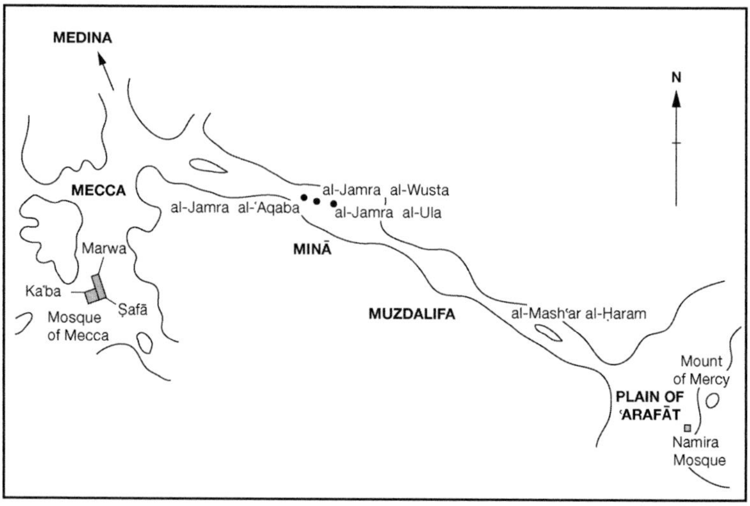

Figure 7.2 Map of the pilgrimage.

Minā, where the night is spent. The next day, a journey to Minā brings them to the stone pillar (*jamrat al-ʿaqaba*) at which seven pebbles are thrown; the column is said to represent Satan. This is followed by a ritual slaughter of sheep, goats, and camels, and a meal, the *ʿīd al-aḍḥā*, "the festival of the sacrifice" (performed by all Muslims whether in Mecca or not and seen as the second major festival of Islam). On returning to Mecca, pilgrims cirumambulate the Kaʿba and run between Ṣafā and Marwa (unless these actions completed prior to the *ḥajj* itself). The state of ritual purity is also abandoned on this day, symbolized by men having their heads shaved and women having a lock of hair cut off. Three days of celebration at Minā generally follow for most pilgrims, with more stones thrown at the three pillars of Satan, all followed by another circumambulation of the Kaʿba. A visit to Medina will also often be included before the pilgrims return to their own homes.

The Qurʾān's major testimony to this ritual is found in *sūra* 2, verses 196–200, and *sūra* 5, verses 95–7. Various parts of the ritual are detailed, as are some of the legal regulations which bear on the participants. However, no full and cohesive explanation is given. An element which does receive mention on a number of occasions is the relationship of some elements of the pilgrimage to the activities of Abraham and Ishmael. The Qurʾān states in *sūra* 2, verse 127, that "Abraham and Ishmael laid the foundations for the House" (that being understood to be the Kaʿba) and that they did a number of the activities which the later pilgrims also do: performed the circumambulation, ran between Ṣafā and Marwa, sacrificed a sheep, and stoned Satan.

Historically, the pilgrimage has given tremendous prominence to Mecca but, as has already been mentioned in Chapter 4, there was a time when Jerusalem may well have been an alternative pilgrimage destination, although clearly the Dome of the Rock was not constructed with a view to facilitating the vast number of pilgrims who now visit Mecca each year. Notably the inscriptions in the Dome do not exhort people to perform a pilgrimage; however, the inscriptions are perhaps to be read while performing a circumambulatory ritual within the domed area.

Other ritual activities

The extent to which Muslim identity is expressed through ritual is not limited to the "Five Pillars," although the prominence of that grouping is obviously high. The *mawlid* festival, celebrating the birth of Muḥammad (not fully established in Islamic practice until about the thirteenth century) and the informal *duʿāʾ* prayers are two additional ritual-type activities which are considered by Muslims to be significant in terms of the expression of their faith. Visits to the tombs of holy men and women are also a popular activity, especially in areas which have been deeply affected by the mystical side of Islam. Such visits are generally used as occasions either to ask favors of the deceased saint or to ask for forgiveness. The power of the saint is believed to reside in his or her ability to intercede on behalf of the individual believer with God.

The interpretation of Muslim ritual

Most noticeable when contemplating the sum of Muslim ritual is the emphasis upon the ritualism of the activities; all events are fully planned and formalized. Beyond that, one may observe a general lack of mythological sense in any of the rituals. The only meaning which can be seen, according to many classical Muslim thinkers and modern scholars of Islam alike, is the sense of participation in ritual being an expression of an individual's piety and obedience to God's command and as an indication of the person's membership within the Islamic community. There is a very real sense of what has been termed "anti-sacramentalism" and also of the rituals being "commemorative" but at the same time "amythical" (Graham 1983: 69). That is, many of the actions in these rituals are done with a remembrance of past actions of Muḥammad or Abraham, but without those actions becoming mythological such that the believer becomes, in any sense, the person of the past. Likewise, the animal sacrifice in the *ḥajj* and the performance of the fast of Ramaḍān for the most part do not take on the character of sacraments, conceived to have specific effects for the believer, but, rather, remain acts which individuals do within their sense of obedience. Overall, ritual is the full manifestation of the special character of Islam, separate from other religions in its conscious decision to be unique in its ritual constituents; that process of creating a separate definition appears to have been carried out, in the case of the development of the ritual practices, in a non-systematic fashion with no overall pattern imposed in creating that "uniqueness" of Islam within the Judeo-Christian milieu. Islam, in the construction of its rituals, is different from Judaism and Christianity and has rejected, or at least greatly modified, the central ritual activities of its two predecessors. In this way, it has created its "uniqueness" through difference, but that does remain a "uniqueness" which cannot be systematized into a cohesive perspective or comparison, at least not within the framework of ritual.

Travel as pilgrimage

The strong emphasis on the pilgrimage to Mecca as a ritual obligation for those who are able to accomplish it has, it is often suggested, resulted in travel in and by itself being seen as a religious activity. There are various factors which add to this overall picture. Some of the emphasis on travel stems from the prophetic notion of *hijra*, the emigration from Mecca to Medina undertaken by Muḥammad. Going somewhere in order to allow one's faith to flourish and to build a Muslim community thus gains a particular sanction through this model.

It was the "search for knowledge" that provided what is likely the most powerful motivator for travel. A *ḥadīth* from Muḥammad states, "Pursue knowledge even to China, for its pursuance is the sacred duty of every Muslim" (this *ḥadīth* is not found in the six canonical collections, however). Muḥammad is also quoted as saying, "The seeking of knowledge is obligatory for every Muslim" (this is found in al-Tirmidhī), and "Whoever leaves home to seek sacred knowledge is on the path of God until he returns home" (also found in al-Tirmidhī). Known in Arabic as *riḥlat ṭalab al-ʿilm*, the journey in search of knowledge gained a particular prominence and religious significance with the rise of the educational institution (*madrasa*) in the eleventh century. It was motivated by several ideas. One, a motif of the loss of knowledge, and thus the need to preserve it, emerged early on in Islamic times, as is demonstrated in stories about the need to assemble the Qurʾān into one standard book before people forgot what was really in it. Second, a strong sense of genealogy that had featured especially in Arab society became manifested in the transmission of knowledge through a face-to-face encounter with someone authorized to pass knowledge on; thus knowledge itself entered into the genealogical framework. Thus travel was necessary as a response to fear of the loss of knowledge, and travel was necessitated as a means of assuring validity.

Travel was a means by which the empire became unified as Muslim. The religious stimulus behind travel meant that people would see distant places—Baghdad in the ninth and tenth centuries, Cairo in the tenth and eleventh centuries, Nishapur in the eleventh and twelfth centuries—as places to go to study with renowned scholars. This did more than spread knowledge, of course, in that such travel became connected to trade and facilitated the spread of goods and innovations across the empire. This was especially because, while the desire to travel was strong, most people also seem to have been deeply motivated to return home at some point. Many stories are told of the great travelers, especially those from Spain it seems (Ibn Baṭṭūṭa in the early fourteenth century probably being the most famous example), who wandered the world and, in doing so, gained a real appreciation for their own homeland. Overall, this extension of the religious significance of the pilgrimage to travel in general was likely stimulated by the reality of what it meant to travel long distances with significant hardship in order to accomplish the pilgrimage.

Valuable insights on travel may be found in Sam Gellens, "The Search for Knowledge in Medieval Muslim Societies: A Comparative Approach," in Dale F. Eickelman and James P. Piscatori (eds), *Muslim Travellers: Pilgrimage, Migration, and the Religious Imagination*, London: Routledge, 1990, pp. 50–65, and Hourari Touati, *Islam and Travel in the Middle Ages*, trans. Lydia G. Cochrane, Chicago: University of Chicago Press, 2010.

Suggested further reading

Gustave E. von Grunebaum, *Muhammadan Festivals*, New York: Henry Schuman, 1951.

Leor Halevi, *Muhammad's Grave: Death Rites and the Making of Islamic Society*, New York: Columbia University Press, 2007.

Gerald Hawting (ed.), *The Development of Islamic Ritual*, Aldershot: Ashgate/Variorum, 2006.

Marion Homes Katz, *The Birth of the Prophet Muḥammad: Devotional Piety in Sunni Islam*, London: Routledge, 2007.

Constance E. Padwick, *Muslim Devotions: A Study of Prayer-manuals in Common Use*, Oxford: Oneworld, 1996 (originally published 1961).

PART III Alternative visions of classical Islamic identity

Significant dates

632	death of Muḥammad
661	death of ʿAlī, fourth caliph and figurehead of the Shīʿa
661–750	Umayyad dynasty
680	death of Ḥusayn, son of ʿAlī
728	death of al-Ḥasan al-Baṣrī
740	death of Zayd ibn ʿAlī of the Zaydīs
750	ʿAbbāsid dynasty begins
765	death of Shīʿī Imām Jaʿfar al-Ṣādiq
767	death of historian ibn Isḥāq
855	death of jurist Aḥmad ibn Ḥanbal
857	death of the mystic al-Muḥāsibī
874	12th Imām Muḥammad al-Mahdī in "lesser occultation"
875	death of the mystic al-Basṭāmī
910	death of mystic al-Junayd
922	death of mystic al-Ḥallāj
941	12th Imām Muḥammad al-Mahdī in "greater occultation"; likely death of traditionist al-Kulaynī
945	Buwayhids take over Baghdad
988	death of mystic al-Sarrāj
991	death of theologian Ibn Bābawayh
1022	death of theologian Shaykh al-Mufīd
1044	death of theologian al-Sharīf al-Murtaḍā
1067	death of traditionist al-Ṭūsī

1072	death of mystic al-Qushayrī
1111	death of theologian/mystic al-Ghazālī
1166	death of Ṣūfī saint al-Jīlānī
1240	death of mystic Ibn ʿArabī
1328	death of Sunnī theologian/jurist Ibn Taymiyya
1501	Safavids ruling in Iran

8 *The Shīʿa*

Islam remained, for the most part, remarkably unified in its religious manifestations during the classical period. It is only the split between the legal and theological schools already discussed in Chapters 5 and 6 and what is known as the Shīʿa of ʿAlī that have produced any degree of cleavage, and only the latter which has produced a true sense of an "alternative vision" of Islam. Of course, such nomenclature reflects only the statistical reality that there are (and have always been) more Muslims who, by virtual of their legal and theological school practices, would be defined as members of the *ahl al-sunna* than there are, and have been, Shīʿite Muslims. Few Muslims would approach these differences as a "choice" to be made on the individual level; rather, in the existence of the Shīʿa and the Sunnīs, we are confronted with the outcome of inner Muslim debates which resulted in different enunciations of Islam and in variant claims over the legitimate (and thus, from each group's perspective, normative) nature of Islam in the world. It may be asserted, thus, that the Shīʿa represent an alternative vision of Islam in the sense that they do indeed hold to different tenets on some very significant points within Muslim theory, dogma, and practice.

A number of treatises were written by various Muslim authors which detailed a tendency toward sectarianism within the faith which would seem to contradict the preceding statement. Famous works by al-Baghdādī (d. 1037) and al-Shahrastānī (d. 1153) provide lists of the seventy-three "groups" into which the Islamic community fractured. Shīʿī writers such al-Nawbakhtī (d. between 912 and 922) did similarly. These works, however, reflect less what would normally be considered true variation in expression of Islamic identity, and more a documentation of variations on specific points of Muslim theology. The books are a part of a tendency towards classification of all sorts of sundry matters which was common in classical Islamic times. They also reflect an interpretation and justification of a tradition ascribed to Muḥammad which speaks of his community dividing into seventy-three (or seventy-one or seventy-two) parts. The important concluding statement of this tradition provides its significance: only one of these groups will actually be saved in the hereafter. It was the job of the authors of these texts, then, to enumerate the multiplicity of groups while, at the same time, providing a clear definition of the group which would be saved: that group, of course, being identical with the author's own allegiances. In some instances, one suspects that, in these books, political rebels have been made into theologically based heretics, thus once again reinforcing the traditional picture of a well-defined "Islam" as existing from the very earliest times.

One of the groups detailed by these "heresiographers," a group divided into numerous sub-divisions according to their classificatory schemes, was the Shīʿa of ʿAlī. Once again, how many of these groups really existed as clearly identified units is questionable and certainly few of them actually survived for any substantial period of time. Several main groupings did become prominent, however.

The Shīʿī understanding of its origins

As was mentioned in the discussion of the rise of theology, the Shīʿa pictures its roots back in the days of ʿAlī ibn abī Ṭālib and the early caliphs. The Shīʿa, or "party," of ʿAlī consisted of those who defended his right to rule the early community in the civil war with Muʿāwiya. They claimed, on the basis of statements of Muḥammad and by virtue of ʿAlī's relationship to Muḥammad (being his cousin and son-in-law), that he had a legitimate claim to rule. Much is made of traditions from Muḥammad, accepted by both the Sunnīs and the Shīʿa, in which ʿAlī is designated as having a special relationship to Muḥammad. One central such instance stems from a place known as Ghadīr Khumm, where Muḥammad stopped on his return from his final pilgrimage to Mecca in 632. There, Muḥammad is recorded to have specified ʿAlī as his favorite follower, closer to him than anyone else. Another example, reflecting general sentiments, is reported by al-Tirmidhī (d. 892, author of one of the canonical Sunnī books of *ḥadīth*): "The prophet said in reply to someone who had complained about ʿAlī: 'What do you think of one who loves God and his prophet and who in turn is loved by God and his prophet?' " Also transmitted is: "The most loved of women to the prophet of God is Fāṭima [ʿAlī's wife, Muḥammad's daughter] and the most loved of men is ʿAlī" (al-Tirmidhī, quoted in Momen 1985: 15). Such traditions tend to fall into a general category of discussion of the "merits of the companions" found in all *ḥadīth* literature, in which each of the early followers of Islam is honored. In this way, their authority as "founding fathers," and subsequently as transmitters of *ḥadīth*, was enhanced, and it seems likely that this was the function of such reports in the beginning. It was only when ʿAlī as an individual had his persona enhanced by the Shīʿa that such reports acquired a greater significance. It would appear, however, that this must have taken place to a great extent after traditions enhancing ʿAlī's position were already in circulation in the early community; ʿAlī's position within the family of Muḥammad is probably sufficient to explain why early sources would consider him an especially prominent person.

From the Shīʿī perspective, there was more at stake in the whole debate, however. For example, what was the nature of the rule of the early community? Was the leader to be one who combined religious with political authority? Or, with the death of Muḥammad, had religious authority passed to each individual believing Muslim? It remains a matter of debate among scholars as to whether ʿAlī received his earliest support because of a nascent belief in his religious significance (which thus suggested that he had authority in religious matters, an element which becomes fully developed among the later Shīʿa), or whether this was a purely political manoeuver which later became colored with religious significance.

However, as was the case for theology, these debates among scholars often tend to accept the Muslim accounts at face value and argue over the various detailed aspects of them, rather than appreciating the ideological viewpoint from which such material was compiled. The impulse to demonstrate a legitimating and detailed view of Islamic origins inheres in all the sources we have available to us on such matters.

The Shīʿa and the Qurʾān

Most significant in the stance of the Shīʿa, *vis-à-vis* their origins, is their general acceptance of the text of the Qurʾān virtually intact, in line with the Sunnīs. While there certainly have been tendencies within the Shīʿī community to debate the accuracy of the text as they have it and even a tendency to suggest some modifications to the text—citing additions, omissions, changes, and alterations to the version promulgated by ʿUthmān—this sort of activity has been relatively restrained. Much of the contemplated modification to the Quranic text is of such a nature as to take place within the legitimated (from the Sunnī perspective) range of "variant readings." An example of this is found in Qurʾān 3/110, "You are the best community which has been produced for humanity," such that rather than reading it as *umma*, "community," the Shīʿa have read the word as *aʾimma* and taken it as referring to the leaders of the Shīʿī community, the Imāms. What this may be taken to suggest is that the differentiation between the Sunnīs and the Shīʿa arose only after the promulgation of an established text of the Qurʾān for all such arguments depend upon a text of the Qurʾān which is fixed and well known.

This view of the historical development of the Sunnīs and the Shīʿa fits in with the account of the rise of Islam and the caliph's authority given earlier in Chapter 4. A fully variant text of the Qurʾān in the hands of the Shīʿa would have indicated an earlier establishment of the Shīʿa than the evidence concerning the rise of Islam as a whole might otherwise suggest. It might also have suggested a "fixed" text of the Qurʾān being established early on, to which the Shīʿa responded with their own version. However, since the Shīʿa do *not* have their own Qurʾān, both the late establishment of the Shīʿa and the Sunnī community as two interpretations of Islam, and the establishment of a fully fixed text of the Qurʾān prior to that division, are historically possible.

The Shīʿa and *ḥadīth*

The other significant element in understanding the rise of the Shīʿa is the observation that the Shīʿa have a distinct body of *ḥadīth* material, much of it traced back to or through the early leaders of the Shīʿī community or, at the very least, containing variants compared to the Sunnī community's versions. In its written form, this material started to emerge during the ninth century. Given the function of the *ḥadīth* in Islam in general, the existence of a separate body of material indicates that the central matter of dispute causing the separation of the Sunnī community and the Shīʿa was one of ultimate authority in the community as a whole and within each group separately. In the early unified community, the caliph appears to have had complete authority, as was discussed earlier in Chapter 4. With the rise of the learned classes in the eighth century, the disputes over authority became more pronounced. The Sunnī community, with its trust placed in fixed written sources of authority, emerged, leaving what became the Shīʿī group continuing to hold to authority vested in an individual.

The authority of the Shīʿī Imām

This understanding of the development of authority makes sense of what is the most prominent and distinct element in the Shīʿa, and that is the person of the Imām. Designated by Muḥammad, ʿAlī was the first Imām for the Shīʿa; this was seen as the designation of a spiritual position, not one of temporal power, and thus the inability of the Imāms in later times to seize power within the community was of no particular concern to their followers. The function of the Imām was to guide his followers by explaining and clarifying the divine law, as well as to direct those believers in the inner spiritual path of Islam. This he was able to do because of his close connection to God, facilitated by *ilhām*, "inspiration" (as distinct from *waḥy*, "revelation," which is the mode through which scripture is produced), and the knowledge passed on to him by the one who designated him. God's mercy and justice indicate that there can never be a time when the world is without an Imām, for, if that were so, people would have no guidance and there would be no proof available of God's beneficence towards His creation. The Imām is thus termed the *ḥujja*, "proof," and *hādī*, "guide." The people who were to be Imāms were designated by God from the beginning of creation, and were even viewed as pre-existent in the form of primordial light according to some mystically flavored interpretations. They are, as a consequence of these ideas, seen as sinless and the best of all creation. The actual existence of an Imām is to be taken as part of God's beneficence towards humanity, for he facilitates the salvation of God's creation by providing a sure guide in the world and a certain answer to issues of dispute.

The most prominent branch of the Shīʿa, known as the "Twelvers" (in Arabic *Ithnā ʿashariyya*) or, more generically, as the Imāmīs, identifies a chain of twelve men through whom the line of authority passed in the formative centuries of Islam. These people were designated by their predecessors and their birth was generally pictured as accompanied by various miraculous signs, confirming this designation. That the clear delineation of this line was, up to a certain point, *ex post facto* would appear likely and is even evidenced by mid-tenth-century Shīʿī sources who speak of people in their community being unsure of the identity of the Imām. It will only have been when the need for authority emerged within the community that the tracing back of a chain of authority (as in the *isnād* of a *ḥadīth*) would have actually been necessary. The established line of the twelve Imāms is as follows:

ʿAlī ibn abī Ṭālib, d. 661
Ḥasan, his son, d. 669
Ḥusayn, ʿAlī's second son, d. 680
Zayn al-ʿĀbidīn, his son, d. 712 or 713
Muḥammad al-Bāqir, his son, d. 735
Jaʿfar al-Ṣādiq, his son, d. 765
Mūsā al-Kāẓim, his son, d. 799
ʿAlī al-Riḍā, his son, d. 818
Muḥammad al-Taqī al-Jawād, his son, d. 835
ʿAlī al-Hādī, his son, d. 868
Ḥasan al-ʿAskarī, his son, d. 873 or 874
Muḥammad al-Mahdī, his son, born 868

The formation of the Shīʿa

Jaʿfar al-Ṣādiq appears to have been the pivotal figure through whom the Shīʿa actually came into existence as a religious movement. Up to that point, the best that one may suppose is that rival groups, whose primary focus was in the political arena, existed in the community; some of these groups saw their right to rule traced back to ʿAlī. As with the emergence of the whole system of Islam itself, the particular elements manifested in the Shīʿa took time to evolve, even though the sources themselves wish to project the origins back to the earliest period. The rise of the ʿAbbāsid caliphate, making its appeal to persons in sympathy with the rights of ʿAlī, would coincide with the dates of Jaʿfar al-Ṣādiq. It is with the sixth Imām and his designated successor, Mūsā al-Kāẓim, that the incipient notions of the Imamate would appear to have originated, based on the information provided by various heresiographical works and Shīʿī tradition itself, which sees Jaʿfar as the formative spokesman. One crucial element here is the establishment of a procedure for the designation of the Imām, rather than that person being determined by a process of battle. The Shīʿī platform can thus defend a quietist attitude despite a lineage

Figure 8.1 Crowds in Baghdad watch the re-enactment of the battle of Karbala, with Ḥusayn here kneeling and lamenting the death of his half-brother ʿAbbās, a dramatic scene in the "passion play" (*taʿziya*) that is the feature of Shīʿī ʿĀshūrāʾ celebrations.
Source: AFP/Getty Images.

which would suggest a need to usurp rule in the world. This process of designation also had the effect of cutting off a tendency towards proliferation of rival claimants to the position of Imām. Another crucial element was the Imām's receipt of esoteric knowledge passed on from the previous Imām. Regardless of these early elements, it is only in the time of the twelfth Imām that we actually have any Shīʿī sources which provide us with detailed information on the Shīʿa and their beliefs, and it is clear that it is in the post-twelfth Imām period that the Shīʿa as we know it today actually came into being.

The occultation of the last Imām

The twelfth Imām is said to have disappeared and to have entered into his "lesser occultation," being hidden from the view of the world. He designated a series of four persons (in parallel with the first four caliphs perhaps) to whom he communicated his commands; this situation lasted from 874 until 941. He then entered into his "greater occultation," in which condition he no longer communicates with the world. This notion of occultation is a necessary consequence of the line of Imāms ending at a particular point in history. If humanity cannot be without an Imām and the line of Imāms has ended, then the last Imām cannot be dead but must be alive; otherwise, a substitute for him must exist. Known as the *ghayba*, the occultation will last until God determines its end. The return of the twelfth Imām in the role of the messianic Mahdī is awaited; this will occur shortly before the day of judgment. At that time, he will be manifested on earth and will lead the righteous into battle against the forces of evil. Finally, good will triumph over evil, and the Imām will subsequently rule over the world in a period of peace.

The notion that there should be twelve Imāms and that the twelfth should permanently "disappear" took some time to solidify within the Shīʿa. Certainly authors writing at the time of the twelfth Imām appear to have expected the line to continue beyond him. Although they admitted that at the time he was "hiding," he was clearly expected to show himself once again. Indeed, the presence of the Imām as a "proof" and a "guidance" was deemed essential and was the major element in polemic against the Sunnī schools, whom the Shīʿa felt were adrift with no guidance. It would appear to be the case, however, that other Shīʿī groups had already developed the notions of a limited chain of Imāms and of the last one "disappearing." All that was really happening, then, was that the Imāmī group was employing already circulating ideas as an explanation of events taking place in their "Twelver-Shīʿī" line. By the time of the Shīʿī writer al-Kulaynī (d. *c.* 941), the idea of there being a line of twelve Imāms was established, although for the rest of the century authors still found it necessary to compose works which would explain and defend this notion of an occulted Imām. Arguments in favor of there being a line of only twelve Imāms were found in Quranic references to the number twelve (for example, twelve months in the year, Qurʾān 9/36) and in Shīʿī and Sunnī traditions which talk of Muḥammad naming twelve successors, which in Sunnī sources are found in texts written in a period before the occultation of the twelfth Imām and perhaps reflect notions regarding "twelve" as a number symbolic of restoration, fulfillment, and authority as in the twelve tribes of Israel and the twelve disciples of Jesus.

There seem to be political reasons lying behind the idea of the "disappearance" of the twelfth Imām which account for it becoming a successful doctrine in Shīʿī circles. As long as the Imām was physically present in the world, he represented a threat, albeit ineffectual, to the ruling powers. The Shīʿa found themselves virtually always persecuted under the rule of the ʿAbbāsids. Removing the worldly reality of the Imām, after enduring some one hundred years of ʿAbbāsid rule, was a way of securing a continued existence for the group, but also may be linked to a growing sense of material prosperity among certain groups of Shīʿīs which they were unwilling to forgo. Cooperation with the ruling powers was far easier without the Imām present, but believing in his "occultation" meant that one's loyalty to him did not have to diminish; cooperation with the rulers brought power as well as a more comfortable existence, something which took place under the pro-Shīʿī Buwayhids in the tenth century and clearly separated political and religious dimensions of existence. The Shīʿī doctrine of *taqiyya* ("religious dissimulation"), by which it was considered acceptable to conceal one's true allegiance in the face of adversity, fitted in with this situation and attitude. It is likely also that, as with Sunnī Islam, a rise in the status and power of the *ʿulamāʾ*, the scholarly classes, put pressure on the Imām, whose actual presence proved inconvenient for the learned classes and their expectations and aspirations. As well, for all practical purposes, by the time of the twelfth Imām the *ʿulamāʾ* had taken over positions of effective authority anyway, the Imām himself generally being kept out of contact with the vast majority of his followers; it was dangerous for the Imām to be in public view, due to his political pretensions. The authority of the learned classes after the *ghayba* resided in the basis of their knowledge of the traditions transmitted by the Imāms. Thus the emergence of the books of *ḥadīth* at approximately the time of the lesser occultation is to be expected.

Shīʿī theology

Much of developed Shīʿī theology follows that of the Muʿtazila, discussed in Chapter 5, with a few crucial differences. It is significant to note that, in a sense, the Shīʿa represents a re-emergence of Muʿtazilī thought, which appears to have lost much of its popular appeal in the Sunnī world in the preceding century or so. The significance and meaning of the Imamate were the major factors which separated the Muʿtazila and the Shīʿa. Further significant differences are really a consequence of this stance. One of the Imām's functions is to intercede on behalf of his followers in the hereafter; this function runs counter to the Muʿtazilī insistence on "the punishment and the threat" as applying to all persons, consistent with their perception of the justice of God. Likewise, for the Shīʿa, there can be no "intermediate position," that of the hypocrite, applicable to those who appear to sin in their actions but declare their belief; those who declare their allegiance to the Imām are quite clearly members of the community and must be accepted as such. Other than these elements, the theological doctrines are familiar: belief in divine unity and justice, in the role of prophethood and the bringing of the law by sinless prophets, and in the resurrection at the end of time.

The Shīʿa did not always hold this theological position, however; the debates in the post-*ghayba* period clearly show an evolution from a tradition-based system to a more fully rationalistic one. Prior to that, however, in the very early period, the information regarding the situation is even less clear and provides at least some evidence of an even greater measure of shift in theological doctrine. However, the fact of the matter remains that there are no sources which can be trusted to be fully reliable, to give us information on the doctrinal stance of the Shīʿa prior to the tenth century. Some scholars have made the suggestion that any sources internal to the group itself suffered destruction at the hands of the later Shīʿa, who found the early doctrines unacceptable. The degree to which these early doctrines were contrary to later ones is suggested, perhaps, by Sunnī sources, specifically al-Khayyāṭ (writing around 882) and al-Ashʿarī (writing around 912). The doctrines of these early groups, dubbed the *ghulāt*, "the exaggerators," included notions of transmigration of souls, an anthropomorphic conception of God, God's willing of the evil deeds of humanity, and the possibility of alteration in God's will. At one point, it is also held that some believed in the absolute divine nature of the Imām, although the later Sunnī sources perhaps reflect the lessening of this doctrine for they no longer make that accusation. The trouble here is that the Sunnī sources are clearly polemical in tone and approach, and the items of doctrine with which the *ghulāt* are associated are precisely those items which bring about the greatest reprobation from the Sunnī schools; to represent these doctrines as being held by the largest Shīʿī school at the time may well be a case of attempting to mislead deliberately.

Ibn Bābawayh

By the tenth century, when the Buwayhid dynasty took over in Baghdad and made the ʿAbbāsid caliph simply a tributary to the ruler, the Shīʿa had become a political force and a clearer picture of its theological stance starts to emerge. Ibn Bābawayh (d. 991) appears to have been one of the leading figures in this movement. He wrote against the notion of anthropomorphism—which certainly suggests that some Shīʿīs still held to such doctrines—and, by the end of his life, also seemed convinced that humanity has a degree of free will under God's law:

> Our belief concerning human actions is that they are created ... in the sense that Allah possesses foreknowledge ... and not in the sense that Allah compels mankind to act in a particular manner by creating a certain disposition. ... And the meaning of this is that Allah has never ceased to be aware of the potentialities ... of human beings.
> (Ibn Bābawayh 1942: 31–2)

At an earlier stage of his life, however, Ibn Bābawayh held to a firmer predestinarian position. What marks all of his works is a reliance on tradition rather than reason and a total rejection of the stance of *kalām*; he states, "The partisans of the *kalām* will perish and the Muslims will be saved" (Ibn Bābawayh 1942: 43). This is similar to the stance of al-Ashʿarī in the Sunnī world, who was reacting to the full force of Muʿtazilī doctrine. Ibn Bābawayh, on the other hand, came before the major impact of Muʿtazilī thought among the Shīʿa, although some tendency in the direction of rationalism is to be noted in writers from earlier in the tenth century.

Later theologians

Muʿtazilī theology proper came into the Shīʿa through the work of al-Shaykh al-Mufīd (d. 1022), al-Sharīf al-Murtaḍā (d. 1044), and al-Ṭūsī (d. 1067). While the basis for the particulars of the Muʿtazilī position was already firmly established in the Shīʿa (and, some would say, was there since the time of Jaʿfar al-Ṣādiq), it is these authors who emphasized the use of reason in support of the doctrine, seeing the need to defend the religion on that basis. Al-Shaykh al-Mufīd argues for a less radical type of Muʿtazilī stance than some of the later authors; he avoids saying that people are the actual "creators" of their own acts and that the Qurʾān is created. Rather, he says that the Qurʾān "originated in time" and acts are "produced" or "made." God's actions in the world are always in the best interest of humanity (this being provided as an explanation of evil in the world). Overall, al-Shaykh al-Mufīd attempted to avoid going beyond what he sees as the limits of Quranic phraseology in enunciating his theology.

With the later authors, the rational position became more pronounced, with reason becoming the basis of all doctrine rather than being the tool by which authoritative doctrine could be defended and enhanced, as it was for al-Shaykh al-Mufīd. Al-Murtaḍā may best be thought of as the Shīʿī al-Ashʿarī in the sense that his writings became the basis for all later Shīʿī exposition of theology, being the virtually unquestioned source.

Why the Shīʿa adopted this rationalist position in theology would appear to be connected to the need for authority. While the Imām was in the world, the source of authority for the Shīʿī community was clear: it was the Imām; being an authoritative source was the very purpose of his presence in the world. The Sunnīs were, in the Shīʿī view, reduced to mere conjecture on all elements of their religion. With the *ghayba* of the twelfth Imām, authority first came through the series of four representatives, who were able to put questions to the Imām and bring back answers. With the greater occultation, however, this could no longer happen, although the appearance of the Imām to a worthy individual, either in reality or in a dream, was at least held to be possible. In the absence of the Imām, then, authority was in the hands of the learned classes. But this was no better than the Sunnī position, which the Shīʿa had criticized for having no sound basis. Muʿtazilī theology provided a way around this problem, by suggesting that reason alone could provide the certitude which is required. Deduction based on reason, therefore, rather than tradition as used by the Sunnīs, was the ideal replacement for the Imām, whose rulings would only conform to the laws of reason anyway. As the line of Shīʿī thought developed, al-Murtaḍā argued that reason could prove the necessity of the existence of the Imām in the first place, providing the proof for the key element of Shīʿī thought that the Muʿtazila lacked. He argued that the office of the Imām was necessary and that

> [t]he way to prove its necessity is reason, contrary to the doctrine of the Muʿtazilites and their like. It is necessary only for bringing those who are under moral obligation close to what is for their interests and for keeping them far from what is harmful.
>
> (Al-Sharīf al-Murtaḍā, quoted in McDermott 1978: 385)

Shīʿī legal thought and practice

In the legal field, a late development among the Imāmīs is quite clear also, as in theology. The tenth-century work by al-Kulaynī, *al-Kāfī fī ʿIlm al-Dīn* ("The Sufficient in the Knowledge of Religion"), marks a pivotal point in the emergence of defined Shīʿī law. This work gathers together traditions, either from the Imāms or from Muḥammad and transmitted through the Imāms, which serve as the basis for all discussions (both legal and theological) in this period. The writing of the book is significant and it contains, by its very composition, a polemical element. The book clearly wants to argue that the Imām in the world is no more. No longer can that source of authority be utilized, and the Shīʿa, like the Sunnīs, must turn to written sources to substantiate their position. The writing of a work such as al-Kulaynī's marks a stage in the emergence of the Shīʿa in which the learned classes, who had control of the sources, were starting to assert their authority; in such a way, it was ensured that any potential claimants to the position of the Imām were effectively silenced. Al-Kulaynī's book is one of four, the others written by Ibn Bābawayh and al-Ṭūsī (the latter having two to his credit), which are considered the counterparts to the six authoritative collections of *ḥadīth* in the Sunnī world.

Without the Imām, or his representatives, in the world, the specific duties assigned to him were said to be lapsed. These included leading the holy war (*jihād*), division of booty of war, leading the Friday prayer, putting juridical decisions into effect, imposing legal penalties, and receiving the religious taxes. The absence of the Imām left the community leaderless, and it fell to al-Tūsī in the eleventh century to enunciate a theory of juridical authority being in the hands of those knowledgeable in jurisprudence, the *fuqahāʾ*. Even then, the role of the jurists was limited and it took several centuries and a number of other theorists to develop a more encompassing theory; it was only in the sixteenth century that the *fuqahāʾ* took over all the duties of the occulted Imām, with the exception of offensive *jihād*, which, it was determined, could only be undertaken by the Imām himself.

The absoluteness of this delegation of the authority of the Imām was tempered by the theological speculation over the return of the twelfth Imām. This expected return, though, was of little practical concern to the jurists, whose role was to create a legal system with no reference to a living Imām, only to one who existed theologically.

The actual theoretical development of the principles of Shīʿī jurisprudence was, for the most part, late in being written (fourteenth to sixteenth centuries), at least in comparison with the much earlier Sunnī development. To some extent, therefore, the Shīʿa depended upon the principles already enunciated within Sunnī thought in order to develop the legal basis of their society; the differences between the two are, as a result, quite slight. The Shīʿa, in this view, are little more than another legal school, parallel to the four major Sunnī schools. Minor differences occur in the prayer ritual and the fast of

Ramaḍān, but these are precisely of a nature which would be seen as a variation between schools of law. Friday noon prayer is not as important to the Shīʿa because of the absence of the Imām who is supposed to lead that prayer, although this became a problem of some seriousness in juridical discussions. Various practices are enjoined such as visiting the tombs of the Imāms, and these visits are conducted with extensive rituals on a par with those of the *ḥajj*.

There are, of course, some significant differences between Sunnī and Shīʿī practices that have become markers of belonging to one group or the other. The phenomenon of "temporary marriage," *mutʿa*, considered to be referred to in Qurʾān 4/24, is specifically forbidden in the Sunnī world, where any limit put on the length of a marriage makes a marriage contract null and void. Divorce and inheritance laws also vary. Most striking is a different form of the *shahāda* employed at some points in Shīʿī history. The phrase "I testify that ʿAlī is the *walī* ['friend'] of God" is added to the two-part Sunnī witness to faith; this is, however, a fairly late addition, mention of it not being made in the earliest texts of Shīʿī law other than that of Ibn Bābawayh, who condemns its usage. The sixteenth century saw arguments in favor of its employment, urged probably by the political aims of the rulers at that time, the Safavids, who instituted the Shīʿī position as the state religion of Iran in 1501. The argument for the basis of the statement as opposed to its ritual employment, however, is to be found quite early in Shīʿī thought, for example in al-Kulaynī, who argues that the belief in the *wilāya* of ʿAlī is a fundamental tenet of the Shīʿa, and that the belief simply in "There is no god but God and Muḥammad is the messenger of God" is not sufficient to ensure salvation; clearly, the third element of the testimony is needed in the belief of the individual, even if in this early period it was not actually part of the ritual repetition of the *shahāda*.

Additionally, Ibn Bābawayh reports the following tradition about Fāṭima bint Asad, the mother of ʿAlī. Muḥammad is quoted as saying that immediately after her death

> She was asked about her Lord, and she said, "My Lord is Allāh." And she was asked about her Prophet and she replied, "Muḥammad." And she was asked about her Imām and *walī* and she faltered and paused. And I said to her, "Thy son, thy son." So she said, "My Imām is my son." Thereupon they [the two questioning angels who appear to everyone after death] departed from her and said, "We have no power over you."
>
> (Ibn Bābawayh 1942: 61)

Undoubtedly, it was the pressure of Sunnī condemnation which did not allow this statement to enter the Shīʿī *shahāda* from the very beginning and it was only after many centuries that it was actually approved under more propitious political circumstances.

A prominent celebration which is not found in the Sunnī world revolves around the commemoration of the death of Ḥusayn, the son of ʿAlī. Culminating on the tenth day of the first month of the year, Muḥarram, the day of ʿĀshūrāʾ, it observes the day of the death of Ḥusayn and his followers which took place at the hands of the forces of the Umayyad ruler Yazīd. This occurred in the year 680. Martyrdom to the cause of the party of ʿAlī became the operative motif in understanding Ḥusayn's death and the celebration of this became the central event of the Shīʿī religious calendar. Visitation of sacred places, especially the tomb of Ḥusayn in Karbala, play an important role in the celebrations on this day. Generally, these ritual differences between the Shīʿa and the Sunnīs have gained symbolic value for the Shīʿa in terms of providing a distinct (and, implicitly, correct) religious identity, especially in times of political antagonism with the Sunnī world.

Variations within the Shīʿa

Given that a fundamental notion among the Shīʿa was the necessity of the identification of an Imām in each generation, it is hardly surprising that rival claimants appeared at various points in history. We thus see the emergence of several branches within the Shīʿa, each of which differed over the line of descent of authority at a certain historical moment. The Ismāʿīlīs, Zaydīs, and Druze (Durūz in Arabic) are three such prominent groups. Some of these splits account for their origins in terms of differences over political strategy. The Zaydīs, for example, picture their origins in armed revolt against the Umayyad rulers. They were formed as a group in support of Zayd ibn ʿAlī, a grandson of Ḥusayn ibn ʿAlī, who was defeated and killed in 740. While in certain situations these small offshoots of the Shīʿa have proven politically volatile, throughout a good portion of history they have been politically quiescent, looking forward to the end of time and the return of the Mahdī. This simply goes along with the doctrine of the occultation of the Imām when faced with the political realities of the historical situation. The Ismāʿīlīs are particularly noted for their "inner" interpretations of much of Muslim practice, looking to make the point that the law was to benefit the soul as well as the body. For them, the person of the Imām is a key link to God who provides the authoritative interpretation of all Islamic matters.

The central issues which separate all of the Shīʿa from the Sunnīs, then, is this issue of the Imām and his role. The answer to this was not, for the Shīʿa, straightforward because of issues related to identifying the person of the Imām and dealing with his absence (in those branches of the Shīʿa which held to that idea). As is always the case, historical contexts affected the way in which this doctrine evolved, but it is clear that the fundamental disagreement between Muslims over the nature of community leadership had a long-lasting and profound effect upon the unity of the *umma*.

The charismatic Imām

The origins of Shiʿism are, like other aspects of the beginnings of Islam, a topic of extensive scholarly investigation and dispute. One critical area that has emerged is how early followers of the Imāms conceived their leaders. The problem is a typical one within the context of early Islamic history: to what extent are the currently available accounts that try to explain the early centuries of Shiʿism back-projections of later conceptions and beliefs?

The Shīʿa was formed around the idea that the legitimate leadership of the community after the death of Muḥammad was to be found in ʿAlī. What should have happened after him, however, became something of a dispute. There was a common understanding that when Muḥammad designated ʿAlī as his successor (as the Shīʿa holds) he also indicated that ʿAlī's descendants would take leadership. How it was to be decided which descendant and what the qualities of that person should be, however, was open to debate both at the time and today in scholarly considerations of the question.

Some scholars have argued that theological issues were central to the debate over the qualities of the Imām and thus also in designating the successor. This revolves around one central concern. Did the Imāms have miraculous powers and knowledge? Or were they "normal" human beings who exercised religious leadership through their knowledge of the Qurʾān and the *sunna*? One theory sees the original conception being the more modest one, which, over time, became affected by the more extremist views (known as the *ghulāt*) that pushed the conception of the Imām towards a semi-divine status for the Imām.

Others, however, have argued that this history needs to be reconstructed differently. The development may well have been from a secretive and extremist form of Shiʿism in which the select inner few were privy to the real nature of the Imām. The significance of this view is that the origins of Shiʿism are then seen to be theologically, rather than politically, stimulated. The issue, within this view of Shiʿism, was not so much over the right to rule but rather over the existence of an esoteric group of followers. While this reading of history has stimulated much debate, no consensus has been achieved among scholars on which view provides the best insights into early Shiʿism. Some have argued that it may well be possible that both views existed from the beginning, and the importance of the "extreme" views only gained prominence later in Sunnī polemics directed against the Shīʿa as a whole as a means of completely discrediting the movement.

An excellent overview of the scholarly discussions of the origins of ideas about the Imāms, along with a full bibliography, is available in Robert Gleave, "Recent Research into the History of Early Shiʿism," *History Compass*, 7/6 (2009): 1593–1605.

Suggested further reading

Tamima Bayhom-Daou, *Shaykh Mufid*, Oxford: Oneworld, 2005.
Heinz Halm, *Shiʿism*, 2nd edition, Edinburgh: Edinburgh University Press, 1987.
Arzina R. Lalani, *Early Shīʿī Thought: The Teachings of Imam Muḥammad al-Bāqir*, London: I. B. Tauris, 2000.
Moojan Momen, *An Introduction to Shiʿi Islam*, New Haven, CT: Yale University Press, 1985.
David Pinault, *The Shiites: Ritual and Popular Piety in a Muslim Community*, New York: St. Martin's, 1992.

9 Ṣūfī devotion

The question of the origins of Sufism (*taṣawwuf*), the mystical aspect within Islam, and its devotees, the Ṣūfīs, seems to have attracted its own particular type of discussion within the academic study of Islam. The reason for this would appear to go back once again to a memory of medieval (and later) polemic between Christians and Muslims. Christians have often pictured Islam as a very sensually based religion: Muḥammad's multiple marriages, the Qur'ān's very physical and sensual portrayal of heaven and its rewards, and Islam's permitting of polygamy and enjoining holy war (*jihād*) have all been featured in these kinds of characterizations. At the same time, however, Christians have been very well aware of a profound ascetic-mystical trend in Islam. Abū Ḥamīd al-Ghazālī (d. 1111), for example, one of the most famous of all Ṣūfīs, became well known in the medieval West especially in his philosophic guise; this was true of a variety of other mystically inspired writers also. In trying to reconcile the two natures perceived within Islam, the implicit suggestion given by some early writers on the subject was that the mystical trend could not be inherent in Islam but must have come from Christianity, a far more elevated religion in their view.

It is the case, then, that raising the question of the origins of Sufism today is no less controversial than the question of the origins of the entire religion of Islam, because behind the questions lies the aura, if not the attitude, of medieval polemic. To suggest that Islamic mysticism is, in fact, a borrowing from outside raises the specter of the denial of the intrinsically spiritual nature of Islam and thence of the spiritual nature of Muslims themselves.

The question of origins here is twofold. The basic point, much argued by Ṣūfīs themselves in their search for legitimization of their spiritual quest, is whether Islam as a religion contained within itself a spiritual-ascetic tendency from the very beginning; that is, does Islam inherently see that the mystical way (defined, for the time being, as the quest for some intimacy with God as induced through certain practices of a meditative, repetitive, or self-denying nature) is the ideal life that should be aimed for? From the Islamic perspective, is that lifestyle inherently pleasing to God?

The second issue is one concerning the origins of Sufism itself. Regardless of where the original spiritual-ascetic impulse came from, were the practices, aspirations, and the mode of expression used by the Ṣūfis elements developed within Islam or were they the result of influences from another source (be that Christian, Indian, Iranian, or whatever) and adapted to an Islamic style?

The source of Sufism in Islam

The problem with answering the first question is, of course, one of interpretation. How do we judge an issue such as "inherent asceticism"? Some would say that a basic world-denying attitude is a part of Judaism, Christianity, and Islam, especially because the overall tradition has been influenced by the radical dualism of Manichaeism, with its distrust of the material world. This attitude is difficult to reconcile, however, with the picture of Islam and Judaism especially as "nomocratic," where a very practical attitude towards life in the here and now, as manifested in the law, is a prime characteristic of the religion. The other aspect of the problem is the common one found in all elements of the origins of Islam and that is the lack of contemporary sources. There simply are no ascertainably early sources which give us a glimpse of a spiritual-ascetic lifestyle from before the ninth century, in common with the lack of documentary evidence for the beginnings of Islam in general.

Muslim arguments on the subject revolve around the citation of the Qurʾān and elements of the *ḥadīth* and the *Sīra*, the life story of Muḥammad, which indicate the possibility of, if not the positive encouragement and enactment of, the ascetic ideal. This approach fully answers the question from the internal Muslim perspective. The Qurʾān and Muḥammad, as Ṣūfis have always said, support the mystical quest. Statements concerning God are popularly cited, for example Qurʾān 2/186, "Whenever My servants ask you about Me, I am near to answer the call of the caller," and Qurʾān 50/16, "We [God] are closer to him [humanity] than his jugular vein!" Looking inward, therefore, becomes the goal and the quest, although Qurʾān 2/115, "wherever you may turn, there is the face of God," adds another dimension to the quest. The wandering way of life of the early ascetic is supported in Qurʾān 29/20, "Travel in the land and see how He began creation." Qurʾān 9/123 asserts, "God is with the godfearing," whose way of life is echoed in the Quranic refrain to remember God always (for example Qurʾān 33/41, "You who believe, remember God often"). The "light verse," Qurʾān 24/35, is the most famous of all verses for Ṣūfī speculation and its very presence in the Qurʾān is often claimed to be proof of the need for the mystic way:

> God is the light of the heavens and the earth. The likeness of His light is as a niche in which there is a lamp; the lamp is in a glass; the glass is just as if it were a glittering star

> kindled from a blessed tree, an olive neither Eastern nor Western, whose oil will almost glow though the fire has never touched it. Light upon light, God guides His light to anyone He wishes.
>
> (Qurʾān 24/35)

As for Muḥammad, his whole experience of revelation and his preparation towards receiving it are seen as models for the ascetic life and its product. This is also true of other Quranic figures, especially Moses and al-Khiḍr, whose stories, as told in *sūra* 18, have been elaborated into accounts of the mystic quest. Many of the traditions about Muḥammad most favored by the Ṣūfīs are not to be found in the major *ḥadīth* collections, generally having been rejected by the collectors as unsound, but the Ṣūfīs kept their traditions going among their own circles. Many aphorisms are found on Muḥammad's lips which are applicable to the Ṣūfī quest, and Muḥammad is also portrayed as following an ascetic way of life. The latter traditions found their way into works such as the *Kitāb al-Zuhd* ("The Book of Ascetic Practices") of Ibn Ḥanbal (d. 855), the eponym of the legal school, who is often seen as a supporter of the early ascetic movement. Poverty especially became an ideal espoused by Muḥammad. For example, Ibn Ḥanbal cites the tradition from ʿĀʾisha, who "was asked what the Messenger of God did in his house. She replied, 'He patched clothes, fixed sandals, and did similar things'." ʿĀʾisha also reported that when Muḥammad died "he did not leave a dinar or a dirham, nor any sheep or cattle, nor did he bequeath anything" (Ibn Ḥanbal 1976: 3).

Even more productive for the Ṣūfīs has been the story of the *miʿrāj*, Muḥammad's night journey (based around Qurʾān 17/1), which is seen as a tale of the supreme mystical experience to which every mystic aspires. While the basic account is found in all orthodox sources about Muḥammad, starting in germ form in Muḥammad's early biographer Ibn Isḥāq, the Ṣūfī understanding and interpretation of the account are, of course, unique. The emphasis frequently falls on the role of the journey as a prophetic initiation, leading the way for all mystics after Muḥammad to journey to their own union with the divine presence, not as prophets but as saints or "friends of God."

Interestingly, there is a marked anti-ascetic tendency within the Sunnī books of *ḥadīth*, especially focusing on the rejection of Christian monasticism. For example, these reports are often used in Islam to support the notion that even Ṣūfīs should marry. Other such elements include a rejection of forty-day food restrictions and pleas against poverty (even to the point of denying excessive charity). Most of this material can be seen as anti-Christian in tendency and as reflecting the tension Muslims felt over the status of ascetic tendencies in early Islam.

However, all of this attention to the Qurʾān, *Sīra*, and *ḥadīth* on the part of the Ṣūfīs simply indicates that they have, like all other Muslims, always gone back to the prime sources of Islam for inspiration as well as justification of their position; in that way they are no different from the jurists in the quest to define the law as closely as possible, for example. For modern historians to take "objective" facts from this type of material and attempt to reconstruct a picture of mystical trends in early Islam is to commit the error of anachronistic reading of texts; one is clearly looking at the texts through the eyes of later people and we learn nothing from them of the earliest meaning given to these sources. The most that may be concluded from this part of the discussion, therefore, is simply to say that Muslims have found the life story of Muḥammad and the Qurʾān itself to be vital sources in their mystical quest. One would not want to discount the possibility that even the early versions of the biography (*Sīra*) of Muḥammad have been affected by early mystics and thus reflect some of their concerns and desires, as is reflected also in the *ḥadīth* literature, with its books devoted to *zuhd*, asceticism, as practiced by Muḥammad. That the Qurʾān might, in fact, contain such ascetic elements is a possibility that needs to be entertained; however, whether the pieces of the Qurʾān which suggest this background were always understood that way by Muslims, and where those pieces of the Qurʾān actually originated, are vexing questions which still must be faced by scholarship.

Sources of Ṣūfī practice

The best solution to this first aspect of the problem of the origins of Sufism, then, would seem to be to put aside the question about the inherent spiritual asceticism of Islam and simply admit that the understanding of the nature of God as contained within the Judeo-Christian–Muslim tradition is one which is potentially amenable to the mystical way of life. There only remains, then, the second question of the development of what we may truly call Sufism in Islam, the influences upon it, and its role in the emergence of Islam. For the early period there is the major problem of definition, of how to determine, for example, whether Ibn Ḥanbal should be considered a Ṣūfī or simply an ascetic Muslim, given his encouragement of that way of life. That he should have combined this role with one of the upholding of traditionalism is significant, of course; one of his works which displays ascetic tendencies is the abovementioned *Kitāb al-Zuhd*, a collection of traditions about the life of Muḥammad. Indeed, for the earliest period, this emphasis on asceticism is the primary element that one can isolate with certainty as the forerunner of the later mystical way. The evidence suggests that it was in the early to mid-ninth century that these sorts of tendencies found their expression in written form; it was only later in that century that this became combined with speculative thought, producing as a result a true system of mysticism which may accurately and meaningfully be called Sufism. The dating of this era for the emergence of Sufism is confirmed within juridical works, where the disdain for the ascetic way of life is displayed and a resultant attempt on the part of the jurists to restrict its scope can clearly be seen; the end of the eighth and early ninth centuries appears to be the era of the greatest disputes on this matter.

Certainly the influence of Christianity on the foundation of asceticism in Islam is clear in some of the earliest writings. Al-Muḥāsibī (d. 857), for example, borrowed heavily from the New Testament for various sayings and commendations of the Ṣūfī way of life. As well, the practice of wearing woolen garments called *ṣūf,* by means of which it is popularly believed that the term "Ṣūfī" (meaning "those who wear rough woolen garments") was coined, is said to have been in imitation of Christian hermits; this was in order to serve as an indication of poverty as well as being an ascetic practice in and by itself.

The development of a mystical litany was also a part of the early enunciation of the movement. Termed *dhikr,* the practice was connected by the Ṣūfīs to the Quranic injunction to "mention God often," as in Qurʾān 33/21. The developed form of this litany consists of the constant repetition of various phrases, often *lā ilāha illā ʾllāh,* "There is no god but God." This practice serves as the focal point of devotions for virtually every Ṣūfī group. Christian modes of worship once again may have provided some of the impetus for this particular element.

Doctrinally, the early mystics are held to have been devoted to the notion of *tawakkul,* "total trust" in God. The characteristics are complete indifference to the world and its affairs and a full dependence upon God supplying the needs of the individual; this attitude was said to demonstrate one's total trust in the power and mercy of God, who will supply those needs. A total lack of possessions and deprivation of any bodily comforts were the marks of such a person. This trend is often seen to have been influenced by Christianity also, that being a tendency of monasticism in the church.

Given the geographical contexts in which Islamic asceticism is generally seen to have emerged—Baghdad, in the environment of the Christian heritage, and Khurasan, a former Buddhist center—it is not surprising that elements of various religions, especially Christianity, as the above examples show, should be present; little would seem to be gained by denying it. However, it has frequently been pointed out that the ascetic lifestyle in Islam developed with a certain overt political motivation. Once again in Islam, a religious position appears to have been used as a rallying point for rebellion against the ruling powers. The whole early ascetic inclination is frequently pictured as a renunciation and rejection of the political strife in the formative Islamic period. The early mystics were the true Muslims who held onto the Islamic spirit in face of the manipulation of the religion by the ruling powers for their own purposes. The emphasis on *tawakkul* would be pictured in marked contrast to the efforts of all other Muslims to secure their places on earth rather than in heaven, at least from the perspective of the mystics. Al-Ḥasan al-Baṣrī (d. 728), famous for his role in the theological debates discussed in Chapter 5, emerges in the literature as one of the central figures of this type of spirituality, going to the extent of denying the value of existence in this world and speaking of the hereafter as the realm free of the contamination of political self-interest. Revolutionary involvement in the political arena was not sanctioned by al-Ḥasan al-Baṣrī, even if that could have meant replacing an unjust ruler by a pious one; the slow persuasion of rulers was about the best that could be hoped for in the effort to improve the lot of all Muslims in the community.

Overall, then, the argument certainly can be made for "foreign influences" on the development of Sufism but, without a doubt, modern scholarship sees the internal tensions of the Muslim community as crucial in the emergence of early ascetic tendencies.

Development of Sufism

The ninth century was marked by a rapid progression of mystics, each famous for adding a certain element to the emergent mystical viewpoint and creating the central tenets of Sufism. Under the influence of neo-Platonism, at least according to some writers, mystical doctrines of the love of God, the beatific vision of the mystical experience, gnosis as the goal of the experience, the image of the mystical ascension, the absorption into God, and the theory of the mystical states are all seen to emerge.

Al-Junayd (d. 910), a pupil of al-Muḥāsibī, is often given the credit for establishing a true system of mystical speculation, bringing together the insights of his predecessors and creating a lasting system for all subsequent generations. He is credited with the elaboration of the doctrine of *fanā*ʾ, the goal of the mystic in "dying in one's self," "passing away," or "absorption" into God, supported by the Quranic, "All that is on the earth will disappear while your Lord's face abides, majestic, splendid" (Qurʾān 55/26–7). The mystic quest is based on the need to return to God, the state in which humanity was before creation. *Baqā*ʾ, the "continuance," is the existence of the mystic after *fanā*ʾ, when he or she lives in God. Al-Junayd combined this goal with an ethical theory which demanded of the mystic who has reached the state of "absorption" a return to society; this was so that the individual would make clear "the evidence of [God's] grace to him, so that the lights of His gifts in the return of his individual characteristics scintillate and attract the community to him who appreciate him" (Abdel-Kader 1976: 89). This meant, for al-Junayd, that the Ṣūfī had the responsibility to return to his community life and fulfill all the obligations of Muslim existence; the knowledge of the individual's absorption into the divine remains a "secret treasure" which shines through the person in everything done in the world.

Al-Ḥallāj

Contemporary with al-Junayd was al-Ḥallāj (d. 922), who, likewise, was convinced of the necessity of the mystic quest, but who was condemned to death for the blasphemy of considering that individuals could recognize their God-nature through mystical experience. Stories relate that al-Ḥallāj proclaimed, "I am the Truth," which was taken to mean that he felt himself actually to be God incarnate in the world. Such Ṣūfīs (another early example is al-Basṭāmī, d. 875) have come to be termed "intoxicated," as compared to the "sober" mysticism of al-Junayd, for they had become so overcome by the mystical experience that existence, as such, had no meaning for them; their utterances became the focal point of their understanding of their experiences and vice versa. The ethical aspect of al-Junayd's doctrine became submerged within their experiences.

Later developments

These authors were only starting to develop a truly systematic picture of Sufism; it fell to authors such as Abū Naṣr al-Sarrāj (d. 988) in the following century to construct general accounts of Sufism, its history, and its meaning in the Islamic context. Al-Sarrāj wrote in his *Kitāb al-Lumaʿ* of the legitimacy of Ṣūfī practice, based upon the precedent of Muḥammad and his companions. With this, he combined a great deal of definitional material in an attempt to distill the essence of the mystical path as it existed in his time. He states, for example:

> The meaning of "passing away" and "continuance" . . . is the passing away of ignorance into the abiding condition of knowledge and the passing away of disobedience into the abiding state of obedience, and the passing away of indifference into the state of continual worship, and the passing away of the consideration of the actions of the servant, which are temporary, into the vision of the Divine Grace, which is the eternal.
>
> (Al-Sarrāj translated in Smith 1950: 43)

The eleventh century brought greater systematization to the theoretical basis of Sufism in the writings of al-Qushayrī (d. 1072). Writing in 1046, al-Qushayrī was concerned with demonstrating that Sufism was not in conflict with Sunnī Islam. Part of this proof was provided by the biography of many prominent Ṣūfīs. He also presented a picture of the theory of the stations through which a Ṣūfī passes on his or her mystic quest and the states which God may grace the mystic with during that quest. Such had already been detailed by al-Sarrāj before him, but al-Qushayrī added further detail to the schema. Forty-five terms are used to describe the quest, starting with *tawba*, "repentance," which is seen as the manifestation of the conscious desire to follow the mystic way, through "patience," "constant awareness of God," and "satisfaction with God," culminating in "gnosis," "love," and "yearning to be with God."

Abū Ḥamīd al-Ghazālī used the basis established by earlier Ṣūfī theorists for promoting the assimilation of Sufism into normative Sunnī Islam in developing his own arguments; his magnum opus, *Iḥyāʾ ʿUlūm al-Dīn*, the "Revivification of the Religious Sciences," written between 1099 and 1102, tried to accomplish just what its title suggests:

bring life back into the orthodox "religious sciences" through the inspiration of Sufism. In the process, Sufism itself would be seen to gain total legitimacy as being an essential part of the Islamic way of life. His work is divided into four sections. The first, "worship," concentrates on the inner meaning of the rituals of Islam. The second, "personal behavior," sees the progression from religious law to mystical training as intimately linked. The third, "deadly sins," details the discipline needed for the mystic quest. Finally, the fourth, "the way to salvation," concentrates on the interpretation of spiritual experience. This progress in the life of the individual reflects al-Ghazālī's overall view of life and the mystic quest:

> If, then, you ask, What is the Beginning of Guidance in order that I may test my soul thereby? know that the beginning of guidance is outward piety and the end of guidance is inward piety. Only through piety is anything really achieved; only the pious are guided. Piety designates carrying out the commands of God most high and turning aside from what He prohibits.
>
> (Al-Ghazālī as translated by Watt 1963: 90)

The Ṣūfī orders

The tendency towards increased intellectual support and systematization of Sufism was developed even further in the Ṣūfī orders which were based on the principle of the relationship between the master and the pupil. The authority of the master who has ascended through the stages of the mystic must be accepted wholly by the pupil, for only with guidance will the union with God be possible. The *ṭarīqa*, the "way" or "path," and later coming to mean the "order" or "brotherhood," emerged as a way of providing a practical and structured way for the initiate to be guided through the stages of mystical experience. Beginning as an informal group, companionship with an acknowledged master was the focal point of the *ṭarīqa*. Groups emerged early on, centered in dwellings known as *ribāṭs*, *khānqāhs*, *khalwas*, or *zāwiyas*, all meaning "Ṣūfī retreats" in one part or another of the Muslim world. Such retreats were not organized in any particular way, however; the participants simply wandered from one such place to another. In the eleventh century the institutionalized *ṭarīqa* movement received a boost with the Seljuq reorganization of the *madrasa*, the Islamic school, and the provision of support and supervision of Ṣūfī dwellings at the same time. This trend was encouraged even further by the success of al-Ghazālī's work in bringing Sufism into the fold of orthodoxy. The process culminated in the thirteenth century with the emergence of special centers of Ṣūfī training; focused on the activities and way of a single man, a center would perpetuate the name, teaching, exercises, and rule of life of that person. The *ṭarīqa* was handed down through the *isnād* or *silsila* of the *shaykh*, the leader of the order, passing on to the spiritual heirs of that person. The initiate swore allegiance to the *shaykh*, and thereby became linked to the spiritual chain. Often incorporated into these *silsila*s were famous Ṣūfīs of the past, such as al-Junayd and al-Basṭāmī; the initial stage of the chain is frequently Muḥammad and from him ʿAlī, although this does not necessarily indicate any Shīʿī leanings on the part of the groups.

All such *ṭarīqas*, formally at the very least, accept the law and ritual of orthodox Islam as binding. In this way, they provide a supplement to the Islamic way of life, rather than a true "alternative vision," although, obviously, their view of the true nature of Islam and its purpose differed from those who remained outside the *ṭarīqa*. The point remained, however, that in order for the *ṭarīqas* to ensure their acceptance by the representatives of the majority (that is, the jurists), the attention to the externals of Islamic life continued to be necessary.

The major *ṭarīqa*s in classical Islam were the Suhrawardiyya, the Qādiriyya, the Rifāʿiyya, the Yasawiyya, the Kubrāwiyya, the Čishtiyya, the Shādhiliyya, the Badawiyya, the Mawlawiyya (Mevlevi), and the Naqshbandiyya. These groups trace their foundations to various persons who lived in the twelfth and thirteenth centuries.

The practices of the Ṣūfī orders

Taking the Qādiriyya as an example of the *ṭarīqa* phenomenon, one may see the role these institutions played in the fostering of the Ṣūfī attitude. ʿAbd al-Qādir al-Jīlānī, the *shaykh* of the movement, was born in Jilan in Persia in 1077 and went to Baghdad at the age of 18; there he became a popular preacher within the Ḥanbalī tradition at the age of about 50, and he died in 1166. There is no evidence that he ever consciously set out to form a Ṣūfī school, although the legends told in great profusion about his life certainly want to picture him as a Ṣūfī miracle worker. The following story is reported by a disciple of al-Jīlānī:

> Once, while I was still a young man, I entered the presence of Shaykh ʿAbd al-Qādir (may Allah be well pleased with him), together with a large group. I had with me a book that dealt with questions of abstract philosophy and the speculative sciences of spirituality. As soon as we entered his presence, the Shaykh spoke to me—to me personally, not to the group as a whole—and before he had examined the book, or asked me about its contents, he said, "That book of yours is a bad companion. You had better go and give it a thorough wash!" I reacted to this by deciding to leave his presence, drop the book into some receptacle or other, and then refrain from carrying it with me after that, for fear of offending the Shaykh. My lower self could not accept the idea of giving it a wash, because I had developed quite a fondness for it, and some of its theories and principles had stimulated my intellectual curiosity. I was about to get up and leave, intending to carry out this plan of action, but the Shaykh gave me

> such a stare, like someone regarding me with incredulous amazement, that I simply could not get up. I felt trapped in a state of paralysis, but then he said to me, "Hand me that book of yours!" So I opened it, and lo and behold, there was nothing inside it but blank paper, with not a single letter written on it! I gave it to the Shaykh, and he thumbed through its pages, then he said, "This is 'The Book of the Excellent Merits of the Qur'ān' by Muḥammad Ibn al-Ḍurays." When he handed it back to me, I saw that it was indeed that book, written in a most handsome calligraphic script! The Shaykh then said to me, "Are you ready to turn in repentance from saying with your tongue what is not in your heart?" I said, "Yes, O my master." So he told me to stand up. I obediently rose to my feet, and I had forgotten all about philosophy and the principles of spirituality! They had been totally erased from my inner being, as if they had never captured my interest.
>
> (slightly modified from Tādifī 1998)

It was to the two sons of ʿAbd al-Qādir that the formation of the school actually fell and, by the year 1300, centers existed in Iraq and Syria, with the major expansion coming in the fifteenth century. ʿAbd al-Qādir himself is famed as a saint and the belief in his power of intercession is what has made the *ṭarīqa* a significant presence throughout the Islamic world.

The Qādiriyya's practices reflect the beliefs of the group itself but also the general Ṣūfī stance on the role of the master and the efficacy of various mystical practices. The initiation procedure contains the promise to "recite the *dhikr* in obedience to the dictates of the *shaykh*" and the *shaykh* accepts the initiate "as a son." The *dhikr* itself is recited by the group seated in front of the *shaykh* and repeated hundreds of times. The novice members repeat *lā ilāha illā ʾllāh*, "There is no god but God," 165 times, while the more advanced members repeat a series of statements praising God and ʿAbd al-Qādir 121 times, followed by 100 repetitions of *sūra* 36, 41 repetitions of *sūra* 72, 121 repetitions of *sūra* 110, 8 repetitions of *sūra* 1, and topped off by one recitation of *sūra* 112. All this is done under the control of the *shaykh* at a pace which increases as it goes on, until individual members, potentially, have a mystic experience appropriate to the level of their spiritual advancement.

Ibn ʿArabī

Muḥyīʾl-Dīn ibn ʿArabī represents the culmination of another strand within Islamic Sufism. Born in Spain in 1165, he traveled throughout North Africa and the Middle East, becoming initiated into Sufism in 1194, and eventually dying in Damascus in 1240. He was a prolific author and wrote *al-Futuḥāt al-Makkiyya*, "The Meccan Revelations," a Ṣūfī encyclopedia, and *Fuṣūṣ al-Ḥikam*, "The Bezels of Wisdom," his most famous work, which summarizes his vision. A difficult writer to comprehend, without a doubt, he was fully educated in the Islamic sciences and brought to his work a vast quantity of learning.

His thought represents a true theosophy, believing in the essential unity between humanity and God. Having brought speculative Sufism to its apogee through his emphasis on gnosis (*maʿrifa*) as the way to the experience of truth, Ibn ʿArabī has been accused of monism, of denying the reality of the separation between God and His creation. The doctrine of God's transcendence is often held to be essential to Muslim orthodox theology, denying as it does any possibility of the incarnation of God in the world, a consequence of its ancient polemic with Christianity. In theory, the theosophical Ṣūfīs got around the problem of the notion of "the reality of Muḥammad" in control of the universe, that being the power to which the Ṣūfīs could aspire in their mystical quest. Ibn ʿArabī argued for the doctrine of *waḥdat al-wujūd*, the "unity of being," where certain implications seem hard to avoid: being and existence are all one and are combined in God; being, which is apart from God, exists only by virtue of His will, but was, prior to its being made separate, one with God; the "perfect human" (*al-insān al-kāmil*) is the one who knows of oneness with God, who loves God, and who is loved by God. For Ibn al-ʿArabī, the concept of the *barzakh*, the barrier and bridge between material existence and the divine world, referred to in Qurʾān 25/53 and 55/20 in a metaphor of "the place where the two seas join," is of central importance because that is the realm of existence in which humans play a critical role. The ability of, or even the necessity for, humans to bridge that gap both in life and in death provides the unity of being but preserves the conceptual tension between the immanence and transcendence of God.

The role of Sufism

The influence of Ibn ʿArabī, despite the complexity of his thought, has been enormous, not only on all Sufism from that point on, but also in the modern scholarly world, which is still trying to come to grips with his ideas. But Sufism was not only of this elevated intellectual type, for the role of the brotherhoods in bringing Sufism closer to the popular level cannot be underestimated. It was the efforts of the brotherhoods which spread Islam into many far-flung corners of the contemporary Muslim world, often facilitated by means of mystical poetry and aided by a tolerant attitude towards local religious practices as long as they were accompanied by the basic spiritual impulse of Islam in its Ṣūfī guise. Such attitudes within Sufism are often seen as key to empowering local culture through its association with the worldly powerful religion of Islam; furthermore, the empowerment of social groups, notably women, has often been facilitated by Sufism, especially given the exclusion of females from many aspects of normative, formal Islam. As well, Sufism has served throughout its history as a source of general religious revival for Muslims, breathing life into institutions when they tended to reach the point of self-suffocation. While many of the representatives of the established legal schools have remained deeply suspicious of many Ṣūfī practices and, at certain points in history (most notably with Ibn Taymiyya, d. 1328), renewal of Islam has been sought by means of a purge of non-mainstream Ṣūfī influences, Sufism has remained alive and well, catering to those who picture life in terms of the "mystic quest."

Rūmī

In 2002, *Time* magazine declared that the bestselling book *The Essential Rumi*, by Coleman Barks (first published in 1995), with more than 250,000 copies in print, was "easily the most successful poetry book published in the West in the past decade" (*Time*, October 29, 2002). Such acclaim for Rūmī has continued in subsequent years.

Jalāl al-Dīn Muḥammad al-Balkhī, commonly known as Mawlānā (Mevlana in Turkish, both meaning "Our Master") and known especially as Rūmī in the West, was born in Balkh, near the border of Tajikistan and Afghanistan, in September 1207, and died on December 17, 1273, in Konya, Turkey, where his family had moved probably in order to escape the threat of Genghis Khan and the Mongols. Rūmī's tomb (known as the Green Dome) is found in Konya and has become a major pilgrimage site for both Muslims and other religious searchers.

Rūmī's fame and accomplishments as a Ṣūfī are such that an order is named after him, the Mevlevis or Whirling Dervishes, so called because of the dance they perform as a mystical ritual. Rūmī was also a prolific writer, being credited with thousands of lines of poetry as well as the massive *Mathnawī*, a didactic poem of about 26,000 rhyming couplets written in Persian (the word *mathnawī*, sometimes written *masnavi* to more closely represent its pronunciation in Persian, means "rhyming couplet").

Perhaps as early as the fifteenth century, Rūmī's *Mathnawī* was referred to as "the Qur'ān in Persian." This suggests not only that the poetry was considered to be of the highest literary quality but also that it is, as a whole, an interpretation or manifestation of the spirit and meaning of the Qur'ān. That is, of course, an incredibly high estimation to be given to any work in the Muslim context. Overall, Rūmī succeeds in making Islam and the Qur'ān central to his work and does so in an imaginative and entertaining manner. This approach worked to Rūmī's advantage: he was able to couch his own message of Sufism in a language and imagery that was familiar to his readers, even going so far as to incorporate the assertion that both the Qur'ān and the *Mathnawī* originated in the same divine inspiration. The overall message of the poem is to highlight the love of God to whom all true believers long to return and to emphasize the need to transcend all worldly concerns in one's devotion through that love.

Some of the famous modern renderings of Rūmī's poetry have been by accomplished contemporary poets on the basis of previous scholarly renditions. In this process, many

Figure 9.1 The *Yeşil Türbe* ("Green Tomb") of Rūmī in Konya, Turkey, built originally in the thirteenth century. Today it is part of the Mevlana Museum (opened in 1927). A virtual tour of the museum may be taken at http://www.3dmekanlar.com/en/mevlana-museum.html.
Source: Martin Gray/Getty Images.

of the truly Islamic aspects of the poetry have been glossed over or obscured, such that a typical reaction to the poetry is that "it sounds like the type of stuff in the *Tao Te Ching*," according to one commentator at rationalskepticism.org. That comment points to the significance of these modern renderings of Rūmī: when they are rendered in this fashion, they express a type of universal spiritualism that is very popular especially in North America today. There is, however, a deeply Islamic content to the poetry, as is seen in its inspiration from the Qur'ān, the life of Muḥammad, and all the Muslim scholarly disciplines.

For more on Rūmī and the Qur'ān, see Jawid Mojaddedi, "Rūmī," in Andrew Rippin (ed.), *The Blackwell Companion to the Qur'ān*, Oxford: Blackwell Publishing, 2004, pp. 362–73. Mojaddedi has also translated the *Mathnawī* (two volumes so far) in an artful yet scholarly way in the Oxford World's Classics series, *Jalal al-Din Rumi: The Masnavi*, Oxford: Oxford University Press, 2004, 2008. On other popular translations, see Amy Standen, "Rumi: No. 1 in Afghanistan and the USA: Translator Coleman Barks Discusses the Bestselling Poet Who's Loved Equally among Yanks and Afghans," Salon.com, October 12, 2001, http://dir.salon.com/people/feature/2001/10/12/barks/index.html.

Suggested further reading

Julian Baldick, *Mystical Islam: An Introduction to Sufism*, London: I. B. Tauris, 2000.

Ahmet T. Karamustafa, *Sufism: the Formative Period*, Berkeley: University of California Press, 2007.

Alexander D. Knysh, *Islamic Mysticism: A Short History*, Leiden: Brill, 2000.

Michael Sells, *Early Islamic Mysticism: Sufi, Qur'an, Mi'raj, Poetic and Theological Writings*, New York: Paulist Press, 1996. (An excellent collection of translated sources.)

J. Spencer Trimingham, *The Sufi Orders in Islam*, New York: Oxford University Press, 1998 (original edition 1971).

PART IV Consolidation of Islamic identity

Significant dates

632	death of Muḥammad
661–750	Umayyad dynasty
750	ʿAbbāsid dynasty begins
813–33	rule of the caliph al-Maʾmūn
889	death of exegete/writer Ibn Qutayba
925	death of philosopher al-Rāzī
945	Buwayhids take over Baghdad
1037	death of philosopher Ibn Sīnā
1111	death of theologian/mystic al-Ghazālī
1144	death of exegete al-Zamakhsharī
1209	death of exegete Fakhr al-Dīn al-Rāzī
1272	death of exegete al-Qurṭubī
1315	death of exegete al-Bayḍāwī
1328	death of theologian/jurist Ibn Taymiyya
1350	death of traditionist Ibn Qayyim al-Jawziyya
1373	death of exegete Ibn Kathīr
1382	death of historian/sociologist Ibn Khaldūn
1392	death of exegete al-Zarkashī
1459	death of exegete al-Maḥallī
1501	Safavids ruling in Iran
1505	death of exegete/polymath al-Suyūṭī
1641	death of mystical philosopher Mullā Ṣadrā
1762	death of reformer Shāh Walī Allāh
1787	death of reformer Ibn ʿAbd al-Wahhāb

10 *Intellectual culture*

In order to study the formative period of Islam, the main evidence we have before us is found embedded in the later Muslim literary tradition. This is a tradition which has been creatively formed and read by Muslims throughout their history. This reading and re-reading is not a process which came to an end at a certain point; indeed, the vitality of Islam—of religion in general—may be seen in the way in which it brings forward the past and reforms it—re-reads it—in ways appropriate to its contemporary situation.

In the emergence of Islam as a religion, there are two major factors displayed in the sources which we have isolated and examined in the preceding chapters. One relates to the formation of Islam as a distinct entity alongside Judaism and Christianity. The other relates to social issues and the emergence of structures of authority in the community. The solidification of the identity of Islam appears to have been a dynamic process, working on several levels all at the same time.

At the base of all of the discussions concerning identity or authority are the Qurʾān and the *sunna*, linked to God and the person of Muḥammad. These are the texts which have gained central symbolic authority within the Muslim community by being connected to both divine revelation and divine protection. In that respect, these sources are following the tradition of the past of which they are re-readings, the tradition of the earlier religious dispensations of the Near East. The basis for the establishment of a new tradition called Islam was created thereby for those who wished to embrace that identity, understanding of authority, and relationship to God. This accomplished, it was possible for a true culture and civilization that had Islam at its base to emerge.

The culture of Islam

The formation of Islam and its emergence as an identity in the world were accompanied by a flowering of an integrated culture. It is a mark of a mature religion, perhaps, that it becomes the motivator, supporter, and basis for many aspects of the social structure beyond those obviously involved in the religio-legal paradigm itself. Examples may be seen in the developments that took place within medicine and science in the Islamic

Figure 10.1 An elephant clock, as illustrated in a fourteenth-century leaf from the work of al-Jazarī (d. 1206), *Kitab fi maʿrifat al-ḥiyal al-handasiyya* ("The Book of Knowledge of Ingenious Mechanical Devices").
Source: The Metropolitan Museum of Art/Art Resource/Scala, Florence. (Folio, A.H. 715/1315–16. Ink, colors, and gold on paper, H. 11 13/16 in. x W. 7 3/4 in. Acc.n.: 57.51.23.)

context. One could also point to the development of the material arts as an additional example. Furthermore, such a mature structure becomes able to tolerate challenges to it and to find ways of integrating those challenges by deeming them to be products of its own culture rather than the result of external pressures. Such was the case with philosophy in the Islamic context.

Medicine, science, and philosophy share a common rigorous, rational foundation and their presence at the time of the flowering of Islamic culture reflects both internal and external developments. The polemical encounters with Christians and the remnants of the Manichean tradition were paralleled by the internal Muslim development of the

Muʿtazila. Greek texts of philosophy, medicine, and science were translated into Arabic not only as a result of Arabic becoming the *lingua franca* of the Christian community in whose possession these texts were, but also because of their appeal to Muslims for their support in developing rational proofs for religious tenets on the basis of empirical data. In the process, the basis was found for the firm establishment of an Islamic civilization in every aspect.

The influence of Greek philosophy on Islamic theology has already been mentioned in Chapter 5. The need for a systematic presentation and defense of the Islamic faith was apparent as Muslims interacted with Christians in the area of Syria and Iraq. But this apologetic tendency acted in consort with the basic appeal of Greek philosophical thinking to produce a desire and a need to study and Islamicize the Greek works. Initially, through the process of translation, these works were incorporated into the Muslim world.

In the same manner, to achieve such ends within the field of medicine required not only the study of the ancient Greco-Roman texts and intelligent people, but also a process of Islamicization of pre-existing ideas. This can be seen in the emergence of a medical tradition which can be called Islamic. Two elements combine to form this tradition: Greek medical texts and popular Near Eastern medical beliefs and practices. Medicine provides a good example of the general tendency in the Islamic world to integrate the assumptions of the Muslim faith about the nature of humanity and the world with pre-existing knowledge in order to create this conceptual entity of culture and civilization which constitutes what we call the "Muslim world."

Medicine

The popular medical beliefs from the time of the formation of Islam which became incorporated into the religion were not unique to the Arabs. Folklore and superstition provided the basis for a common approach to sickness. Such practices were transmitted and supported through custom, and they were referred to by the word which became the common term used for medicine of the developed Islamic system, *ṭibb*. Remedies included the use of plants and herbs as medicines, and incorporated various physical approaches such as cupping and cautery. These fundamentals were intermixed with, and sometimes based upon, beliefs in the power of spirits, *jinn*, and related malevolent tendencies such as the evil eye. Thus, magical remedies and precautions were an integral part of this tradition. Incantations, charms, and amulets were important defenses. Evidence for these sorts of practices has frequently been discovered in items such as magic bowls with inscriptions and talismanic squares of letter combinations.

At the same time, there existed a learned Greco-Roman tradition of medicine based upon formal investigation and isolation of causes which was continued within the

Eastern Christian monasteries and which was then encountered and incorporated into the Islamic context. The study of the Greek texts (and their Christian Syriac translations) within the Islamic world likely started in the eighth century, but it did not become systematic until the ninth century. This, of course, coincides with the emergence of an educated elite in Islamic culture and the solidification and flourishing of that culture itself. The interaction between Muslims and Christians, as was so crucial in the development of Islamic theology, exposed Muslims not only to Greek philosophy in a limited sense but also to the medical tradition from which it cannot really be separated. There was even specific support for theological argumentation to be seen in medical texts:

> Galen in particular offered powerful evidence for the ancient and much-used argument from design—if the parts of the body worked together for the benefit of the whole, for example, and accord to some principle of harmony and order, then this necessarily implied the giver of harmony and order, i.e., God.
>
> (Conrad 1995: 103)

The translation of Greek texts into Arabic entered an enthusiastic phase with the caliph al-Maʾmūn (ruled 813–33), whose support for the rationalist Muʿtazila encouraged the pursuit of the Greek tradition for its value in providing a rigorous foundation to discussion and argumentation. One manifestation of this support was the foundation of the *bayt al-ḥikma* ("house of wisdom," meaning a library) in Baghdad in 832, in which this translation movement set to work. Hundreds of texts were rendered into Arabic, especially works by Galen, before the demise of the school came about in the wake of the loss of caliphal support for the Muʿtazila towards the end of the ninth century. This did not spell the end of the translation of Greek works by any means, for such efforts continued through the tenth century as well, although as time went by original Muslim research became more highly valued and relevant than the remaining untranslated Greek classics.

The work of Galen thus established the *principal* element of the agenda for Islamic medicine, just as the terminology used in the translations set the vocabulary for later generations. The translation movement was also conscious of the need to incorporate the material upon which it was working within the Islamic framework. References to pagan deities were eliminated and specific works were ignored in the translation efforts.

The final manifestation of this is in the Arabic literary tradition, which emerges from the tenth century on, of writing about medicine on the basis of original work. Here, persons often associated famously with philosophy are also seen to have written about medical topics, for example Rhazes (d. *c.* 925) and Avicenna (d. 1037). The end result is the emergence of vast compendia of medical information following a variety of organizational patterns.

Islamic basis of medicine

The Qurʾān says little about medical matters. Statements about the *lame, blind, and sick* tend to fall into moralistic, symbolic exhortations common to the monotheist tradition. One statement about the curative power of honey (Qurʾān 16/69: "Then there comes out of [the bees'] bellies a drink of diverse shades in which is a healing [*shifāʾ*] for people") is the only substantive statement. The fact that the Qurʾān does mention the *jinn*, however, and makes reference to the purveyors of spells and the like, was also an element in the emergence of the Islamic medical tradition. Some of these elements created controversy. The use of the Qurʾān as a talisman was likely one of the earliest ways of bringing together Islamic elements and popular practices. Such procedures included the Qurʾān's use in amulets, on magic bowls, and in potions (by the washing off of the ink of the written text). More significant than the support of the Qurʾān, however, was the tendency in this popular approach to medicine to use the example of Muḥammad to support various activities. The emergence of *ḥadīth* reports dedicated to the "Medicine of the Prophet," gathered together in medieval works by people such as Ibn Qayyim al-Jawziyya (d. 1350) and al-Suyūṭī (d. 1505), indicate the attempts to suppress those elements considered inappropriate to the Islamic framework and to support those popular practices that were deeply embedded in society. Accounts of early Muslims have also been retold in order to bridge the gap between ancient medical traditions and the ideas of Islam. Anecdotes are told of al-Ḥārith ibn Kalada, who was an "Arab doctor" who used popular remedies in his cures but who is spoken of at the same time as acquiring knowledge of medicine from Persia. Muḥammad used to send people to him for help in their illnesses. The treatments spoken of were "uncomplicated, commonsensical, and self-sufficient," reflecting folk tendencies, while the knowledge which al-Ḥārith tapped was foreign and ancient. The combination was legitimized through the person of Muḥammad.

The plague

Perhaps the most significant way in which disputes about medicine versus religion emerged is to be seen in the attitudes towards epidemics, a concern which has been the focus of scholarly study. The plague was a recurring and severe problem at several points during medieval history. Following earlier Greek thought, its cause was generally thought to be spread through bad quality air (miasma) which upset the balance of the four elements (fire, air, water, and earth) within the human body. Ibn Khaldūn (d. 1382), a historian and philosopher who is also often spoken of as an early sociologist who studied the rise and fall of societies, reports:

> In the later [years] of dynasties, famines and pestilences become numerous. . . . The large number of pestilences has its reason in the large number of famines just

> mentioned. Or, it has its reason in the many disturbances that result from the disintegration of the dynasty. There is much unrest and bloodshed, and plagues occur. The principal reason for the latter is the corruption of the air [climate] through [too] large a civilization [population]. It results from the putrefaction and the many evil moistures with which [the air] has contact [in a dense civilization]. Now, air nourishes the animal spirit and is constantly with it. When it is corrupted, corruption affects the temper of [the spirit]. If the corruption is strong, the lung is afflicted with disease. This results in epidemics, which affect the lungs in particular.
>
> (Ibn Khaldūn, quoted in Dols 1977: 90)

Astrological factors and evil spirits were also thought to play their role in the spread of epidemics. However, ideas of contagion as a cause were certainly present but frequently downplayed. The recognition that corpses could be the source of the plague, for example, was certainly known and experimentally confirmed. But supposed corrupt air was always firmly held to be the vehicle for such transmission. Fleeing to an area of pure air was generally seen to be the best preventative step, along with fumigation of one's place of dwelling. Blood-letting was the main method of treatment.

These ideas about the plague were constrained and directed by religious factors in many instances. Three factors have been isolated:

1 A Muslim should not enter or flee from a plague-stricken land.
2 The plague is a martyrdom and a mercy from God for a Muslim and a punishment for an infidel.
3 There is no infection (contagion).

The first and second factors go together, although the first does suggest a certain medical attitude and understanding of the nature of epidemics. However, one cannot, and should not, flee from one's God-given fate, for such is an expression of disbelief. Epidemics before Islam and those which befell non-Muslim populations were God's means of rendering justice in the world; when the Muslim population was afflicted, the incident had to be understood as an opportunity to reach paradise, just as in dying in battle (*jihād*) for Islam. Such notions were supported by *ḥadīth* reports from Muḥammad. That religious thought did not accept the notion of contagion finds its basis in the idea that God is the cause of all things and is supported once again by appeal to *ḥadīth* reports. Such attitudes were widespread regarding medicine in general and some people argued that medical cures were an attempt to "contravene the omniscience and omnipotence of God" (Rosenthal 1969: 523).

The link to philosophy

As in medicine, so it has been observed in other scientific endeavors that an uneasy relationship existed between those who continued within the "folk" traditions and those who pursued the rational basis. Procedures regarding how to determine the start of a lunar month (especially crucial for Ramaḍān) and how to align a mosque in the direction of Mecca were established by rigorous approaches to astronomy yet they were rarely incorporated into Muslim religious practice. Rather, the time-tried methods of observation and approximation were continued, despite significant advances in mathematical reckoning. Underlying the conflicts in these and many other fields of thought on the part of those Muslims who had certainly been influenced by the rational basis of medicine, science, and philosophy but who felt the need to protect Islamic theological dogma was a distrust for those who wished to support the philosophical project wholeheartedly. Those who pursued in-depth study of philosophy (and, frequently, medicine at the same time) were often seen (sometimes justifiably so) to pose a challenge to Islam in their thought. Famous in this regard is Abū Bakr al-Rāzī (d. *c.* 925), known in the West as Rhazes. As a philosopher, much of al-Rāzī's written legacy has been lost (he states that he wrote about 200 works on medicine, logic, philosophy, theology, natural sciences, alchemy, astronomy, and mathematics), but it is clear that he was a Platonist and a "free thinker" whose challenge to Islam was fully informed by Greek philosophy. He argued for the eternal existence of five principles—the creator, the soul, matter, space, and time. Through the study of philosophy, the soul can be released from the cycle of birth and rebirth. Humanity has no need of a belief in prophets and revelation as reason is sufficient as a guide. Material existence poses a constant challenge to pure intellectual existence, the soul always being tempted by the pleasures of nature.

As a doctor, al-Rāzī headed up hospitals in Rayy and Baghdad. Among his significant extant works are a tract on smallpox and measles and two compendia on diet, hygiene, anatomy, physiology, and pathology, along with general descriptions of diagnosis, therapy, and surgery. In his work *Fī 'l Ḥaṣba wa 'l-Judarī*, al-Rāzī distinguished smallpox from measles, a considerable achievement for the time. The details provided are based upon observation rather than dogmatic assumptions:

> The eruption of the smallpox is preceded by a continued fever, pain in the back, itching in the nose and terrors in sleep. These are the more peculiar symptoms of its approach, especially a pain in the back with fever; then also a pricking which the patient feels all over his body; a fullness of the face, which at times comes and goes; an inflamed colour, and vehement redness in both cheeks; a redness of both the eyes; a heaviness of the whole body; great uneasiness, the symptoms of which are stretching and yawning; a pain in the throat and chest, with a slight difficulty in breathing and cough; a dryness of the breath, thick spittle, and hoarseness of the voice; pain and heaviness of the head; inquietude, nausea and anxiety; (with this difference that the inquietude, distress of the mind, nausea, and anxiety are more frequent in the measles

> than in the smallpox; while, on the other hand, the pain in the back is more peculiar to the smallpox than to the measles;) heat of the whole body; an inflamed colon, and shining redness, and especially an intense redness of the gums.
>
> (Rāzī 1848: 34)

One feature of al-Rāzī's medical system which often gets noted is the emphasis on cures through diet, combined with an acknowledgment of the influence of psychological factors on health. He used animals for the testing of remedies and introduced the use of alcohol for medical purposes. This latter element and related matters created some of the adverse attitude and suspicion of the Islamic religious leaders towards medicine in general. The use of substances banned by the *sharīʿa* could not help but draw their attention.

Ibn Sīnā

Ibn Sīnā, known in the West as Avicenna (d. 1037), is another example of the physician-philosopher. He is credited with having written 250 works, the most famous of which in the medical field is his *al-Qānūn fī'l-Ṭibb*, "The Canon of Medicine," a rigorously organized treatise based on Aristotelian principles concerned to see medicine within the context of the whole of the natural sciences. The "rational sciences" for Ibn Sīnā were divided into two groupings. One was the "speculative," which searched for truth through physics (which included medicine, astrology, and physiognomy), mathematics, and metaphysics. The other was the "practical," including personal morality, domestic morality, and politics. Philosophy thus covered every item of value to humans.

Neoplatonism was the foundation of Ibn Sīnā's philosophy but he combined that with a mystical aspect and spoke of

> the intellectual urge of the soul to achieve contact or conjunction (*ittiṣāl*) with the Active Intellect, or conversely the divine Nous of Plotinus, rather than union (*ittiḥād*) with, or even vision (*kashf, mushahadah*) of, God, who both for Plotinus and Muslim Neoplatonists continues to be unattainable.
>
> (Fakhry 1997: 48)

The soul aims to exist in conjunction with God (or the "Active Intellect") which will thereby allow the beauty and goodness of the world to be perceived; in that lies true happiness and the meaning of human existence. Such an end can only be reached by the philosopher or the prophet, whereas most people must rely upon the message of the prophets for guidance and, at best, would be able to experience only a shadow of the true happiness after their death.

Attitude to philosophy

Certainly, philosophical thought challenged Islam in this period. This did not mean, however, that it did not flourish, or that the associated ideas of the medical tradition did not have a tremendous impact. Rather, for most Muslims during this period of intellectual development and consolidation, the role of reason as conveyed within the philosophical tradition was accepted as God-given and as a useful tool in the development of human existence. Even those more closely associated with traditional approaches to learning in the early period saw the benefits. Ibn Qutayba (d. 889) wrote:

> Knowledge is the stray camel of the believer; it benefits him regardless from where he takes it: it shall not disparage truth should you hear it from the polytheists, nor advice should it be derived from those who harbor hatred; shabby clothes do no injustice to a beautiful woman, nor shells to their pearls, nor its origin from dust to pure gold. Whoever disregards taking the good from its place misses an opportunity, and opportunities are as transient as the clouds. . . . Ibn ʿAbbās . . . said: "Take wisdom from whomever you hear it, for the non-wise may utter a wise saying and a bull's eye may be hit by a non-sharpshooter."
>
> (Ibn Qutayba, *ʿUyūn al-Akhbār*, quoted in Gutas 1998: 159)

That such attitudes did not continue throughout Islamic history is also true and philosophy as such was perceived by many to be a danger to true Islamic belief. The ramifications of that attitude are still being felt today, as will become clear in Chapter 16. That this attitude did not necessarily extend to all aspects of Greek learning is important to keep in mind, although the tendency to "reclaim" the knowledge by ascribing it to Arab or Biblical predecessors of the Greeks was known in medieval times (just as it is today).

Hashish

The Assassins are famous in history for the legends concerning their use of hashish to drug their followers into willingness to assassinate their enemies. Such notions are likely misunderstandings and fanciful developments that arose during the Crusader period. However, it is a fact that medieval Muslims knew hashish well, studied its medical and scientific properties, and tangled with its legality for many centuries.

The word *ḥashīsh* in Arabic originally meant a dried herb but came to be applied to the hemp drug known in India as *bhang* (as compared to *ganja*, which is the resin from the plant that is collected). References to hashish abound in *The Thousand and One Nights*, which likely took its final literary form around the thirteenth century.

Abū ʿAbd Allāh Muḥammad al-Zarkashī, an Egyptian Shāfiʿī jurist and scholar who died in 1392, has among his many legal works of note a book on hashish called *Zahr al-ʿarīsh fī taḥrīm al-ḥashīsh*, "The Flowers of the Grape Trellis Concerning the Prohibition of Hashish."

The work details the physical hazards of hashish consumption and the moral impact of the substance. From a legal point of view, al-Zarkashī pointed out that there was no mention of the substance in the Qurʾān (not that some people did not try to find references to it in the *zaqqūm* tree of Qurʾān 56/52 or in references to "green garments" in Qurʾān 18/31 as part of the picture of the hereafter) or the *sunna* (even though *ḥadīth* reports were occasionally circulated that claimed to deal with the substance). Thus, arguing on the basis of analogy, al-Zarkashī deemed that the effects of the substance were parallel to those associated with wine and intoxication; hashish was declared forbidden. At the same time, he did admit to some of hashish's positive (and legal) anesthetizing abilities. It was the use of hashish for enjoyment and pleasure that raised the ire of al-Zarkashī, as it did for most every Muslim jurist.

Abū Manṣūr al-Harawī in the tenth century wrote about the use of hemp for the manufacture of rope. He also wrote of the success in using hashish itself for headaches and earaches. This medical information was acknowledged to be a legacy of the Greek tradition. Hippocrates and Galen were both cited as authorities on the nature and use of the drug. It was consumed in solid form (not smoked), and the doubtful legal status of the substance led to a good deal of mixing of popular and medical beliefs regarding its use. Al-Zarkashī reported that it could cause sudden death, mental confusion, fever, consumption, dropsy, and effeminate behavior. Overall, he suggested that the drug simply destroys the human being physically and mentally as well as attacking any sense of religious responsibility. At the same time, he suggested that it can be a cure for epilepsy, can dissolve flatulence, and can clear up dandruff; it may also be used as a type of anesthetic to control hunger (as an intoxicant).

The standard work on this topic is Franz Rosenthal, *The Herb: Hashish versus Medieval Muslim Society*, Leiden: Brill, 1971.

Suggested further reading

Peter Adamson and Richard C. Taylor (eds.), *The Cambridge Companion to Arabic Philosophy*, Cambridge: Cambridge University Press, 2005.

Michael W. Dols, *Medieval Islamic Medicine: Ibn Riḍwān's Treatise "On the Prevention of Bodily Ills in Egypt", translated with an introduction*, Berkeley: University of California Press, 1984.

George Makdisi, *Ibn ʿAqil: Religion and Culture in Classical Islam*, Edinburgh: Edinburgh University Press, 1997.

Peter E. Portmann and Emilie Savage-Smith, *Medieval Islamic Medicine*, Edinburgh: Edinburgh University Press, 2007.

Boaz Shoshan, *Popular Culture in Medieval Cairo*, Cambridge: Cambridge University Press, 1993.

11 *Medieval visions of Islam*

Despite the emergence and definition of Islamic identity in the earlier centuries, Muslim thinkers did not cease in their efforts to enunciate the substance of their faith, each responding to the needs and conditions of his (and virtually every name which is known to history is male) time. The period from the thirteenth century through the eighteenth century saw a continuance of the distillation of Islam in textual form. The structures employed for this varied, however, often in mutually opposing ways. Super-commentaries emerged, encouraging reflection upon and preservation of some of the great intellectual achievements of the past. Distillations become more popular, in response to general educative aims. Expansions of previous work, ever accumulating the knowledge of the past in celebration of the endless potential of tradition, were popular. Reformulations, often involving a contraction of tradition in response to a perceived need to avoid certain excesses, also abounded. The writings in a discipline such as Quranic exegesis, *tafsīr*, illustrate this, while emphasizing at the same time the continuing perception of the relevance of Islam but also the need to keep the faith ever adaptable, albeit in different ways.

Tendencies in medieval exegesis

Abū'l-Qāsim Maḥmūd ibn ʿUmar al-Zamakhsharī (d. 1144) was a philologist, theologian, and Qur'ān commentator. For most of his life al-Zamakhsharī lived in the region of his birth, Khwarizm in Central Asia, although he did spend some time studying in Bukhara and Baghdad, and twice he visited Mecca. Motivated by a great appreciation of Arabic (although he was a native Persian speaker) and influenced by rationalist Muʿtazilī theology, al-Zamakhsharī wrote one of the most widely read commentaries on the Qur'ān, called *al-Kashshāf ʿan Ḥaqāʾiq Ghawāmid al-Tanzīl*, "The Unveiler of the Realities of the Secrets of the Revelation." Despite what came to be regarded as a heretical theological slant, the work has been an essential part of the curriculum of religious education throughout the Muslim world for centuries. It attracted many super-commentaries which attempted to explain its terse style and intricacies, as well as

Figure 11.1 Manuscripts and tablets containing the Qurʾān and *ḥadīth* texts as found in a library in Chinguetti (Shinqīṭ in Arabic), Mauritania. Founded as a trading center, the city was important as a gathering spot for pilgrims from the Maghreb on their way to Mecca and became important as a place of religious learning and pilgrimage in its own right.
Source: Stuart Freedman/In Pictures/Corbis.

refutations (e.g. by Fakhr al-Dīn al-Rāzī, d. 1209) and bowdlerized versions (e.g. by al-Bayḍāwī, d. probably 1315–16). Al-Zamakhsharī commented on each phrase of the Qurʾān in sequence, providing philosophical, lexicographical, and philological glosses, while displaying a concern for the rhetorical qualities of the text. His text is also imbued with his theological vision, which is characterized by a thoroughgoing de-anthropomorphization and support for the doctrines of human free will and the notion of the created Qurʾān. Al-Zamakhsharī also wrote a number of other works, including works on Arabic grammar, rhetoric, and lexicography, and a collection of proverbs.

The significance of al-Zamakhsharī's work was recognized quickly, with the emergence of explicit commentaries on it written by Ibn al-Munayyir (d. 1284) and Sharaf al-Dīn al-Ṭībī (d. 1343), for example. Super-commentaries such as this are not very common within the *tafsīr* tradition, but the form itself certainly emerged earlier in other disciplines such as grammar. Their existence indicates the nature of learning and of the consolidation of Muslim identity in society in general at the time.

Al-Bayḍāwī's work *Anwār al-Tanzīl wa Asrār al-Taʾwīl*, "The Lights of Revelation and the Secrets of Interpretation," plus a commentary on it by al-Khāṭib al-Kārūnī

(d. 1553), has continued to be an important element in the course of studies at the Muslim religious university al-Azhar in Cairo. Al-Bayḍāwī's text, short, succinct, yet exhaustive, presents the essence of Sunnī doctrine and has attracted a large number of other commentaries as well. While clearly dependent upon al-Zamakhsharī, although avoiding those points of Muʿtazilī doctrine which he deemed unacceptable, al-Bayḍāwī was also indebted to a good deal of the general tradition of exegesis which preceded him.

The commentary on the Qurʾān by Muḥammad Aḥmad al-Qurṭubī (d. 1272), *al-Jāmiʿ li-Aḥkām al-Qurʾān*, "The Compendium of the Rulings of the Qurʾān," indicates by its title that a major concern of this medieval Quranic exegete was to support the use of the Qurʾān as a source of law with Islam. However, al-Qurṭubī's work is not limited to that for it provides a vast source of opinion on the meaning of the Qurʾān, much of it presented with little indication of the author's preferred meaning of the text. Rather, the point of the work seems to be the demonstration of the potentiality of the text for conveying a multiplicity of meanings.

According to Norman Calder,

> the process of citing authorities and providing multiple readings is, in part, a declaration of loyalty. It defines the tradition within which one works. It is also a means to establish the individuality or the artistry of the commentator. The selection, presentation, and organization of citations constitute always a process that is unique to one writer.
>
> (Calder 1993: 103–4)

Although such compilations may strike us today as mere repetition of the ideas of others, they constitute a creative act that is the result of dedicated work of the author. Finally, the books themselves are, of course, one element in a theological message: the possibility of the community and the text containing a multiplicity of interpretation while remaining one community and one text is asserted through this process.

The desire to distill tradition into compact units suitable for study and for reflection may be seen in the work of Jalāl al-Dīn al-Maḥallī (d. 1459) which was completed by Jalāl al-Dīn al-Suyūṭī (d. 1505) known as *Tafsīr al-Jalālayn*, the "Commentary of the Two Jalāls." The work focuses upon grammatical issues which are presented succinctly in a manner appropriate to those who have a solid training in the subtleties of the Arabic language. Yet at the same time, al-Suyūṭī also complied another work of exegesis, *al-Durr al-Manthūr fī ʾl-Tafsīr bi ʾl-Maʾthūr*, "Scattered Pearls in the Interpretation (of the Qurʾān) by Tradition," which is a vast compendium of older sources brought together complete with abbreviated *isnāds* in order to provide an overview of opinion. This latter work is more in keeping, in fact, with the overall character of al-Suyūṭī's work. He was a polymath whose compilations on many subjects set the tone for a general understanding of this age of consolidation. His aim was clearly to compile, in card file fashion, a sum of useful knowledge as it had been transmitted from the past. Much of the same material finds itself repeated in multiple works, all by al-Suyūṭī; the apparent vast number of his books is exaggerated by the tendency to create separate works on individual subjects which are also found in his larger compendia. His classic work on the Quranic "sciences," *al-Itqān fī ʿUlūm al-Qurʾān*, "The Perfection Concerning the Sciences of the Qurʾān," brings together about eighty subjects, each related to the Qurʾān and its study: where pieces of it were revealed, how they were revealed, what difficult words there are in it, what foreign words there are in it, what metaphors there are, and so on. This encyclopedist tendency provides a categorization of knowledge that is functional rather than necessarily original, although the classification system itself may be innovative in some cases; al-Suyūṭī himself builds upon a tradition of such matters in this case, working on the model provided by al-Zarkashī (d. 1392) in his *al-Burhān fī ʿUlūm al-Qurʾān*, "The Disclosure of the Sciences of the Qurʾān."

Counter-tendencies in exegesis

However, this expansive, encyclopedist tendency also came in for criticism in a manner which resulted in a contraction of available information. Two names stand out in medieval times for this tendency: Ibn Taymiyya and Ibn Kathīr. ʿImād al-Dīn Ismāʿīl ibn ʿUmar ibn Kathīr was born in Basra in 1300 and moved to Damascus when he was six, where he studied with some of the most famous scholars of his time, including the Ḥanbalī theologian, jurist, and reformer Taqī al-Dīn Aḥmad ibn Taymiyya (d. 1328). Ibn Kathīr became known as a scholar of law and a teacher of *ḥadīth* as well as being praised as one of the most respected preachers and lecturers in Damascus. He died in 1373. His major work, a commentary on the Qurʾān entitled simply *Tafsīr al-Qurʾān*, provides a synopsis of earlier material in a readily accessible form, a factor which gave the work much popularity in subsequent generations. His reliance is totally upon *ḥadīth* material; the era of Ibn Kathīr, in fact, marks the final submersion of rationalism under the powers of traditionalism. No longer did even the minimal measure of explicit personal opinion displayed in the work of al-Ṭabarī or al-Zamakhsharī have any substantial place in the understanding of the Qurʾān. Ibn Kathīr frequently structures his commentary around extracts from the classical books of *ḥadīth*, citing those reports relevant to the passage in question. In doing so, the tradition of *tafsīr* is being contracted severely; no longer are the intellectual disciplines of grammar, law, and theology being brought into dialogue and debate with the text.

It was Ibn Taymiyya who provided the theoretical basis to Ibn Kathīr's approach, through his emphasis in his *Muqaddima fī Uṣūl al-Tafsīr*, "An Introduction to the Principles of *Tafsīr*," on the steps which one must take in explaining the Qurʾān:

> If someone says, "What is the best method of *tafsīr?*" the answer is [as follows]. The most sound method is that the Qurʾān be interpreted by the Qurʾān. What is summarized in one place may well be explained in another, and what is abbreviated in one place may well be expanded in another.
>
> If that [approach] thwarts your efforts, then you should [interpret the Qurʾān] by the *sunna*, for it is a commentary (*sharḥ*) and an elucidator of the Qurʾān. . . . About this the Messenger of God said, "Is it not that I was given the Qurʾān and the like of it with it?", that is, the *sunna*. The *sunna* was also revealed to him by revelation (*waḥy*), just as the Qurʾān was revealed. It is just that it is not recited as the Qurʾān is recited. . . . The objective of this [approach to understanding the Qurʾān] is that you search for the interpretation of the Qurʾān within itself and if you do not find it [there], then from within the *sunna*. . . . Whenever you do not find an explanation in the Qurʾān nor in the *sunna*, you should look concerning that matter at the statements of the companions of Muḥammad (*ṣaḥāba*). They are the most knowledgeable in that regard because of what they witnessed [of the revelation] of the Qurʾān and the circumstances by which they were distinguished and because they have complete understanding and sound knowledge. This is especially so of their scholars and elders who include the four rightly-guided Caliphs and the rightly guided *imāms*. . . . When you are unable to find the interpretation in either the Qurʾān or the *sunna* and you cannot find it on the authority of the Companions, in that situation most learned people go to the statements of the Successors. This includes people such as Mujāhid ibn Jabr, for he is a mark by which *tafsīr* is known. This is as Muḥammad ibn Isḥāq said, saying that Abān ibn Ṣāliḥ told him on the authority of Mujāhid ibn Jabr that he said, "I went through the Qurʾān with Ibn ʿAbbās three times from beginning to end, stopping at each of its verses and asking him about them."
>
> (Ibn Taymiyya 1978: I, 76–81, excerpts)

The goal of both Ibn Taymiyya and Ibn Kathīr was to render the Qurʾān accessible and intelligible through an assertion of authority of the *ʿulamāʾ*. Elements of classical exegesis that were deemed unnecessary and impractical were excluded and condemned as lies or even the material of the enemies of Islam. The emphasis on Muḥammad, the person, and his revelatory *sunna*, along with his closest followers as the focus of authority in Islam, rather than the intellectual tradition, is covered in the term *salaf*, the "pious ancestors."

Clearly, such tendencies in all these exegetical works and their conflicting aims can be explained to some extent by the differing audiences which the authors contemplated for their works. However, it is important to recognize the ideological stance which is conveyed within these books, especially in its attitude towards the past. The "acquisitive" nature of the works of al-Qurṭubī or al-Suyūṭī, their gathering together of material from the past in a celebration of the significance of the living Islamic tradition is opposed to the more monovalent attitude of Ibn Kathīr. Of course, these expansive and contractive tendencies show the power of religion to renew itself through a constant movement of reinterpretation.

Developments in Sufism

A survey of works in the field of history, theology, or law would reveal the same variety of tendencies and liveliness in intellectual activities among Muslims of the post-thirteenth century. Some special attention is needed to Sufism in this period because it, too, went through a period of development, significantly consolidating institutionally in the post-sixteenth century, and starting to follow new lines in ritual. The setting of the stage for the developments of the nineteenth and twentieth centuries is clearly to be seen both in terms of the developments within Sufism and in the reactions against it during this period.

Most of the Ṣūfī *ṭarīqa*s were rather loosely organized for much of their history, with individual branches within a given order existing independently. It would not necessarily have been possible for a Ṣūfī to recognize a follower of his own order from a different area; no common mode of dress or practice was implemented. The commonality of such Ṣūfīs was located only in their respect for the founder of the order. Even the person of the *shaykh* was nominated by the local centers, with no centralized control. The Ṣūfī orders were, therefore, of no particular significance in terms of general social movements in the earlier period; their influence was regional and not political.

This started to change first within the context of the sixteenth-century Ottoman empire, where the Mawlawiyya (Mevlevi order) and Bektāshiyya were prominent and had significant influence with the people and were, to some extent, controlled by the government as a result. Such organizational movements became more widespread in the eighteenth century, with, for example, Shaykh Khālid (d. 1826) of the Naqshbandiyya order creating a network of more than one hundred subsidiary *khalīfa*s or "deputies," each with his own geographical region of control. At the same time, the notion of dynastic succession (rather than spiritual selection) in the designation of the *shaykh* became more common.

Furthermore, a tendency emerged towards requiring allegiance to a single Ṣūfī order. In earlier times, the spiritual benefit of Sufism was thought to be such that more such benefit could be gathered by belonging to more than one order. It is common to read of people being initiated into multiple orders. Furthermore, many Ṣūfī orders displayed (and continue to display) a syncretic nature in terms of matters of authority and ritual. Ṣūfī saints who are apparent key figures in one order will be appealed to by members of another order. Rituals commonly associated with one order, such as the whirling dance of the Mawlawiyya order, will be employed by another order which is normally associated with other rituals, such as the deep breathing Rifāʿiyya. However, the Khalwatiyya in eighteenth-century Egypt emphasized the need to belong to this one order and to leave all others behind. Such an attitude created a similar effect in other orders, notably the Tijāniyya of Aḥmad al-Tijānī (d. 1815) and its rival, the Qādiriyya in North Africa.

These changes tended to elevate the status of individual *shaykhs* in a manner which became reflected in ritual activities also. The centralized leadership of Shaykh Khālid of the Naqshbandiyya, for example, became the focus of devotional activities rather than the local leader (who, as the "spiritual guide," had formerly been the center of attention). Other changes reflect more on the desire to popularize and spread Sufism rather than simple organizational maneuvers. An interesting shift in the practice of the *dhikr* is to be noted within disparate and different Ṣūfī orders, including the Naqshbandiyya in China and the Khalwatiyya in Egypt in the eighteenth century. The *dhikr* can be performed either silently by individuals or out loud by a group. The former procedure tended to be considered more orthodox, and those who wished to maintain a respectable image for Sufism were concerned to see that the tradition was maintained, especially since the vocal *dhikr* was often accompanied by music and dance, which was frequently condemned by more conservative religious leaders. In moving to a vocal *dhikr*, it has been suggested that a larger number of common people were attracted to the performances, making the message of the orders that much more widespread but also indicating the greater influence upon society which these groups had despite the reaction which some of their practices provoked.

It is apparent from the perspective of later history that all of these elements of change are significant within the development of Sufism and its impact upon Muslim society in general in the nineteenth and twentieth centuries. A strong organization coupled with a good deal of popular appeal made the Ṣūfī orders a force to be reckoned with. However, the changes in Sufism were not limited to the *ṭarīqas*, but may also be noted in the emergence of several significant figures who added to the body of the imagery and theory of Sufism in particular ways. Ṣadr al-Dīn al-Shirāzī, known as Mullā Ṣadrā (d. 1641), is perhaps the most significant. Working within the developed tradition of Sufism in the wake of Ibn ʿArabī in the context of Shīʿī thought, Mullā Ṣadrā's works reflect an integration of those two elements with Greek philosophy.

Purification movements

A certain backlash against Sufism can also be seen within the medieval period. Ibn Taymiyya argued strenuously for purging Islam of various practices prevalent in his time, especially popular Ṣūfī practices such as excessive asceticism, tomb visitations, and saint worship, along with beliefs such as miracle working. Although Ibn Taymiyya appears to have aligned himself personally with Ṣūfī orders and was thus not opposed to Sufism as such, he argued against these specific activities by appealing to the Qurʾān and the practice (*sunna*) of Muḥammad; anything within Sufism that could not be justified on this basis was to be rejected. Thus, music and song were to be considered non-Islamic, for example. The entire Ṣūfī proposal of the ecstatic experience of God was not a valid criterion by which to judge what is right and wrong (which is one of the arguments which al-Ghazālī had used a few centuries earlier to legitimate Ṣūfī practices). Similar thoughts arose in the eighteenth century as well, primarily in the Arabian movement which became known as the Wahhābiyya, once again a movement against Sufism and the Shīʿa. Led by Muḥammad Ibn ʿAbd al-Wahhāb (1703–87), the movement argued that the attitude of reverence towards saints had led to a blind acceptance of their authority and this was to be rejected and replaced by the sole authority of Islam, the Qurʾān and the *sunna*. Shāh Walī Allāh (1702–62), a mystic-theologian, represents a similar tendency in the Indian context, but he placed greater emphasis on gradual reform rather than the strident confrontations of Ibn ʿAbd al-Wahhāb.

A prolific writer, Ibn ʿAbd al-Wahhāb includes among his many tracts one with the title *Nawāqiḍ al-Islām*, "The Things which Nullify Islam," which harkens back to the moral stance of the Khawārij. This work sets out in point form the limits to what a Muslim may believe or do and still maintain membership in the community. The text appears to be a distillation of many of the central points of Ibn ʿAbd al-Wahhāb's most famous and emblematic text, his *Kitāb al-Tawḥīd*, "The Book of Unity." The document *Nawāqiḍ al-Islām* needs to be seen within the context of Muslim discussion of defining community membership with a view to understanding the political ramifications of theological issues. Such discussions show a remarkable evolution through time, adapting to the situation of the writer and, in doing so, reflecting the perceptions of the social and political pressures of the day. The text reads as follows:

Know that the greatest matters which nullify your Islam are ten:

1 Ascribing partners in the worship of the one God who has no partners. The indication of that is in His saying, "God does not forgive setting up partners with Him but He forgives whom He pleases for sins other than that." [Qurʾān 4/116] This includes slaughtering animals in the name of someone other than God, as in slaughtering the name of the *jinn* or [spirits connected to] tombs.
2 Setting up intermediaries between oneself and God, making supplication to them, or asking their intercession with God is unbelief by the consensus of the community.
3 Anyone who does not consider the polytheists to be unbelievers, or who has doubts concerning their unbelief, or considers their way to be correct, is an unbeliever by consensus.
4 Anyone who believes any guidance to be more perfect than the prophet's, or a decision other than his to be better, is an unbeliever. This is like those who prefer the rule of evil to his rule.

5 Anyone who hates any part of what the messenger of God has brought, even though he may act in accordance with it, is an unbeliever by consensus. God has said, "This is because they hate what God has sent down, so He has made their deeds fruitless." [Qurʾān 47/9]

6 Anyone who ridicules any aspect of the religion of God, or any of its rewards or punishments, is an unbeliever. The indication of that is in God's saying, "Say: Was it God, and His signs and His Messenger that you were mocking? Make no excuse; you have disbelieved after you had believed." [Qurʾān 9/65–6]

7 The practice of magic. Included in this, for example, is causing a rift between a husband and wife by turning his love for her into hatred, or tempting a person to do things he dislikes using black arts. One who engages in such a thing or is pleased with it is outside the fold of Islam. God said, "But neither of these two [angels, Hārūt and Mārūt] taught anyone magic until they had said, 'Indeed, we are a trial; so do not disbelieve.' " [Qurʾan 2/102]

8 Supporting and aiding polytheists against the Muslims. The indication of that is God saying, "Whoever among you who takes them as allies is surely one of them. Truly, God does not guide the wrongdoers." [Qurʾan 5/51]

9 Anyone who believes that some people are not required to follow Muḥammad is an unbeliever and that leaving its *sharīʿa* is possible just as al-Khiḍr left the *sharīʿa* of Moses, is an unbeliever.

10 To turn completely away from the religion of God, neither learning its precepts nor acting upon it. The indication of that is God's saying, "And who does greater wrong than he who is reminded of the revelations of his Lord and turns aside there from. Truly, We shall exact retribution from the guilty." [Qurʾan 32/22]

It makes no difference whether such violations are committed as a joke, in seriousness or out of fear, except when done under compulsion [i.e. from threat of loss of life]. We seek refuge in God from such deeds as entail His wrath and severe punishment.

(Ibn ʿAbd al-Wahhāb 1977: V, 212–14)

The concern of a text such as this one is the clear delineation of the community combined with high moral expectations and a closed definition of what Islam stands for. The sense of the cumulative historical community fades in such a presentation, to be replaced by an authoritarian definition which demands support and control by a central authority which will make decisions regarding rightful membership. Such efforts establish their sets of standards by isolating those factors that are not in keeping with the desired ethos of the group (a culturally conditioned factor) and declaring all such attributes to be "mere" (and illegitimate) cultural intrusions into the purity of Islam. It is, however, the willingness to declare someone a non-Muslim, harking back to the early Muslim discussions of "commanding right and forbidding wrong," that marks this position of Ibn ʿAbd al-Wahhāb as so particularly strident.

The movements connected to Ibn ʿAbd al-Wahhāb and Shāh Walī Allāh may be termed "pre-modern," in the sense that they developed before the impact of the industrialized West had been felt. They may be best termed "purification" movements and they certainly sowed the seeds for later social and legal change in the Islamic world. They seem to have been caused by a dissatisfaction with the more rigid formulations of medieval Islam, especially in the legal schools. The movement also picks up on a well-established tradition in Islam regarding the *mujaddid*, or renewer of the faith, believed to be an essential part of each age. Fazlur Rahman has characterized these pre-modernist groups as having the following traits:

1 a deep and transforming concern with the socio-moral degeneration of Muslim society;
2 a call to "go back" to original Islam and shed the superstitions inculcated by popular forms of Sufism, to get rid of the idea of the fixity and finality of the traditional schools of law, and to attempt to perform *ijtihād*, that is, to rethink for oneself the meaning of the original message;
3 a call to remove the crushing burden of a predeterministic outlook produced by popular religion but also materially contributed to by the almost ubiquitous influence of Ashʿarī theology;
4 a call to carry out this revivalist reform through armed force (*jihād*) if necessary.

(Rahman 1979a: 317)

The birthday of Muḥammad

Such stances towards Sufism also reflect some of the developing attitudes within ritual and law. An example may be seen in the festivities connected to the celebration of the birthday of Muḥammad. Known generally as *mawlid al-nabī*, "the birth of the prophet," the celebration of this day does not have full community consensus behind it. The commemoration of the day is not recorded in the classical texts of Islamic law and it has no connection to the *sunna*. When jurists did contemplate it in later centuries, they often termed it a *bidʿa ḥasana*, a "commendable innovation." Historically, the present festival is thought to stem from the twelfth century; this is when the historians of the period start to record various practices related to the twelfth day of the month of Rabīʿ I, which was designated as Muḥammad's birthday. The activities within the celebration are characteristic of general Muslim approach toward honoring local saints. *Mawlids* were, and still are, held for the most popular holy men and women of Islamic history as a part of mystical devotion. A holy day is stimulated by a connection with a holy person, a day on which celebrations and devotions may be expected to bring great merits and benefits. The central events of such days are processions (frequently lit with candles or the like), chanting, singing, and telling stories. A fair is often organized for children. The celebrations culminate in religious devotions to the holy person, producing "exaltation, fervor, rapture and in many a tranquil contentment" (Berger 1970: 83). Today, in most parts of the Muslim world, the birthday of Muḥammad is celebrated in a similar manner. Each area has its own particular form of celebration and in many countries it has become an official state holiday. This official character is reinforced by the presence of the head of state, who will frequently attend the festivities held at the main mosque in the capital city.

Characteristic of the celebration is the recitation of poetry in praise of Muḥammad, often known as *mawladiyya*. Much of the material found in the poems recited even today is derived from classical sources, which emphasizes the continued role of and devotion to the learning of the past, and the significant role that Muḥammad's miracles and his human qualities have played in the practiced faith of Islam. As well, the characteristics of the poetry reveal a definite mystical element which has permeated Muslim belief. One example of the Ṣūfī influence may be seen in the theory espoused in much of the poetry regarding the pre-existent "Muhammadan light," an element of the miraculous but also the salvific nature of the conception of Muḥammad through which this world is connected to the divine domain. A typical poem contains the following lines:

> The lights of Muḥammad streamed upon us,
> The full moons have hurried away; we have never seen such beauty.
> Only you are the face of happiness.
> You are a sun; you are a full moon.
> You are light upon light.
> You are an elixir, very precious
> You light up (our) hearts, my Beloved Muḥammad.
> You are the bride of both East and West
> You are firmly backed (by God) and honored,
> You are the Imām of the two *qiblas*.
> Whoever gazed upon your face felt elated.
> You are from distinguished parentage and your background is peerless.
>
> (Waugh 1989: 189)

Together with the recitation of poetry in honor of Muḥammad on these occasions, a more definitive element of Ṣūfī practice makes its presence felt. The poetry is often followed by litany of a *dhikr*. This will not always be the case on the actual day of the celebration of Muḥammad's birthday, but it frequently occurs on other occasions in which the person of Muḥammad is invoked for blessing, such as in marriages. The performance of the *mawlid* poetry becomes the task of entertainers hired for the purpose. The poetry is not limited to praise of Muḥammad, but that theme always "brackets the proceedings" (Waugh 1989: 100).

Reactions against the *mawlid*

The entire celebration of the *mawlid*, whether connected to Muḥammad or to specific Ṣūfī saints (the latter celebration often referred to by a variety of names), frequently raised the ire of those Muslims who wished to purify Islam of all elements that could not be explicitly supported by the regulations of the Qurʾān or the practice of Muḥammad.

However, the power of Sufism, both in its institutionalized form and in the way that its general influence has been felt in Islam as a whole, was such that that Ṣūfī brotherhoods and their associated practices remained a vital part of the religious environment and have done so down until today. The desire for an emotional aspect to religious life, in combination with the appeal of images which glorify Muḥammad and, indeed, the divine, has a substantial place in Islam and this is frequently provided by the Ṣūfī tradition. Grouped around a spiritual leader and following certain practices designed to stimulate the experience of God, Ṣūfī brotherhoods flourished throughout the Muslim world, even if they were not always condoned by governments or establishment religious forces.

Paper as a legal issue

While Islamic law during the late medieval period is often portrayed, especially by nineteenth-century modernist Muslims, as an unchanging entity that was preventing Muslim society from developing, the law had, in fact, always been able to adjust to the new challenges that arose. The notion that the law was fixed once and for all time is simply false. The process that the law went through in medieval times to accommodate developments can be illustrated with all sorts of examples: tobacco, narcotics, and coffee all posed particular challenges that were addressed, not without controversy certainly, but eventually the matters were resolved.

One area of challenging examples is to be seen in the introduction of European technological innovations, such as public clocks, mechanized printing, and paper. Paper itself was not an issue: paper had been known and produced in the Islamic world, likely from as early as the eighth century, and was introduced to Europe from there early in the twelfth century. At that time in Europe, official deeds were written on paper imported from al-Andalus and elsewhere in the Muslim world. By the fourteenth century, however, Europeans had created a substantial paper industry and started exporting their product around the Mediterranean. While a paper industry remained viable in places in the Middle East such as Iraq, the limited markets in other places meant that European paper came to dominate and what local manufacturing industry there had been soon disappeared.

The legal question that arose related to European paper was thus a response to the local domination of a non-Muslim product and not the actual product itself. The Christians who made this paper were, after all, pork-eaters and wine-drinkers, and it was felt that it was possible that their wet and impure hands would contaminate the paper during its manufacture. As well, this European paper often had watermarks that were Christian in character: the Paschal lamb, an angel, crusader shields, and the Latin or Greek cross were all known to be there, lurking under the surface, able to be seen with a strong light. How could such paper be used by a believing Muslim at all, let alone employed to write a copy of the text of the Qur'ān, for example?

In the fifteenth century, the jurist Ibn Marzūq (1364–1438) of Tlemcen, Algeria, was asked for a ruling on the legality of the use of foreign paper. This was a question that, obviously enough, had not been dealt with in the Qur'ān or the *sunna*, and so a decision needed to be made on the basis of analogy. The task was to determine the practical benefits versus the religious costs. Ibn Marzūq saw parallels in the instance of clothes being bought from Christians and he noted that they were not deemed inherently impure; Muḥammad himself had taken tribute from Christians in the form of clothing. He also considered Christian books, written on parchment, which, according to historical records, were taken as booty in battles and then washed of their ink and reused (as was common practice with any parchment text). No problems had previously been seen to emerge in these cases. He also spoke of the phenomenon of churches being converted into mosques, which similarly was deemed unproblematic. He therefore argued that writing an Islamic text on Christian paper transformed the religious character of the paper itself, meaning whatever concerns there might be about the paper, especially regarding the watermarks, could be put aside—the Muslim writing would destroy the integrity of the image of the Christian idolatrous symbols. Ultimately, he argued on the basis of *maṣlaḥa* ("public interest") that the benefits of using the paper were greater than any possible danger of impurities that might be present. There being no local industry to make paper meant that Muslims were, in fact, dependent upon European paper.

For a full treatment of Ibn Marzūq's legal reasoning, see Leor Halevi, "Christian Impurity versus Economic Necessity: A Fifteenth-Century Fatwa on European Paper," *Speculum*, 83 (2008): 917–45. For paper in general, see the exemplary study in Jonathan Bloom, *Paper before Print: The History and Impact of Paper on the Islamic World*, New Haven, CT: Yale University Press, 2001.

Suggested further reading

Jonathan Berkey, *The Transmission of Knowledge: A Social History of Islamic Education*, Princeton: Princeton University Press, 1992.

— *Popular Preaching and Religious Authority in the Medieval Islamic Near East*, Seattle: University of Washington Press, 2001.

Farhad Daftary (ed.), *Intellectual Traditions in Islam*, London: I. B. Tauris, 2000.

Nikki R. Keddie (ed.), *Scholars, Saints and Sufis: Muslim Religious Institutions in the Middle East since 1500*, Berkeley: University of California Press, 1972.

Nehemia Levtzion and John O. Voll (eds.), *Eighteenth-Century Renewal and Reform in Islam*, Syracuse: Syracuse University Press, 1987.

PART V Modern visions of Islam

Significant dates

632	death of Muḥammad
1798	Napoleon lands in Egypt
1897	death of reformer al-Afghānī
1898	death of reformer Sayyid Aḥmad Khān
1905	death of Modernist Muḥammad ʿAbduh
1935	death of Modernist Rashīd Riḍā
1938	death of Modernist Muḥammad Iqbāl
	death of the founder of Republican Turkey, Atatürk
1956	death of the writer Muḥammad Ḥusayn Haykal
1966	death of Islamist Sayyid Quṭb
1979	death of Islamist Mawdūdī
1985	death of Modernist Ghulām Aḥmad Parvēz
1988	death of scholar Fazlur Rahman
2006	death of the writer Najīb Maḥfūẓ
2010	death of scholar Naṣr Abū Zayd
	death of scholar Mohammed Arkoun

12 *Describing modernity*

> In 1798 Napoleon landed in Egypt, ostensibly to protect French merchants there from local misrule, but more especially as a base of operations against the British in India. The Egyptian Mamluk troops were helpless against him, having maintained even less than other Ottoman troops an awareness of modern military developments. The population generally was likewise relatively parochial in outlook. The French set up as much as they could of the apparatus of the Enlightenment on Egyptian soil: modern hospitals, impersonal administration, scientific laboratories (they set about, among other things, recording in scientific detail the non-technologically based ways still prevailing, which were presumed about to vanish before modern French civilization); they invited the astonished local savants to inspect the show and acknowledge the moral superiority of the Revolution—claimed to be true Islam.
>
> (Hodgson 1974: 216)

With the French occupation of Egypt, the Middle East (and other parts of the world, of course) was confronted directly by a technologically advanced and expansionist Europe. The impact on Muslims has been both substantial and significant, especially as they debate whether or not Islam itself can or should change, and how it should change if it should, to meet the current challenges and remain relevant to the lives of individuals.

Studying modern Islam

It is hazardous to make generalized judgments about an entity as manifold as modern Islam from Indonesia to Morocco, in times so turbulent; whatever is said must be suitably modest and tentative. It is especially dangerous, although many observers often seem to miss the point, to view the entire world as revolving around developments in Europe, as if the rest of the world had no significant existence prior to and independent of Europeans or has been irrelevant to the creation of what modern Europe is now. It is an important corrective to keep in mind that the transformation of European society over the last five centuries is not the culmination of a straight line from ancient Greece and Rome to modern France and Germany, but the result of the interplay of general human history.

Certainly, a major transformation of European society did take place between the late 1500s and the late 1700s. It is highlighted by two significant changes: the industrial revolution ushering in the technological age, and the French revolution, which altered basic social values. This transformation not only affected Europe, where it initially took place, but the rest of the world as well, especially through the rise of European colonial expansion. However, one should not think that everything which has happened in the Muslim world and elsewhere during this period is simply a response to those changes on the "outside"; the Muslim world continues on its own path of organic growth and change which interacts with the rest of the world. Change is very much a two-way street.

One area which proves a great stumbling block in the study of modern Islam is the implicit (and even on occasion explicit) moral valuation of progress as it has manifested itself in the West through the transformations of the technological age. Countries which have benefited most from progress are seen to be "more advanced" or "better" than those which have not. However, while various useful changes in human life have come about, not all of them may be championed as necessarily good. Certainly some of them may well be thought of in this mode—modern medical advances and the eradication of smallpox, for example—but a facile judgment of the state of modern progress in one society versus another does not satisfy the demands of careful scholarship, nor the understanding of human societies in their multiplicity.

The terms "traditional" and "modern" are a part of this value-laden system in common parlance, where traditional stands for the irrational, non-scientific world view, and modern for everything which opposes that. But it is possible to use these terms meaningfully, if carefully done. Traditional refers to taking the attitude that one is doing things in the way in which they have always been done, that is, looking to the past for authority on a given matter. Modern then becomes identified with the technological age, not necessarily more rational than the traditional way, but with a different view of the past, the authority of which has been displaced. The trouble is that the division is not as clear as such a definitional stance wishes to pretend. There is a tendency to assume a process of evolution from traditional to modern, but, in fact, the situation is far more fluid. The traditional world deals with change by rejecting or subtly altering its inherited conceptions (and thus the traditional world most assuredly does change), while the modern world never frees itself totally from the authority of the past. The modern aspects of a society are generally seen as following along hand in hand with its traditional ones. In sum, one might say that the terms are, at best, generalizations and that they do not reflect the realities of life as it is lived but are intellectual abstractions which can, if used reflectively, aid understanding. "Modern" refers to the embracing of the technological aspects of contemporary society, that being understood in the broadest manner; "traditional" does not mean the rejection of the modern but the continuation in certain aspects of life in a mode authorized by the past, notably in areas of life where other people have changed to a modern view.

The methodological dilemma is somewhat further confused by the fact that many nineteenth- and twentieth-century Muslim spokesmen (and there have been, until more recent times, very few spokeswomen) adopted the chauvinistic European mode of understanding the world: that the highlight of world existence is, in fact, in the West, that the rest of the world had to evolve and progress to that level, and that the Islamic world had been unchanging since the rise of the Mongols in the twelfth century. Time and again in reading Muslim sources this kind of apologetic, which accepts the European perspective on the question, is encountered. So, methodologically, we become even further tangled. We wish to understand contemporary Muslim world views and to do so we must recognize the cultural biases with which we approach the subject. Yet those biases are precisely what much of the material is interacting with, responding to, and even adopting. And that is, in fact, what we are interested in: how modern Muslims have constructed their world views.

The phenomenon of modernity

> The real challenge that the Muslim society has had to face and is still facing is at the level of social institutions and social ethic as such. And the real nature of this crisis is not the fact that the Muslim social institutions in the past have been wrong or irrational but the fact that there has been a social system at all which now needs to be modified and adjusted. This social system has, in fact, been perfectly rational in the past, i.e., it has been working perfectly well, as perfectly well as any other social system. The disadvantage of the Muslim society at the present juncture is that whereas in the early centuries of development of social institutions in Islam, Islam started from a clean slate, as it were, and had to carve out *ab initio* a social fabric—an activity of which the product was the medieval social system—now, when Muslims have to face a situation of fundamental rethinking and reconstruction, their acute problem is precisely to determine how far to render the slate clean again and on what principles and by what methods, in order to create a new set of institutions.
>
> (Rahman 1979b: 214)

While Fazlur Rahman, the author of the above passage, is enunciating a particular position within the Modernist Muslim debate, he strikes a central point common to all who try to contemplate the relevance of Islam today by speaking of a modern situation of "fundamental rethinking and reconstruction" in which Islam now finds itself. But, before tackling the proposed answers to that question, something more basic must first be approached: why and how has this situation of "fundamental rethinking and reconstruction" arisen? What are the characteristics of the modern age which have created this situation? Why has Islam had to face them? And why does facing them seem to be such a problem?

The characteristics of the "modern era"

There are many ways of analyzing the idea called "modernity." At its simplest level, it might be said that modernity is that which renders the past problematic. Notably (and this is what makes this definition so significant), once tradition—the past—has been questioned and examined, there is no going back. The ideas of the past (for example in terms of historical facts) can never have the same weight again, even if the challenge of modernity is ultimately rejected.

Modernity is that which has created fundamental changes in behavior and belief about economics, politics, social organization, and intellectual discourse. Once again, it is important to keep in mind that changes have happened throughout the world; this is not just a matter of Western influences on the rest of the world. Modernity must be seen as a world phenomenon.

In the economic sphere, change is seen in terms of industrialization and consequent economic growth, the formation of large capital sums, the growth of science and the emergence of new classes of people and social mobility. In the political arena, it is the growth of political parties (and the belief in the moral evolution resulting from that growth), unions, and youth groups. In the social dimension, the change in relations between the sexes (with its economic implications), mass communications, urbanization, travel, and generally increased mobility are especially marked. In the intellectual realm, the prominence of the idea of progress, the emergence of secular-rational norms, and the rise of historical studies all make the phenomenon of change so apparent. All of this has brought with it or brought about as a consequence a change in the historical reality in which we live.

The five pillars of modernity

Many attempts have been made to try to define more closely the characteristics of the modern period in order to say just how it is different from past eras. "Toward a Critique of Modernity" by Peter Berger has become a classic statement of such a definition. He speaks of five "dilemmas of modernity":

1 Abstraction (in the way life confronts bureaucracy and technology especially).
2 Futurity (the future as the primary orientation for activity and the imagination, and life governed by the clock).
3 Individuation (the separation of the individual from any sense of a collective entity, thus producing alienation).

4 Liberation (life viewed as dominated by choice and not fate; "things could be other than what they have been").
5 Secularization (the massive threat to the plausibility of religious belief).

(Berger 1977: 70–80)

Harvey Cox has modified these into a slightly more positive form and speaks of the aptly named (for this context) "five pillars of modernity." The modern period is said to be characterized by the following aspects:

1 The emergence of sovereign national states as legally defined entities in a global political system, most of which emerged in their present form at most 200 years ago.
2 Science-based technology as a principal source of images for life and its possibilities.
3 Bureaucratic rationalism as a way of organizing and administering human thought and activity, where institutions take on their own intellectual life producing people who feel alienated, powerless and apathetic ("I only work here").
4 The quest for profit maximization as a means to motivate work and distribute goods and services (thus both within capitalism and socialism) as manifested in, for example, the capitalist mode of production and marketing.
5 Secularization and trivialization of religion and the use of the spiritual for profane purposes manifested in the removal of religion's concern with politics and economics.

(Cox 1984: 183)

Secularization needs further comment, given the context of our investigation. This concept may be defined as the process of emancipation of certain areas of social, cultural, and political life from the dominance or control of traditional religious ideas; it has been both a contributing factor in modernization and a result of it. The terms used to describe the modern era—enlightened, secular, rational, disenchanted (i.e. the loss of magic), scientific, post-traditional—all indicate the tendency of secularization.

In fact, the attitudes towards religion are central elements of what many people identify as modern, at least in popular parlance. For example, the demolition of the truth of the Bible, the rejection of the divinity of Jesus, and the doubts expressed about the value of much that has been taught for generations are all the most obvious elements within Christianity. But these are negative elements, matters which have created fear and terror along with an almost perverse attraction to this modern age. Speaking positively of the modern age as coinciding with the emergence of the philosophical principle of the self as the judge on matters of truth and validity, Descartes's "I think therefore I am" remains the only basic certain truth as opposed to traditional religious values and their claims to eternal validity.

Some observers have noted that this tendency towards secularization especially, but the other aspects of modernity also, happened in Europe initially but has become of crucial significance for the rest of the world. Therefore, European religion (Christianity) has had to respond to this situation from the beginning of the age of industrialization and the ways in which it has done so have become paradigmatic (at least to some extent) for other religions. To a degree, this would appear to be intrinsically true, but it is also a position urged by some writers: that Muslims should learn from the Christian experience and be prepared to relinquish certain aspects of their traditional faith while maintaining others. This kind of writing about Islam especially has received a great deal of criticism recently but continues nevertheless.

Other people, perhaps with a greater political (rather than religious) orientation towards life, have isolated another series of adjectives which characterize the modern period: colonial, imperialist, missionary, Western invasion. There can be no doubt that isolating such elements is important in understanding the perceptions of the modern period in the Muslim world. However, this view tends to see the modern world in terms of confrontation between the West and the Islamic world; other people may wish to subsume these elements under broader categories, however, such as the worldwide emergence of nation states. Still, the reality of this perception cannot be underplayed.

Characteristics of the modern era in the Muslim world

How has modernity made its impact on the Muslim world? The sense of the tension created in the modern context is one of the first things which strikes many travelers and may be seen in many films and other media portrayals: the absurd and distressing confrontation between modern and ancient ways of life. Donkeys still vie for a place on the road as decrepit cars and trucks, amid the Mercedes, whiz by; the importation of the McDonald's–Coca-Cola global consumer culture exists in the face of vast wealth and abject poverty, creating tensions and raising expectations that cannot be met. This becomes a powerful conservative argument against the West, for appealing to Western values and aspirations is seen to be the cause of contemporary frustrations. Yet the Muslim world has, in certain ways, adapted to the modern world through the use of its ancient resources; these have proven a source of strength as well as a source of tension. The utilization and re-utilization of modern materials—the implicit rejection of the throwaway society and the planned obsolescence of the West—are frequently startling and encouraging to the observer accustomed to North American-style consumerism.

The impact of modernity on the Islamic world has been felt in a vast number of ways. Some can easily be isolated: the cycle of ascendancy and decline through which the Islamic world feels itself to have been historically, the impact of the nationalist and socialist challenge, the impact of Zionism and the creation of Israel, and the impact of oil revenues, among many others.

Figure 12.1 Symbols of nationalism, globalization, and religious heritage combine in Turkey. Source: Time & Life Pictures/Getty Images.

Ascendancy and decline

A recognition of the impotence of the Islamic world in the face of the newly emerged power of Europe along with a shared memory of a powerful past has produced a great deal of soul searching and analysis. What are the reasons for this decline into subjugation and exploitation? The answers have frequently been religious, a response fostered and encouraged by negative post-Enlightenment attitudes towards religion in general and towards Islam in particular.

Haunting all of the discussions within the Muslim world is the notion of the failure of Islam. Has Islam somehow fallen by the wayside, become unable to cope with the emerging world and the contemporary human situation? This, of course, is a shattering thought for any religion, but it is especially so for Islam because the idea of success in the world has been central to Islamic ideology from the very early period of Islam. Acting as a paradigm for later Islamic thinking, Muḥammad is pictured as moving from Mecca to Medina (the *hijra*) in the midst of his preaching career in order to be successful. Islam would not have been revealed to the world, as God's last statement, if it were not divinely preordained to succeed. God's word cannot be frustrated by human obstinacy. Islamic history and the golden age of Islam, in the same time period as the dark ages of Europe, only reinforce the notion of the success of the religion in further, very tangible terms. The rise of Europe as a colonialist power, therefore, shattered a deeply held Muslim idea—even, it might be said, one of the basic presuppositions of Islamic existence. A crisis of identity faced those who did not get carried away on the Western bandwagon and who wished to investigate the roots of the problem. The modern situation was perceived to be one of fundamental challenge to Islam, therefore; the failure to be able to respond would be the failure of Islam as a religion. What, then, is the status of Islam when it is not in political ascendancy in the world?

The answers to this problem have been varied: the extent to which Islam itself might be seen as the cause of the gradual decline of its civilization is, in part, the subject in debate. Is it Islam itself which needs modification in the modern world or is it Muslims who have not lived up to the demands of Islam and consequently the civilization has declined? This question arises most frequently in discussions over science and technology. The failure to embrace modern science (which, it is often proudly proclaimed, stems from Muslim medieval advances) along with the scientific mentality as embodied in the Western educational system was the cause of Islam's decline according to some. Others, however, would say that it is faith in God which is more crucial than the technology itself and thus they reject this entire argument.

Some have pointed to the irony present in this Muslim self-conception when they note the reality that "Islam today is a monumental success story, its popularity reflected in overflowing mosques from Panama to Peking" (Murad 2003: 7). The so-called crisis of Islam is, in this view, an external perception dependent upon the impact which some elements of Islam have had on the non-Muslim world and has nothing to do with the values of Islam itself. Judging Islam on the initial basis of its worldly success is a mistake, it would be claimed. This response, however, is a part of a Modernist platform which separates out Islam as a faith from Islam as a civilization, precisely in order to grapple with this factor of ascendancy and decline. Be that as it may, the contemporary success of Islam in terms of the willingness of individuals to adopt the religion, complete with its external symbols and values, is certainly of note for considering the role Islamic identity plays as a source of resistance to an assumed ascendancy of a global modernity.

Nationalism and socialism

Modern political ideologies have been seen by some as a way out of the present dilemma of decline but also as attractive modern options in and by themselves. Especially in the twentieth century, socialism attracted attention both as an alternative to Islam and as a way to construct an entirely new society. But it was also seen as the true embodiment of Islamic principles, especially in aspects of equality and social justice, and as anti-Western capitalism. In this view, Muḥammad established socialist principles in his state, which means that such a structure of society should take precedence over capitalism. After the period of occupation by European nations, democracy as a system of government, in the argument of many people, has lost its glamour and its moral claim to supremacy. Yet the civic virtues of Europe still held their appeal for many. The impact of more recent developments—the collapse of the colonial empires—has resulted in further confusion in the overall picture. The emergence of new political states, areas which formerly had little unified identity in many cases, has fostered the new phenomenon of nationalism in ethnic and/or cultural terms, which often does not include Islam, at least not as that religion has been classically portrayed. Contemporary discussions in Egypt which seek to find a way to unite Christian Copts and Islamist tendencies under the banner of the state of Egypt—a vision facilitated by an enhancement of the shared heritage of Pharaonic times—is just one manifestation of that. There continue to be significant changes in, and pressures on, traditional, pre-modern loyalty patterns brought about by nationalism.

Zionism and the establishment of Israel

Zionism has led to a strengthening of Islamic identity according to many observers, although most would also comment that, even so, no united front has appeared among the Islamic nations, especially the Arabs. The sense that the existence of Israel represents the absolute trough of the decline of Muslim civilization is felt by many. Whether Israel is perceived as a punishment for Muslim errors in the past or as a part of a continued Western presence in the Middle East, the insult that the nation represents to the Muslim world cannot be underestimated. Some people have argued that Israel's success as a nation—economically, politically—is evidence of the need to adopt Western ways. But, for the most part, many feel that Israel represents further evidence of the sinful ways of Muslims and the need for a purification of Islam. The 1967 war between Israel and the Arab world deeply affected the collective psyche of the Muslim people in the wake of the defeat of the Arab troops. The rise of fundamentalist movements, a renewed interest in the symbolic role of Jerusalem, and a host of other factors are frequently attributed to this war. Today, the sense in which the Israelis are regarded as an outpost of

Euro-American civilization (often viewed as a tool of American foreign policy) in the vanguard of the attack upon Islam continues to be strong throughout the Islamic world.

Oil

Oil revenues have produced an ambivalence similar to that caused by the existence of Israel: they are either a curse or a blessing, according to the perspective taken. The impact of the vast revenues has been to take Muslims away from Islam, to the point that Saudi Arabia is frequently pictured as the most corrupt and un-Islamic nation in the world, a land of wine-drinking multimillionaires who repress the less fortunate citizens of their own country and do nothing to enhance Islam. The Iraqi invasion of Kuwait and the various justifications which emerged for it, especially as revealed in statements from Muslims outside the Arab countries, echo this sentiment to a great extent. The opposite argument, that oil revenues now put the population of the Muslim world in a position of affecting the world, giving them the possibility of standing up for their own rights and permitting the propagation of Islam within the context of the modern world, is also frequently made: oil revenues are a gift from God to allow the Muslim world to function in the modern context. The impact of oil is, of course, only a part of the whole discussion of the modern industrial-technological civilization and its impact upon the economic and social life of individuals in society.

Beyond this ambivalence stands another factor related to the increased wealth of the oil-producing countries which looms large in many contemporary discussions. Increasing attention is paid, especially by more radical Islamic groups, to the autocratic nature of the regimes who rule in many of these countries. It is the wealth from oil which keeps such regimes in power because they are able to make a considerable financial commitment to maintaining their own position through amassing armed forces and the like. The context of the worldwide dependency on oil also brings international alliances into play in the support of such regimes. It is in the strategic interests of many countries to maintain the political stability of the oil-producing countries in order to ensure a continuing flow of oil. The fear of the unknown consequences of a move to a democratic system of government, for example, leads to the pragmatic support of autocracies by the international community. It is the United States, of course, that has been particularly isolated as being responsible for this state of affairs, as its involvement in world affairs becomes more widely known. This manifests itself in a strong anti-American rhetoric among many Muslim groups who cite the attempts of the United States to manipulate the internal politics of some Muslim countries (notably Iran, Iraq, Afghanistan, and Saudi Arabia) to its own financial and political advantage. The United States is often seen to be a major inhibitor to the growth of democracy in the Muslim world because, it is suggested, the outcome would have the potential to constrict American economic growth. This has sometimes been phrased in more recent times as the hypocrisy of the United States, and that charge takes on a moral tone when the criticism is made that democracy is spoken of as an essential value but, through the actions of the United States, democracy is not encouraged or is even thwarted. Furthermore, the critique of the United States extends further into questioning the honesty of all the values with which the United States has been associated, not only democracy but pluralism, secularism, and peace as well. The portrayal of the United States as a country ruled by evangelical Christians whose mystique of violence and victory guides their every move accentuates the extent to which attempts to control political regimes within the Muslim world are seen as an overwhelming conspiracy against the interests of Islam in general. Even when the rhetoric reaches this level, it must be remembered that underlying all of this is the basic point about the global economy based in oil and its impact on Islam; linking this to a general critique of the foreign policy of the United States characterizes the contemporary discussion.

Other factors

In presenting the situation of the modern Islamic world, Emmanuel Sivan (1985: 11) speaks of television (now arriving through satellite) as the most obvious and blatant symbol of the contemporary invasion and the most effective tool in modernity's propagation, certainly among the broadest segment of the population, for whom the twenty-first century's dominance of the internet is only a theoretical point. Loose morality, instant gratification, life as centered in love and pleasure while oblivious to religious beliefs are all a part of the Hollywood image which is bringing the Islamic world into the global village. Other points may be raised. Education makes no attempt to relate the modern scientific world to Islam, the modern family is reinforced over the traditional structure, and nationalism and the nation state are more firmly established than the concept of the Islamic community. Of course, this analysis of society and its ills is by no means unique to Islam. With their own cultural forms and their own socio-cultural assumptions, these same sentiments are echoed by certain segments of the population throughout the world. Clifford Geertz has said:

> [In face of the modern world, people] lose their sensibility. Or they channel it into ideological fervor. Or they adopt an imported creed. Or they turn worriedly in upon themselves. Or they cling even more intensely to the faltering traditions. Or they try to rework those traditions into more effective forms. Or they split themselves in half, living spiritually in the past and physically in the present. Or they try to express their religiousness in secular activities. And a few simply fail to notice their world is moving or, noticing, just collapse.
>
> (Geertz 1968: 3)

The role of Islam in the modern world

A basic point needs to be made in understanding the various discussions which relate to the role Islam should or could (or should not and could not) play in the modern world. Religion, and Islam specifically, is classically thought of as the element which provides the grounding for an individual's life, the interpretative core through which life's experiences may be understood. But the past-oriented nature of religion as it acts to preserve that grounding has meant that its role in the contemporary period has been problematic. The issue then revolves around the form Islam should present to the world in order to take its place in modern society.

As has already been suggested, much of the character of the modern period could be termed the impact of secularism upon a traditional religious system; in that way, the threat to Islam is the same as that posed to Judaism and Christianity. Whether Islam is viable in the modern world is the question, especially since Islam has classically been conceived (if not always manifested in history this way) as a politicized religion. The reality of the matter is that, in the modern context, politicization is even further distant than it was in medieval times for the majority of Muslims. In those ancient times, at least the presence of the caliph as a religio-political authority figure was maintained, even if that person was, during many periods, powerless in front of the military rulers and the independent scholarly elite. The office of the caliphate was officially eliminated with the rise of Republican Turkey in 1924. The perception of some Muslims in the modern period is that secularization is thus attacking the heart of the theoretical basis of Islam.

Islam is the civilizational basis of the Muslim world in politics, in society, and in life. In modern terminology, it provides the linguistic basis by which life is experienced, delimits how things are to be perceived, and sets the limits to discourse. Can Islam continue with this role in the modern world? Should it even try to? These are the fundamental questions which some Muslims have chosen to face, and continue to face. It is the nature of religion in and by itself which has rendered the questions so difficult.

Some would say that it is the traditional nature of religion as it is manifested in its attitude to authority, based upon a notion of sacredness, and which sees authority as stemming from the past in a continuous flow up to the present, that jars so much with the modern ethos. A value is placed on the past because it supports the authority of the religion as it exists today. But modernity involves rapid and multifaceted change. Religions have always had to face changing circumstances and they have developed a number of mechanisms by which this is handled. New ideas, whether emergent, borrowed, or acquired, are legitimated in a number of paradigmatic ways: change is seen as a legitimate unfolding of the past; new ideas are proven to have been present always; new ideas are proven to have legitimacy by saying that they should have been present but the faithful have ignored/suppressed them so that a more legitimate continuity with tradition is discovered through change; or new ideas are accepted through a cultural revolution, the most radical of all strategies.

Under the impact of the rapid change which the modern world has inflicted, many Muslims have experienced a severe weakening of the traditional conception of the eternal, unchanging Muslim legal code, the *sharīʿa*. At the same time, it is within the *sharīʿa* that various strategies have been employed in order to try to face the challenge of change. The Muslim law had been firmly established by the great jurists of the past. Within the traditional framework, there is room for interpretation and modification, but there cannot be a questioning of the nature and the basis of the authority and the relevance of the law. How to assess the law today, then, in light of the characteristics of modernity, has proven to be a challenge, to say the least. This is especially a problem because of the range of topics covered by the *sharīʿa*: while matters such as politics and taxation remained only theoretically under the guidance of the religious code in medieval Islam, areas of personal law—marriage, divorce, inheritance—remained the stronghold of religion. It is, however, precisely in many of those areas that the contemporary world has effected a great deal of change and where the pressures, especially of nineteenth-century European values, have been felt the most. Equally problematic has been the fact that during the nineteenth century (if not earlier) most Islamic states either adopted or had imposed upon them European law codes which simply displaced the traditional *sharīʿa*. This process provided a means by which to introduce reforms, for example in areas of women's and family rights, but the result has been that those who wished to see religion continue to play a significant role in their societies had to either demonstrate that their religion, in fact, supported the reforms (and this became the position of those commonly termed the Modernists) or demand that the secular law codes be repealed and simply replaced by Islamic ones (a stance characteristic of more conservative elements).

The response of modern Muslims to this situation has been of every conceivable type. For some, the solution to the question of the role of Islam today is found in Islamic "totalism": that Islam should govern every part of life, from politics to personal conduct to scientific investigation. At the other end of the spectrum, some have argued that the former Muslim ideal of a religio-political mix is the main stumbling block to the modernization of Islam, itself a desirable aim; religion should be a personal, interior matter, an issue between the believer and God, and only in that way will Islam remain a vital force in today's world. In between these two responses remain a variety of compromise solutions and non-solutions which do not foster an integrated way of being for the individual. How choices are to be made—such that some Muslims emphasize the wearing of the head scarf (*ḥijāb*) or assert the permissibility of marrying four wives but do not deem slavery to be an acceptable practice despite clear Quranic provisions for the practice, for example—remains the biggest challenge that individuals face and the greatest threat to the unity of the community.

The post-modern phenomenon

For those on the outside, however, some of the Muslim discussions of this confrontation with the modern period often seem rather quaint. The arguments often seem to revolve around the relevance or danger of Darwin, Marx, and Freud, as if those figures represent the state of Western thinking. There is little evidence of the impact in the Muslim world as a whole of what is called in some circles post-modernism. Certainly, radical Marxism is present and that may be viewed as a reaction within the post-modern framework; it is one, however, that calls for a total rejection of Islam and thus it can hardly be termed an Islamic post-modern ideology. The post-modern questioning of the basic presuppositions of religion within a religious framework—the structures of authority, its orientation to the past, its fixation on success—is extremely limited.

Furthermore, to some people the descriptions given above of what characterizes the modern world are woefully inadequate. The world has already entered a new period of challenge, it may be suggested. Mass communications have made the existence of independent states anachronistic; a world community is emerging, but its character is extremely unclear. Recognition has come about of the limits to progress in science and the impact that faith in science has had on the world; the perception of an ecological crisis is a large part of this. The recognition of the threat of technology has raised questions of whether just because something can be done it should be done. Despite earlier optimism, technology has not managed to solve the basic problems of the world such as starvation, certainly not without raising its own new set of issues related to genetic engineering. Faith in the moral evolution of humanity (especially the trust in democracy) was destroyed in the furnaces of Auschwitz; the reality of continuing racism and of the potential for evil that lurks in humanity is felt. The impact of the industrialization of the world in terms of unemployment, pollution, poor distribution of goods, and the merging of cultures has been recognized. Feminism and the assertiveness of less-developed countries (with a view to directing their own future through their own value systems) have both accompanied and perhaps been precipitated by post-modernism. These issues are manifested in general terms by the post-modern realization of the powerlessness of the individual to effect change on what have become living institutions. To paraphrase the words of Harvey Cox (1984: 186–7), if the problem of Modernism is termed "We cannot pray," the problem of post-modernism is "We cannot (and others cannot) eat." Post-modernism entails confrontation with the social issues of the day, here conceived within a religious framework: feminism, peace and war, minority expressions of theology, political stances, economics, and so forth.

Whether the post-modern situation is taken seriously is one of the differentiating factors in trends in modern thought in general. Fundamentalism tends not to confront the reality of the situation; it proposes in its crasser forms, for example, that homeless people are those who simply choose to live that way. The emergence of critical theology in Christian and Jewish circles is marked by a willingness to confront the post-modern condition with compassion and thoughtfulness.

To the extent that Muslim post-modernism does exist, its greatest manifestation is to be found outside the cultural sphere of the Muslim countries themselves. The future may offer a different situation, in some people's estimation, with the rise of women's movements and the potential inversion of power structures which could result within the Muslim world. It is worthy of note now, however, that even here the positions brought forth seem limited: we do not see many women enunciating a new *sharīʿa* that displaces the male prerogative, nor many who work on a theology based upon a female (or all-inclusive, gender-neutral) language, for example.

Classification of Muslim approaches to modernity

The main issues for Islam in the contemporary situation relate to the place of religion in public life—social, economic, legal, political, intellectual. It is precisely those dimensions which are crucial to a definition of modernity and which thus create the problems to be faced. The dimensions of the phenomenon of modernity focus on the changes which have taken place in all these aspects of public life. That the focus of the conflict is found in this sphere is confirmed by the complementary principle that, to an almost complete extent, there has been no calling into question of Islam itself as a private need or mode of personal devotion, nor have there been many major attempts at a theological reformulation of the faith in light of the modern world. Therefore, studying the reactions of Muslims to modernity is primarily a matter of addressing the question of what specific place the religion is to have in modern life rather than questioning the existence of the religion as such. Can answers to the dilemmas and problems of modern life be found in the religion? If so, how? Can religion at least provide a way to cope?

A tri-part division of religious ways of interacting with the modern age is suggested by many analyses: Traditionalist (sometimes termed Normative or Orthodox); Islamist (sometimes termed Fundamentalist, Neo-Normativist, or Revivalist); and Modernist (sometimes termed Acculturating or Modernizing). A simple, although controversial, example can serve to illustrate how this sort of division works in the case of Islam: polygamy.

The Traditionalist group may be characterized by their acceptance of multiple-wife marriages, suggesting that to think otherwise is to accept Western standards; Islamic tradition has allowed polygamy and that is the way things should be.

The Modernist group would suggest a position based on the premise that men and women are equal and monogamy is morally good because it aims towards a concept of social welfare, while polygamy has potentially negative effects on family life; it is often argued that the Qurʾān supports this position.

The Islamist group will start from the Qurʾān and say that the Qurʾān was aiming for monogamy all along but made allowances for ancient habits which no longer have any relevance.

It must be remembered that these three divisions are theoretical categories only; people, in the realities of their life situations, can rarely, if ever, be fitted neatly into one position or the other. The categories are heuristic, helpful to indicate tendencies but rarely sufficient to support a full analysis. Furthermore, such categorizations do not allow for historical change within the categories themselves, as will become clear. Modernists, for example, have a substantially different face today than they did at the start of the twentieth century. While the characterizations of these groups, along with refinements to be added later, will be employed in subsequent parts of this book, they are too schematic and reductive to provide structure for a full analysis. The value of these characterizations lies in their ability to reflect the overall dimensions of discussions in modern Islam and thereby provide some tools for more critical analysis.

The Traditionalist group

Each of the above three main categories may be said to display a different attitude towards the authority of the past. The Traditionalist group holds to the full authority of the past and believes that change should not and does not affect the traditions of the past. Change is to be rejected. Such an expression of the essence of the Traditionalist group is misleading, however: to some extent it falls captive to the group's own rhetoric. Islam, as a cultural entity, has, after all, always been able to cope with change and has built into its structures ways of dealing with change. New situations were ably managed by the institutionalized juridical system. Certainly it is true that the basic sources of Islam—the Qurʾān and the *sunna*—are viewed as unchanging, for they are, in some manner, representations in the world of the unchanging God. But this conception, contrary to some suggestions, did not curtail all reaction to changing circumstances. Rather, the issue for the Traditionalists in the contemporary period has been one of substantial challenge to well-established patterns of life and methods of legitimizing change. The Traditionalist group contains within it many of the learned scholars (*ʿulamāʾ*) who might be thought to have a vested interest in maintaining the *status quo*, many of the mystically oriented Ṣūfī groups, and the vast majority of those who have not been exposed to modern education and thus to a great extent have not experienced the challenge of modernity to such a degree as to consider it a personal problem.

One trend within Traditionalism can be termed "Neo-Traditionalism." This is a tendency which has been seen as a transitional position from Traditionalism to any of the other groups. It may be, however, that as a position it has its own inherent permanent protagonists; such a position (displayed in S. H. Nasr's writings and, perhaps, in the Iranian revolution) urges a gradual change, seeing the advantage in certain elements of modern technology, for example, but wanting to withstand the rush of the acceptance of it all. In the short term urgent change may be required but in the long run Islam will reign supreme.

Islamism and revivalism

The Islamist group, in contrast to the Traditionalists, is characterized by its desire to accept change in a controlled fashion; it therefore uses the authoritative sources of the past to legitimize changes in the present day. This group has a long intellectual history in Islam, or, at least, that is the perception of its adherents. Picking up on the line of thought from Ibn Taymiyya through Ibn ʿAbd al-Wahhāb, these revivalist tendencies emphasize the absolute character of the sources of authority in Islam—the Qurʾān and the *sunna*. This reliance on texts results in what is frequently termed literalism or fundamentalism but, at the same time, it opens up the possibilities for independent reasoning through the rejection of authority by that very process of the return to the texts and the ignoring of traditional interpretation of those texts. Such thinking also tends toward an anti-intellectualism, especially anti-philosophy. This is perhaps one of the key points for differentiating between Modernists and Islamists.

These trends in thought are crucial to the writings of people associated with contemporary expressions of Islamic revivalism led by the Islamists. Abūʾl Aʿlāʾ Mawdūdī (1903–79) is a prime example. His call was for a return to the Qurʾān and a purified *sunna* so that Islam might be revitalized; this could only truly happen if Islam became the constitution of the state and this was the political goal towards which he worked in Pakistan. Sayyid Quṭb (1906—66) of Egypt provides another example. He became the intellectual spokesman for the Muslim Brotherhood. He championed a return to "pure Islam" and a move away from the materialism of the West, which he perceived as contaminating Islam. Allegiance should be to Islam alone, for that provides the perfect social system for all humanity, one which will cure all the ills of the modern world. Once a truly Islamic state is established, all aspects of life will fall into their proper place. Both of these thinkers will be dealt with in later chapters (Mawdūdī in Chapters 13 and 14, Quṭb in Chapter 14).

Revolutionary radical Islamism—that fringe element which dominates the media picture of Islamic fundamentalism—is somewhat distinct in the emphasis it places on the corruption to Islam from within the community. True Islam is the cure and must be applied through armed uprising. Also notable is the tendency to view things as opposing spheres: for example the Government of God versus the Great Satan in Iranian propaganda. Thus, for someone such as Sayyid Quṭb, everything is *jāhilī*, that is, in a state of barbarism, except for true Islam.

The Islamist movement is sometimes called "fundamentalism," although that latter term involves the use of a designation borrowed from early twentieth-century Christianity which some people see as inappropriate. In its application to religious groupings, the word "fundamentalism" arose in the United States and was used by a coalition of theologically conservative Protestants who came together in 1920 to struggle against Modernism and Liberalism; it was coined because these people were said to be holding to the great fundamentals of their faith. For Protestant Fundamentalists, the key fundamental is the inerrancy of the Bible, which is a defense of basic religious ideals—the seriousness of sin, the need for redemption, and the idea that Jesus has granted that redemption. There is a great stress placed on individual salvation and personal morality. Fundamentalists are prepared to do battle for their fundamentals. The best examples are seen in court cases against the teaching of evolution in the 1920s and in the more contemporary Moral Majority movement.

In the Islamic world the term "fundamentalism" has been applied (mainly by Westerners) to those who call for a strict implementation of the *sharīʿa*, including the call for an Islamic state. Opposition to Western ways and to the perceived corruption of Muslim society is important, and even, according to some, the most important element uniting fundamentalists of all religious persuasions.

The issue of scripture marks a difference between Muslim and Christian fundamentalists. Virtually all Muslims are "fundamentalist" in their attitude to scripture. Protestant doctrines, on the other hand, which are seen as intimately linked to inerrancy (for example the resurrection of Jesus) are rejected by all Muslims. Likewise, while Muslim fundamentalists stress political goals and implementation of religion in all areas of life, Christian fundamentalists can go either way and some become secularists by Muslim standards, wanting to keep all aspects of the state separate from their religion.

The oppositional stance of both Christian fundamentalists and Muslim Islamist groups is significant; they both "do battle" with Western Modernism. (Muslims also frequently attack elements within their own societies and desire a total restructuring.) That element of militancy (taken in either a figurative or literal sense) on behalf of God's way in the world unites both groups. The claim to be the authentic expression of the tradition is also prominent; somewhat ironically, then, both groups—Christians and Muslims—emphasize the distinctive elements of their own faith. Both groups wish to take scripture very seriously (if not always literally, although in theory they may be more inclined that way than more Modernist groups). Absolutism in ethics follows from this and both groups emphasize the supernatural, seeing God's will at work in the world in very direct ways.

Islamic Modernism and its history

The Modernist group has seen that greater advantage is to be found within the modern circumstance by embracing change and making religion itself subject to change. The Modernist position is frequently based upon a principle of differentiating basic moral precepts from specific legal prescriptions. This movement, too, has had a substantial history. It developed in the nineteenth century with people such as Jamāl al-Dīn al-Afghānī (1839–97), Muḥammad ʿAbduh (1849–1905) and Rashīd Riḍā (1865–1935) in Egypt, and Sayyid Aḥmad Khān (1817–98) and Muḥammad Iqbāl (1876–1938) in India. Al-Afghānī is famous for his idea of Pan-Islamism, which he saw as a way of reviving and uniting Islam against Europe; this idea was to be combined with an embracing of philosophy and science, which, he argued, transcend particular communities. He greatly influenced ʿAbduh and, through him, Riḍā, who worked further to synthesize those features of the West which seemed desirable (especially its scientific rationality) with the essential truths of Islam. The situation in India was very similar. Aḥmad Khān argued that modern knowledge and the use of reason were what was required in order to bring vitality back to Islam. Essentially, this involved a separation between Islam as a religion of ritual and law, and reason or science, which was not seen to be under the control of religious law although it was in keeping with the true principles of the faith itself. Deep down, the argument went, there was no conflict between Islam and modernity, for they both functioned on different planes. Islamic law is not fixed but must change in each situation, especially in the social realm. Iqbal's message, frequently couched in mystically inspired poetry, urged the same return to the essentials of Islam, to be found in its true sources.

Reconstruction, *iṣlāḥ*, became the catchword for this trend. As a movement it may also be seen to have had a substantial influence on the Islamists as well, with its call to go "back to the sources." But its emphasis on elements of the West as having some value for Islamic culture (as opposed to the self-sufficiency of Islam) and its tendency towards a definition of religion centered on the individual in his/her relationship with God, along with its flexible attitude towards the social aspect of the faith, mark the Modernists as distinct. A number of factors may be isolated as contributing to the rise of the Modernists, which illustrates once again that speaking simply of Modernism as a reaction to Europe does not represent an accurate summary of the issues involved. According to the analysis of Ali Merad (1977: 108–27), the pressures of pre-modernist fundamentalism, the development of the printed word as a result of the introduction of the printing press in Arab countries around 1822, the influence of Western culture, the liberal evolution of the Ottoman regime (for example the introduction of a code of civil liberties in 1839), and the structural renovation of the Eastern Christian churches showing an example of "zeal in the service of a faith," all contributed substantially to stimulating an Arab "renaissance," *nahḍa*, which has become identified with the Modernist trend.

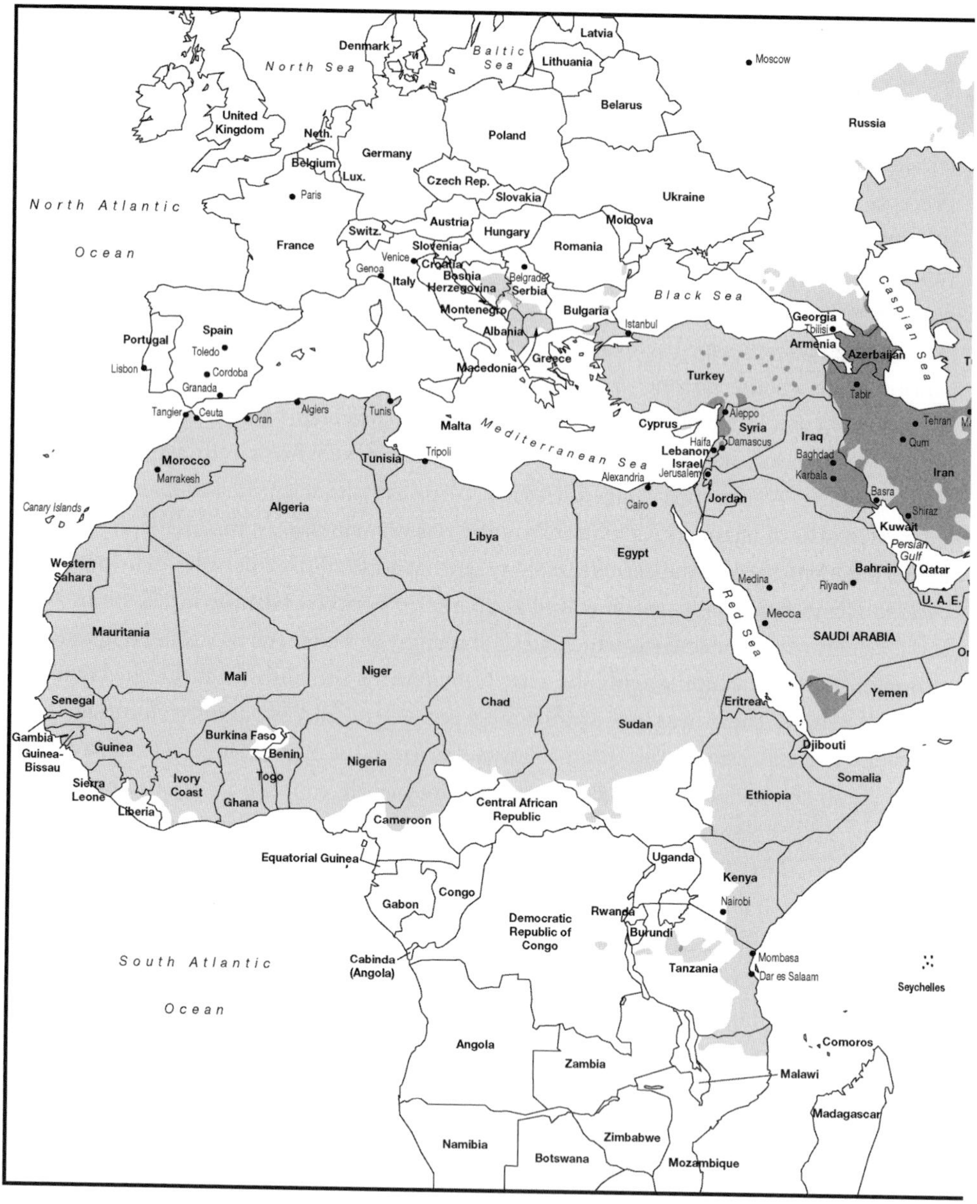

Figure 12.2 Map of the Islamic world in the twenty-first century.

Muslim Distribution
Sunni
Shī'a
Scale 1:40,000,000 at the Equator
Russia
Mongolia
Kazakhstan
Lake Balkhash
Aral Sea
Uzbekistan
Kyrgyzstan
Tashkent
Bukhara
Samarkand
Tajikistan
urkmenistan
Marv
Nisabur
Herat
Kabul
Afghanistan
Indian claim
Chinese line of control
Lahore
New Delhi
Pakistan
Nepal
Bhutan
Bangladesh
Oman
Gulf of Oman
Arabian Sea
India
Bay of Bengal
Andaman Islands (India)
Nicobar Islands (India)
Sri Lanka
Burma
Laos
Thailand
Cambodia
Vietnam
China
Beijing
North Korea
South Korea
Japan
Taiwan
Hong Kong
Pacific Ocean
Philippines
Brunei
Kuala Lumpur
Malaysia
Singapore
Indonesia
Jakarta
Indian Ocean
Australia

Islamic Modernism wants Islam to be the basis for political life as well as the religious, but it perceives a need to reinterpret those structures in light of contemporary needs, frequently with a clear and unapologetic adoption of Western notions. This generally reflects an idea of the flexibility of Islam such that modern ideologies may be seen as fitting in with Islamic ones. Generally, Modernists (such as Fazlur Rahman and Ghulām Aḥmad Parvēz, to be discussed in Chapter 14) argue that the juridical basis of Islam must be put aside for the modern use of independent judgment based on the Qurʾān and (perhaps) the *sunna*. This is a way of limiting the binding nature of the past, thus allowing some flexibility, but note that it does not deny its authority. Rather, the position allows for a radical reinterpretation of the past, enabling principles of the past to be seen in light of modern ideals, such as democracy, freedom, equality, tolerance, and social justice. In fact, these and other ideals become general principles that Islam is seen as standing for, and through which Islam must be implemented in today's world. Other examples are to be seen in the value of work and the redistribution of excess wealth. Matters which do not fit within these ideals are deemed superstitions and must be done away with, for they are not in keeping with Islam. Notable, too, is the frequent Modernist appeal to the Islamic basis of many Western ideas: democracy being found in the early Islamic community; *dhimmī*—non-Muslim subjects living under Muslim rule—being the foundation of religious pluralism; and so forth. This sort of tendency can lead to apologetics where the superiority of Islam over all things Western is argued, a tendency also to be seen, although perhaps less frequently, in Islamism. Modernism, then, differs from secularism by the efforts it makes to find support in the Qurʾān and the *sunna*; from the critic's point of view, this method is only "a cover for what secularists do more openly" (Shepard 1987: 313).

In looking at these three main divisions, Traditionalism, Islamism, and Modernism, another factor differentiates or becomes crucial in the definition: the attitude toward what is termed "Islamic totalism." To what extent is Islam seen as encompassing all of life in its social, political, and economic spheres? To what extent is Islam seen as a guide to social action and public legislation? The extent of this can range from Islam governing the full social structure to Islam being a "religion" in a Protestant sense, that is, as a matter for the individual and his/her conscience alone. Here, too, for Islamists, as we shall see, it is possible to separate modernization from Westernization. That is, Islam can modernize without being Western: Islam can be pictured as providing the basis for all of life without having anything to do with Western ideas, and, at the same time, change may be embraced as fully as is desired in order to allow for that modernization.

There are other possibilities for a solution to the dilemmas which Islam faces which come from a rejection of Islam *per se*. For example, the arguments for agnosticism and atheism present themselves. The former, perhaps also to be seen as a simple embracing of secularism, is as rampant in many Muslim countries as it is elsewhere. Some may well argue that it is not really a solution as such; rather, it is a platform displaying a failure of nerve, the inability either to commit oneself to religion or to leave it totally. It is for many, however, a pragmatic solution where issues of religion are simply not as important in life as are matters of finding a job and maintaining a family. Our concern here, however, is primarily with those who are active in trying to find a religiously based answer to the questions of today.

Violence in the name of Islam as a new factor?

The factors of ascendancy and decline, nationalism and socialism, Zionism and the creation of Israel, and oil have been isolated as being attributes of the impact of modernity on Islam and the countries of the Muslim world. Some have argued that this list can now be supplemented by a new factor: the rise of violence in the name of Islam. That suggestion needs to be considered from two angles.

First, this violence (often termed "terrorism" by those on whom it is inflicted) in its contemporary appearance takes full advantage of every aspect of modernity: social, political, and technological. Whether the violence may be the result of those very modern factors themselves certainly needs to be considered. The key to defining these random acts of violence is that they are designed to provoke fear and terror: the goal is to emphasize the instability of the modern social and political order by intruding on the public space in places where any of us could be. While not all acts of this type of violence are perpetrated in the name of religion, many are at the very least motivated by a world view that has religious resonances. For the perpetrators, the world is at war with their world view and their own community, and a response that involves violence is, from within this viewpoint, justified. Through their acts, the perpetrators appear to hope that they will gain influence in the world. Such people see themselves as militants on behalf of a just cause in a violent world. These militants operate in a globalized world in which social and political certainties have long since disappeared. Those who commit these acts of violence are not campaigning on a "return to the past" platform: they have embraced all the aspects of modernity, particularly in its means of communication (especially the internet) and its weaponry. In that sense, as the scholar Olivier Roy suggests, groups such as al-Qaeda encapsulate a new understanding of Islam cloaked in Western revolutionary ideology.

Second, this violence has created the greatest challenge to Muslim identity in the twenty-first century. The tension between the perpetrators of violence and the vast majority of any religious community is a key characteristic of what gets called terrorism. (Non-militant) Muslims disagree with the motivation, the tactics and world view of those who use violence in the name of Islam. Yet, ironically, at the same time that very violence has brought religion back to the forefront of public discussion, and has forced a recognition of the power and value of religion. Further, aspects of the militants' platform resonate deeply: that economic and cultural globalization has led to oppression and to the violation of basic rights is a common theme. Thus, the presence of violence in the name of Islam has demanded that all other Muslims enunciate their own religion in a manner that is appropriate for the modern world and for the continued peaceful existence of individuals; but they must do this without demonstrating that they have done just what the militants claim, that is, fallen victim to secular and liberal values that can no longer be identified as "Islamic." The challenge that the militants create, therefore, is one internal to the religion of Islam itself. However, given the dominance of violence in the name of Islam at the beginning of the twenty-first century, Muslims feel that Islam as a whole has become tarnished in the eyes of others—and there is a good deal of evidence to suggest that such is so, as we witness indiscriminate anti-Muslim backlash around the globe today.

To understand violence and terrorism as global phenomena of the modern word, an excellent overview is provided in Mark Juergensmeyer, *Terror in the Mind of God: The Global Rise of Religious Violence*, Berkeley: University of California Press, 3rd edition, 2003. For an interview with Olivier Roy entitled "When Religion and Culture Part Ways," see www.signandsight.com/features/2025.html.

Suggested further reading

Richard W. Bulliet, *The Case for Islamo-Christian Civilization*, New York: Columbia University Press, 2004.

Yvonne Y. Haddad, *Contemporary Islam and the Challenge of History*, Albany: State University of New York Press, 1982.

Samira Haj, *Reconfiguring Islamic Tradition: Reform, Rationality, and Modernity*, Stanford: Stanford University Press, 2009.

Francis Robinson, "Crisis of Authority: Crisis of Islam?" *Journal of the Royal Asiatic Society*, 3(19) (2009): 339–54.

Amyn B. Sajoo (ed.), *Muslim Modernities: Expressions of the Civil Imagination*, London: I. B. Tauris, 2008.

13 *Muḥammad and modernity*

It is crucial to any understanding of religion in the modern world that an assessment of the attitude towards the past be undertaken: how is the authority of the past dealt with in the modern situation? In the Islamic case, the many specific issues which arise stem from one major question: what is the status of Muḥammad and the Qurʾān in the view of modern Muslims?

In dealing with Muḥammad, there are a number of approaches that may be contemplated in order to embrace the totality of the subject. Muḥammad's role as a source of authority through the accounts of what he actually did during his lifetime, summed up in the word *sunna*, is crucial. There are other, more subtle ways in which Muḥammad is discussed in the modern context, however, each of which reflects the impact of modernity and differing conceptions of Islam. They are frequently implicit positions, as compared to the explicit ones found in the discussions of the *sunna* and its authority. Even more notably, they are frequently more popular and significant in terms of their influence.

The role of biography

All Muslim groups in the modern world join in their veneration of Muḥammad. In fact, within the context of the modern world, that must be taken as one of the defining elements of what it means to be a Muslim. The writing of biographies of Muḥammad is, therefore, a singularly appropriate enterprise for all concerned, and it provides, thereby, a glimpse into the adjustments Muslims have made as a response to the modern context. Biography is a powerful mirror for the reflection of ideals, as well as standards, of the age in which they are written and thus may be seen to reflect the contemporary situation of their authors in the very construction of the facts that the works intend to record.

Because of Muḥammad's role in Islamic society as "teacher and exemplar"—ideals embodied in the concept of the *sunna*—his life story has been used constantly as an inspirational source, manifesting itself in the writing of biographies. With the impact of change in the modern world, it has become necessary for a biographer to create a life story

Figure 13.1 A woman in Karachi, Pakistan, holds a sign that says, in Urdu, "We can sacrifice our lives for the name of Muḥammad." She was part of a protest, organized by the Jamāʿat-i Islāmī, against Facebook on May 19, 2010, because of the use of the website to promote "Everybody Draw Mohammed Day," to be held on May 20. A ban of the website in Pakistan was sought.
Source: REHAN KHAN/epa/Corbis.

which may be read as having some relevance to contemporary times: a relevance which will reflect the ideals and aspirations of the writer's perception of the needs of the Muslim community. For example, encouraging the use of reason, the pursuit of education, and the fostering of science have frequently been pictured as cures for the ills of the Muslim world. Providing women with a more active role in society has become another common goal. The support that the actual details of the life of Muḥammad can provide for these ideas is crucial to the process of legitimizing the change which is deemed necessary. The sense of legitimization is important for most reformers; if Islam is to remain relevant to human life, then the changes deemed desirable must be incorporated within it and they must be legitimated in an Islamic manner. There is also a pragmatic reason for the appeal to legitimization by Muḥammad: literature, especially of the biographical type, is a powerful tool of propaganda.

Furthermore, for reformers, biographies can become the vehicle for reform by being a message couched in traditional terms and thus not so subject to attack from the more conservative elements in society. The example of widely criticized reformers from the nineteenth century made a number of twentieth-century reformers feel the need to veil their ideas in a form acceptable (or less easy to reject out of hand) to religious authorities.

The character of biography

A number of motifs are found repeatedly in modern biographies of Muḥammad which are worthy of attention. Among these are the following:

1 The treatment of the process of revelation versus the role of reason—can the traditional view of revelation as a supernatural event be maintained in light of reason?
2 The issue of Muḥammad's sinlessness—does it really make sense that Muḥammad never committed an error during his life as has been traditionally held?
3 The nature of Muḥammad's heavenly journey, undertaken early in his prophetic career, according to traditional accounts, when he traveled on the back of a winged horse to Jerusalem and ascended to heaven in order to meet the former prophets and receive a vision of God—was it in the body (as was classically emphasized) or by the soul only (perhaps as a vision)?
4 The general status of miracles in Muḥammad's life—can they be accounted for by rational scientific explanations?
5 Muḥammad's personality as a husband and as a statesman, with *jihād*, "holy war," a major part of the issue—can these sorts of activities be accepted in a modern context?

These topics reflect two concerns, both prominently displayed in the biographies. One is the impact of modern scientific thought and ways of understanding phenomena such as prophecy and miraculous occurrences. The other is the impact of Orientalism and general Christian attacks on Islam, especially in charges of Muḥammad's "immorality" (as reflected, for example, in concerns over the number of his marriages) and "war-mongering" (as reflected in the assessment of the many battles which he led against the various tribes in Arabia). This last point is somewhat more complex. Orientalists, especially those who worked within the framework of colonialist regimes, frequently spoke of Islam as being counter to modern ideals and progress—that latter concept being glossed to include morality and ethics. That is, the morality encouraged by Islam was not in keeping with the modern ethos and would only hold Muslims back from being able to embrace science and progress. An example would be the horror expressed by some writers at the idea of Muslim men being able to have four wives; no man could possibly be an active member of an industrialized work force and cope with four wives! Therefore, these two topics—modern scientific thought and the moral character of Islam—are frequently intertwined. Thus the Muslim pro-science argument will frequently be anti-Orientalist at the same time.

With regard to the Orientalist attention to Muḥammad, while Muslim devotion to their prophet was obvious enough, Christian desires to discover the "historical Jesus" were undoubtedly being reflected in some of the attention being given to Muḥammad. The temptation towards implicit or explicit comparisons between Jesus and Muḥammad—always being conducted from the viewpoint of the superiority of Christianity, to be sure—was undoubtedly too hard to resist for many Orientalist writers.

The question of the historical reliability of sources and the rise of historical criticism has also affected the Muslim biographical enterprise to a great extent. In embracing ideals of modern scientific thought and in rejecting Orientalist aspersions cast upon Islam, a method of historical-critical writing arose. This rise of the study of history is one of the characteristics of the modern period, as was noted above (p. 184). There was, therefore, on the part of some modern Muslim writers, an effort to foster a historical-critical approach in their writings about Muḥammad. No longer, it was said, could events simply be narrated as they were in the past, but the sources must be subjected to analysis for bias and implausibility. For those reformers bent on introducing the scientific method into the Muslim world, what more appropriate (but potentially dangerous!) vehicle could there be than the biography of Muḥammad? Many writers, therefore, certainly raise these sorts of issues in their work, but in many instances the actual implementation of the historical method has been quite minimal. That fact, however, should not detract from the attention given to the influence the idea itself has had.

Biographies and history

The emphasis in many (but certainly not all) of the modern biographies is not on Muḥammad's actions as such—that is, not on the historical narratives found in the classical books written by people like Ibn Isḥāq—but on his spiritual attitude, his general outlook, and his morals. In this sense, Muḥammad is portrayed as the truly modern man, and once that idea is fully understood Islam may not only be seen to be compatible with the modern era, but also be seen to embody it fully.

As with the classical biographies of Muḥammad which provide a mythic portrayal of a pristine society at the time of the foundation of Islam, a picture of the Islamic ideal, so too the modern ones. Each wishes to portray the ideals of the community, but the fact is that those ideals have changed over time. For the classical biographer Ibn Isḥāq, valiant battles led by the divinely appointed leader of the community served as an example for all to follow. Muḥammad's special relationship to God was displayed by the permission granted to him to marry many wives. These were aspects of the argument for Islam at the time of Ibn Isḥāq. But for modern writers the ideals and aspirations are different, and narrating the factual realities of Muḥammad's life (as recorded in these classical sources) does not necessarily accomplish the desired goal of contemporary relevance. In fact, Muḥammad as a real, live person tends to fade in many of the modern biographies, slipping into the light of unreal absolute perfection in his heroic role, while at the same time there is a downplaying of the "irrational" prophetic elements in his life. Muḥammad's greatest miracle for many modern writers, unlike the ancient writers such as Ibn Isḥāq, is not the splitting of the moon, or the sighing palm trunk as he walked by, or talking sheep, but the moral and spiritual transformation that he accomplished in society.

Another aspect appears in some biographies which needs attention. The biographies frequently reflect the socio-political environment of the writer to the extent that support for specific political parties becomes manifest. The past becomes a source of inspiration, especially for nationalists, and nationalism was rife in Egypt in the 1930s, for example, reflecting internal developments but also trends in European political thought; Islam and Muḥammad became ideal channels through which nationalism could be expressed. There was a wave of biographical writing in Egypt during this period; as a result, treatments of Muḥammad became popular elsewhere in the Arab world, the biographical form being adopted as a vehicle for reform. Looking at some of these biographies briefly will indicate some of their scope. Most of the attention falls on Muḥammad Ḥusayn Haykal, the most significant and the most studied of all contemporary biographers.

Muḥammad Ḥusayn Haykal

Muḥammad Haykal was born in 1888 and died in 1956. He studied law in Cairo and then pursued further education at the Sorbonne in Paris. He received his doctorate in 1912 for studies in economics and law. He worked as a lawyer and educator as well as a member of the government, as a novelist, and, most significantly, as a journalist. His first work, *Zaynab*, was written while he was in Paris and was published in 1914; it is generally cited as the first Arabic novel. He also founded a newspaper with a weekly literary supplement in the 1920s and much of his later work appeared in it.

Haykal was most concerned with establishing the rationality of Islam and rejecting every Orientalist objection to, and criticism of, the religion itself. Islam is, for Haykal, fully in keeping with modern life and reason. Modern rational standards may, in fact, be identified as inherently and originally Muslim, Greek, and Egyptian. Writes Haykal:

> Long before the times of Moses and Jesus, the science of ancient Egypt as well as its philosophy and law had passed to Greece and Rome, which had then spread their dominion. It was Egypt that contributed to Greek philosophy and literature their

> noblest ideas. The new rationalist awakening thus produced, warned and convinced people that miracles constitute no argument at all . . . it was God's pattern that reason shall constitute the apogee of human life, as long as it is not composed of empty logic, not devoid of feeling and spirit, and as long as it martials [*sic*: read "marshals"] all these faculties in a synthesized effort to discover the secrets of the universe and achieve intimate knowledge of the cosmic pattern. Thus, it was decreed by God that soon the Prophet of Islām would rise to call men to the truth through reason, complemented by feeling and spirit, and that the one miracle of such a gnoseological synthesis should be the Holy Book revealed to His Prophet Muḥammad.
>
> (Haykal 1976: 579–80)

Much of this paragraph is a reaction against Christian missionary and Orientalist prejudice and is spoken of as a scientific inquiry into Muḥammad, away from the biases of the Europeans. Haykal does use European studies of Muḥammad as the basis of his work, however, for he considered the traditional Arabic sources to be full of superstition and impossible stories. To some extent, Haykal suggests, the Orientalists are not to blame for their distortions of Islam, for irrational elements are clearly to be found in the classical sources. It should not be thought, however, that Haykal's method employs the historical-critical method as expounded in the modern Euro-American tradition; rather his biography of Muḥammad is guided by the ideals and spirit of Islam and by the sources molded by the methodological principle that things "must have been" a certain way. It is generally not a critical analysis entailing a comparison of various traditions, but simply a choosing of the appropriate historical report through the elimination of any elements deemed superstitious or in error according to the modern sensibility.

Notably, Haykal also sees his approach as a rejection of Muslim conservative elements. What is holding Muslims back is not Islam but the tradition which is so fervently maintained by the religious elite. Furthermore, the attitudes displayed by the conservative religious authorities only give the Orientalists and the Christian missionaries more ammunition. The sources used by these unfriendly writers are those dominated by the conservative elements, and the conclusions which those critics come to are the result not of the methodology which they employ—a methodology which Haykal argues should be followed—but of the sources themselves.

The only absolutely reliable source for talking about Islam is the Qurʾān. Interpreting the other sources in light of the spirit of the Qurʾān would correct all misunderstandings. For Haykal, the message of the Qurʾān is clearly one of rationality and the search for scientific wisdom, and that is a message which the religious classes have perverted over the ages. Further, the Qurʾān supports ideas of social order and individual freedom, keys to a truly modern Islamic society and in agreement with Haykal's own political position.

Haykal's Muḥammad

Haykal's work *The Life of Muḥammad*, published as a book in 1935, has been extensively read, translated, and studied, both in a popular way as well as in scholarly analyses. Its aim is to provide a fully modern biography, one written in accord with modern scientific reason. At the same time, it is not a critical biography: for the most part it is a reiteration of facts from the classical sources with no critical stance. Haykal started the work in 1932 and published pieces of it periodically over the following two years. The work has been through at least ten editions, gaining a few extra sections in the process.

Haykal argues that all biographers reflect the standards of their own day. That Ibn Isḥāq, for example, should speak of certain events as miraculous simply reflects his understanding of the workings of the world at that time. Likewise, the early biographers display a materialistic slant towards an issue such as Muḥammad's multiple marriages (emphasizing elements like tribal alliances and so forth) and fail to see the spiritual element implied by the prophet's activities.

Several points prove crucial in Haykal's biography, as they do in most modern biographies, for they reflect the central issues which have been emphasized in Western attacks upon Muḥammad and Islam. This apologetic response of the biographers is frequently their most notable element. Haykal discusses the trustworthiness of Muḥammad in order to counter some of the charges laid against him. Involved here is the notion of Muḥammad's sinlessness. One special aspect of this is in regards to the Satanic verses, concerning which it is declared inconceivable that Muḥammad could have been deceived by Satan into uttering certain verses supposedly to be in the Qur'ān (but later withdrawn) which compromised the monotheism of Islam by allowing minor goddesses to be viewed as intercessors with Allāh (a story told in many classical sources). Muḥammad's marriages are dealt with in detail, especially those to Zaynab and Māriya, where images of lust and seduction were often conjured up. The treatment of Muḥammad's use of violence, minimized as much as possible by Haykal, is especially noticeable in comparison with older texts, in which Muḥammad's fighting is often seen as a part of his successful strategy and nothing to be played down: fighting took place under God's will and command. All these areas are focused upon by Orientalists, and Haykal clearly rejects the Orientalist conclusions and argues against the Orientalist methods.

Finally, Haykal speaks from a certain time period in Egypt when democracy was being promoted; his biography clearly reflects those ideals as stemming from, and therefore legitimized by, the time of Muḥammad:

> While the non-Muslim inhabitants began to fear Muslim power—knowing well that it stemmed from the depth of hearts which had tasted sacrifice and persecution for the sake of faith, the Muslims collected the fruits of their patience and enjoyed their

> religious freedom. Their peace and freedom were now made constitutional by the Islamic principles that no man has any authority over any other, that religion belongs to God alone, that service is to Him alone, that before Him all men are absolutely equal, and that nothing differentiates them except their works and intentions. . . . The theater was ready and the stage was set for Muḥammad to constitute by his conduct the ideal exemplification and embodiment of these teachings and principles, and for his laying down the foundation stone of Islamic civilization.
>
> (Haykal 1976: 184–5)

Because of Haykal's sense of rationality, he sees fewer miracles playing a role in Muḥammad's life but puts an emphasis on natural processes to explain some of them. The heavenly journey is taken as psychological, for example. As well, the picture of Muḥammad is framed in terms of modern ideals—loving, forgiving, perfect.

ʿAbd al-Raḥmān al-Sharqāwī

Al-Sharqāwī (1920–87) was an Egyptian novelist and critic who, in 1962, published *Muḥammad, the Messenger of Freedom*. His previous writings were famous for their poetic spirit as well as their political commitment. His treatment of Muḥammad was not designed as a biography to replace the classical ones in their recounting of history; "everything has been said" on that topic, according to the author. Rather, he was attempting to portray an image of Muḥammad as a man whose aim was to produce a unified humanity based on notions of love and mercy and whose ultimate goal was to produce a better future for his people. Inherent in Muḥammad's message were progress and liberation through a veritable revolution.

Al-Sharqāwī hoped to provide a positive picture for non-Muslim readers, a potentially large and fruitful audience given the large population of Christian Copts in Egypt. His work also, and perhaps more successfully, reflects the political climate of Nasserite Socialism in Egypt, a revolt against capitalism (and thus against Europe). This is conveyed by picturing Muḥammad as a worker, rising up on behalf of others against the rich Quraysh tribe and the Jews; the latter are pictured throughout the work as the rich enemies whom Muḥammad constantly tried to befriend. Downplayed are the prophetic and miraculous elements in Muḥammad's life; his experiences are seen as dreams of the perfect state of human existence, free from the type of oppression which was prevalent in pre-Islamic Mecca, where everything was done for the benefit of the rich. Al-Sharqāwī's biography, then, is apologetic while pursuing the clear political end of a modern vision of society legitimized through Muḥammad's life. As such, it aroused some opposition within Egyptian clerical circles for its failure to treat the traditional religious values of Muḥammad's career and Islam as a whole.

ʿAbd al-Raḥmān ʿAzzām

ʿAzzām (1893–1976) was an Egyptian diplomat and served as Secretary-General of the Arab League from 1945 to 1952. In 1938 he wrote an Arabic work entitled *The Hero of Heroes or the Most Prominent Attribute of the Prophet Muḥammad*. A revised English version was published in 1965 as *The Eternal Message of Muḥammad*. The format of the book is worthy of attention. The life of Muḥammad itself is briefly sketched in a short twenty pages. Following that are sections dealing with the basic message of Islam, social reform, the state, international relations, dissemination of the message, the causes of world disturbances, and the search for "a spiritual bulwark for civilization." The point is clear: Muḥammad, through his person and his action, has something to say about each of these aspects of modern (political) existence. Bravery, love, the ability to forgive, and eloquence are all attributes of Muḥammad that are emphasized, leading to the conclusion that the diplomatic nature of Muḥammad's life is one that provides an example for today in the resolution of conflicts:

> The Message of Muḥammad recognizes neither nationalism nor racism in their modern contexts; the fatherland of the Muslim admits of no geographical delimitations—it coexists with the faith. . . . Racism, or a fanatic attachment to tribe, nation, color, language, or culture, is rejected by the Message as a product of pre-Islamic idolatry.
>
> (ʿAzzām 1965: 204–5)

Political manoeuvres and military insights are also championed:

> Recognizing the inherent and manifest evils of war, the Message of Muḥammad circumscribed warfare with common rules of right conduct (*adab*), defining its aims and limiting it to the repulsion of aggression, the protection of the freedom of belief, and the termination of battle with just and durable agreements. . . . Certain states nowadays prefer surprise attacks on their enemies without any previous warning. Preliminary precautions prior to attack are such that the aggression-bent state can surprise its enemies completely by pretending all along to favor peace; often the true motives and pretenses for waging war may not be revealed prior to combat. . . . There is nothing more distasteful to Islam than this, and the tenets of Muslim law reject it in spirit and in practice.
>
> (ʿAzzām 1965: 141–2)

Underlying this presentation is the common Modernist approach to the issue of *jihād*, here presented as only defensive and hedged by rules compatible with contemporary moral standards, in themselves superior to the practice (rather than the theory) of other modern nations. The centuries of Muslim discussion regarding *jihād* and its obligations and flexible application are discarded and replaced by an invocation of modern liberal standards.

Najīb Maḥfūẓ

Awarded the Nobel Prize for Literature in 1988, Najīb Maḥfūẓ (in English usually written Naguib Mahfouz; 1911–2006) is probably the best known of all contemporary Arab writers. He published his first novel in 1939 at a time when the Arabic novel as a form was in its infancy. His major works include *The Cairene Trilogy*, written 1956–7, which traces the story of three generations of a Cairo family, putting into novel form the changes in the daily life of middle-class people in the first half of the twentieth century. His works were cited by the Nobel Prize committee as being "rich in nuance, now clearsightedly realistic, now evocatively ambiguous."

Maḥfūẓ, in at least some of his writings, critiques the stance and values of traditional religion, Islam included. Religion has not accomplished what it set out to do. The divine has become irrelevant to modern life because of the way in which He has been made absent from human existence. The prophets, sent by God, have had little effect on human existence, "unable after their demise to ensure any abiding salvation for mankind from the burden of being human" (Cragg 1985: 159).

Maḥfūẓ's Muḥammad

Published first as a serial in the newspaper *al-Ahrām* in 1959, *Children of Gabalawi* is an allegory of God, His messengers through history, and their interaction with the world. Its treatment of Muḥammad is not therefore traditional biography by any means, although elements of his life as depicted in early works are clearly discernible in the character of Qāsim and his environs of the streets of Cairo. The names are changed "to protect the innocent," but the story remains the same. The book is even divided into 114 sections, echoing the 114 *sūra*s of the Qurʾān.

Maḥfūẓ's Muḥammad is a deeply committed man who challenges the established secular and religious powers. He leads a band of vigilantes whose aim is no less than setting the stage for a world where human rights are respected and the law of God is enacted; this they set out to accomplish by force, in a manner pictured as being midway between Moses' war-mongering and Jesus' pacifism. Muḥammad's character embodies all the values that should be emulated, and this includes his ability to love women; no modern apologetic is needed to excuse Muḥammad's multiple marriages.

Maḥfūẓ's main interest, however, is in the frustration of the goal of Muḥammad by later followers, and this is what the work goes on to explore in its final section. Science has become the prophet. The leaders of the past have been made into legends. The story finally leads to the death of Gabalawi (i.e. God). Muḥammad, in this way, is no different than the earlier prophets talked of in the book (Adam, Moses, Jesus), whose mission should have been sufficient to set the world aright but, in fact, matters did not work out that way. Muslims are now without God, even while they claim to be surrounded by Him; this is the result of the failure to pose the necessary and penetrating questions concerning the nature of God and existence.

This is a biography for the modern world, one in which the message is deeply veiled by the curtain of the medium and the form. One cannot help thinking of Salman Rushdie's attempt at the same feat, and this parallel has been pursued by some observers. Maḥfūẓ's work created an outcry at the time of its publication and it did not appear in book form until it was published in 1967 in Beirut (the venue for many a dissident Egyptian work). Kenneth Cragg's assessment of the work is fitting:

> Its haunting, wistful scepticism presents a searching challenge to ordinary believers. Served by eminent narrative skill and literary art, it invites them to look into a void, to think themselves stripped of their familiar securities, to divest themselves of assumptions about God and His messengers which have always been instinctive to their minds and culture. It confronts them with the unthinkable, with the implication that everything on which they had relied might need, for its own sake, to be called in question.
>
> (Cragg 1985: 157–8)

Fatima Mernissi

The work *Women and Islam: An Historical and Theological Enquiry* by Fatima Mernissi (b. 1940), a sociologist and university teacher in Morocco, is as close as one might conceive to a feminist biography of Muḥammad. The root problem of Muslim society today, according to Mernissi, one which the intrusion of the West has forced Muslims to confront, is that women have not been treated as full members of the community.

Mernissi does not see Islamic gender segregation as an isolated social phenomenon of a religious nature, but as a political expression of a specific distribution of power and authority and an economic reflection of a specific division of labor, both forming a total and coherent social order. When this Islamic segregation is shaken, the coherence of the traditional social order as a whole is put into question, especially if social reform is not able to set up an acceptable new system of values governing male–female relations.

Women may have gained the right to vote in a country such as Morocco, from where Mernissi writes, but they have not gained the right to be elected, she says. Men continue to consider power the privilege of the male and cannot conceive of the need to have women participating in decisions regarding the future. Furthermore, in order to support their position, appeal is made to the foundations of the faith of Islam. This accounts for the current surge in Islamist membership, where men find comfort against the inroads of female demands.

To counter these sorts of appeals to religion, Mernissi returns to the sources to extract a picture of Muḥammad as the supporter of women's rights: though her picture is a mixed one. On one level, she seems to say that Islam is inherently male oriented and there is a need to move "beyond": "One wonders if a desegregated society, where formerly secluded women have equal rights not only economically but sexually, would be an authentic Muslim society" (Mernissi 1987: 9). But, at the same time, she looks back to Muḥammad for inspiration and legitimization. This is an attempt perhaps to battle Islamist elements (glossed consistently as anti-women) on their own grounds—inter-Muslim apologetics. Muḥammad is the champion of women whose opinion is even overruled by God on occasion (the implications for the status of the Qurʾān in Mernissi's books will be a topic for consideration in Chapter 14), who seems to have been more influenced by the pragmatics of male-oriented power structures than His prophet. The tendency towards reinforcing male power has been further aggravated by male interpreters of the sacred texts who saw only their own prerogatives at stake and who thought nothing of ignoring Muḥammad's intentions of improving the lot of women.

For Mernissi, Muḥammad's character reflects precisely what is lacking in contemporary male–female relations:

> Muhammad was a chief of state who publicly acknowledged the importance of affection and sex in life. And, during expeditions, his wives were not just background figures, but shared with him his strategic concerns. He listened to their advice, which was sometimes the deciding factor in thorny negotiations.
>
> (Mernissi 1991: 104)

The institution of the *ḥijāb*, "veiling"—here to be taken to mean the entire social system which separates men and women in Muslim countries, as will be explored further in Chapter 16—became a part of Islam only because of male concerns for their own privileges and was put in place against the general principles which Muḥammad had initiated. Attacks were made on Muḥammad because of his private life, in which his wives enjoyed a great deal of freedom and authority, contrary to the established practices of society at the time:

> Hurt and weakened, [Muhammad] lost his ability to stand up to ʿUmar [pictured here as the spokesman for the male prerogative], and he agreed to the confinement of women. He gave his consent to the *hijab*. He gave his consent to the reestablishment of male supremacy.
>
> (Mernissi 1991: 163–4)

Muḥammad, for Mernissi, aspired to the ideal society, but the pressures of the situation—a situation into which he had introduced radical change—would not allow these platforms to be maintained. But the equality of men and women and the freedom of women to control their own lives and to be a valuable part of society are what Muḥammad stood for, and this is the true core of Islam. The pragmatic value of providing safety for his wives had overcome his principles. Those principles are reflected in the very basis of the religion of Islam, except, it would seem, when it comes to dealing with women. Islam, for Mernissi, stands for the use of the intellect as the means by which good is to be separated from evil. The veiling of women imposed the language of violence and power, whereas individual responsibility was the essence of the society which God wished to be instituted. But the ignorant forces of male power could not accept that responsibility:

> Muhammad put great emphasis on politeness. He himself was very shy. Several verses [of the Qurʾān] attest to this aspect of his character, which . . . in the absence of tactfulness on the part of some men of his entourage forced him to adopt the *hijab*. He did not consider that having a house open to the world had to mean that people would invade his privacy. The *hijab* represented the exact opposite of what he had wanted to bring about. It was the incarnation of the absence of internal control; it was the veiling of the sovereign will, which is the source of good judgment and order in a society.
> (Mernissi 1991: 185)

Mernissi's biography is not a traditional one, then. While it covers a great deal of the life of Muḥammad, its focus is on the women around him and his attitude towards them. This is no different, albeit substantially more explicit, than Haykal arguing for the rationality of Muḥammad. That is, the point of the biography is made more explicit to the reader; it could well be that, with the rise in general literacy levels, works like that of Mernissi have become more appropriate and more convincing. No longer is it necessary to embed one's ideas so deeply in stories.

ʿAlī Dashtī

Biographies of Muḥammad are, of course, not limited to being written by Arabs. ʿAlī Dashtī was an Iranian journalist, novelist, and politician with a classical religious training; he served in the Senate of Iran from 1954 to 1979. His book *Twenty Three Years: A Study of the Prophetic Career of Mohammad* was published anonymously in 1974. He died shortly after the Iranian revolution at the age of about 85 under vague circumstances.

Dashtī's biography presents a full rationalization of prophethood and is a fairly extreme example at that. Muḥammad's experience of prophethood was his own conscience or inner mind speaking to him. Nothing supernatural occurred in

Muḥammad's life; everything can be accounted for by modern psychology and sociology. Muḥammad's infallibility is rejected, and thus the "Satanic verses" are accepted. The Qur'ān—Muḥammad's book rather than God's—is spoken of as being full of grammatical errors, as should be expected from an illiterate man such as Muḥammad, and was taken from a variety of sources. The miracle of the Qur'ān lies in its results, not its literary formulation—it is as untranslatable as a poem by the famous Persian poet Ḥāfiẓ. This comparison is noteworthy because of its Iranian emphasis; Dashtī, in fact, accuses the Arabs of being responsible for most of the problems of Islam, especially as it is manifested in today's Arab Islamism. With the rise of Islam, "the Arabs did not suddenly lose their materialistic outlook, their inability to think in abstract terms, their unconcern with spiritual matters, and their unruliness and obstinacy" (Dashti 1985: 158). Only after a few centuries of Islam did the Iranians place "no value on their nationhood and [imagine] the Hejaz to be the sole source of God's blessings to mankind" (Dashti 1985: 208).

The lack of rationality in matters of belief has caused the spread of superstition and illusion, according to Dashtī. Religion in general is seen to blunt human reason, although there is no reason why this should be so. If people would just accept that Muḥammad was fully human, then they would understand that everything he did in his life may be seen to fit with general psychological reactions and human emotions. Muḥammad's actions must be assessed in the context of the social environment and in terms of their benefit to the community. No standard of firm ethics can be expected from Muḥammad. Apparently inhumane principles were used by Muḥammad based on expediency and not on consistency with any spiritual or moral principle. Laws from the time of Muḥammad are, in today's context, frequently useless and meaningless, as are even some ritual practices, for example the pilgrimage. Concerning Muḥammad's wives and various references to them in scripture, Dashtī says, "Every reader of the Qor'an must be amazed to encounter these private matters in a scripture and moral code valid for all mankind and for all time" (Dashti 1985: 137). In the context of a radical biography such as this, all traditional understandings of both the person of Muḥammad and his authority, along with the authority of the Qur'ān, are brought into question.

Biography and reform

The examples and the geographical distribution of these biographies of Muḥammad from the modern period—both at the beginning and at the end of the twentieth century—could be multiplied substantially. Earlier publications from outside the Arab world—for example of Aḥmad Khān and Ameer Ali in India and Umar Cokroaminoto in Indonesia—indicate that the phenomenon is much larger than what has been sketched above. In fact, one could also point to a similar use of the biography and ethos of the

Shīʿī Imām Ḥusayn ibn ʿAlī by Ayatollah Khomeini in the Iranian revolution of 1978–9. Khomeini's appeal to the life story of the leader of the nascent Shīʿī community who was killed by the Umayyad ruler, Yazīd, in the year 680 was both vivid and effective. This story is one which speaks to every member of the Shīʿa about the need to rebel against an unjust ruler and to be prepared to sacrifice one's own life on behalf of the good of the community. Such actions are seen as redemptive for the individual believer. By alluding to this story and suggesting implicitly that he himself could be viewed as Imam Ḥusayn, Khomeini was able to rally support for political and social reform in Iran despite the overwhelming odds which the clerics faced when confronted by the Shah's power. This paradigmatic use of Ḥusayn achieved literary manifestation in the book by Shaykh Muḥammad Mahdī Shams al-Dīn called *The Rising of al-Ḥusayn*. Originally written in Arabic by this Lebanese Shīʿī leader, the book's English translation (published in the wake of the Iranian revolution, in 1985) has a foreword which summarizes well the continuing relevance of religious biography in Islam:

> Imam al-Ḥusayn, peace be with him, created a momentous Islamic revolution, which has continued to live as history has gone by and still provides writers with vitality and inspiring material. Despite the passing of time, it is a revolutionary torch whose light guides revolutionaries and those who struggle to proclaim and support the truth and to resist and oppose the symbols of falsehood. For more than thirteen centuries, writers of different groups, inclinations and ideas have continued to write books and studies about this revolution. Yet neither has its spring been exhausted nor have the streams which flow from it run dry. It is the same as it was at the blessed time it took place in terms of its great significance.
>
> (Shams al-Dīn 1985: xiii)

The use of the English word "revolution" (in Arabic, *thawra*) is significant here and its usage continues throughout the translation. Furthermore, the author alludes to its contemporary relevance:

> From the time of Muʿāwiya ibn Abī Sufyān, the Shīʿite Muslim has endured different kinds of persecution, harassment and terrorisation. He has been pursued by the authorities and has seldom felt secure . . . .
>
> The tragic situation for the Shīʿite has continued for long periods. Out of this situation, under which generations and generations have lived and died, a man has emerged who carries, in the depths of his being, a feeling of sorrow and a spirit of revolution. This situation has made him keep close to his historical symbols, in the vanguard of which is the revolution of Imam al-Ḥusayn, in particular, and the history of the Imams, in general.
>
> (Shams al-Dīn 1985: 23)

The outpouring of biographical material related to Muḥammad and other religious heroes seems endless. There appears to be good reason for this, too. The appeal to authority is a necessity, it would seem, and the life of Muḥammad is an obvious focal point with which to deal with the issue of reform. The life stories of Muḥammad have no authoritative status themselves; they are not the actual source of the *sunna*, although they certainly have relevance in understanding the context of both Muḥammad's actions and the Qur'ān. Therefore, the subtle rewriting of his biography (as displayed in the examples above) or even the maintenance of the traditional picture (and there are many examples of that in the contemporary world also) does not raise substantial doubts over the basis of Islamic faith, at least on the surface. It is notable, however, that embedded in a number of the biographies, especially the more recent ones, are some far more radical views of the value both of the *sunna* and of the Qur'ān as well.

Issues of authority

Lying behind and presumed within all biographical treatments of Muḥammad is the belief that Muḥammad has something to say to modern Muslims. Clearly, all Muslims would agree that the story of Muḥammad has didactic value; that is, there are lessons and wisdom which can be learned from the life story itself. Furthermore, there is fundamental religious inspiration to be gained from reading the story of the founder of the religion, his trials and tribulations, his victories and defeats. But a question still remains that underlies all of these treatments: to what extent is Muḥammad's life, in the sense of all those things which he did in his life, actually binding upon Muslims? Are there simply general principles to be learned from Muḥammad's life or are the very details themselves elements which should or must be emulated? One Muslim scholar, Aslam Jayrājpūrī, the teacher of Ghulām Aḥmad Parvēz (who will be discussed later in this chapter), has explicated his views about this in the following way:

> There is a difference between obedience to the Prophet in his quality of prophet and obedience to him in his quality of *amir* [i.e. leader of the community]. In his quality of prophet he is to be obeyed until the Resurrection, since the Koran is for all times. But in his quality of *amir* he was only obeyed during his lifetime. . . . Instructions resulting from his *amir*-ship, will always remain temporary, because circumstances change.
>
> (Baljon 1958: 225)

The rebuttal to this position, representing another point of view, is to say that the two roles cannot, in fact, be distinguished: Muḥammad's example, his *sunna*, covers both aspects and only by following that *sunna* can salvation be assured.

Religion is, as has been mentioned several times before, traditional. It orients itself from the past with a view to the present; it sees authority as vested in and stemming from the past. Adherence to *ḥadīth* material, the source of the *sunna*, has generally been pictured as maintaining this cultural continuity within Islam. But at the same time, it has been argued that the material gathered in the *ḥadīth* reports often hampers attempts to adapt Islam. Thus, questions have arisen: are the *ḥadīth* reports an essential part of Islam? Is it that they are essential but that they must be subjected to a total reassessment? Are they fully applicable? Or are they totally irrelevant and illegitimate as a source? It is noteworthy that the authority of the Qurʾān remains virtually unquestioned, although, as will be seen in Chapter 14, different ways of interpreting it have been urged and do, to some extent, bring its status into question also.

The *sunna* today

The overall question to be raised here, then, is what is the authority of the *sunna* today? Is it felt to give legitimacy to contemporary patterns of life, social and ethical codes? Two opposing paths may be used as examples and both will recall the discussion of biographies. On the one hand, Muḥammad is the "perfect man," a perfect embodiment of the message of the Qurʾān. His example, therefore, must be authoritative, although in modern discussions it is not as common to see this conceived to be actual revelation as it was in classical times. On the other hand, Muḥammad is merely human, therefore capable of error and conditioned by his time and circumstances. His example is, as a consequence, not overly relevant or at least not compelling for the modern person. From the Modernist position, this removal of the constraints of Muḥammad's example provides an opening for evolution or progress in Islam.

It should be asked, however, why it is that the *sunna* specifically has become the focus of these sorts of discussions, rather than the Qurʾān? What is the point of these discussions? For those who enunciate a position which involves extensive questioning of the *sunna*, the aim is to distil Islam down to its essentials and thereby more easily facilitate the incorporation of modern ideals. Those who speak from this position certainly desire the survival of the relevance of Islam; this is true despite the rhetoric of their opponents, who picture them as attempting to destroy the religion. Furthermore, one could also say that all parties desire an intensification of Islam. All parties agree with the concept of Islamic law, that is, that religion should have something to say about legal issues, but they disagree on matters of jurisprudence, that is, the extent to which the decisions of the past are binding on the present. As well, the character of that Islamic law—whose Islam? Which Islam?—continues to fragment the various groups.

The Modernist vision is one of an Islam which will more readily incorporate change and, thus, the *sunna* has become the target for criticism and an avenue for aspirations. Part of the reason for targeting the *sunna* is because the custodians of the sacred law were those who were perceived by many reformers as doing the most to prevent the modernization of the Islamic world. Many of the critics came from a lay background; they were not fully trained in the traditional legal sciences of Islam and did not have great admiration for such educational methods. Added to this is the use of Orientalist notions regarding the *ḥadīth* by some reformers. The reports of what Muḥammad had done and said during his life were subjected to critical historical analysis by Europeans, especially by Ignaz Goldziher at the end of the nineteenth century, who emphasized the weakness of traditional Muslim evaluations of the material and, even more, the tendentious nature of many of the reports themselves. Some Muslims picked up on this and used these sorts of doubts about the veracity of the material to attack the authority of the *sunna*. This was primarily an Egyptian phenomenon; the criticism of the *sunna* as a whole, however, has much earlier roots, especially in India, where the problem was attacked in more of a theological manner than a historical one.

Discussions in India

The fact that many of the discussions concerning the status of the *sunna* took place in India, and continue to take place in areas distant from the Arab countries, may be significant. The way in which the *sunna* embodies, in a very literal way, Arabian customs may be the jarring point, such that, while the Arabs may feel secure in their identity as reflected in the *sunna*, the same may not hold true for those in other parts of the globe. Some have suggested that the more direct contact of Europeans with the Indian population could also have been a factor in this movement, at least to the extent that the pressure to adopt European ways was felt more strongly by some people. Also, the Indian heritage of discussions about the *sunna* is long: Shāh Walī Allāh, in the eighteenth century, is famous for his encouragement of a critical attitude towards *ḥadīth*, for example.

Arguments between two contemporary Indo-Pakistani figures display precisely the dimensions of the issues conceived to be at stake in the authority of the past for Muslims. Ghulām Aḥmad Parvēz represents what is clearly a minority position today in arguing for the illegitimacy of the constraints of the example of Muḥammad, the *sunna*. Abū ʾl-ʿAlāʾ Mawdūdī is a far more significant figure in terms of Pakistani politics but also the general Islamic resurgence worldwide. His position, which urges a reassessment of the *ḥadīth* reports which underlie the *sunna* but still acknowledges the authority of the concept itself, is far more widespread than that of Parvēz. The discussions between the two indicate the tensions between the different reform positions within modern Islam.

These arguments did not start in India with Parvēz and Mawdūdī; in fact, the basic issues have been discussed ever since Indian Muslims have tried to grapple with European rule and the relative status of Islam. Sayyid Aḥmad Khān represents an example of nineteenth-century Modernist thought, and, on this point, is clearly a precursor to the twentieth-century discussions.

All three of these writers—Aḥmad Khān, Parvēz, and Mawdūdī—challenge the traditional religious classes, the *ʿulamāʾ*; none of them emerged from the context of the religious scholarly elite. There was, therefore, no way for their views to be declared heretical since the people promulgating the ideas were not subject to expulsion from the religious circles of authority. However, at the same time, "none of them [is] advocating a situation in which every Muslim can believe as he likes" (McDonough 1970: 3); the communal sense of Islam remains, just as do the limits of the authority of the past.

Aḥmad Khān

Sir Sayyid Aḥmad Khān was born in 1817 to a noble family of Delhi. He died in 1898. He joined the East India Company in 1839 and was loyal to the British during the uprising of 1857–8. He urged that all that Muslims needed in India was the freedom to perform public religious rituals; the British should be supported, therefore, as long as they protected the Muslims rather than suppressed them. Ultimately, he saw the separation of the Muslims from the Hindu majority as the only way that an independent India could allow for Muslim survival. Until that goal was achieved, rule by benevolent foreigners was a better solution. He was knighted in 1888.

Aḥmad Khān may be characterized as a rationalist: he considered the proposition "religion in conformity with human nature" as absolute. All elements of supernaturalism must be declared false; this would include miracles and the like. Ethics and practices, therefore, should be based in nature; the law of Islam gives further guidance only. Education about the natural world is essential. His major life involvement was in Muslim education, and he devoted his retirement from 1876 on to the establishment and development of the Anglo-Muhammadan Oriental College at Aligarh. Education was the only way in which Muslims were going to be able to recapture their proper status. The school in Aligarh was traditional in the sense that it was a Muslim theological college, but it accepted students from all denominations—Sunnī, Shīʿī, and Hindu—and "aimed at the liberalization of ideas, broad humanism, a scientific world view, and a pragmatic approach to politics" (Ahmad 1967: 37). Its goal was to have its graduates enter government service and thus eventually pave the way for Muslim separatism within India under this new leadership.

Aḥmad Khān and the authority of the past

Deeply influenced by European ideas of history and change, Aḥmad Khan embraced the notion that Indian and Islamic history should be studied within the perspective of Western methodologies. He wrote a work on the life of Muḥammad (1870), using manuscript sources found in London. This opening of the past to re-examination also led to the possibility of questioning the basis of its authority. His approach was also supported by his theological attitude, which saw the need to reopen the discussions concerning very fundamental ideas of Islam; all of this was marked by a severe anti-Traditionalism and a strident nineteenth-century Modernism. The past interpretations of Islam had become too embroiled in minor details and had lost the essence of the faith. In fact, Muslims had built themselves a structure of law based not upon an infallible source but upon the ideas and attitudes of Muslims from the first centuries of Islam; this was embodied in the *ḥadīth* material.

While the authority of the *ḥadīth* had been established in the past, Aḥmad Khan felt that the issue needed to be reopened so as to provide a basis for re-evaluating the *sharīʿa* as a whole; individual reasoning, *ijtihād*, must be used. This argues, as Sheila McDonough suggests, that nineteenth-century people are as much in touch with determining the norms of Islamic society as the earlier ninth-century community which set the standards still followed in Islamic societies. Thus, authority itself is not being questioned, only the formulation of it. The only valid *ḥadīth* reports are those which are in agreement with the statements of the Qurʾān, those which explain Quranic injunctions, and those which deal with basic issues not alluded to in scripture.

Aḥmad Khan critiques the institution which has maintained the *sharīʿa* and the idea of that institution itself. Foreign influences are seen as one of the problems in the corruption of the *sharīʿa*. His aim was the liberalization of Islamic law in light of modern demands and the rationalization of other elements deemed to be essential.

Underlying Aḥmad Khan's ideas is the principle that true religion does not change but worldly affairs do and the two must be separated. "In his view," says McDonough,

> true religion should always be carefully distinguished from worldly affairs. True religion, he said, is unchanging, but worldly affairs are always changing. Originally, the great *ulema* used their personal opinions to give judgments on worldly affairs. This was in itself, he says, a valid thing for them to have done. Later, however, these opinions on temporary issues became identified with unchanging truth. This meant, he says, that the *ulema* were considered law-givers in the same sense as the Qurʾan; their human opinions became identified with the will of God.
>
> (McDonough 1970: 14)

It is important to notice that, in this conception, the status of the Qurʾān as non-contingent in terms of worldly affairs is not challenged: only the legal structure of Islam needs to contend with change.

Parvēz

Ghulām Aḥmad Parvēz (in English sometimes Parwez) was born in 1903 in East Punjab, India, and died in 1985. He was raised in a religious home and was deeply influenced, according to his own account of his life story, by Muḥammad Iqbāl, who pointed out for him the idea of a pure Islam without the centuries of foreign influence. He worked as a civil servant in India, which is often seen as a career that set the pattern for him to see the need for definite planning and instruction for the future of Islam. His first book, a political tract against the Soviet Union, was published in 1926 or 1927 and it appeared anonymously because his government job allowed no political involvement. He also wrote articles for Abū'l Aʿlāʾ Mawdūdī's *Tarjumān al-Qurʾān* and other magazines. In 1938 he started publishing the magazine *Ṭulūʿ-i Islām* ("The Dawn of Islam"), which has remained the main vehicle for his ideas since then and is now published in Karachi. He moved to Pakistan in 1948 and worked there as a government official until his retirement. He was a fervent opponent of Pakistan's religious classes, whom he saw as the protectors of elite interests, not of true Islam and true rationality. His audience appears to have been mainly well-educated young people, those who had presumably been deeply influenced by the West but were also searching for meaning within their own heritage.

Parvēz saw that *ḥadīth* had been treated as a revelatory source by the religious classes of the past. This was not legitimate for him. The *sharīʿa*, the "path" of life which Muslims follow, was, as a result of the status given to the *sunna* as a source of revealed knowledge, fundamentally wrong. All of the Muslim past, with the exception of the time of Muḥammad and the first four "righteous caliphs," must be rejected and considered a corruption of true Islam, because foreign influences, especially Byzantine and Persian, had become fully embedded in the *sharīʿa*. For Parvēz, the Qurʾān alone can function in taking people from their complacent, destructive ways toward becoming full persons; reason is a base human instinct (but one which demands cultivating certainly) and needs revelation to complete it. At the time of Muḥammad there was the ideal political situation, everything being before God, with absolute authority vested in the leader. To restructure society into its pure Quranic foundations was Parvēz's goal. In this way, the decline of Muslim civilization—in terms of its power and conditions—would be halted.

Parvēz on *ḥadīth*

Parvēz's argument has a number of aspects. The Qurʾān explains everything that an individual needs and no further source is needed. The Qurʾān contains no ruling saying that *ḥadīth* must be followed. Traditionalists claim that the word *ḥikma* in Qurʾān 2/129, "teach them the book and the *ḥikma*," refers to the *sunna* of Muḥammad, but Parvēz contends that this word is meant in the general sense of "wisdom." Likewise, *sūra* 59, verse 7, "Whatever the messenger gives you, take; whatever he forbids you, give over," relates only to distribution of spoils after battle for Parvēz, not to general things which Muḥammad proclaimed. Muḥammad himself, on the basis of *ḥadīth* itself, argued against the continuing relevance of his person: "Do not write down anything from me except the

Qur'ān." The historical background to this *ḥadīth*, it should be noted, is undoubtedly to be found among those people who in the early centuries of Islam also took Parvēz's position on *ḥadīth*, seeing the Qur'ān as the only legitimate source. *Ḥadīth* and its authority were the result of a compromise, according to Parvēz, reached between the rulers and those who wished to uphold the Qur'ān alone.

Ḥadīth reports occasionally contradict the Qur'ān; for example, the punishment for adultery is 100 lashes in the Qur'ān but stoning in the *ḥadīth*. Thus, for Parvēz, *ḥadīth* cannot be considered reliable. The unreliability of *ḥadīth* transmission also undermines its validity; any source will be garbled over time (except the Qur'ān, which was widely transmitted in uniform style). Subjective judgments were made in the past regarding the transmitters of *ḥadīth*. According to Parvēz, even the companions of Muḥammad may have erred in their transmissions; this is a position which opposes all traditional theological statements, which hold the companions of Muḥammad to have transmitted the material perfectly, limited only by their own perspective on the event being reported.

Furthermore, Muḥammad was an ordinary man according to Qur'ān 18/110 and he could have erred. The *ḥadīth* reports frequently include repugnant material, mixing ethical and doctrinal matters. The *ḥadīth* reports have fixed numerous elements of society in a static way in areas not governed by the Qur'ān; for example, in the Qur'ān it is commanded to give *zakāt*, "charity," which is seen to legislate the principle of "giving," whereas in *ḥadīth* it is stipulated that such and such an amount should be given. Says Parvēz, "If it had been the will of God that [the rate of *zakāt*] had to be 2 1/2 percent [as the *sharī'a* stipulates] until the Day of Resurrection, He would have stated it in the [Qur'ān]" (Parvēz, quoted in Baljon 1958: 224).

Significance

Parvēz's position, in a manner similar to that of other Modernists, tends to separate existence into two parts. For Parvēz, the distinction is between *madhhab*, the ethnic (principally Iranian) elements implemented in revenge for military defeat at the hands of the Arabs (and now to be identified with society), versus *dīn*, "religion," which is the Qur'ān. His overall platform of urging people to go straight to the Qur'ān is one which accommodates the greatest possibilities for change while staying within a traditional understanding of the authority of the scripture; the Qur'ān is, after all, far less precise and detailed than the *sunna* as elaborated in medieval Islam, and thus adaptation is far easier to legitimize.

Much of the emphasis in Parvēz's arguments is methodological and theological. Historical questions of whether Muḥammad did or did not do such things—questions which have motivated many scholarly studies of *ḥadīth*—seem subsidiary; the concerns are internal Muslim ones, despite the likelihood that Western influence accounts for some of the impetus of the discussions. The overall impact of these arguments, for Parvēz, is that the decisions of the past made on the basis of *ḥadīth* are all open to question. Fazlur Rahman (1955: 873) points out, however, at least one danger in this position: "The historical validity of the Koran itself is vouchsafed only by the tradition." Some may not agree that the Qurʾān depends upon tradition to that degree, preferring to see the status of the scripture vested in the results it has had in society, for example. The point does demonstrate, however, the potential need for those who enunciate such positions to elaborate a full theological vision of Islam.

Mawdūdī

Parvēz found his opponent in the figure of Mawlānā Abūʾl Aʿlāʾ Mawdūdī (1903–79). Mawdūdī was raised in a professional and religious family and was educated within a private, family setting in Hyderabad, India. He received no formal religious training, but his education was based on traditional Islamic knowledge. He learned Arabic and Persian in addition to his mother tongue, Urdu; later, he taught himself English and read widely in modern thought and science. He became a journalist at an early age, and by 1921 was editor of the Delhi newspaper *Muslim*; from 1925 to 1928, he was editor of *al-Jamʿiyyat*. Both these papers were sponsored by an organization of Muslim scholars known as the *Jamʿiyyat ʿulamāʾ-i Hind*. He started his personal writing, translating, and involvement in political activities during this period. In 1933 in Hyderabad, he became editor of *Tarjumān al-Qurʾān*, a monthly magazine which became the major vehicle for the enunciation of his views. His early writings of this period concentrated on the conflict between Islam and the Western world view, all being judged on the basis of the Qurʾān and the *sunna*.

By the middle of the 1930s, Mawdūdī became more involved in political issues. He argued strenuously against nationalism as being a foreign invention and anti-Islamic, and he felt that within India such nationalism would result in the destruction of Muslim identity. In 1941 he founded Jamāʿat-i Islāmī, the "Islamic Society," and remained its head until 1972. The goal of this organization was to effect a change in the life of Indian society, to make it more properly Islamic. However, in 1947, events forced Mawdūdī to emigrate to the recently formed Pakistan, and there he vowed to help establish a truly Islamic state; if this state for Muslims was to exist, he argued, it should be an Islamic one. His methods for urging this formation were the involvement of the Jamāʿat-i Islāmī in Pakistani politics, constant criticism and inciting to action of the political powers, and a stream of writings all of which aimed to explain the Islamic way of life. This political agitation led to prison terms for Mawdūdī, even to the sentence of death for a "seditious" pamphlet in 1953 (a sentence which was eventually commuted to two years in jail). He remained active in Pakistani politics throughout the 1960s.

Mawdūdī's vision of Islam

Many of Mawdūdī's works clearly illustrate his basic view of Islam and portray him as an Islamist. His largest work, *Tafhīm al-Qurʾān,* is a translation and explanation of the Qurʾān in Urdu. Its aim is to present the message of the Qurʾān in a clear style for people of today, using the commentary to display how that message is relevant to modern-day concerns.

The fundamental structures of Islam all revolve around God, who is in complete command of the universe and to whom all allegiance is owed. The natural order demands that people "submit," become Muslim. In order to facilitate that, God has sent prophets who bring the guidance which is needed for all humans to govern every aspect of their lives; this guidance is based on the idea of total loyalty to God. Any allegiance to something other than God—nationalism, Modernism, and the like—is anti-Islamic. Anything other than God which demands allegiance from a person belongs to the *jāhiliyya,* the term used in the Qurʾān for the non-Islamic ethos. Islamic guidance, the form of divine guidance which is the most complete and totally pure and which directs full allegiance to God, is embodied in the Qurʾān and in the *sunna* of Muḥammad. The understanding and interpretation of these sources are not vested in the religious learned classes but are available to all by use of personal judgment; those judgments will be made by the yardstick of "Is it Islamic?" rather than "Is it rational?" as is done by so many Modernists.

Mawdūdī and the authority of the past

Mawdūdī argues, on the basis of the Qurʾān, that Muḥammad is to be taken as a good example for all Muslims at all times. Muḥammad as a prophet is inseparable from his being a full example. The very purpose of revelation is to use a person to enact the message; otherwise, God would have just sent an angel with a book and been done with it. Mawdūdī suggests, however, that the idea of Muḥammad as an exemplar does not validate slavish adherence to everything Muḥammad did. Not everyone should marry an Arab woman, for example! It is worth mentioning at this point that, for a Modernist, the issue remains in Mawdūdī's position of how to distinguish what should be followed from what should not. Parvēz certainly perceived this problem. J. M. S. Baljon (1958: 225–6) notes that Parvēz accuses Mawdūdī of "denying tradition" when convenient, as in the length of his beard not necessarily being the same length as that of Muḥammad, yet condemning others for doing the very same thing—denying tradition. The accusation is made that those who claim to be able to determine which elements of the *ḥadīth* reports are to be followed and which are to be ignored—as Parvēz would suggest Mawdūdī is doing—are really claiming for themselves the status of prophethood. This is a veiled reference to the problems in Pakistan with Mīrzā Ghulām Aḥmad of the Aḥmadiyya (discussed in Chapter 16). The ultimate answer to this direction of the debate must lie in the concept of *ijmāʿ*, the consensus of the Muslim community, embodied in a more general notion of tradition. The real question, then, is to what extent are twentieth-century Muslims going to maintain those basic elements of the past in their search for modern Muslim identity?

Mawdūdī, like Parvēz, wants to find an Islamic flexibility which would legitimize change and allow Islam to continue to be relevant to life in the contemporary context. He is concerned, however, that the position which Parvēz argues *vis-à-vis* the *ḥadīth* reports, especially where it raises issues concerning their historical value, would eventually be applied to the Qurʾān, and Islam would crumble as a result. On the question of whether Muḥammad's example should be emulated in all times, he asserts that the Quranic evidence argues that it must; the prophetic example is the guarantor of the meaning of revelation and is indispensable to accepting the Qurʾān as revelation. The *ḥadīth* reports are reliable as texts because memorization was a highly developed skill among the Arabs and Muḥammad was an important person whose words and actions people would have remembered. Certainly, fabrication of *ḥadīth* reports did occur, but this is no reason to dismiss the entire package. The scientific procedures of the past used to assess *ḥadīth* reports were good but subject to error and were only based upon probability. In an argument typical of Mawdūdī's rationalism, the point is made that all of life is based upon probability and we all must use our God-given judgment to decide what to trust. "Blind imitation," *taqlīd*, is no longer sufficient, even though from a traditional standpoint that imitation is the best anyone can attain. To put one's trust in the learned people of the past and follow their interpretations is, from the traditional viewpoint, the appropriate manner of behavior rather than following one's own insights, which will be sure to be influenced by personal desires and lack of knowledge. Mawdūdī rejects this; for him, the learned classes have failed to preserve true Islam and are only acting to preserve their own self-interest. In Charles Adams's words:

> Mawdūdī puts particular emphasis on the argument from probability, saying once more that the fact of a piece of information being only probable does not make it necessarily either wrong or untrustworthy. The proper thing for a serious man is neither to reject all the *ẓannī ḥadīth* [probable reports] nor to accept them all but to investigate each one individually. The vast majority of *ḥadīth*, because they are *akhbār-i-āḥād* [reports transmitted via one *isnād* only] fall into the *ẓannī* category. One should accept those he is able to prove to be reliable, reject those which he cannot prove, and reserve his judgment about any that fall in the neutral ground between proof and its lack. This he holds to be a reasonable stand and one that is in accord with Islam since Islam is a reasonable religion.
>
> (Adams 1976: 35)

Mawdūdī's answer to modernity is rigorous discipline and self-sufficiency along with revolt against Muslim rulers who do not support Islam appropriately. His call is to a return to

Medina, the perfect political time of Muḥammad when true Islam existed and true interpretations were available; the faithful collectivity of the Muslim community in this period is the final goal of the present time. However, this will only be arrived at by an initial return to the Islamic revolution through quiet conversion as displayed in Mecca. Parvēz's call, on the other hand, is to Mecca alone: Islam is internal, and Mecca was the era of pure faith, before time and place constricted Islam in Medina.

Authority

The controversy over the *sunna*—and it has taken place throughout the Muslim world, not only in India and Pakistan—points straight to the heart of the views about Islam in the modern period. What is the essential part of Islam that must be maintained and passed on to future generations and what may be discarded as trappings from the past? This is the universal problem for all religions today. All parties in these discussions agree that Islam needs to be revitalized so that its relevance to modern life can be perceived and felt to be advantageous for individual believers. But what is the proper Islamic way of deciding the basic question of the authority of the past? Does the *sunna* in fact have any authority within an Islamic framework or was this, as Parvēz suggests, simply a construct created in the past for political expediency? Is the *sunna* a vital part of Islam which has simply become mired in the analyses of the past? These are very fundamental questions about the structural bases of Islam, and the answers to them produce radically different views on what Islam might be in the future. Most answers, when they are in fact produced, seem to urge a gradual reassessment of the past, one which will not produce a severe fracture with practices which are already a part of Muslim society. For some, this is too slow a solution and for them a more radical approach is needed. Others may try to sidestep the issue and instead turn to the Qur'ān, the agreed-upon locus of Islamic identity, and attempt a positive formulation of Islam on that basis. Chapter 14 pays attention to the implications of these discussions concerning the Qur'ān.

Muḥammad on film

Because of the widespread sentiment among Muslims that suggests that Muḥammad should not be portrayed in representational form, movie producers have struggled to find ways to tell the story of the prophet's life without actually having him be a presence in the film.

The earliest attempt, *The Message*, made in 1976, was a live-action film with Anthony Quinn playing Hamza, Muḥammad's uncle, and had Muḥammad himself always off-camera. The film was well received by Arabic- and English-speaking audiences (two versions were made, the Arabic one having different actors and being released under the title *al-Risāla*). The producer-director Moustapha Akkad (1930–2005)—who later went on to produce the *Halloween* series starting in 1978—worked with Egyptian Sunnī and Lebanese Shī'ī religious authorities to produce a film that would prove religiously acceptable. The ground rules were explicit: Muḥammad, his wives, his children, and 'Alī, his son-in-law, could not be depicted. (In 2004, Azhar authorities decided that films should not portray Muḥammad's companions either, and Akkad's effort became subject to censorship.) The portrait of Muḥammad in the film is a typically Modernist one and displays sensitivity to issues that arise in the contemporary world: Muḥammad is portrayed almost as a pacifist, abhorring violence and always ready to forgive, in a manner that stands in contrast to that of his opponents. Somewhat ironically, because it is a result of the imposed

(a)

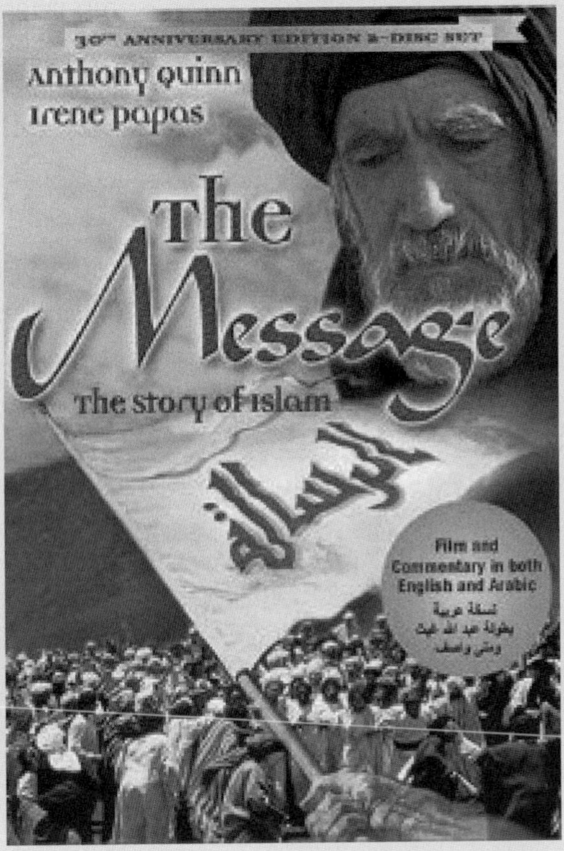

Figure 13.2 **(a)** *The Message*; **(b)** *Muhammad, the Last Prophet.* Neither movie poster illustrates the person of Muḥammad himself.

(b)

Figure 13.2 Continued

restriction on not portraying his wives, Muḥammad is also pictured as apparently celibate, with no close friends or family members (an image, as has been pointed out, that is appealing to Christian, Hindu, and Buddhist audiences, given their own image of what is appropriate for holy men). Akkad is quoted as saying:

> I did the film because it is a personal thing for me. Besides its production values as a film, it has its story, its intrigue, its drama. Beside all this I think there was something personal, being [a] Muslim myself who lived in the West I felt that it was my obligation, my duty, to tell the truth about Islam. It is a religion that has a 700-million following, yet it's [*sic*] so little known about it, which surprised me. I thought I should tell the story that will bring this bridge, this gap to the West.
>
> (www.imdb.com/name/nm0002160/bio#quotes)

One more recent, Syrian-backed, effort was the production of an animated feature, *Muhammad, the Last Prophet*, using a total of 196,000 drawings. Directed and produced by Richard Rich and released in 2004, the film portrayed Muḥammad's presence by a blinding light, a technique that harkens back to fourteenth- to sixteenth-century miniatures that portray Muḥammad's face in this manner (as well as God). Even then, Muḥammad does not speak in the film and his words are passed on by a persecuted but loyal follower. The film was ultimately approved by religious authorities, although not without incident: it was reported that the chief censor in Egypt was angered by scenes in which Muslims destroyed pre-Islamic idols that looked like Pharaonic statues; nationalism can be as strong a motivator in reacting to such a film as can religious sensibilities.

An Iranian film, *Soheil Star* ("Star of the Canopus"), produced in 2007 and directed by Amir Ghavidel, is a filmic biography of Uways al-Qaranī (Oveis-e Qarni), an early convert to Islam from the Yemen who never met Muḥammad in person but whose faith was so secure that it could not be broken by the Persian rulers of his homeland. Muḥammad appears very briefly as a figure of blazing light and speaks through his (Persian) spokesperson, Salmān al-Fārisī; ʿAlī ibn abī Ṭālib appears at one point but his face is never shown.

Other films have been produced about Muḥammad but most have been presented as documentary educational-type films (typically including interviews with academics or other individuals). One example is PBS's *Islam: Empire of Faith* (2000), which devotes its first fifty minutes to the life of Muḥammad.

For more on Akkad's film, see Freek L. Bakker, "The Image of Muhammad in *The Message*, the First and Only Feature Film about the Prophet of Islam," *Islam and Christian–Muslim Relations*, 17 (2006): 77–92.

Suggested further reading

Daniel W. Brown, *Rethinking Tradition in Modern Islamic Thought*, Cambridge: Cambridge University Press, 1996.

G. H. A. Juynboll, *The Authenticity of the Tradition Literature: Discussions in Modern Egypt*, Leiden: Brill, 1969.

Aisha Y. Musa, *Ḥadīth as Scripture: Discussions on the Authority of Prophetic Traditions in Islam*, New York: Palgrave Macmillan, 2008.

Sayyid Vali Reza Nasr, *Mawdudi and the Making of Islamic Revivalism*, New York: Oxford University Press, 1996.

Omid Safi, *Memories of Muhammad: Why the Prophet Matters*, New York: HarperOne, 2009.

14 *The Qurʾān and modernity*

In a manner which would seem to be quite exceptional within contemporary world religions, there is an impressive amount of activity occurring in writing works of Qurʾān interpretation throughout the Muslim world. The reasons for this must be examined.

Clearly, the search for Islamic identity, for the Islamic answer to the problems of the modern world, has led many Islamic thinkers to make recourse to the original resources of Islam: it has led them back to the Qurʾān. This tendency is widespread and not overly surprising; Islam has always been a scripturalist faith and few have wanted to question that basic orientation to the revealed text. Be that as it may, the writing of commentaries on scripture still needs some explanation to account for its prominence and significance.

The field of *tafsīr*, the Arabic word for "commentary," is a traditional one. The act of writing a *tafsīr* is an expression of individual piety on the part of the writer, but it also acts to enunciate each writer's particular view of Islam and its relevance to his or her age. Therefore, each writer faces a basic difficulty anew (although each does work initially on the basis of what had been said in previous generations): how to make the text communicate meaningfully within his or her own time and cultural framework. Clearly, explaining the text to Malaysians in the twenty-first century requires a different approach than it would have in Arabia of the tenth century.

The mode of commentary writing has not changed substantially since its emergence in classical times, although the use of certain modern forms—magazines, newspapers—may be noted. Modern Qurʾān interpretation is marked, in many of its manifestations, by three interrelated principles:

1 The attempt is made to interpret the Qurʾān in light of scientific reason and methodology. "To interpret the Qurʾān by the Qurʾān" is the phrase frequently used to express this, implying the rejection of all the extraneous material provided by tradition in the form of *ḥadīth* reports and earlier commentaries.
2 Following from the previous principle, the attempt is made, through the expediency of interpretation, to divest the Qurʾān of all legendary traits, primitive ideas, fantastic

stories, magic, fables, and superstitions; symbolic interpretation is the primary means for such resolutions.
3 The attempt is made to support doctrine by finding it in, or justifying it by, the Qurʾān.

Overall, it is common to find in modern commentaries an emphasis on the spiritual content of the Qurʾān and its guidance. As well, some Modernist approaches are marked by an attitude of viewing the Qurʾān as the work of Muḥammad's mind, at least to the extent of speaking of the text not as descending from heaven in its actual wording (as was classically expressed and is still held in many circles), but as being the spirit of revelation filtered through Muḥammad's psyche and thus being expressed within the limits of his intellect and linguistic abilities. As has been remarked by Fazlur Rahman (1955: 872), however, this has not always led to "historical inquiry into the Koranic revelation on scientific lines, [but] has enhanced the emotional intensity for the Prophet's person." The ramifications of that have been sketched in Chapter 13.

Figure 14.1 In a 1948 stained-glass competition, Egyptian calligrapher Aḥmad Muṣṭafā rendered Quranic verses that refer to the bounty of the sea as made available by God for human consumption. Works such as this display the continued vitality of Quranic calligraphy in the Muslim world.
Source: Hussain A. Al-Ramadan/*Saudi Aramco World*/SAWDIA.

The beginnings

The earliest focal point of Modernist *tafsīr* activity was in India. Sayyid Aḥmad Khān (1817–98) wrote the first major explicitly Modernist commentary, entitled simply *Tafsīr al-Qur'ān*. His book was directed towards making all Muslims aware of the fact that Western influences in the world required a new vision of Islam, for Islam as it was actually practiced and believed in by most of its adherents would be seriously threatened by modern advances in thought and science. Where, therefore, was the true core of Islam to be found? How was its center to be defined? For Aḥmad Khān, these questions were to be answered through reference to the Qur'ān, which, if it were properly understood through the use of the powers of reason, would provide the necessary answers. The basis of the required social and educational reforms, for example, was to be found in the Qur'ān. By returning to the source of Islam, the religion would be revitalized and the proper future would be secure.

Muḥammad ʿAbduh

Generally considered the most significant Modernist figure in the crucial nineteenth-century developments in Egypt, Muḥammad ʿAbduh lived from 1849 to 1905. He was born in lower Egypt and was educated at the home of Islamic orthodoxy in Cairo, al-Azhar. He studied philosophy with Jamāl al-Dīn al-Afghānī and started writing on social and political issues, reflecting many of Afghānī's views. In 1877 he started teaching at al-Azhar and shortly after that at Dār al-ʿUlūm in Cairo. When the British invaded Egypt in 1882 (after the Egyptian army had taken over governing the country from the ruler Ismāʿīl), ʿAbduh, who had emerged as a leader of the civilian wing of opposition to Ismāʿīl, was exiled for a time to France along with Afghānī. He taught for a period in Beirut, and his lectures there form his book *Risālat al-Tawḥīd*, "The Theology of Unity," one of the few explicit attempts made to write a Modernist Islamic theology. In 1888 he returned to Egypt and spent the rest of his career as a jurist (*muftī*) giving decisions (*fatwās*) which embodied his Modernist stance. He became the chief *muftī* of Egypt in 1897.

For ʿAbduh, the central problem which had to be faced was the decay of Islamic society. Changing circumstances, unforeseen by Muḥammad in forming the Muslim community, had resulted in the status of Islam deteriorating within the community. New codes of law were being imposed, ones which some felt were more compatible with modern economic and social realities. New schools and institutions were emerging throughout society. These changes created a basic issue which had to be confronted: what is it that actually makes Muslim society Muslim?

ʿAbduh saw change as inevitable and beneficial, but he also saw the danger of the increasing separation of Islamic spheres of influence and areas controlled by the modern sense of human reason. Bringing these two together became the central platform of his Modernism. The simple transplantation of European law, for example, would not provide a viable basis for an Islamic society. Traditional Islamic schools were stagnant and modern schools were devoid of a religious ethos, and this resulted in the further splitting of Egyptian society into traditional and European-influenced sectors.

ʿAbduh's answer to this dilemma was to link the principles of change to Islam; Islam would be the controller of change, providing the criteria for selecting what was good and necessary in modern life. His aim was not to convince the traditional learned classes of the need for change, but rather to demonstrate to the more secular-influenced group that it was possible to be devout in the modern age. He hoped thereby that a new learned class would emerge which would be able to articulate the new, revitalized, rational Islam. His book *The Theology of Unity* is a good example of the way in which he worked out this position. The book is structured in the form of a classical work of theology, starting with epistemology and moving through the topics of God, prophets, revelation, and Islam. Throughout the work the emphasis is on logical argumentation such that the conclusion that Islam is the one, true religion must be accepted by all rational people. The logical argumentation, however, avoids the "excesses" connected to probing into matters declared to be "unprofitable" for speculation.

Fundamental to this revitalized Islam was the identification of elements in traditional Islam which were consonant with modern thought. Islam was to be seen as a "civilization" and an activity in life. *Ijmāʿ*, the principle of consensus in law, was to be identified with public opinion. *Shūrā*, consultation of the elders, was, in this view, parliamentary democracy. *Maṣlaḥa*, a legal principle reflecting the ideal of the public interest, could be identified with utilitarianism, in which legal opinion always aims toward the position from which the greatest good will flow.

In order to accomplish his aims, ʿAbduh urged a "return to the sources" in order to reassess them in light of the modern predicament and with the assistance of human reason. This task is reflected in his Qurʾān commentary and has made him the reference point for many Modernist writers as well as Islamist groups, who highlight his scripturalist emphasis.

ʿAbduh and the Qurʾān

Leading the way for a changed Quranic interpretation, ʿAbduh struggled against the traditional enterprise of *tafsīr*. He argued for the need to make Qurʾān commentary available to the people as a whole. The intellectual efforts of the past had made the text "illegible"; any sense of a distinction between what was important and what was not had been lost. As well, the efforts of the past did not respond to the needs and questions of his day. ʿAbduh thus embarked on a commentary that would be minus the theological speculations, the detailed grammatical discussions, and the obtuse scholarship which characterized the commentaries of the past. The similarities in impulse and direction to those of the Protestant Reformation of Europe may be noted: for one, Luther's Bible translation took the text out of the hands of the clergy alone and gave it to the common people; as well, the impact of the printing press is to be noted, this being a major factor in the development of Egypt, with the first press established there in the 1820s.

ʿAbduh's Qurʾān commentary, which was published and completed by his follower Rashīd Riḍā under the title *Tafsīr al-Manār* and was based upon his class lectures and the texts of his legal decisions, is marked by a moderate rationalist spirit coupled with an emphasis on the moral directions for the modern world as provided by the spiritual and religious guidance of the Qurʾān. The search for knowledge, the use of the intellect, the need for education, and the prerequisite of political independence were all to be found in and justified by the Qurʾān. What is unknown should be left unknown, rather than embrace the traditional folk tales that attempt to explain them. Any ambiguity which exists in the Qurʾān as a result is there for a reason: in order to divert attention away from the material world toward the spiritual. "If more details were useful, God would have added them." This, it should be noted, leads to a marked attitude of rejecting interpretations which find modern science in the Qurʾān. This tendency is even more pronounced in the work of Rashīd Riḍā, who completed ʿAbduh's *tafsīr* after the latter's death. For ʿAbduh himself, the Qurʾān certainly tolerates (even encourages) scientific investigation, but science is not seen to reveal the true meaning of the Qurʾān. References in the text of scripture to telephones and spaceships are functions of the imagination according to ʿAbduh and are not based upon sound principles of interpretation, contrary to the opinion of some other prominent writers discussed later in this chapter.

That the moral point of the Qurʾān is the text's highest and ultimate aim in ʿAbduh's view may be nicely illustrated by his commentary on the Quranic passage dealing with marriage of multiple wives:

> God has made the condition that one keep far from injustice to be the basis for his giving of a law [concerning marriage]. This confirms the fact that justice is enjoined as a condition and that duty consists in striving for it.
>
> . . . Polygamy is like one of those necessities which is permitted to the one to whom it is allowed [only] with the stipulation that he act fairly with trustworthiness and that he be immune from injustice. . . . In view of this restriction, when one now considers what corruption results from polygamy in modern times, then one will know for certain that a people . . . cannot be trained so that their remedy lies in polygamy, since, in a family in which a single man has two wives, no beneficial situation and no order prevail.
>
> (ʿAbduh, as translated in Gätje 1976: 249)

Abū'l-Kalām Āzād

Āzād, who lived from 1888 to 1958, was an Indian politician who was influenced in his Modernism by Aḥmad Khān and thought highly of his educational ideas. Āzād is also said to have been in contact with Muḥammad ʿAbduh's ideas when he traveled in the Middle East in the early 1900s. He started his career as a journalist and continued to work for his political causes through journalism throughout his life. He was president of the Congress Party in India in 1923 and 1940, and was Minister of Education from 1947 to 1958 in independent India. Journalism was his main activity but in everything he wrote he manifested his aims concerning the nation of India. He opposed the creation of a separate Muslim state in India and served, from 1937 on, as Gandhi's adviser on Muslim issues. He urged the necessity for Hindu–Muslim cooperation in India in the struggle for independence from the British.

True religion is universal for Āzād, echoing a stance of modern Indian pluralism and of opposition to the India–Pakistan split. To recognize this unity is to recognize the unity of humanity. Antagonism between religions has emerged only because people have come to think that they have a monopoly on truth within their own faith; in fact, all religions share in the truth. All religious people should return to the true form of their own religion; this is what the Qur'ān instructs. All should submit to God and lead a life of right action according to their own religion. This religious spirit of cooperation reflects Āzād's ideals concerning the Indian political situation. All Muslims should return to the Qur'ān and the *sunna* and purify their religious tradition from all foreign additions. Care must be taken not to over-emphasize the importance of ritual and law of any faith, for this is what has produced conflict between religions in the past.

Āzād wrote his *Tarjumān al-Qur'ān* in the late 1920s as an explanatory translation, but his treatment of *sūra* 1 is a full commentary which presents all the basic concepts of Islam. *Dīn* is what has been given to all prophets everywhere and this is Islam. *Sharīʿa* or *minhaj*, used by Āzād to refer to the path of Islam, varies with time and conditions, although it is an absolutely necessary and desirable part of all religions.

The Qur'ān presents its message as one based on truth, justice, and righteousness. Its method of presentation is equally important:

> The primary and the most important feature of the method of presentation followed by the Qur'an is the appeal to reason that it makes. It lays repeated emphasis on the search for truth, on the need of exercising one's reason and insight, of reflecting over the outward experience of life and drawing valid conclusions. In fact, there is no chapter in the Qur'an wherein it has not made an earnest appeal to man to reflect upon everything.
>
> (Āzād, as quoted in Faruqi 1982: 73)

Āzād's comments on *sūra* 1, verse 4, "[God is] the Lord of the Day of Judgment," illustrate how he finds the theme permeating the text:

> The current religious beliefs had invested God with the characteristics of an absolute and moody monarch who, when he was pleased, showered gifts all around him or, when he was displeased, inflicted dire punishment. Thus arose the custom of offering sacrifices to appease God's wrath and win His favour. The Quran's conception of God, however, is not that of an arbitrary ruler who governs according to his moods and whims. On the contrary, the law of divine reward and retribution is a natural law of cause and effect which has universal application. We see its operation in the physical world around us all the time and should therefore have no difficulty in understanding its operation in relation to our spiritual conduct . . . .
>
> So, just as man needs the protection of God the Preserver and the grace and bounty of God the Merciful [as presented in the previous verse of the Qur'ān], he cannot do without the divine quality of justice, which makes for organised good life and eliminates, or at least minimises, the elements of harm and mischief.
>
> (Āzād, as quoted in Husain 1960: 68, 69)

Sayyid Quṭb

Born in 1906 and executed in 1966 for his role in plotting against the rule of Egyptian President Abdul Nasser, Sayyid Quṭb was spokesman for the radical manifestation of the Islamist Egyptian Muslim Brotherhood, al-Ikhwān al-Muslimūn, and continues to be a powerful, martyred voice for the movement. He represents, therefore, not the Modernism of ʿAbduh, but an activist Islamic totalism, one initiated by Ḥasan al-Bannāʾ (1906–49) in 1928 and a major force in Egypt in the 1940s and 1950s. The thrust behind the Brotherhood was the desire to purify Islam of the corruption of Western morals and influence in general. This was to be done through revolutionary social action, bringing Islamic policies into action in Egypt. Islam was argued to be a comprehensive ideology, one which held the only possible answer to the ills and despair of the day. Islam would and should regulate life totally, and with the full acceptance of the *sharīʿa* in public life, social justice and political freedom would follow. Reason and public welfare are the operative principles in life, but these must work within the moral principles of Islam alone. Islamic order rests on three basic principles: justice of the ruler, obedience of the ruled, and the notion of consultation (*shūrā*), by which the ruler is elected, controlled, and, if need be, deposed. It is thus a political platform under which all political parties would be outlawed, the law reformed to the *sharīʿa*, and administrative posts given to those with religious education. This type of Islamism has proven very popular in many places in the Muslim world, especially among the better-educated young who have rejected both the traditional approach to scripturalism (as manifested in the works of the scholarly elite) and Western modernity. Mawdūdī, whose ideas have already been examined, and Quṭb represent the most successful manifestations of the enunciation of this Islamist tendency.

Quṭb himself embraced Westernization early in his life but became disenchanted with it, so it is reported, after Israel's formation and after experiencing first hand what he spoke of as the anti-Arab sentiment in the United States during a stay there in 1949–51. He did not think much of the entire Western way of life:

> I do know how people live in America, the country of the great production, extreme wealth, and indulgent pleasure. . . . I saw them there as nervous tension devoured their lives despite all the evidence of wealth, plenty, and gadgets that they have. Their enjoyment is nervous excitement, animal merriment. One gets the image that they are constantly running from ghosts that are pursuing them. They are as machines that move with madness, speed, and convulsion that does not cease. Many times I thought it was as though the people were in a grinding machine that does not stop day or night, morning or evening. It grinds them and they are devoured without a moment's rest. They have no faith in themselves or in life around them.
>
> (Quṭb, as quoted in Haddad 1982: 90)

These attitudes towards the West and its materialistic trappings are reflected in Quṭb's *tafsīr* called *Fī Ẓilāl al-Qurʾān*, "In the Shade of the Qurʾān." Islam is the "final, comprehensive, perfect and accomplished message" from God. This Islam is not merely the religious principles of the Modernists, but a full system of life, perfect in its integration of freedom, equality, and social justice, one which is in perfect accord with the cosmic order. This is expressed in the *tafsīr* in the following way:

> "Those who believe and do righteous deeds are the best of all creatures" [Qurʾān 98/7]. This is also an absolute verdict that makes for no dispute or argument. Its condition is also clear, free from any ambiguity or deception. The condition is faith, not merely being born in a land which claims to be Islamic, or in a family which claims to belong to Islam. Neither is it a few words which one repeats again and again. It is the acceptance of faith which establishes its effects on the actual life, "and do righteous deeds." It is entirely different from the words which go no further than the lips. As for the "righteous deeds," these are everything which Allāh has commanded to be done in matters of worship, behaviour, action and day-to-day dealings. The first and most important of these "righteous deeds" is the establishment of Allāh's law on this planet, and the government of people according to what Allāh has legislated.
>
> (Quṭb 1979: 249)

Everything outside Islam is, as for Mawdūdī, *jāhiliyya*, derived from the spirit of barbarism and contrary to everything Islam stands for. Unbridled individualism and depravity are the marks of the modern world, and these have culminated in moral and social decline. Islamic society has not simply degenerated; it has, in fact, left Islam and become non-Muslim by negating God's sovereignty and substituting materialism. Modernization and development are plots to colonize, in material, moral, and cultural ways, the entire Muslim world. The reassertion of Islam and the condemnation of *jāhiliyya* are the ways to combat this threat. There can be no compromise; Islam must be fully implemented according to the *sharīʿa*. A group such as the Muslim Brotherhood must exist in order to create an alternative counter-society which will produce a model generation of true Muslims. Such a society will substitute divine rule for human rule, for the latter is the key marker of the *jāhilī* attitude.

A study of Quṭb's commentary reveals the careful way in which his vision of Islam and society is embedded in the text. A. H. Johns (1990: 143–70), for example, has looked at the way Quṭb treats the story of Moses in the Qurʾān. Moses is the "great figure of moral and social liberation" and provides Quṭb with a fitting vehicle for his ideas. Pharaoh is the tyrant ruler of every age who wishes to destroy religion; Moses is the model for all who wish to proclaim the triumph of God's word. Egypt—despite Quṭb's emphasis on the whole of the Islamic community, as Johns points out—is the "cradle" of the world, a green, fertile valley providing all the necessities of life. Threats of jail made by the tyrant to the devotee of God do not cause loss of self-control but only produce demonstrations of the truth of the message, guided by God's power. And this message will resound in the hearts of the people who have lost their faith because of the humiliation they have suffered at the hands of the tyrant. The remnant of their faith which remains in their hearts will be rebuilt. All of this, of course, while acting to interpret in vivid fashion the story of Moses as told in the Qurʾān, is a reflection of Quṭb's life itself, his struggles on behalf of religion against the hypocritical powers of the world, a struggle which radical Islamists continue down to today.

Quṭb also based his position on an argument about the merits of the Qurʾān, and his style of presentation in his commentary reflects this urge. The lack of artistic appreciation of the text on the part of Muslims has meant that the holistic emphasis of the message has been missed; this is especially the fault in traditional commentaries, which took an atomistic approach to the text. The unity of the Qurʾān as a book, as reflected in its artistry, is a mirror of divine unity and an image of the cohesive unity of Islam, the religion and social order. The dramatic elements of the Qurʾān are a reflection of the drama of human life and the text must therefore be lived for it to be meaningful. Quṭb reveals here his own earlier avocation as a *belletrist*.

Ṭanṭāwī Jawharī

As has already been mentioned, both Aḥmad Khān and Muḥammad ʿAbduh were intent on encouraging their compatriots to welcome the scientific outlook of the West in order to share in the progress of the modern world. Often this effort involved little more than simply stating that the Qurʾān enjoins its readers to seek and use rational knowledge. However, at other times, it also involved the historical claim that the Islamic world had developed science in the first place and had then passed it on to Europe, so that, in embracing the scientific outlook in the present situation, Muslims were only reclaiming what was truly Islamic. A more distinctive trend in *tafsīr* emerges also, for example in the writings of Ṭanṭāwī Jawharī (1862–1940), an Egyptian secondary school teacher who published, among many other educational, religious, and spiritualist works, a twenty-six-volume work entitled *Al-Jawāhir fī Tafsīr al-Qurʾān* ("Jewels in the Interpretation of the Qurʾān") between 1923 and 1935.

Jawharī's writings are permeated by two main themes, common to much Modernist writing from the turn of the twentieth century: first, Islam is in perfect accord with human nature; and, second, Islam, as found in the Qurʾān, contains within it an explanation of the scientific workings of the world. God would not have revealed the Qurʾān had He not included in it everything that people needed to know; science is obviously necessary in the modern world, so it should not be surprising to find all of science in the Qurʾān when that scripture is properly understood. Jawharī also makes reference to the classical notion of the miraculous character or inimitability of the Qurʾān (*iʿjāz*), which he takes to refer primarily to the content of the text in terms of its knowledge concerning matters which are only now becoming clear to humanity. Since the scientific knowledge contained in the text is proof of its miraculous character, references are found in the Qurʾān for numerous modern inventions (electricity, for example) and scientific discoveries (the fact that the earth revolves around the sun). Jawharī always claimed that his exegesis was no more far-fetched than the traditional legal approach to the text. Scientific exegesis stems from a view of the Qurʾān and the *sunna* as providing all the knowledge that people would need. The Qurʾān therefore anticipates modern science. What is more, as a tendency in interpretation, this exegetical approach has an honorable pedigree with classical precedents, for example in al-Mursī (d. 1257) who found astronomy, medicine, weaving, spinning, agriculture, and pearl-diving mentioned in the Qurʾān.

The tendency to scientific interpretation (although now markedly out of date in the actual scientific information provided in the instance of Jawharī himself) has become widespread, and it is often used as a popular means of trying to convince non-Muslims of the divine nature of the Qurʾān and Islam. A startling example which was in circulation in Turkey in an English-language publication (and thus presumably designed for tourist/non-Muslim consumption) comments in the following manner on Qurʾān 66/6, "The fire whose fuel is men and stones":

> A vast amount of energy lies locked in the nuclei of matter. In accordance with Einstein's equation, $E = mc^2$, it is known that a single gram of matter, if converted into

> energy, would yield energy equivalent to that contained in 2500 tons of coal. If the atoms of men and stones could be converted directly to energy, we would be faced with inexhaustible amounts of fuel.
>
> (Nurbaki 1986: 44)

The real aim of the sacred verse, then, is to direct our attention to this fact. In other words, it intends to teach us the truth hidden in the essence of matter.

Apologetics is not the only accomplishment of scientific exegesis, however. Muslims have found their faith enhanced and renewed through exposure to these types of claims. Typical is the following testimony from an Egyptian Doctor of Pharmacy, published in a 1991 textbook of world religions:

> Some of the statements in the Qur'an had no meaning at that time, 1400 years ago, but they have meaning now. For example, "We have created this universe and we have made it expanding." "We have made the earth look like an egg." Such statements cannot come from just an average person living 1400 years ago. Among ancient Egyptians, ancient Syrians we cannot find this information. I started to believe that someone was giving the knowledge to Muhammad. I'm not a very good believer—don't ask me to believe just because there is a book. But this information cannot come from any source except One Source.
>
> (Fisher and Luyster 1991: 277)

Many other such science-based proofs are appealed to by contemporary Muslims. Extremely popular, for example, have been numerically based schemes that manage to find unexpected patterns in the letters, words, verses, chapters, and so forth in the Qur'ān. Essentially such approaches are modern variations on ancient gematria—the "science of numbers"—often powered by computer analysis. The number nineteen has a long heritage in these speculations and a recent work has managed to accomplish the same thing using the number seven. There is a definite selectiveness with the data that goes on in making these arguments (how to define a "word" in Arabic is notoriously problematic, for example). It is also likely that patterns of a similarly striking character could be produced by an analysis using any number, given statistical probabilities of a small range of numbers and a reasonably large textual basis.

The main argument against the scientific type of approach, as enunciated by some Muslims, is that it suggests that the language of the text was not that of Muḥammad and his times; that is a lexically unsound approach, according to these critics. The word *samawāt* (literally "heavens"), translated as "universe" in the previous quotation, for example, would have conveyed a certain meaning to Muḥammad and his followers which would have been quite different from what is conveyed by the word "universe" today. As well, of course, such interpretations are opposed to the common Modernist idea that the

Qurʾān's value is in its spiritual and general guidance and it is not a source book of facts. The ever-changing scientific ideas of the nineteenth and twentieth centuries should not be identified with the unchanging value of the Qurʾān, say many opponents. Shabbir Akhtar points out that these "arguments, if indeed that is the appropriate term for them, carry conviction only with devotees." Rarely, Akhtar notes, is the criterion of scientific consistency applied throughout the text:

> If the koranic claims tally with scientific views, it is cause for celebration in the religious camp; if not, it is declared either that the beliefs currently prevalent in the scientific community are, conveniently enough for Muslims, erroneous or else that secular scientific truths are irrelevant to judgements about the truth of revealed claims. . . . For to accept a consistent application of the criterion is, as the religionists themselves vaguely sense in some moods, in effect to impose a very exacting demand upon revelation. Is the Koran's authority, then, dependent upon its being able to achieve conformity with current scientific scholarship?
>
> (Akhtar 1990: 54)

Scientific interpretation of the Qurʾān is a particularly modern approach to scripture because it reflects a very modern assumption: that science holds a single objective truth and scripture, for it to be valid, must conform to and confirm that truth. This is a value system which is markedly at variance with that of medieval times, in which science was treated as a separate endeavor which contained multiple attempts to describe the world, as compared to the absoluteness of the Qurʾān.

Tafsīr in other parts of the Islamic world

The writing of commentaries goes on throughout the Muslim world, not just in India and Egypt. Ibn Bādis (1889–1940) was a famous Algerian Modernist reformer who turned to *tafsīr* to provide a vehicle for his ideas about contemporary political questions. In Iran, Sayyid Muḥammad Ḥusayn al-Ṭabāṭabāʾī (1903–82) published an Arabic work entitled *al-Mīzān* ("The Balance"), some of which is available in English translation, which presents a totalist vision of Islam with a Neo-Traditionalist flavor. In Indonesia, people such as Ahmad Soorkatie presented the Modernist ideas of Muḥammad ʿAbduh in the form of Quranic commentary embedded in lectures given in Arabic.

As should be apparent from the above discussions, books of Quranic interpretation have become a vehicle for the spread of diverse ideas in the Islamic world. Support for various conceptions of Islam are found in the scriptural text, along with many passages which are deemed to have the answer to the dilemmas faced by Muslims and their faith in the modern world. All such works urge the relevance of Islam to the modern day, but

Figure 14.2 A class in Mali for teaching young boys to memorize and recite the Qur'ān. Source: James L. Stanfield/Getty Images.

it must be an Islam that is properly understood; and that is where the differences between the approaches begin to appear. Each approach argues for its own definition of what is essential in Islam. It is notable that the discussions and presentations thus far illustrated have not raised fundamental questions about the nature of the Qur'ān and how that is to be understood in the modern world.

Types of critical approach

Practical examples of looking at texts from the Qur'ān provide the best illustration of the issues which are at stake in talking about types of Muslim critical approach to the Qur'ān, the problems which they raise, and the limits which the interpretations will reach. Here is a good exercise for the reader: read the following three sections of the Qur'ān and consider their problematic aspects within the modern context. Assume the stance of a Modernist Muslim: what do you perceive as problematic? Assume the stance of an Islamist: what is your response to a Western perception of difficulties with these texts? Assume the stance of a Traditionalist: how would you interpret the passage?

The first example

Sūra 56, verses 11–24:

> These will be
> Those Nearest to God:
> In Gardens of Bliss:
> A number of people
> From those of old,
> And a few from those
> Of later times.
> (They will be) on Thrones
> Encrusted (with gold
> And precious stones),
> Reclining on them,
> Facing each other.
> Round about them will (serve)
> Youths of perpetual (freshness),
> With goblets, (shining) beakers,
> And cups (filled) out of
> Clear-flowing fountains:
> No after-ache will they
> Receive therefrom, nor will they
> Suffer intoxication:
> And with fruits,
> Any that they may select;
> And the flesh of fowls,
> Any that they may desire.
> And (there will be) Companions
> With beautiful, big,
> And lustrous eyes,—
> Like unto Pearls
> Well-guarded.
> A Reward for the Deeds
> Of their past (Life).

This sensual picture of the rewards of heaven can evoke a variety of responses. For the Modernist, such portraits are potentially objectionable for what they imply about the relations between the sexes and for their material imagery in dealing with the rewards in the hereafter. Furthermore, Modernists will react to the Orientalist-missionary suggestion that this afterlife picture is somehow unspiritual (with the insinuation that Christianity has a more elevated view). Such a position may wish to propose that the picture is to be understood as mythic; this is not a description of reality as such, but is a figure which is expressed in a language which would appeal to those at the time of Muḥammad and would motivate them to convert and "submit" to the will of God. Such a resolution of the perceived problem suggests a certain relativization of the Quranic message in history such that parts of it may only be directly relevant to a certain age.

Muslims of the Islamist persuasion will insist that the passage reflects a reality, but that the reality is spoken of in metaphors and similar figures of speech. The "Companions," often translated less euphemistically as "fair maidens" (in Arabic: *hūr*) are not maidens at all, but priests who will minister to all, for example. The accuracy of the text, therefore, is not to be relativized but to be reinterpreted in a fashion amenable to the modern spirit—but the reality is still there in the text.

Traditionalists have no difficulty with such a passage. There is no reason to suggest that the hereafter will be the least bit different than its literal description as provided by God in the Qur'ān. The only evidence which we have for the nature of the afterlife is provided in scripture and God will have described it accurately and will have designed it in a manner pleasing to Him and to humanity.

The second example

Sūra 23, verses 12–18:

> Man We did create
> From a quintessence (of clay);
> Then We placed him
> As (a drop of) sperm
> In a place of rest,
> Firmly fixed;
> Then We made the sperm
> Into a clot of congealed blood;
> Then of that clot We made
> A (foetus) lump; then We
> Made out of that lump
> Bones and clothed the bones
> With flesh; then We developed
> Out of it another creature.
> So blessed be God,
> The Best to create!

After that, at length
Ye will die.
Again, on the Day
Of Judgment, will ye be
Raised up.
And We have made, above you,
Seven tracts; and We
Are never unmindful
Of (Our) Creation.
And We send down water
From the sky according to
(Due) measure, and We cause it
To soak in the soil;
And We certainly are able
To drain it off (with ease).

The previous passage suggested a situation for which humans have no evidence other than scripture. Here we are dealing with issues which relate to our knowledge of the natural world: birth, the notion of heavens ("tracts"), and rain. From some perspectives this information must be either right or wrong. For the Islamist, all this information must correspond to scientific knowledge, when both are properly understood. The very translation of the words relating to birth, for example, already reflects the assumption that the words were understood at the time of revelation in a semi-scientific fashion which agrees with current investigations into the stages of development of a fetus. More problematic, perhaps, is "seven tracts" or "heavens," but, even there, various layers in the earth's atmosphere can be identified with these seven. It is significant to note the implication here that the proper interpretation of these passages would only have become clear to Muslims in the latter part of the twentieth century, according to this view.

Scripture, for the Islamist, cannot be relativized to the point of saying that the text reflects the state of knowledge of the world at the time of Muḥammad, as would be the position of some (more radical) Modernists. These passages, Modernists might suggest, do not attempt to tell us of the facts of the world. Rather they reflect basic ideas that all suggest the glory and power of God; the importance of the text lies not directly in what it says but in what it points to.

For more traditional thinkers, any apparent conflict between such passages and modern science only illustrates the changing nature of scientific knowledge. The reality of the world is in the accurate description given by God. When observation of the world is done properly (and investigation is generally to be encouraged), the truth of the Qurʾān will be borne out.

The third example

Sūra 4, verse 34:

> Men are the protectors
> And maintainers of women
> Because God has given
> The one more (strength)
> Than the other, and because
> They support them
> From their means.
> Therefore the righteous women
> Are devoutly obedient, and guard
> In (the husband's) absence
> What God would have them guard.
> As to those women
> On whose part ye fear
> Disloyalty and ill-conduct,
> Admonish them (first),
> (Next), refuse to share their beds,
> (And last) beat them (lightly);
> But if they return to obedience,
> Seek not against them
> Means (of annoyance):
> For God is Most High,
> Great (above you all).

It is unlikely that any other passage in the Qur'ān has created more furor in the contemporary period than this. Pivotal is the word *wa-ḍribūhunna*, translated as "(and last) beat them (lightly)"; other translators soften the tone further with "chastise them" or other similar sentiments. The Arabic word is commonly used to mean "beat," and there is no doubt that traditional Islam has taken the word in that physical sense. For the Islamist, there are two options, depending on the view of society and family values. First, the passage can be taken literally but with an emphasis placed on the legal requirements which are associated with the passage. For example, the necessity to "fear" disobedience would have to be taken very seriously. The strict application of the passage could then be argued to be "for the woman's own good," to protect her from herself. Implicit here (and, in fact, frequently made explicit) is the rejection of what is considered to be a Western norm of family and male–female relations that would suggest that using physical force to ensure obedience is necessarily wrong. Some would claim that the ethical code promulgated by this passage under this interpretation is, in fact, the way things should be; the failure to embrace a proper (that is, Islamic) family structure is what has led to the degeneracy of the West—the "spare the rod, spoil the child/woman" syndrome.

However, another Islamist position on this passage would be to reinterpret the word "beat them." Phrases such as "chastise them" leave the text of scripture intact, and suggest that Islam has its own standards which are, in fact, better than those encouraged in the West but are fully respectful of the responsibilities of both men and women.

It is Modernists who encounter the greatest problem in dealing with this passage. To declare the law appropriate for an earlier time, appropriate for a stage when people were still evolving morally, is to suggest that even the legal content of the Qurʾān is contingent upon history; only the basic religious impulse of the Qurʾān—the existence of God, His omnipotence and majesty—remains as the everlasting message of scripture.

This position of the contingency of the law is not accepted by many among the vocal promulgators of Islam in the contemporary period, for the absolute nature of the law of the Qurʾān is generally considered one of the central tags for the identification of Islam. Many Muslims fear—especially those of the Islamist persuasion, but the feeling is more widespread than that—that relativizing the Qurʾān to the standards of today (as in equality between men and women) will lead to "immorality" and similar sins, and will eventually lead down a "slippery slope" to the abandonment of Islam.

The issues at stake

There are two main questions which arise in modern discussions of the Qurʾān which illustrate, in a more abstract fashion, the limits to which these critical approaches may go in dealing with the contingency of the text. The first begins from the question of the miraculousness of the Qurʾān and moves into the general question of the rationality of the Qurʾān, and the second raises the question of the difference between legal and moral regulations. Both of these are interconnected, one leading to the next, at least in the thought of some people.

The miraculousness of the Qurʾān

Classically, the doctrine of the *iʿjāz* ("miraculousness," "inimitability") of the Qurʾān has been seen to assert the totally non-contingent nature of the text: it is fully divine and the language is that of God. The Qurʾān is the word of God *per se*. It has no relationship in its form to the passage of historical time. It literally descended from heaven, having been written on the pre-existent divine tablet. Any conflicts created by this attitude to the ultimate authority of the Qurʾān have always been solved by pointing to the limits of human knowledge—we simply do not fully understand.

Some Muslims have urged a somewhat modified understanding of the miraculousness of the Qur'ān. In general, this conviction may be viewed as an aspect of the anti-supernaturalism and the support of rationalism which has already been noted, especially in discussions of Muḥammad's biography. But the question remains, to what degree can anti-supernaturalism go regarding the Qur'ān without destroying Islam, while remembering that underlying that question is always a second one, what is Islam?

A frequent response, as in the case of ʿAlī Dashtī, is that the miracle of the Qur'ān lies not in its form, which is the most important aspect of the classical statements on the matter, but in the divine guidance which the book provides and the success which it has had. Thus the elevated, divine status of the Qur'ān (and, therefore, in one sense, its miraculousness) is maintained, but the traditional interpretation of each doctrine is done away with. This, then, allows two further thoughts for some people: a removal of all other supernatural elements within the Qur'ān and a questioning of the precise understanding of the non-contingency of the text.

Another common tendency is to conceive the Qur'ān not as revealed literally but as installed in Muḥammad's heart and then spoken through the human faculties of the prophet. The language, therefore, is Muḥammad's, although it is still possible to hold that this is ultimately God's word also.

The impetus behind these discussions rests with the basic drive of the Modernist movements: the need to modernize, reform, and rejuvenate Islam. The means to do this is found in removing what is envisioned to be the stumbling block: anti-rationalistic ideas along with norms which are perceived as not being in keeping with modern society.

In addition, there has been the methodological influence of the historical-critical method as developed in Europe. Basic to this method are a number of assumptions—all revolving around the scientific rational impulse—that history moves by causality and that those causes may be determined and studied. History must be studied according to the laws of reason for that is the way the world works. Religion is nothing special in this regard: it is like any philosophy or literature and like nature itself. It must be coherent, logical, and capable of being incorporated into an understanding of human history. Biblical scholarship of the eighteenth century enunciated this stance quite plainly, for example in the case of Johann Salamo Semler, who published a study of the Bible between 1771 and 1775 which "called for a purely historical-philological interpretation of the Bible, in the light of the circumstances surrounding the origin of the various books, without any concern for edification" (Krentz 1975: 19). Detached from theological and philosophical restraints in the nineteenth century under the impact of Schleiermacher, Biblical studies in the early twentieth century "made impartial and objective research the ideal" (Krentz 1975: 24). The end result of this is summarized in the following:

> The only scientifically responsible interpretation of the Bible is that investigation of the biblical texts that, with a methodologically consistent use of historical understanding in the present state of its art, seeks via reconstruction to recognize and describe the meaning these texts have had in the context of the tradition history of early Christianity.
>
> (Krentz 1975: 33)

For the most part, the impact of the historical-critical method has been slow to be felt in the Muslim world, at least within the study of the Qurʾān. The reasons for this lie within the traditional discussions concerning the nature of the Qurʾān which have just been mentioned. It must be remembered how much Muslims perceive to be at stake here. The existence of Islam classically depends upon the miracle of the Qurʾān. Thus, for those who have determined that this is the reform route to follow, caution is a continuous feature. Assessment of the basic character and nature of the Qurʾān must be accomplished first, and that means raising questions of the rationality of the text and of its relationship to historical fact. The issue still lingers, as the following examples will show, of just how far Muslims can go in pursuing these questions while still remaining Islamic.

Muḥammad Khalaf Allāh and historical specificity

Rationality or anti-supernaturalism is one area where the limits of interpretation are confronted; the desire to see scripture as fully in keeping with reason can only be taken so far before those who maintain a more traditional view of Islam raise their objections. Another area where these limits are confronted is seen in the relationship between the text and historical reality, often spoken of in terms of the conflict between "truth" and "reality." Muḥammad Aḥmad Khalaf Allāh (1916–97), in a thesis submitted to Cairo University in 1947, brought this issue to prominence in the Islamic world. While the issue had been broached by others before him, especially his teacher Amīn al-Khūlī (1895–1966), in Khalaf Allāh's instance public reaction was fairly rapid. He wrote that the prophetic stories in the Qurʾān were not historical as such but kerygmatic: that they were being repeated for their moral/religious aims, and were reiterated in different forms according to Muḥammad's needs in a given situation. They were therefore contingent upon history even in their aims. This is the distinction between what may be termed "truth" (in a spiritual sense) and "reality" (as reflected in historical fact).

Khalaf Allāh was accused of "atheism and gross ignorance" and had to rewrite his thesis several times before it was accepted; it was published in 1950–1 but he was subsequently forced out of his university teaching post. Traditionally, all the stories of the Qurʾān have been seen to be of equal value and to be of a historical nature. This position raised a number of questions in the modern world, however. What of stories which did not seem to be in agreement with other, earlier sources? For example, in the Qur'ān Hāmān is presented as Pharaoh's minister, while in the Bible he is a minister to the Persian king of a much later period. What is a modern Muslim to believe? Are the facts of the Qur'ān all necessarily true historically and all other sources false? How will this attitude work in conjunction with the historical-critical method, which clearly values older sources over newer ones? One of Khalaf Allāh's concerns was apologetic: how to save the Qur'ān from the attacks of the Orientalists who continued to cite all these problems within the text.

Khalaf Allāh's resolution of the problem was to say that the concern of the Qur'ān is to employ striking literary expressions through which psychological and religious truths are expressed. Its concern is not necessarily with historical or material truth (that is, "reality"). Literary genres, specifically historical-literary, parable and allegory, have been employed within the Qur'ān to embody these spiritual truths. The aim of the Qur'ān was to "admonish and exhort," not to instruct in history. Hence, information about time and place is generally missing in the Quranic narratives.

Such controversies continue to be replayed down until today. Another scholar in the tradition of al-Khūlī, Naṣr Abū Zayd (1943–2010), was charged with apostasy in 1995 before the Egyptian Family Court. The Court found him guilty on the following grounds:

1 He had allegedly denied the existence of angels and devils referred to in the Qur'ān.
2 He had described certain images in the Qur'ān used of heaven and hell as mythical.
3 He had described the text of the Qur'ān as a human production (it is a "historically determined and culturally constructed" text).
4 He had advocated the use of the intellect to replace concepts derived literally from the text of the Qur'ān, especially in regard to matters related to inheritance, women, Christians and Jews, and female slaves.

For these writings, Naṣr Abū Zayd was held to be an apostate and his marriage was annulled. He and his wife fled the country as a result. Abū Zayd's response was simply to note that such ideas have a long heritage in Islam. They were the key notions held by the Mu'tazila during the formative centuries of Islam. Such ideas cannot simply be readopted within Islam, however; there is a need for a new modern theology of Islam which will accept the literary study of the Qur'ān. In his more recent writings, Abū Zayd speaks of the Qur'ān as "discourse," suggesting that scripture is more than the text between two covers as it has classically been treated. The book, characterized by its multiple speaking voices and its style of dialogue and negotiation, cannot be limited to a literal or even a metaphoric reading but must be approached in its own spirit of openness, communication, and relationship. Abū Zayd admits that the problem remains one of determining the nature of the universal principles that one may identify with the

Quranic discourse, the common Modernist dilemma solved only by the assertion of basic elements of human rights and dignity to which no one, it is claimed, could object.

The examples of Khalaf Allāh and Abū Zayd raise issues about the limits to which Muslims are prepared to take reinterpretation of the Qurʾān. Rationalism, the underlying principle of the historical-critical method, is fully applied in these cases in order to resolve the problems perceived within a general Modernist tendency. Neither writer actually doubts the authenticity of the text of scripture, only whether the words themselves are to be taken as intending to convey precisely what it has been traditionally thought that they say.

A contemporary response

Much of the response to Khalaf Allāh's work at the time of its publication dealt with it by saying that the author was using history as a criterion of truth higher than the Qurʾān, something which no Muslim could accept. The ultimate truth of the text of scripture exists, in these responses, *a priori*. A more subtle argument is made by Shabbir Akhtar, who does not raise the example of Khalaf Allāh specifically but certainly deals with the principle in his book *A Faith for All Seasons*. He approaches the problem as though it had only affected the Christian study of their scripture; he may well not have been aware of the extent to which Muslims have already broached these questions. Regardless, the case of the "sophisticated Christians" (as an example he cites Richard Swinburne) provides a cautionary tale for Muslims, according to Akhtar, who wish to maintain their faith in light of philosophical approaches to scripture. Akhtar points out that it was Darwin who made it so necessary for Christians to distinguish between "the false non-religious husk and the concomitant true religious kernel" (Akhtar 1990: 69). This has gone to the extent now that Christians are willing to talk about false cultural trappings in which scripture has expressed truths for ignorant people of the past. Some statements of the Bible, or the Qurʾān, in this view, may be taken as "unempirical or false." For Akhtar, the problem with this is: how can one be sure that the underlying religious claims which have been embodied in these false statements are necessarily true? There is no way, he contends, to "distinguish in any unquestion-begging way ... between the religious message presumed to be true and the culturally specific incarnation presumed to be false" (Akhtar 1990: 70–1). After entertaining several possible ways around this problem—that God incorporated errors in scripture to keep us on our toes, or that apparent errors are matters which are simply beyond human reason—he concludes by saying that any concession to the idea of false claims in scripture must be resisted. If this is not so, then:

> [while] today we disown what we take to be factually erroneous, perhaps tomorrow we will reject apparent moral anachronisms—such as scriptural claims about the

> relatively low status of women or the impropriety of deviant sexual behaviour, not to speak of the occasional questionable doctrine about the nature or activity of the Deity.
> (Akhtar 1990: 74)

Revelation, for Akhtar, is an all or nothing affair; that is the only way to construct a philosophically defensible Islam. Watering down the doctrine of the non-contingent nature of the text too far will lead to no defense against claims that the entire basis of the religion may be false.

The contingent nature of Quranic law

Khalaf Allāh did not confront the question of the nature of the law; in fact, he studiously avoided raising the issue. Neither did he question the divine nature of the Qur'ān. It should be noticed that, from his perspective, it is not necessary to question the Qur'ān's status as the actual word of God; God may reveal speech which does not have the intent of providing historical facts, but it may still be conceived of as God's word. But when this kind of approach confronts the legal parts of the Qur'ān, further issues arise. Are the laws contingent, that is, applicable only to the time of Muḥammad? Are they embedded in the history of the early Muslim community or are they expressions of the eternal will of God?

Fazlur Rahman

Fazlur Rahman (1919–88) was Director of the Islamic Research Institute in Pakistan from 1962 to 1968 but, after pressure from conservative elements in that country, was forced to leave; he became Professor of Islamic Thought at the University of Chicago in the United States and achieved a reputation of being one of the great scholars in the field.

Rahman was a fervent Modernist. In approaching the text of the Qur'ān, he wished to differentiate legal regulations from moral regulations, the former being contingent, the latter non-contingent. Legal rulings must be considered binding in a moral sense, even if not in their literal wording. Much of the law of classical Islam has been wrongly formulated because the jurists ignored the moral ideal behind the text and the words were read as literal legal enactments, according to this view. The Quranic acceptance of slavery, a form of ownership of people which has fallen into disrepute under the impact of modernity, is treated in the following way by Rahman:

> As an immediate solution, the Qur'ān accepts the institution of slavery on the legal plane. No alternative was possible since slavery was ingrained in the structure of society, and its overnight wholesale liquidation would have created problems which it would have been absolutely impossible to solve, and only a dreamer could have issued

> such a visionary statement. But at the same time every legal and moral effort was made to free the slaves and to create a milieu where slavery ought to disappear. . . . Here again we are confronted by a situation where the clear logic of the Qurʾānic attitude was not worked out in actual history by Muslims. . . . These examples [also including women and wine,] therefore, make it abundantly clear that whereas the spirit of the Qurʾānic legislation exhibits an obvious direction towards the progressive embodiment of the fundamental human values of freedom and responsibility in fresh legislation, nevertheless the actual legislation of the Qurʾān had partly to accept the then existing society as a term of reference. This clearly means that the actual legislation of the Qurʾān cannot have been meant to be literally eternal by the Qurʾān itself.
>
> (Rahman 1979b: 38–9)

It is not only on legal topics that Rahman has approached the Qurʾān in this manner, although it is in that area where the extent of his demythologization becomes most clear. The psychological intention of the text as opposed to the descriptive meaning is frequently employed as a principle in his work *Major Themes of the Qurʾān* (1980). God's power, humans being predestined, intercession in the afterlife, divine punishment of humans, and the existence of the *jinn* are all interpreted not for their literal sense but for what they were driving at in terms of motivating humans toward the proper attitude regarding God, life, and creation.

This position fits into an overall Neo-Modernist stance, according to Rahman himself, one which recognizes the complexities of life as opposed to the Islamist idea of everything (especially Islam) being "simple." Once again, it is the history of Islam which has taken Muslims away from the proper understanding of the Qurʾān; the text of scripture itself is still a perfect reflection of standards as they should be, as long as it is properly understood. Rahman blames the educational institutions developed in the early Muslim centuries for the failure to appreciate the true import of the Qurʾān. The educational system created what it called the Quranic sciences along with the legal structures of society. It separated these religious sciences from the rational or secular sciences (Rahman traces this division back to al-Ghazālī), and with the growing disrepute of the latter studies Islamic civilization fell into stagnation. The worst consequence of this was the rejection of Islamic philosophy, which could have kept open ways of enquiring into the foundations of Islam, but was unable to. No longer was the Qurʾān treated as a "vibrant and revolutionary document"; rather, it became "buried under the debris of grammar and rhetoric," a trend reaching its apex with the notion that only super-commentaries could and should be written (Rahman 1982: chapter 1). The way Islam can free itself from this burden of the past is by studying history critically, in order to comprehend how the impetus of the Qurʾān has been understood in the past and how Muslims have interacted with it. Thereby, the essentials of the faith may be differentiated from that which has simply attached itself unnecessarily.

Pushing the "limits"

Some Muslims would take this further or perhaps even question the very presuppositions of the historical-critical method and approach the issue in a totally different way. We saw in Chapter 13, for example, how Fatima Mernissi perceives the Quranic attitudes toward women: that they reflect male ideas put in the mouth of a male God. The law of the Qur'ān—through language—is culturally conditioned from beginning to end.

The same sense emerges from the writings of Mohammed Arkoun (1928–2010). In dealing with the Qur'ān specifically, Arkoun pays attention to the historical development of interpretation of the scripture, a process which serves to establish how the Qur'ān takes on meaning in the Islamic context. This then leads to the observation that, from within the modern context, Muslims are attempting to read the Qur'ān as if modern reason was in all ways identical to the linguistic shape of the Qur'ān and Muḥammad's epistemological environment. The logic of the Qur'ān from Arkoun's perspective, however, is a poetic logic rather than a rational logic. Ironically perhaps, it is precisely because the Qur'ān is written with this poetic logic that it can be read as if modern rationality were reflected in it. For Arkoun, of course, the Qur'ān conveys a mythical discourse rather than a historical one, but by that very fact it allows a historical interpretation.

The necessity today is, for Arkoun, to approach the Qur'ān with today's categories, which are composed of the totality of the human sciences. The selection of these forms a refrain—even a litany according to one of his reviewers: ethnology, anthropology, history of religions, psychoanalysis, semiotics, and with human consciousness to be viewed mythically, historically, socially, economically, politically, philosophically, morally, aesthetically, religiously, and so forth. The aim of this is to discover the way in which all elements of culture are bound ideologically with history. All of human existence is founded upon and created by history and only through the realization of this can the past, present, and future become clear. This is demythologization at its extreme.

As an example of what this might mean in a practical sense, an issue of law is useful. For Arkoun:

> The basic difference between the Quran and the Sharî'a is that the first makes use of contingent data in order to emphasize the relationship between God and man and to fill men's minds with a consciousness that there is a world beyond this world of events, values, norms and possessions. All this is clothed in mythical language and structure

> which opens the way to problems rather than excluding them. The second, on the other hand, systematizes, within the framework of a code of law, the pragmatic solutions that were adopted at an early period. It is understandable, then, why it is wrong to call norms that have been included in this code and perpetuated by an inflexible teaching Islamic.
>
> (Arkoun 1979: 78)

The Qurʾān then does not provide answers but problems, ones which must be struggled with in human life.

It is the aim of Arkoun's method to get "outside" the dualities of contemporary discussions which still deal with the understanding of the world in historicist terms. The historical-critical method is not the answer, given the needs of the Muslim consciousness in the latter part of the twentieth century.

This approach does not even seem to entertain the idea of Rahman's moral ideals within the Qurʾān. Could it be said that Mernissi and Arkoun get to the point of challenging the authority of the Qurʾān text itself? In traditional understandings of "text" and "authority" they clearly do. Their understandings seem to call for a re-expression of the Qurʾān—one that stands, however, completely within the Muslim ethos. Mernissi wonders, for example, if an Islam which gave women freedom could really be called Islam at all. It might be termed post-Islamic, I would suggest. One of the reasons for the radicalness of these positions is that neither writer stands within the now-traditional method of historical criticism, although the reasons for this may well be different in the two cases. Mernissi's use of the feminist interpretative framework brings her face to face with the historical issues, and there is a tendency in her writings to step back from what might seem to be the inevitable conclusion. Arkoun, on the other hand, wishes to change the very terms of the discussion and eliminate the duality of the discussion between contingent and non-contingent, for example, for those very terms imply that there can be human knowledge which is outside the framework of historicity and language. From this perspective, "limits" to critical approaches make little sense, for the limits are those imposed by linguistic structures; the deconstruction of those limitations is the entire purpose of the exercise.

A Syrian engineer studies the Qurʾān

Muḥammad Shaḥrūr was born in 1938 in Damascus and is an Emeritus Professor of Civil Engineering at the University of Damascus. He was trained in his profession in Syria, the Soviet Union, and Ireland. He has written extensively about Islam, arguing that the religion must conform to modern philosophy as well as the rational world view of the natural sciences. His first work, *Al-Kitāb wa'l-Qur'ān: Qirā'a Mu'āṣira* ("The Book and the Qur'ān: A Contemporary Interpretation"), was published in 1990 with the declared goal of "formulating an Islamic theory of divinity that is at once both human and universal." He was widely censured for the work, which was subsequently banned in many countries, although that did not stop it from becoming a bestseller. The book was followed by a series of further treatises on politics, faith, jurisprudence, and terrorism, all developing the ideas put forth in his first book.

Shaḥrūr echoes the common Modernist refrain that medieval exegesis of the Qur'ān has obscured the meaning of the text, and the juristic reading of scripture has misled Muslims and taken them away from the true faith. But the implications of his theory and the basis on which he has argued it—through an intensive personal reading of the Qur'ān with no traditional or academic training in the area—separate him from many other contemporary figures. The uniqueness of his ideas can be measured by the resistance that has been expressed to them by established religious authorities. Dozens of books, reviews, and sermons have been written condemning him.

Shaḥrūr's overall argument urges the compatibility of democracy, individual freedoms, and human rights within an Islamic notion of civil society. The main political point of his work is to argue for democracy, with an emphasis on political pluralism involving opposition parties and freedom of expression. Only in that way, he says, can the Islamic principle of "commanding right and forbidding wrong" be truly implemented.

Underneath this platform is an approach to the Qur'ān that prioritizes reason as an interpretative tool, dependent upon the historical circumstances of the interpreter. Legislative verses of the Qur'ān must always be interpreted and those interpretations are historically conditioned, such that any given juristic interpretation cannot be presumed to be valid for all times. There is a basic covenant between God and humans which is conveyed in verses of the Qur'ān that are factual and reflective of a reality known by God and discoverable by science. The legal and ethical parts of the Qur'ān, however, are always subject to human choice, as shown by the way in which Muḥammad explained and enacted those provisions.

Shaḥrūr's detailed analysis of Islam and the Qur'ān is based on rigorous philosophical and scientific attitudes. In the words of Andreas Christmann (2009: xlvii), "No other modern Muslim writer, except perhaps Fazlur Rahman, has managed to combine both a theoretical critique and a concrete analysis of the qur'anic text that covers such a large area of Islamic law."

For an analysis of Shaḥrūr along with translations of some of his work, see Andreas Christmann, *The Qur'an, Morality and Critical Reason: The Essential Muhammad Shahrur*, Leiden: Brill, 2009.

Suggested further reading

J. M. S. Baljon, *Modern Muslim Koran Interpretation (1880–1960)*, Leiden: Brill, 1961.

Massimo Campanini, *The Qur'an: Modern Muslim Interpretation*, London: Routledge, 2011.

Kenneth Cragg, *The Pen and the Faith: Eight Modern Muslim Writers and the Qur'an*, London: George Allen and Unwin, 1985.

J. J. G. Jansen, *The Interpretation of the Koran in Modern Egypt*, Leiden: Brill, 1974.

Suha Taji-Farouki (ed.), *Modern Muslim Intellectuals and the Qur'ān*, Oxford: Oxford University Press, 2004.

15 *Issues of identity: ritual and politics*

In the discussion of the emergence of Islam in the seventh through tenth centuries, three matters were isolated that provided the key elements of Islamic identity. Theology, law, and ritual were crucial to those activities which would serve to identify Islam as a religion over against other faiths (primarily Judaism and Christianity) and to provide Muslims themselves with a sense of commonality with one another. This motif has remained stable throughout Islamic history down to current times, although the background against which that identity must be read is now much more multifaceted than in previous centuries. It is still possible to isolate the same three elements as crucial, although theology perhaps has taken substantially more of a back seat to law, which now manifests itself primarily within the arena of politics and the role of Islam within it. Ritual, on the other hand, remains a very important aspect, both from the perspective of self-identity and for identity from the outside.

Each era has its way of interacting with these symbols of identity. Subtly altered understandings of the basic ritual activities of Islam illustrate some aspects of the transformations which are taking place in modern Muslim faith. Once again, these changed understandings and interpretations flow from changes in attitude toward the fundamental sources of Islam, the Qurʾān and the *sunna*. In most instances, however, the abstract intellectual discussions regarding these sources are not brought to the forefront when Muslims conceptualize their basic religious practices within the modern context. What continues to be of interest for our purposes is the way in which the issues and approaches as employed in the considerations of the Qurʾān and the *sunna* are also manifested in the approaches to the various issues which surround the role and function of ritual practice in the contemporary context.

The pillars of Islam

The traditional definitional elements of Muslim faith—the summaries of belief and the ritual "Five Pillars"—remain virtually intact in the modern context. Any movement toward prayers being said in the vernacular rather than Arabic, for example, or being able to perform the fast of Ramaḍān during a more "convenient" month, has proven singularly unsuccessful. But this should not be taken to suggest that the modern world has not had its impact felt in Muslim practice at all. Attention to Islamic ritual activities and their practice provides a means of looking at ways Muslims have attempted to express their religiosity in general; within the modern context, several factors lead to these ritual aspects of Islam having a significant bearing on the question of the contemporary manifestation of Islam.

What might be termed the politicization of Muslims, a worldwide phenomenon in Islam but especially prevalent in diaspora populations in North America and Europe, has led to a heightened sense of identity being felt through the affirmation of distinctive Islamic practices. Another way of expressing this is as "the Islamization of the self," and the use of Islamic symbols to provide identity on a personal level. This tendency is connected not only with the move of individuals from a rural to an urban society, but also, one might contend, with the move from a "Muslim" society to a "non-Muslim" one. Village society has always been characterized by the idea that "the life of the village is the religion of the village"; that is, the rhythm of life reflects the Islamic way and is integral within each member's life. Modern society, especially that of a predominantly non-Muslim country, displays a separation between religious life and secular life which has led to a tendency toward affirming various aspects of Muslim existence—notably those associated with ritual activity and self-study of the Qurʾān—as central tenets of identity. Identity in these cases is a personal one, not a collectively affirmed one as in the community-based village life. The idea of women's veiling, *ḥijāb*, being a personal, home-focused idea serves as a specific example of this reorientation. Such personalization of faith is frequently a core element of Islamism, it may be remarked.

This tendency toward personalization of faith may be the result of the general globalization of Islam within the world community. While Islam certainly spread widely in previous centuries, the present-day mobility of world populations along with massive dislocations of various groups within many countries has had some significant consequences. The status of Muslim minorities around the world has become an issue for Muslims, not perhaps impinging upon their self-definition within Islam in the same way as did the creation of a diaspora-centered Judaism but significant nevertheless, and it may well have an even greater impact in the future.

Islam has always defined itself ritually as being focused on the "Five Pillars." In connection with each ritual, the impact of the modern world may be noted, not so much in the practices themselves but in the interpretation which is put forth of the activities. It is, therefore, not a matter of continuing to legitimize the activities themselves in the modern context but a question of how to mold them to the modern age within an Islamic framework and how to conceptualize them in relation to ideas of self-definition. It is this principle which displays, in a very practical sense, the ramifications of the approaches toward reinterpretation of the Qur'ān and the *sunna*, as discussed earlier in the previous chapters.

Witness to faith (*shahāda*)

The *shahāda*, or "witness to faith," is the first of the classical Five Pillars of Islam, repeating in Arabic the two phrases "There is no god but God" and "Muḥammad is the messenger of God." An example of the contextualization of the *shahāda* in contemporary American society is provided by the following statement within a wedding ceremony, addressed to the bride, who intended to convert to Islam:

> "There is no priesthood in Islam. Anyone can perform the [wedding] ceremony, even you yourselves, or a trusted representative of the bride and groom. I do not like the term conversion. Sister, you are not converting, you are reforming. Islam is not only the religion of Muhammad, it is also the religion of Moses and Jesus. The term Christianity was not used by Jesus but only by later generations, who modified his teachings. Thus, when we say, 'There is only one religion and that is Islam,' we mean that all the prophets carried the same message from the same God. Sister, you are not obliged to convert to Islam. You may keep your religion intact if you wish to do so." Sue indicates her need to "reform." Nasem says, "Then let it be so." He explains the three foundations of Islam: oneness of God, prophethood, and resurrection . . . .
>
> Then come the two testimonies: "Sister, repeat after me, I witness there is no God but God, Muhammad is His servant slave and His messenger." Then prayer: all present raise their hands and pray that she might be a good Muslim and have a happy, prosperous life. Then the marriage ceremony.
>
> (Fischer and Abedi 1990: 303)

Islamists have often attempted to define Islam in terms of the witness to faith alone, by emphasizing the concept of *tawḥīd*, the oneness and unity of God, as expressed in *shahāda*. This follows from a statement made by Muḥammad as reported within the *ḥadīth* material to the effect that he brought nothing more important than the *shahāda*. The idea of *tawḥīd*, then, for the Islamists, expresses everything which Islam stands for and is the basis of all Islamic thought; such a summary is a crucial part of the suggestion that Islam is a "simple" religion, in that once the truth of this affirmation of the oneness of God is perceived, then everything else in Islam flows from it.

> So, when you recite these words [of the *shahāda*], you should be conscious what an important commitment you are making to your God, with the whole world as your witness, and what a great responsibility you are taking on as a result of your commitment. Once you have made the affirmation consciously, the Kalimah [literally

> "the word," meaning the words of the *shahāda*] must inform all your thoughts and reign supreme in your whole lives: no idea contrary to it should form part of your mental furniture. Whatever runs counter to the Kalimah you must always consider false and the Kalimah alone true . . . .
>
> If you recite the Kalimah in this manner, only then can you become true Muslims, only then is created that overwhelming difference between man and man.
>
> (Mawdudi 1985: 71)

The statement of the *shahāda*, then, is the essence of the Islamist totalism in the vision of Islam.

Prayer (*ṣalāt*)

Five specific periods of prayer a day are a ritual requirement in Islam. The globalization of the Muslim population has created a number of incongruous situations illustrating the way in which Islam has been confronted with the realities of the modern context. In Surinam, Indians, brought by the Dutch to that country in the period 1873–1916 (in 1982 there were 50,000 such people), are members of the Ḥanafiyya in their legal school alignment. They conduct their sermon (*khuṭba*) during the Friday noon prayer in Urdu, and they face the east (their *qibla*) during all the prayer. The Javanese present in Surinam, on the other hand, are members of the Shāfiʿiyya according to their legal school and have a *qibla* to the west. These people were indentured laborers brought by the Dutch in the period 1850–1931, and in 1982 there were 90,000 of them. "The qibla is towards the west simply because it is in this direction in Java, although Mecca is situated from Surinam in the easterly direction," according to Rolf Reichert (1981: 123), who researched this issue. This is, of course, not a "problem" for Islam in any sense; that any group of people would continue to follow their traditional direction of prayer in any given place does not impinge upon significant elements of Muslim self-definition. It does indicate, however, that as the process of globalization continues, such elements may continue to grow and may well provoke questioning on the part of Muslims themselves.

A similar, and likewise essentially trivial, element is presented by Muslims flying in outer space and locating the direction of prayer and the time of prayer; this latter point also applies to those in polar regions where timings as related to the sun's position provide the suitable intervals for prayer. In most such situations, people agree that the timings of prayer in Mecca should be followed. The point here is that the modern context provokes a situation in which the fundamental principles of ritual activity in Islam must be faced. The solutions are argued on a legal basis, employing well-established juristic principles, extrapolated for the required situation.

More substantial issues related to prayer most certainly do exist and they reflect the extent to which Muslims have been willing to adapt ritual to the social context in which they live. The implementation of Sunday as the day of congregational prayer (*jumʿa*) rather than Friday has been one such issue. In 1935, the Turkish leader, Atatürk, made Sunday the weekly day of closing for offices, factories, and so forth. Such a "day of rest" had not been instituted during the pre-industrial age of Islamic society and had never been seen as a religiously based necessity (the Qurʾān suggests that the Sabbath as a day of rest was a special legal provision for the Jews). Atatürk's action was justified by him in terms of practical concern for life in the modern age. Such a step did not, however, transform Muslim worship with its focus on Friday noon for communal prayer. In other countries, however, especially those with Muslim groups living within a primarily Christian context, the move to Sunday became an entire transformation of the Muslim day of communal gathering. Like similar movements within Reform Judaism which tried Sabbath worship on Sundays rather than Saturdays within the context of European (Christian) society, this was a relatively short-lived accommodation to the society around them. For Muslims, Friday was (re)asserted to be the day which was attached to a very basic sense of Islamic identity. What still remains in more contemporary times is the use of Sunday as a "family day" with mosque-centered activities (for example "Sunday school" as religious training for children).

For the performance of the Friday communal prayer, a prayer leader, *imām*, is required; his function is to lead the community in prayer, keeping the actions in unison, and he will frequently (but not always) be called upon to deliver the *khuṭba* or sermon. This has raised another issue related to the wide dispersal of Muslims today in countries where Muslims are not the majority of the population. In many instances, an *imām* is recruited from outside the country. This is often done as a way of helping to maintain the identity of the minorities, but in some situations this only emphasizes the foreignness of a minority group. Furthermore, these imported *imāms* are often felt to be out of touch with the realities of life in the new countries in which they are living. Malise Ruthven has pointed this out as a factor in exacerbating the "Rushdie affair" in England. The *imāms*, in this case brought in from Pakistan to Bradford, reinforced

> the ties with the homeland, creating an anchor with the certainties of the past. It also reinforces isolation: few of the *imams* know English; fewer still are aware of the wider British society around them with its complexities and diversified spiritual resources. The leaders add spiritual authority to a vision of society already viewed, one might say distorted, through the prism of faith: the society that corresponds to the *jahiliyya* of the Prophet's time, a godless, materialistic society wholly dedicated to the pursuit of worldly wealth and sensual pleasure.
>
> (Ruthven 1990: 72)

Equally significant in this regard, however, is the extent to which these prayer leaders have been thrust into a situation of adopting a general counseling, ministerial role, something essentially foreign to the nature of the office in the past and also in predominantly Muslim countries today. A new institution has essentially arisen within the North American and European context for Muslims.

Overall, the interpretation of prayer in modern Muslim discussions has often taken on a certain spiritualized interpretation which may be usefully compared to the general remarks about the character of ritual at the conclusion of Chapter 7. Rarely is prayer presented as simply a duty to be fulfilled because it has been decreed by God. Rather, prayer is described as the primary defense of the Muslim against the encroachment of worldly concerns, for "it prevents an individual from all sorts of abominations and vices by providing him chances of direct communion with God." The spiritual leader of Iran, Ayatollah Ali Khamenei, is reported to have suggested the following:

> No other channel is a better means for communicating with the Almighty, and . . . a "Salat" said with full cognizance of its deeper meanings and with a full heart is the best safeguard against a tendency to succumb to a feeling of absurdity and moral weakness.
>
> (*Hong Kong Muslim Herald* 1991: 2–2)

Fasting (*ṣiyām, ṣawm*)

Abstention from all food and drink, as well as avoidance of sexual intercourse, during daylight hours is the mark of the Muslim thirty-day period of fasting, undertaken during the month of Ramaḍān. Ramaḍān has always been considered by most Muslims as the most important of the ritual duties. Even if a person does not comply with the requirement of five prayers a day, observance of the fast may well still be practiced. Contemporary Muslim fast participants do, however, exhibit subtle changes in the interpretation of their actions. While in earlier times a sense of the penitent value of fasting was certainly present, this has been downplayed in the interpretations of recent decades. For many Modernists and Islamists, the fast is performed because it has been commanded by God, not for any individual benefit which may accrue to the individual in terms of his or her fate in the hereafter. Moral benefit in the here and now, however, is emphasized. The fast is a means of social leveling and of reinforcing notions of social responsibility. When even the rich are hungry, the fate of the poor will be evident, so the argument goes. Even more, there is an overall sense of Muslim unity celebrated during the fast, especially in the festive aspects of nightlife during the month.

Various attempts have been made, especially under government impetus, to modify this area of Muslim practice. President Bourguiba of Tunisia, in February of 1960, for example, urged the avoidance of Ramaḍān observances for government employees. Religion should serve to ameliorate life, not make it more difficult, his argument went; in the present state of Tunisia's attempts to thrive as an independent country, fasting would only worsen the economic condition, and the suffering which would result from the month of fasting was a type of penitence foreign to Islam. Certain religious scholars supported this stance on the grounds that *jihād*, "holy war," was needed in order to build the country economically, and fasting for those fighting in times of *jihād* was not necessary according to Islamic law. Similar suggestions were reported in Egypt in the mid-1950s. These "reforms," based upon an impetus toward greater efficiency in (capitalist) society, did, however, prove extremely unpopular, even among those who did not participate in the fasting. Those who argued against changing the requirements of Ramaḍān said that the legislation imposed by God could not be changed by the opinion of a lowly human being. Fasting, according to the argument against change, is intimately tied to hardship; that is the essence of it in fact. ("Where is the fasting person who does not suffer hardship in fasting?" it was asked.) Just because economic hardship might result from fasting did not give a reason not to fast; if it did, then nobody would bother to fast, everyone claiming that it involved hardship. In fact, the whole logic of fasting was to provide the experience of hardship for those who might otherwise never experience it. The argument for the rationality of Islamic ritual is notable. Overall, these types of arguments and the tide of public sentiment led governments to a compromise position of restricting working hours in government offices and factories during the month.

It has been pointed out by some observers that the concern which Muslims expressed over this issue of Ramaḍān observance was far more severe than that expressed regarding many other changes which were taking place in the Muslim world at that time. Polygamy, for example, was banned in several countries during this period. The issue, therefore, was not perceived to be one of changing the law, as such, but one of an attack on Muslim identity:

> Ramadan had become in modern times the great manifestation of the unity of Islam, the month when Muslims believing or unbelieving became conscious of their past and affirmed their links with their ancestors, and the criticism [of the practice of Ramaḍān] was perhaps resented not because it ran counter to the Shariʾa but rather because it threatened the solidarity of the Muslim community.
>
> (Hourani 1983: 350)

The role of Ramaḍān as a social rather than religious requirement has also become apparent in recent times, with some young people declaring that fasting during Ramaḍān "is the thing to do" even, apparently, if one is not Muslim.

The extent to which fasting is a significant element of Muslim identity today is emphasized within the context of the often-noted assertion of Muslim identity in situations in which Muslims live as minorities. One interesting instance of this contemporary politicization of Muslims may be illustrated through an incident at my own university. During the spring of 1991 and the winter of 1999, the final examination period for students fell during Ramaḍān. This, of course, is not the first time such would have happened, with Ramaḍān moving some eleven days earlier each solar calendar year. However, in recent years the university administration has experienced an apparently new phenomenon: requests for "deferred final examinations" from Muslims on the grounds of the religious requirement of fasting during daylight hours, which would, reasonably enough, it was argued, make undertaking an examination difficult. It is the focus on Ramaḍān that is significant. North American society, after all, ignores all aspects of the Muslim ritual calendar. Students have not demanded that classes not take place during prayer times (not even Fridays) or that those wishing to go on pilgrimage to Mecca be excused from any academic responsibilities. (Christmas and Easter remain central to the academic schedule, however.) Ramaḍān is an individual religious action which is particularly amenable to the general North American religious ethos; the assertion of its prominence in the ritual calendar may be seen, therefore, as a part of the contextualization of the Muslim community in the modern world.

Determining when Ramaḍān should start and the precise hours of fasting on any given day is increasingly accommodated to modern technology and sense of order. Traditionally, the religious calendar has been established each month through the sighting of the moon. For some people, this raises a question about the role of science within Islam. Science can now tell us with great accuracy when the month of Ramaḍān starts and ends. Back in Muḥammad's time, the only practical means of determining the month was by observation of the moon. It only makes sense (and God urges such in the Qur'ān), so the argument goes, that today Muslims should embrace the scientific accuracy which is available.

The traditional practice of the recitation of the Qur'ān during the nights of Ramaḍān continues, celebrating the revelation of the Qur'ān to Muḥammad during that month. Modern media participate in the event, with radio stations playing Qur'ān recitation. Even in officially secular Turkey, the publication of the appropriate one-thirtieth section of the Qur'ān in Turkish translation each day in the newspaper is an ongoing practice.

Charity (*zakāt, ṣadaqa*)

The giving of alms (*zakāt*) has been, within the juridical system of classical Islam, a fully regulated system. Modern terminology and principles have been applied to *zakāt*, especially in countries outside the Muslim heartlands where the economic systems presuppose, if not demand, certain forms of financial participation. Thus we see "*zakāt* returns" just like "income tax returns," where statements of net worth are subject to calculation of the tax owing. Such "returns" often present an uneasy compromise between the realities of modern Euro-American life and the traditional categories of items on which *zakāt* is collectable; they may also feature certain aspects which might not be seen as being fully in keeping with a system of "Islamic economics" as that is proposed, and partially enacted, by some Islamists (such as taking into account interest paid on mortgages and loans).

Similar problems with the payment of *zakāt* must be faced in the more central Islamic lands also. Is *zakāt* to be paid on types of property unknown in classical Islamic times? Just what do stock certificates represent? Should the tax be paid in stock certificates or in cash? In what percentage? Likewise, an issue over who should receive the *zakāt* arises, with the traditional list of the poor, new converts, travelers, missionaries, those who collect the tax, slaves (for buying their freedom), and those who have debts due to public service frequently being extended to include modern charitable institutions. Such issues are generally solved through the processes of Islamic law, such as reasoning by analogy, but the significant fact, of course, is that the issues do have to be faced.

Zakāt and politics have mixed extensively in Pakistan, where charity and income tax have often been equated; it has been argued that only the modern state apparatus can actually handle the equitable distribution of these funds, given the complexities of modern life. Likewise, *zakāt* and the idea of egalitarianism as fitting in with the socialist platforms were especially prominent under Abdul Nasser in Egypt of the 1960s. Islamic charity is equated to a system of responsibility fundamental to Islamic social structures and social assumptions. The sharing of wealth legitimizes one's own possession of material goods and emphasizes the communal aspects of ownership in Islam. "To pay Zakat is a cleansing process for the wealth and its owner. Allah not only promises reward in the hereafter but also to bless an enterprise so that it becomes more profitable" (Badawi 1999: 32).

Finally, another way of solving the entire problem of how *zakāt* is to be understood in the modern world has arisen. There has been a tendency to remove *zakāt* altogether from its juridical context and simply make it freewill offerings. This is one more aspect of the emergence of a personalized and individualized Islam, common among the Islamist group. But this exists in tension with ideas of Islamic economics, in which the only legitimated system of taxation (and taxation would seem essential to the modern nation state, Islamic or otherwise) is that of *zakāt*. It is also argued that *zakāt* must be given in the proportions which have been established in the *sunna*, regardless of whether they are needed or not; the basis of a secular taxation system, however, is that the amount "given" varies with the needs of the government. Fundamentally, this is an issue of whether or not charity is to be viewed as a purificatory rite for the devout: if so, then demands by a government to extract it subvert that sense of offering which seems essential to a purificatory view. Could Muslims ever view a compulsory tax which is assessed and deducted from one's pay check as a religious offering? At the same time, the sense of the communal nature of Islam and the legitimizing of the political aspects of the religion through the model of Muḥammad leads more frequently to an assertion of the state's responsibility for collection of the tax. This would appear to be the motivation behind a 1991 suggestion in Malaysia that the government should legislate for the giving of *zakāt*, with penalties of up to three years in jail, an $1,800 fine and six strokes of the cane for non-payment. Even the threat of such legislation would seem to be having an effect, according to authorities, who saw a 75 percent rise in contributions to the Islamic Treasury in 1991 compared to 1990. Other approaches are also suggested for Muslims in the diaspora:

> The imposition of an organised Zakat collection system should be the objective of every Islamic state, both for the benefit of social peace and religious fulfilment. This might create a problem where Muslims live side by side with non-Muslims. It would not be just to charge the Muslim with both civil and religious taxes while the non-Muslim neighbour pays only one tax. In the past, non-Muslims used to pay Jizya which was the counterpart of Zakat. This, however, is no longer the practice. The solution, therefore, should be to deduct Zakat from the secular tax. As Zakat is ear-marked for social benefits, it is of service to all citizens.
>
> (Badawi 1999: 33)

Pilgrimage (*ḥajj*)

Lasting up to seven days, the pilgrimage focuses upon Mecca and its environs. The pilgrimage presents ritual, legal, social, administrative, symbolic, and ethical aspects, all of which have a particular and distinctive flavor in the modern period. There is a tendency in apologetic works towards rationalism in aspects of pilgrimage ritual. Regarding the black stone lodged in the side of the Kaʿba which pilgrims attempt to touch while circumambulating the shrine, for example, a symbolic status alone is often attributed to it; any connection of the stone to pre-Islamic times and to stone worship, as was classically affirmed by Muslim writers, will be ignored. The stone is just a natural stone from Mecca, according to the religious scholar Maḥmūd Shaltūt of Egypt. Such interpretations exist in tension, however, with those that emphasize the power of the stone and thus affirm its pre-Islamic significance. Such issues have arisen primarily because of the confrontation of modern historical questioning and traditional religious conceptions. Some aspects relate to "irrational" matters: is the black stone really a rock descended from heaven as was held in the past? How could that possibly be?

More generally, according to one study of contemporary popular religious literature, there is a marked reluctance on the part of many writers to acknowledge any continuation of pre-Islamic practices within Islamic rituals such as the pilgrimage. The "Islamization" of pagan rituals is ignored, for it is felt, apparently, that such historical research may well be destructive to Islam, even though observations about these connections were widespread in classical Islam. The preferred view today is to see all elements of Islam as having been revealed by God, sometimes even to the point of ignoring the idea that there had been a pre-Islamic pilgrimage. Interestingly, Sayyid Quṭb provides a contrary view:

> in these verses [of the Qurʾān] we see how Islam turned the [*ḥajj*] into an Islamic commandment, removed its pagan roots and made it into one of the supporting pillars of Islam, adorned it with Islamic notions and cleansed it from its blemishes and dregs . . . indeed, this is the way of Islam with every custom and ceremony which it deemed right to maintain.
>
> (Quṭb, quoted in Lazarus-Yafeh 1981: 111)

The most popular way of understanding all the pilgrimage rituals is to emphasize their symbolic and spiritual value. For example, throwing stones at the pillars represents not the external Satan but the internal Satan in the individual's heart. In general, the acts of the pilgrimage may appear "irrational" but their performance provides a way for the individual to show devotion to God; interpretation or relating the elements to their historical symbolic referents is unnecessary, if not undesirable, therefore. The pilgrimage is portrayed as an event in which the power and grandeur of God may be experienced by all Muslims, regardless of their origin or social status. In some of the more imaginative symbolic interpretations, such as that of the Iranian ʿAlī Shariʿātī, various aspects of the *ḥajj* become symbols of Islamic life: the *saʿy*, which in its historical interpretation is the running back and forth in search of water of Hagar, becomes "activism," the struggle of life in the world for what is needed in daily living and the struggle against economic and political oppression. *Ṭawāf*, the circumambulation of the Kaʿba, is symbolic of "endeavor," especially in the striving toward a correct, divinely oriented life of devotion.

Beyond the interpretation of the activities of the pilgrimage, there are substantial issues related to the level of participation. Somewhere between one and two million people have participated every year over recent decades. The Saudi Arabian government counted 2,521,000 people at the 2009 *ḥajj*, including 1,613,000 pilgrims who arrived from foreign countries and 154,000 from within Saudi Arabia, the majority of whom were non-Saudi residents. (There were an additional 753,000 pilgrims who did not have valid *ḥajj* permits, according to official news releases.) Of the participants arriving from outside the country, generally somewhat over 50 percent are male.

The total number of pilgrims in any year can vary because of political circumstances. For example, in 1989 the total number was 774,560. This was a substantial drop from 960,386 in 1987, and may be explained by the absence of pilgrims from Iran (who in 1987 numbered 157,395). Behind this variation in number, then, is another modern issue for Islam, one which vexes Muslims tremendously. The pilgrimage, a ritual required for all Muslims who are able to undertake it, takes place not solely on a personal level but also as a ritual which is performed in a modern nation state, Saudi Arabia. It is, therefore, both under the control of that state and also that state's responsibility. Thus one can see the emergence of complex visa regulations allowing for entrance into the country limited to the period around the pilgrimage. In 1987, over 400 pilgrims, mainly Iranians, were killed during violent demonstrations. As a result, the Saudi government cut ties with Iran and limited the number of Iranian pilgrims to 45,000. Iran retaliated by refusing to allow participation in the *ḥajj* at all. This situation lasted until 1991, when Iranians once again joined in. Similarly, Iraqis who wished to come overland to do the *ḥajj* faced a problem due to the closed border between Iraq and Saudi Arabia in the wake of the Kuwait war in 1991. By 1999, this led to a war of words between the two countries over who was responsible for the problem. The Saudi Arabian government declared that it "will not under any circumstance use the *Hajj* occasion and the performance of religious duties, for any political purpose" (Embassy of Saudi Arabia press release, March 20, 1999), underlining its consciousness of the Muslim perception of the issue. The idea that participation in a fundamental ritual of the religion should be controlled by a given political regime has created substantial difficulties for some Muslims; calls for the internationalization of Mecca are sometimes voiced as a result. The political aspects of the issue—the alliances between Saudi Arabia and the United States being a focal point of many allegations—result in the pilgrimage frequently becoming a symbolic element in the struggle between modern nations. Ayatollah Khomeini of Iran, for example, described the pilgrimage as the most important time for Muslims to demonstrate their unity and their rejection of imperialism:

> What is the solution, and what is the responsibility of the Muslims and oppressed for dispelling these illusions [of their powerlessness]? The primary solution, from which emerges all other solutions for cutting the roots of these problems and eradicating corruption, is the unity of Muslims, rather the unity of all oppressed and enslaved peoples in the world. This unity is gained through widespread *tabligh* [missionizing] and invitation. And the centre for this invitation and *tabligh* is the holy city of Makkah [Mecca] during the congregation of Muslims to perform the Hajj. This was started by Ibrahim, continued by Muhammad and will be followed by Hadrat Mahdi [who, the Shīʿa believe, will return at the end of time]. It was enjoined on Ibrahim to call people to Hajj to attend to their needs—that is, the political, social, economic and cultural issues of the society—and so that they, could witness how God's Prophet laid upon the altar the fruit of his life, for the sake of God . . . .
>
> We renounce the infidels during the Hajj rituals. This is a political-religious renunciation that the Prophet Muhammad, upon whom be peace, enjoined.
>
> (Khomeini 1985: 98–9)

The politicization of the *ḥajj* has recently manifested itself in a variety of other ways. In 2004, in the aftermath of the Iraqi war, the Saudi government paid special attention to receiving pilgrims from Iraq, for example, with arrangements being made for an anticipated contingent of 33,000 people. Additionally, American Muslims have recently expressed concern at the treatment which they have experienced during the *ḥajj* when they are identified as coming from the United States (over 10,000 visas were issued in the United States for travel to the *ḥajj* in 2004); so far, however, there have been no reports of encountering any substantial physical danger as a result of this.

On top of the question of political control of access, other implications also arise as a result of modern conveniences allowing participation in the pilgrimage. Most pilgrims now fly directly to Jedda in Saudi Arabia before setting out on their way to Mecca. (In 2004, 1,252,612 foreign pilgrims arrived by air, 23,658 by sea, and 143,436 by land.) The number of pilgrims handled in Saudi Arabia has increased tremendously (in 1869, some 110,000 foreigners participated; in 1907, 250,000) but the implications of this are felt all over the Muslim world, especially in the social significance which results from participation in the pilgrimage. Richard Antoun (1989: 165) reports that in the Jordanian village which he studied a general rise in annual income (resulting from working in the Saudi Arabian oil industry), modern, safe, and rapid transportation methods, and government encouragement of local pilgrim guides had all resulted in a marked rise in the proportion of the inhabitants who had performed the pilgrimage between the years 1959 and 1986. This was accompanied, however, by a change in the ethos related to pilgrimage performance. It used to be, according to Antoun, that performing the pilgrimage brought both status within the community and the requirement from the pilgrim of appropriately pious behavior; it was, therefore, something which was reserved for the older men of the community who, it was felt, would be able to carry the burden of that responsibility. Today, a far greater proportion of younger men (under 40 and generally well educated) undertake the pilgrimage as a means of asserting religious identity.

Flying to Jedda to commence the pilgrimage has some direct ritual implications. Traditionally, the state of sanctity represented by the clothing known as the *iḥrām* (along with other associated rituals) would be entered before passing into the region of the *mawāqit* or boundaries of the sacred area, within which Jedda sits. Pilgrims coming by airplane, therefore, as a rule put their pilgrimage costume on in their home country before boarding the plane, although it is considered possible to do it in Jedda if one sets out with the intention to perform a visitation (*ziyāra*) to the holy sites first and then perform the *ḥajj* afterwards. Certain other aspects of the rituals are now likely to be spread over a number of days rather than have all the pilgrims accomplish them all at once. This fact was brought home once again by an accident at Minā in 1998 in which 118 pilgrims died when a stampede occurred as the participants headed towards the area for the ritual stoning of Satan. For the 1999 pilgrimage, much effort was put into the coordination of the twenty-one hospitals (with a capacity of 7,103 beds) to be able to deal with an emergency. In 2009, due to the fear of H1N1 swine flu, vaccinations were given to all those working in Saudi Arabia in *ḥajj*-related jobs, and in order to receive a *ḥajj* permit visitors had to submit proof of having been vaccinated; 68 confirmed flu cases, including some deaths, were reported. As well, physical safety is emphasized:

> Undersecretary for Pilgrimage Affairs Hatem Qadi announced that in order to avoid overcrowding at the Jamrat area in Mina, arrangements have been made with the *Tawafa* organizations for the stoning ritual to be performed by their pilgrims in groups at specified times. He stated that the success of the group system to be implemented this year depends upon the cooperation of all pilgrims and *Hajj* missions. Electronic instruction boards will be installed on the Jamrat bridge to inform pilgrims in various languages on the situation in the area, and pilgrims will be urged to wait for some time if the area is crowded, and not proceed with the stoning.
>
> (Embassy of Saudi Arabia press release, February 14, 1999)

Despite these precautions, the 2004 *ḥajj* was marred once again by the death of 251 pilgrims at Minā due to a stampede (an additional 280 people died from natural causes during the *ḥajj* period). The cause of the problem was blamed upon a substantial number (estimated to be over 250,000) of "unlicensed" pilgrims who tried to perform the ritual stoning without having a scheduled time allotted. The proposed solution is to build a nine-story terrace to replace the existing two-level structure; when it is complete, it is anticipated that the stoning ritual could be accomplished by nine million people in one day. There will be escalators and elevators for the disabled.

The crush of people attending has also required an extra story to be built at the mosque of Mecca, something which is considered in legal terms an innovation, yet one which was necessary. Some people have urged that the pilgrimage be stretched over a longer period of time so that everyone may be accommodated. Substitutions for the animal slaughter which is an integral part of the activity have been suggested, such that a person needs to give up (i.e., sacrifice) something "held dear," just as Abraham was willing to give up his son, the action which the sacrifice recalls. As it stands, the sacrifices have become centralized. The Islamic Development Bank's Sacrificial Meat Utilization Project is in charge of coordinating the annual sacrifice ritual and subsequent distribution of the meat. A sheep (of which 587,723 were used in 2004; 5,076 camels and cows were also slaughtered) is then slaughtered on behalf of the pilgrim in four modern abattoirs (built at a cost of $128.3 million, employing 20,000 people to administer and perform the program) according to prescribed Muslim ritual slaughtering methods. The meat is quick-frozen and later distributed to refugee populations in twenty-seven countries around the Muslim world. Modern issues of hygiene clearly dictate that over half a million animals cannot be slaughtered in the outdoor environs of Mecca. Such hygienic and safety concerns are also raised in relation to housing and facilitating the massive influx of pilgrims themselves; much publicity was given in 1999 to the construction of the required tent cities out of fireproof material due to accidents in previous years.

Identity and the Qurʾān in cyberspace

Ritual is not, of course, the only aspect of Muslim identity that has been affected in the modern context. The rapidity of change in the contemporary world is one of the few constants of life which many people say they experience, and it occurs in every area of existence. As was remarked earlier (p. 194), the concerns and responses of many of the voices within Modernist Muslim visions of Islam quickly become quaint or irrelevant in the face of these quickly altering structures of modern life. No better illustration of this can be found than in the transformation which scripture is undergoing under the influence of the internet and new media, and the impact that is having on Muslim society. It has already become a cliché among scholars to remark on the impact this move of the Qurʾān into its new cyber existence is having on Muslims in general and, potentially, on Islam itself, even though the process is still underway and no definitive study of the phenomenon is truly possible at this time.

The impact of the cyber Qurʾān on access to knowledge and all the resulting changes which may come about because of shifting social, political, and intellectual power structures have already become apparent at least in legal fields, where the invocation of the Qurʾān does, of course, play a central role. The influence of an internet-based jurist can extend far beyond the geographically bound areas previously experienced by Muslims in their search for answers to day-to-day questions that arise in a life lived in an Islamicly conscious fashion. Further, the theoretical accessibility of the internet to anyone (restricted primarily by economic resources) has resulted in a shifting social composition of those who can provide legal opinions on subjects. The anonymity of the internet means that anyone may assert his (or her, for gender, too, is hidden) qualifications as a *muftī* and the appropriate citation of sources is no longer limited to those who have undergone a traditional education in the religious sciences or even those who have access to a physical library of books. While authority is frequently still being asserted through the invocation of sources which come from the past and that very fact does signify a substantial level of learning (the classical works of law or Quranic commentary are not easier to understand simply because they are available on the internet), it is clear that the composition of the scholarly classes among Muslims is being altered. This is also the result of a fundamental shift in literacy levels among Muslim populations, which, combined with other forces such as the personalization of religion, a distrust of established power structures, and the global context of knowledge production, has transformed the way in which many individuals relate to their religious heritage. One outcome of this is seen in a shift to Qurʾān-centeredness in Muslim practice simply for pragmatic reasons related to the difficulties involved in digesting the enormous body of *ḥadīth* literature, while at the same time most Muslims have acquired the level of literacy that makes intimate, intellectual contact with the Qurʾān possible.

An effect on the recitation of the Qurʾān is also to be observed as a result of the emergence of the cyber Muslim community. The process of putting recitations on record and then cassette has been going on for almost a century now and the controversies which that initially engendered appear to have fully subsided. It is thus the internationalization of certain recitation styles and voices which is primarily being enhanced by the presence of the recited Qurʾān on the internet. Some observers have commented on the increasing sense of the commoditization of the Qurʾān under the impact of this sort of technology. On the internet one now finds the Qurʾān alongside (in a digital sense) the less-refined aspects of human behavior. This might be argued to be true of a library as well, but the uncontrolled nature of the cyber context does change the sense of this. With the Qurʾān available to anyone, for free, open to whatever changes it might be subjected to with very little effort—and with an awareness of this context being felt by Muslims themselves—the sanctity of the text and the emotions which that evokes are being subjected to subtle but substantial change. The impact on the status of the Qurʾān through its manifestation in an electronic form is still being absorbed by Muslims, with questions regarding the need for purity in interacting with a digital Qurʾān and the problem of the impermanence of the image of the text when it is displayed on a screen being grappled with by those whose frame of reference remains the memorized and recited text. Online *fatwā*s often try to address such questions. For example, among the rulings provided at Islamicity.com, special attention is paid to whether or not one must be in a ritually pure state when reading the Qurʾān on the internet (or, for that matter, from a CD); the answer provided is that it is not required—because this is not the same as a tangible, physical text—but it is desirable to maintain purity while interacting with the text regardless of the form it is in. However, one should certainly avoid taking tapes, CDs, and computer versions of the Qurʾān into a bathroom when using the toilet. Encountering the recited Qurʾān by hearing it play as a background track on a website also raises questions; this practice of web design is determined to be objectionable because those encountering the recited Qurʾān in such a context would not necessarily pay the appropriate attention to the recitation, given that the purpose of their visit to the website would presumably be to another end.

A significant transformation in interaction with classical religious texts is to be noted due to their move to digital formats. Such texts are now fully searchable electronically. Given that it is not always predictable where a Quranic word or idea may be treated within a work of exegesis, for example, having a full text which is searchable by individual words suggests a major transformation in investigative methods on every level. We witness in this use of technology what has already been recognized as fundamental transformation of knowledge in global terms, but it still needs to be remarked specifically within this context: this is a wholesale change in access to knowledge which alters fundamental aspects of exegetical procedure. As was observed earlier (p. 166), one of the presuppositions of the entire method of classical Muslim exegesis is the cumulative nature of the enterprise and how the person involved within the process needs to be immersed not just in the Qurʾān itself but in the world of *tafsīr* literature, in grammar, in lexicography, and so forth. The authority of one's pronouncements on meaning is intimately tied to one's ability to be able to cite cross-references, authorities, information, rules, and opinions. Such abilities demand training, dedication, intelligence, and acumen. This is what electronic access and searchability truly transform.

As is well known, the internet is also an extremely active venue for modern polemics. Sites such as "Islamic Awareness" and "Answering Islam" are replete with tracts on the Qurʾān from the Muslim and Christian perspectives respectively. These are resources to which the unwary are drawn and to which the convinced contribute. The very sophistication of such sites is both their appeal and their danger in their glossing over of

Figure 15.1 An Iranian *mulla* in Qom works on the website of saanei.org, dedicated to the Grand Ayatollah Yūsuf Ṣāniʿī [Ayatollah Yusef Saanei] (b. 1937). Available in Arabic, Urdu, English, and Persian, the website provides an illustration of the efforts made in Iran to use technology to spread the message of Shiʿism and to assert the authority of individual Ayatollahs in the country. Ṣāniʿī was a pupil of Ayatollah Khomeini, and served on the Iranian Guardian Council in the 1980s; more recently he has become quite controversial because of his reformist views.
Source: AFP/Getty Images.

critical questions while asserting the veracity of what they claim on the authority of established academic scholarship. The internet has also fostered intra-Muslim polemic, with Iranian websites being very active in providing Ithnā ʿAsharī Imāmī interpretations of the Qurʾān and Saudi Arabian sites promoting a conservative Salafī view. The group known as "The Submitters," based in the United States and following notions promulgated by Rashad Khalifa in relationship to the Qurʾān (especially the role of the number nineteen), have garnered much greater attention as a result of their presence on the Web than would otherwise have been the case. The internet can thus be a place for the creation of a community of like minds but can also be a place for the aggravation of contemporary contention, strife, and disagreement.

Islamic identity and politics

In contemporary Muslim life much attention is given to the attempt to implement Islamic ideals within society in general. This may be summarized generally as the impact of Islam upon politics, although its basis in Islam is in the field of law. Primarily associated with the Islamists' totalist vision, the idea that Islam "encompasses all of life" has become the central pivot for political aspirations. Religion also becomes a political tool in this framework, as in the frequent charge that Islam is used by many political leaders simply to justify change and to keep the masses quiet. Here it is a matter of the social use of Islamic symbols rather than the personal use of them. It is here, then, that we realize that Islam as a faith in the modern world has two faces: the personal, ever-searching and flexible, and the institutional, firm and imperialistic.

The background to this search for the public, political face of Islam may best be considered in light of the growth of secularism, especially as promulgated by governments in countries which identify themselves as constituted by a majority Muslim population. Secularism exists in many different forms in these countries, but it always manifests itself in those who argue for Islam in the modern world as a purely religious phenomenon without political force, an argument which allows for massive social reorganization without having to take the full Islamic factor into account. The extreme form of this is radical secularism as was found in mid-twentieth-century Albania, where the aim had been to replace all of Islam. This is, therefore, not an Islamic example as such, although the people involved were Muslims by heritage and they were seeking a way to live within the modern world. More common is the type of secularism found in Turkey, where there has been a total separation of religion from politics and public life as a whole, at least symbolically. Mustafa Kemal Atatürk (1881–1938) was the Turkish nationalist leader responsible for much of the character of that country as it is today. After leading the drive to expel the Greeks from Turkey after World War I, he moved the country towards official secularism, best typified symbolically by the change in the way Turkish was written: the Arabic script which had been used for five centuries under the Ottomans was abandoned and replaced by the Latin alphabet, modified slightly to account for certain peculiarities of Turkish. The suppression of Islamic legal and educational institutions and the outlawing of mystical Ṣūfī groups were other steps in the removal of religion from the apparatus of the state. While certain elements of these positions have been modified in recent years with the back-and-forth movement of the parties in power and the continuing significant role of the armed forces, Turkey remains firmly secularist even while certain Islamic symbols become ever more prominent. The contemporary debates in Turkey over female veiling, *ḥijāb*, demonstrate, however, how tenuous and variable the line between secularism and Islam can become.

Islam in officially secular countries is replaced on an ideological level—that is, as the system of thought which orients and interprets an individual's life within society—by nationalism, capitalism, or socialism. Other cited examples of secularism are seen in the multi-faith system found in Indonesia and Muslim secularism as in the Egypt of the 1970s, where religion (or Islam specifically) had a role and a standing politically but was not the full basis of the society. The evidence for this may be seen in the way in which law codes were implemented and adopted. While the Muslim religious legal code, the *sharīʿa*, was replaced in secular countries by other law codes, in each instance the dividing line between religious and secular varies, especially when compared to Euro-American models of secularism, as, for example, in the religious control of divorce and marriage. One other way in which secularism is characterized is by state control of all religions. Secularism has been used to champion progress and also to enhance unity in countries, especially where there are significant non-Muslim minorities. This, it is said, has been the most important factor in pushing countries such as Egypt and Indonesia toward official secularism.

It is against this background that the emergence or resurgence of Islam as a political force manifest in the Islamist groups must be seen. Starting in the 1970s, Islam thrust itself into world headlines with the revolution in Iran, the assassination of Anwar Sadat, the killings in Algeria, the Taliban in Afghanistan, the Iraqi invasion of Kuwait, September 11, 2001, and al-Qaeda, and the wars in Iraq and Afghanistan. The heritage of this resurgence goes back much further, of course, but the modern movements have had a particular focus upon the presence of Islam as a political identity and have created their own ideologies suitable to the context of today.

The continuing pressure of the Islamists has led to an uneasy balance in many countries. Governments are using Islam to a greater extent, while cracking down on the more radical aspects of the Islamist groups. In recent years, some have spoken of a "post-Islamist" mood emerging among many people, because of the significant re-emergence of Islam as a factor in established political parties, which has undermined the need for the more moderate (and generally accepted) aspects of the Islamist agenda. This has been accomplished through a governmental appeal to Islam as the social basis of legal statutes, while being accompanied by a careful limiting of the realms in which the Islamic *sharīʿa* is to be implemented. To those in power, this often makes a good deal of pragmatic sense, since the difficulties in determining how the *sharīʿa* can give guidance on current issues such as gun control, import duties, and industrial monopolies are well understood. Discussion of such issues by Islamists has produced a number of responses, for example that the *sharīʿa* is designed for a "minimal" government (as in the platform of Ḥasan al-Turābī in the Sudan) or that one may weigh the rulings of the *sharīʿa* against the greater interests of the country (as in the platform of Ayatollah Khomeini in Iran).

The rise of an Islamic political consciousness and the resultant wish for participation within the political system among a good portion of the general Muslim populace have had their own ramifications. While such political movements may have started with numerically insignificant groups of people, the rise of mass higher education and the emergence of inexpensive means of mass communications have produced the desire and the opportunity for many more people to become involved. This rise in participation has had the effect of producing a significantly fractured voice within the Islamist movement; the greater the number of people involved, the greater the number of opinions. Because of this, it has become difficult, if not impossible, to say that such a "movement" actually exists in any real sense. Consequently, governments have been able to use their authority to fill the resultant lack of Islamist unity.

The challenge of diversity

Along with the impact of modern technology and the changing face of communications in the world today has come an even greater challenge to Muslim identity in the twenty-first century, which may be summed up by simple reference to key words: Taliban, al-Qaeda, *jihād*, September 11, Islamic terrorism. The significance of all of these aspects of the modern world lies not in what they say about the character of Islam itself—for the movements themselves are on the periphery of anything that could claim to be Islamic—but rather in the crisis of identity which they have created for Muslims.

The events of the twenty-first century have aggravated the fractures which were so apparent within the Muslim community as it evolved in the twentieth century. The pressures of terrorism and the wars in Iraq and Afghanistan on Muslim identity and self-conception have forced the lines between Muslim groups to be exacerbated and have created a situation in which talk of Muslim "communities" in the plural becomes a much more accurate description of reality.

The moral dilemmas of the past remain as vital as ever. The discussions from the formative period concerning who is and who is not a Muslim become as pressing as ever. The sense of the responsibility of the individual Muslim for the state of the Muslim community and the state of the world proves as overwhelming today as it did for the Khawārij in the early centuries, Ibn Taymiyya in the thirteenth century, or Ibn ʿAbd al-Wahhāb in the eighteenth century. This may be illustrated by looking at a version of "The Things Which Nullify Islam" associated with Ibn ʿAbd al-Wahhāb, discussed in Chapter 11, and now circulated widely in English and in Arabic on the internet under the title "Ten Things Which Nullify One's Islam," with authorship credited to the Saudi cleric Shaykh ʿAbd al ʿAzīz ibn ʿAbd Allāh ibn Bāz. Ibn Bāz was born in 1912 in Riyadh, Saudi Arabia; blind from the age of twenty, he was appointed vice-chancellor of the Islamic University of Medina in 1961, and chancellor of the University of Medina in 1970. In 1992, he was appointed the official *muftī* of Saudi Arabia, responsible for expounding the Islamic law and providing *fatwās*, "legal opinions," when needed. Ibn Bāz was also appointed to the Saudi posts of presidency of the Committee of Senior Scholars and presidency of the Administration for Scientific Research and Legal Rulings. He continued to hold other posts until his death in 1999.

The eighteenth-century version of the document attributed to Ibn ʿAbd al-Wahhāb may be compared with this late-twentieth-century one in order to display the changing concerns of Islam in the modern world when it is a matter of upholding the principles of the religion while adhering to the same exacting standards of moral behavior as in the past and asserting one's ability to judge the performance of fellow Muslims. Such a position is a strident, activist one; its tone emphasizes the potential for fractures within the community of Muslims as it makes clear that some self-declared Muslims are really unbelievers.

At the beginning of the document which is available on the internet, Ibn Bāz adopts a proof text with a more apocalyptic tone and changes the examples in order to take the emphasis away from the ritual of animal slaughter as Ibn ʿAbd al-Wahhāb had it, by restating the point as follows:

> "Truly, whosoever sets up partners with God, then God has forbidden the Garden for him, and the Fire will be his abode. And for the wrongdoers there are no helpers." [Qurʾān 5/72] Calling upon the dead, asking their help, or offering them gifts or sacrifices are all forms of *shirk* [ascribing partners to God].
>
> (http://www.fatwa-online.com/FATAAWA/CREED/SHIRK/9991120_1.HTM)

When dealing with Muslims who might not consider polytheists to be unbelievers, Ibn Bāz makes it explicit that these categories can include Jews and Christians. He also clarifies a point of classical Muslim discussion by adding that Muslims should also not believe that it is possible that such people will enter paradise. The text then goes into an extended discussion of the status of Jews and Christians because of their disbelief in Muḥammad, providing the Catholic and Protestant view of the doctrine of the Trinity, which is cited as contrary to the explicit statement of Qur'ān 5/73 ("Those who say that God is the third of three and not that of gods there is only the one God, disbelieve"), and the Orthodox view of the divinity of Jesus deemed contrary to Qur'ān 5/72 ("Those who say that the messiah, the son of Mary, is God, disbelieve"). The Jews already declared their non-belief by rejecting Jesus, as reflected in Qur'ān 3/52 ("When Jesus came to know of their disbelief, he said, 'Who will be my helpers towards God?' The disciples said, 'We are the helpers of God. We believe in God and we bear witness that we have submitted [become Muslims].' "). Ibn Bāz is inevitably far more concerned with the Euro-American-Israeli threat to Islam than Ibn ʿAbd al-Wahhāb.

Dealing with challenges to the notion of the perfection of the *sharīʿa*, Ibn Bāz extends the matter extensively by citing three examples (listed as 1, 2 and 3 below). The following items are all deemed ways of violating Islam:

1 To believe that systems and laws made by human beings are better than the *sharīʿa* of Islam; for example, saying that the Islamic system is not suitable for the twentieth century; or that Islam is the cause of the backwardness of the Muslims; or that Islam is a relationship between God and the Muslim that should not interfere in other aspects of life.

All of the specific examples listed under this point have been common refrains of Modernists in Islam since the nineteenth century. The rejection of the privatization of Islam in the Protestant Christian mode is especially telling and represents a rejection not only of modern tendencies and debates over civil society, but also of the heritage of *taqiyya*, a doctrine associated with Shīʿī Islam that allows for the hiding of the outward manifestation of one's religion in face of oppression.

2 To say that enforcing the punishments prescribed by God, such as cutting off the hand of the thief or the stoning of an adulterer, is not suitable for this day and age.

3 To believe that it is permissible to give a rule based on something God did not reveal when dealing with commercial transactions or matters of law, punishments, or other affairs. Although one may not believe such things to be superior to the *sharīʿa*, in effect such a stance is affirmed by declaring a thing which God has prohibited, such as adultery, drinking alcohol, or usury, to be permissible. According to the consensus of the Muslims, one who declares such things to be permissible is an unbeliever.

When dealing with "ridiculing" Islam, Ibn Bāz speaks of making fun of God, Muḥammad, any aspect of the law that might be considered a distinctive Muslim marker (including aspects of beards, clothing, gender relations, and using a *siwāk* as a toothbrush), or those who uphold the traditions of Islam.

Ibn Bāz has updated Ibn ʿAbd al-Wahhāb. The concerns of the late twentieth century are clear. The ghost of Salman Rushdie, for example, lurks behind a number of the statements, especially when the matter of the possibility of apostasy comes up; Ibn Bāz declares that any Muslim who believes that it is possible for someone to leave Islam is him- or herself an unbeliever. The existence of Israel is reflected in the renewed emphasis on the Jews, and theological disputes with the Christians revived from the Middle Ages are clear in the discussions around the doctrine of the Trinity. The rejection of the modern conception of the notion of religion as an internal matter and the rejection of modern animosity to certain religious symbols are clearly conveyed. As an aside, note should be made of the impact of translation in the move from an Arabic-reading audience to an English one and the influence of the worldwide context of the internet in producing a softening of some aspects of Ibn Bāz's statement (which remains recognizably strident even in its more polite English version as circulated electronically).

Examination of such theological debates allows us some modest insights into the complexities of the situation. Times of crisis in Islamic history have been marked by tensions between Muslims regarding membership in their community. A threat to the unity and stability of the community, widely felt and deeply perceived, tends to provoke a spirit of Islamic renewal which has been, in some of its manifestations, oriented towards a strict delimitation of the boundaries of Islamic identity. The Wahhābī movement is one such tendency and that continues today in the Salafī movement in Saudi Arabia. The pressures are there—the threat of people leaving Islam, especially due to the attractions of the world around—and the desire to be able to tell friend from foe becomes more critical. There are definite authoritarian aspects to these proclamations and those who support them are firm in their belief that they are correct. That violence may erupt in such a situation is, unfortunately, a reality. That may clearly be seen in the career of Osama bin Laden, whose criticisms of the Saudi government are trenchant but whose notions of Islamic moral purity clearly fit within the conservative tendencies of Arabian Islam. There is, of course, nothing uniquely Islamic about authoritarian responses emerging in a situation of authoritarian repression.

It is the absoluteness contained in such documents and attitudes that marks the nature of this approach to Islam. The struggle for the definition of the relationship between Islam and the state and to establish the state's responsibility for maintaining an Islamic culture and ethos has led, as Shirin Ebadi, the Nobel Peace Prize winner for 2003, put it, to the emergence throughout the Islamic world of "state religion" rather than "religious states." The defense of Islam becomes a vehicle for the oppression of the population and results in the emergence of a notion (popular at least in the Euro-American press) that Islam and human rights are incompatible. Stories emerge from Iran, for example, of "vigilante groups" bursting into Tehran dormitories and homes searching for VCRs and satellite-TV receivers to smash, attacking couples holding hands in the street, and burning down movie theaters. They are storming into restaurants in search of women wearing their scarves too loosely. According to such reports, the command to enforce Islamic social values is fiercely enacted by these groups, who seem to have no doubts about the answer to the question "Am I my brother's keeper?" as the age-old debate rages on over commanding right and forbidding wrong all around them.

Identity in the modern context

The interpretation of Islamic ritual and political activities illustrates the tension which would seem to be present in some of the conceptualizations of Islam today. Bringing the personal and the institutional together in a rapidly moving world of conflicting interests seems beyond most discussions, and when they do occur they often take on the air of unreality, as for example in the treatment of "Islamic economics" or "Islamic ways of knowing." Underlying them all are the basic motifs already noticed in discussions of the place of Muḥammad and the Qurʾān: anti-supernaturalism, an accommodation with science, a debate over legal provisions versus moral imperatives. The presentations of Islam often seem to be on the defensive: Muslim activities are seen as the final bulwark of the individual against modernity. It is not surprising, then, that for many Muslims ritual has become the keystone of their self-identity as Muslim. It should not be forgotten, however, that for many Muslims this resurgence of or added emphasis on ritual is a feature only of those alienated from their Islamic roots anyway. The integration of Muslim life in the more rural parts of the Muslim world continues as it ever has and may well continue in that manner for many generations to come.

Women leading prayer

On March 18, 2005, Dr. Amina Wadud, an American academic, served as prayer leader at a Friday noon prayer. Men and women joined together in prayer in New York's Synod House, at the Cathedral of St. John the Divine, an Episcopal church, being led by Wadud. While this was not the very first time a woman had served in the role of *imām*, the event did garner a good deal of press coverage as well as the condemnation of religious authorities in the Arab world and the United States.

The goal of the Progressive Muslim Union—one of the sponsors of the event—was to draw attention to the continuing disenfranchisement of women in mosques, which continue, even outside core Islamic countries, to privilege men. Muslim law schools are unanimous (with some minor exceptional circumstance allowed in the Ḥanbalī school) in ruling that women may only lead other groups of women in the prescribed daily ritual prayer; only within a family home would it be permissible for a woman to lead both genders. Al-Nawawī (a Shāfiʿī jurist who died in 1278) is often cited as providing the clear ruling that if a man prays behind a woman, then his prayer is invalid. In traditional Islamic custom, women are required to pray in rows behind men or in an entirely different part of the mosque.

During an interview, Wadud said the following:

> The idea that patriarchy has a grip on human development is not unique to Islam. And certainly the way in which this grip has been abused—that is, the way in which it has been utilized in order to justify abuse—I think the idea of a link between Islam and patriarchy is not inherent in Islam itself, but inherent in the context of Islamic origin. So it is very easy to go back in Islamic history or tradition, or even in [Islamic] intellectual development, and find justification for maintaining patriarchy and giving it an Islamic slant.
>
> The question is—and I certainly think that the most important work that is before us in terms of progressive Islamic thought—is to wrestle the eternal system away from its contextual foundation. And that foundation is a time–space reality, that is, Islam had to come into being into the mundane world, but it is not the universal. In order to be able to cast the universal into its many, or say, its pluralistic guises, we have to be able to determine that patriarchy is in fact a limitation, it's not a liberation.
>
> (www.pbs.org/wgbh/pages/frontline/shows/muslims/interviews/wadud.html)

Amina Wadud's work *Inside the Gender Jihad: Women's Reform in Islam*, Oxford: Oneworld, 2006, provides a full expression of her point of view. For the conservative reaction to the issue, see, for example, the ruling of Yūsuf al-Qaraḍāwī available at www.iio.org/article.php/20050417005930119.

Suggested further reading

Mohammed Ayoob, *The Many Faces of Political Islam: Religion and Politics in the Muslim World*, Ann Arbor: University of Michigan Press, 2008.

Robert R. Bianchi, *Guests of God: Pilgrimage and Politics in the Islamic World*, New York: Oxford University Press, 2004.

Marjo Buitelaar, *Fasting and Feasting in Morocco: Women's Participation in Ramadan*, Oxford, Providence: Berg, 1993.

Gary R. Bunt, *iMuslims: Rewiring the House of Islam*, Chapel Hill: University of North Carolina Press, 2009.

Peter Mandaville, *Global Political Islam*, London: Routledge, 2007.

PART VI Re-visioning Islam

16 *Women, intellectuals, and other challenges*

With the move into the twentieth-first century, the question may well be asked, what of Islam (or, indeed, religion in general) in the new millennium? Few doubt that Islam will continue to exist. Rather, it is the variety of forms in which it will be found that is of interest. Doubtless, the main trends which have already been sketched in the preceding chapters will be the most significant. Islam, however, will face challenges on a variety of fronts which will likely both change it and strengthen its determination in the ongoing march of human history. Some of those challenges will come from within; others will come from without. Some of the modern thinkers within Islam, such as Fatima Mernissi, Mohammad Arkoun, and Shabbir Akhtar, who may well stimulate these new lines of thought, have already been mentioned previously in the context of discussions of Muslim sources of authority. Others, such as Farid Esack, who attempts to face human problems from his own sense of Muslim identity not constrained by traditional Islamic practices, are just starting to make their impact. Still others present a revolutionary Islam that will topple existing social structures. From the outside, it is not only the forces of creeping secularism but strident humanist and feminist voices who pose a new challenge, along with rival religious groups. Among the latter, it is groups whose origins are from within the Islamic milieu that are particularly significant, since their appeal is precisely to those familiar with Muslim claims and activities. Other religions, including Hinduism and especially Christianity, play a major role as a challenge to Islam as well, of course, but they fall outside the purview of this book, although their influence is to be noted in many places.

The intellectual discussions conducted in Muslim circles over the past two centuries have attempted to enunciate an understanding of the basis of Islam in its contemporary context. Certainly not all Muslims have taken part in the actual discussion of these issues sketched earlier, but they all do, in fact, have a position on them, whether they enunciate it or not. How the Qurʾān is to be understood and how Muḥammad is to be conceived are the hermeneutical fundamentals upon which Islam is based, and even those who simply follow what has "always" been thought on these topics are taking a position within the debate. Furthermore, it is clear that some of the discussions taking place today have had a profound impact upon the face of Islam as a whole, not only in its intellectual and ideological formulations, but also in its practical ramifications, as may be seen in the modern discussions surrounding ritual activities and politics.

No doubt, Muslims as individuals are far more concerned with the implementation of their religion as a vital part of their lives than they are with the theoretical understanding of the underpinnings of their faith. Islam is a "simple" religion, says a popular phrase in Islamist circles, and it is not in need of these intellectual discussions. And yet the point remains that the basic principles which surround the intellectual conceptualization of the fundamental elements of Islam—the Qurʾān and Muḥammad—make their mark even in the basic aspects of modern Muslim daily life, despite these claims. One area in which this may be demonstrated revolves around the discussions dealing with women's place in modern Islam, especially as this reflects further issues concerning the entire structure of Muslim society. In fact, it is in tangling with this concern that many thinkers believe the traditional face of Islam will encounter its greatest challenge and from where new visions of what Islam might be in the future will emerge.

Obviously enough, women comprise about 50 percent of all Muslims. While all Muslims, male and female, would agree that Islam stands for and aspires to a single religion regardless of the gender of the adherent, the sociological facts speak otherwise. Islamic society has both encouraged and allowed specifically female modes of religiosity within the overall framework of the religion. This is the result of a number of factors which could be termed both negative and positive. The exclusion of women from the power structures of institutionalized Islam, along with the specific religious requirements for women, have jointly brought about specific female-oriented ramifications. Islamic law, with its enunciated roots firmly in the Qurʾān, has instituted a social system based upon the presumption of an extended family grouping within a patriarchal system. This has existed, quite successfully, in creative tension with the notion of the Muslim *umma*, the community within which all are one under their relationship to God. Within that overall social system with its assigned roles for women, certain women-focused religious activities have emerged. Feminists would say that women have sought to build a world to replace the one from which they have been excluded.

The modern age has had a severe impact upon the social system of Islam, as has already been noted several times. At the same time, the place of the family within that social system remains central to much of the sense of Muslim identity. Not surprisingly, therefore, issues of women in the context of the family receive what might considered a disproportionate amount of attention in the discussions of Islam in the modern context. This focus on women is not necessarily an apologetic response to the pressures of the day, nor is it necessarily "anti-Islamic" to focus upon it, as is sometimes suggested. Family roles have always been fundamental elements of Islamic identity, and thus women's issues are central. Furthermore, the question of women's roles in society is an enormous problem at the present time for a number of reasons. The traditional assumptions about the way in which family life is structured are being questioned daily, not simply by intellectuals and Western-educated individuals, but by the urban masses as well. The transition from rural to urban society, resulting in overcrowded cities, mass transit, poverty, unemployment, and all the other characteristics of modern life, has meant a severe disruption in the roles played within the family. Education has also exaggerated the problem, not just by creating a reflective group of people who recognize that knowledge is power (only to have that insight rendered meaningless frequently by their failure to achieve any significant social power despite their education), but by radically changing the social structure. Both men and women have tended in recent times to delay marriage while education was being undertaken. This has resulted in the emergence of a group of people not even contemplated in the traditional Islamic social system: unmarried adolescents. The prime focal points of the traditional jurist's social system are the female child and the married woman.

The question therefore emerges for Muslims of every persuasion: what is to be done to make Islam relevant and even helpful in this new situation? It is the discord felt between modernity and the traditional religious forms that is stimulating the need for change. It is not that accusations are necessarily being made that Islam is somehow "at fault," but rather that attempts are being made to draw on traditional religious resources to find the answers for today. Islam has functioned, through its divinely authorized social system, to provide identity for its members by drawing the social boundaries of individual existence in relationship to other members. Under the pressures of today, the identity provided is no longer commensurate with the aspirations of some people, many of whom are women; or, at least, the straightforward answers of the past no longer prove sufficient in responding to modern questioning. The issue of women, then, is one which displays, in a very vital form, the implications of the intellectual debates which have been discussed earlier and suggests, in some of its ideas, an emerging new vision of what Islam as a social system and even as a "religion" might be in the future.

Traditional patterns of women's religion

In practice, women have been excluded from substantial areas of Islamic ritual. Menstruation, while not implying a ritual contagion in Islam (for "pollution" does not get transmitted from one person to another in Islamic thinking), serves as a barrier to ritual performance for the woman concerned. Thus, while men have nothing to fear from women being present at prayer, the ritual status of a woman would be on communal view if her attendance at public worship, for example, were to be required whenever she was able to attain a ritually pure state. Islam, therefore, instituted what might be termed a paternalism, generally excluding women from public performance of the daily prayer for the benefit of their privacy. Other reasons for this exclusion are frequently proffered, especially within apologetic presentations of Islam. Women prove a distraction to men at prayer, some claim, not allowing the believers to concentrate fully upon the divine; praying separately is therefore advantageous for both genders. In addition, women have other responsibilities within the family structure which preclude their participation in regularly scheduled events; this explanation for different ritual requirements according to the gender of the believer is also common in Jewish apologetics.

The result of this separation has not been the establishment of rival formal female-dedicated institutions in which women may perform their rituals separately. Rather, in many places in the Muslim world, informal popular religious practices often associated with mysticism and saint worship (something which many Muslim reformers have targeted as "non-Islamic") have emerged, activities which exist outside the male-dominated institutionalized forms of Islam. Such cults are seen to have provided women with a sense of solidarity and independence from men. The magical aspects of this worship, manifested in trances, vows, and oaths, are viewed as powerful tools in the relationship between men and women. Fear is often seen to be instilled in men because, through their wives' activities in these saint cults, power is believed to be held over a man's virility and fertility.

Another popular Islamic institution, resulting from the legal institution of ritual cleansing and from the practicalities of society, is the public bath. Here, women gather within the intimacy of their own gender and participate in social circles beyond their own kin grouping. Observers have noted that women emerge with a significant form of power from this structure because they are able to move between family groupings in these contexts to a far greater extent than men are able to in male-oriented situations. The "inside track" on social, political, and economic movements is available to women, frequently then to be shared with their husbands within the confines of their own homes, a factor of some value in domestic power arrangements.

Seclusion

Seclusion of women has become the most firmly lodged image of Islamic society in the Western popular imagination. That is an image which reflects a reality and a basic principle of the Islamic social system, although the precise form which it takes varies with geographical location (and implied cultural differences), social status, and a variety of other factors. The honor of the family is what is traditionally seen to be at stake, although this is critiqued frequently by pointing out that it is the male sense of honor which is being protected on the assumption of a female tendency towards independence and uncontrolled sexuality which must be restrained. The behavior of the female is therefore to be controlled to preserve male honor.

The word used to refer to this seclusion varies: *ḥijāb* and *purdah* both refer to a principle which frequently becomes manifest in the clothing of women which is expressed more accurately in contemporary terms as *al-ziyy al-Islāmī*, Islamic modest dress, and denotes a covering of the hair and an obscuring of the shape of the body. Seclusion as a whole is an ideal aspired to but which cannot always be afforded economically. For women in total seclusion, servants are required in order to run errands; this was, and is, beyond the means of many families. As well, in the modern world it is often easier for a woman to find a job to provide a source of income for her family than it is for an uneducated man to do so; this means that a woman will, of necessity, be thrust into society outside the home. In rural societies, the restrictions on the movement of women were always of little consequence; the family, within which a women has no restrictions, was seen to extend throughout the village and thus freedom of movement (required for women to participate in agricultural tasks and so forth) created no difficulty.

The concept of seclusion has produced a great deal of debate in Islam, with some people stating that seclusion is not a part of the religion, and others saying that it is. As is frequently the case, this is as much a matter of definition of words as anything else. The total veiling of women—taken as a way of implementing a "movable seclusion"—is not stated as a requirement in the Qurʾān and, on that basis, it is often suggested to be simply a cultural trait and not a part of Islam. Such is true only, however, if attention is paid to the outer form of clothing alone. Veiling is, in fact, the logical (although, strictly speaking, perhaps not necessary) outgrowth of various Quranic statements taken to their limits. Full veiling institutes the Islamic attitude towards social interactions between men and women in its fullest degree, in a manner that ensures that violations are extremely difficult. Of course, why this specific issue—the seclusion of women—should be the one that Islamic jurists took to such an extreme formulation as compared to other aspects of Islamic law may well be questioned. Overall, however, one of the implications of the symbolism which seclusion suggests is that women are conceived to have power, while needing (in the male view, it would seem) to be restrained at the same time.

In terms of legal standing in the Islamic system, women's rank, logically enough, reflects the assumptions of the social structure. This is how it should be, after all; a social system is unlikely to function well if the confines of that system do not allow a group of people to assert the status which the system grants. Thus the Qurʾān establishes that the testimony of two women is required to equal that of one man (Qurʾān 2/282). The portion of a woman's inheritance is less than that of a man (Qurʾān 4/11). Divorce is allowable upon the woman's instigation only for a set number of reasons, whereas a man needs no specific pretext at all. A great deal of concern is displayed over establishing the lineage of children: while men are free to remarry after divorce, women must wait (while being supported by their ex-spouse) to see if they are pregnant. The male rules the house in all matters. The religion of the male is presumed to be the religion of the entire household; thus a Muslim male may marry a Jewish or Christian woman, but a Muslim female may marry only another Muslim (Qur'ān 5/6). A man may marry up to four wives at a time, but a woman may marry only one husband. Discipline (Qur'ān 4/34) and sex (Qur'ān 2/223) are the prerogatives of the male, to which the female is subject.

There is a sense conveyed in the Quranic statements which suggests that women will not wish to cooperate in society and will need to be coerced. For example, that a woman must wait a certain period after divorce or after becoming a widow in case she should be pregnant so that paternity may be firmly established would seem necessary only on the assumption that a woman would wish to hide relevant information about her sexual liaisons. Additionally, Fatima Mernissi (1987: 82) has argued that Islam is based not on the misogyny which characterizes Western society, but on the fear of heterosexuality. Mernissi's view is echoed by other writers, for example in the fiction of Alifa Rifaat (1985). The women of these short stories, poignantly illustrated by the unnamed woman of the title story *Distant View of a Minaret*, at first seem to crave more love and life, and yet they are constantly disappointed by their male companions. As a result they find their only solace in performing the worship of God within the context of female religious practices.

It might be possible to invert Mernissi's argument and say that this guarded attitude toward sex is precisely what is appropriate. The Islamic social system is set so that women will not distract men from worship and are themselves then forced to worship for their own comfort. But the objection would remain that this had been accomplished at the price of the full humanness of both genders. If it is thought that the purpose of religion in general, and Islam specifically, is to allow the achievement of that humanness, then the existence of a problem will be felt.

Modern demands

"Equality" has become a catchword worldwide when speaking of women's issues. The concept is slippery, however, and needs a clear definition in order to be able to anchor an analysis. In most cautious feminist discussions, equality does not mean "sameness," as some opponents might try to suggest in their attempts to trivialize the issues. Equality refers to the potentiality of humanness, a self-determination for "life options." These are issues of opportunities, not roles. The experience of gender is the most prominent aspect in the discussions of the issue. The social process of the internalization of gender is seen to determine the limits in achievement of humanness, which, it is suggested, we are all entitled to. There is, in Judeo-Christian-Muslim society in general, a relationship between power and gender, and gender internalization is a means of control to the advantage of patriarchy; gender roles and the control involved thereby serve to advantage the already established prerogatives of the male in society. Mernissi (1987: xv) summarizes this aspect of the problem of being a woman: "Why can't I stroll peacefully in the alleys of the Medina?" That is, the very fact of being a woman in society limits the activities which she might wish to undertake, and these activities are ones which men take for granted in their lives.

Another term frequently used in discussions about women is "status," but that, too, is rather evasive conceptually. "Status" frequently seems to imply that there are some given categories into which social roles may be categorized and that these may be used to compare social functions. This, however, ignores the fact that different social systems reflect different assumptions; looking only at something called "status," therefore, views only the superficial manifestations of a social system and not its underlying structure, which would seem to be far more of a key to understanding.

Notably, a great deal of the analysis of gender structure is specific not to Islam itself, but to patriarchy in general as a worldwide phenomenon. And Islam's assumptions certainly reflect a patriarchy within its society. Thus, from some points of view, Islam has not allowed the possibilities for women that it has for men; if the social system of Islam reflects the best possible solution for all, then why is it that a woman cannot stroll around the Medina, to repeat Mernissi's phrase? "Inferiority," a popular idea of what the complaint of women is all about when it comes to discussion of their status, really misses the point. Mernissi argues that the issue is really one of subjugation. That is, society does not reflect ideological positions regarding women which are necessary to its functioning as such, but rather reflects assumptions about power structures.

The idea of the complementarity of the genders is often used in talking about the Islamic understanding of the roles of men and women in society; the concept is especially popular in Islamist circles whose approach to the Qurʾān necessitates the continuation of legal differentiation between men and women. Women have their role to play in society as mothers and home-makers, while men shoulder the responsibilities for maintenance of the family in financial ways. The question from this position is not one of "subjugation" or "inferiority," but rather "natural order" reflected in the concept "equal though different."

The complementarity notion suggests that women want and need to be isolated in society and do not wish to play a more active role in the world at large; this, the theory suggests, is "natural":

> The function of the husband and wife are quite distinct, and each is entrusted with the functions which are best suited for his or her nature. The Holy Qurʾān says that God has made man and woman to excel each other in certain respects. The man excels the woman in constitution and physique, which is capable of bearing greater hardships and facing greater dangers than the physique of woman. On the other hand, the

> woman excels the man in the qualities of love and affection. Nature, for her own purpose of helping in the growth of creation, has endowed the female among men, as well as the lower animals, with the quality of love to a much higher degree than the male. Hence there is a natural division as between man and woman of the main work which is to be carried on for the progress of humanity. Man is suited to face the hard struggles of life on account of his stronger physique; woman is suited to bring up the children because of the preponderance of the quality of love in her. The duty of the maintenance of the family has therefore been entrusted to the man, and the duty of bringing up the children to the woman. And each is vested with authority suited to the function with which he or she is entrusted. Modern civilization is ultimately coming round to the opinion that the true progress of humanity demands a division of work, and that while the duty of bread-winning must be generally left to man, the duty of the management of the home and the bringing up of the children belongs to the woman. Hence it is that men are spoken of as being the maintainers of women and women as "rulers over the household and the children."
>
> (ʿAlī 1950: 646–7)

Furthermore, any of the so-called restrictions on women resulting from this assessment of the situation are argued to be for the benefit of women themselves, and are seen to be based upon the differences in nature between men and women, differences which are, after all, at the bottom of any assertion about complementary roles:

> Possessors of beauty are comparatively few in number, and the natural course of life changes the appearance of those and renders them homely. When women without the veil mingle with men, the favourable attention of the latter will be drawn only to beautiful women and charming young girls. Naturally unattractive women would be considered undesirable, and this would result in their being cut off from society and companionship. This would mean, on the one hand, a decrease in the population and, on the other hand, since men are not always able to procure beautiful wives, that their attention would be drawn to handsome children. Therefore if one looks at this question from the standpoint of reason and justice, he will see that the veil prevents corruption.
>
> (Yusuf 1943: 209)

Objectors to the theory of complementarity note that it is based upon an idea of men and women having antagonistic wills such that the two genders need to be separated into different spheres of competence, since, it would appear to be fundamentally assumed, they could never cooperate. These assumptions, however, are cultural constructs according to feminist critiques; they are ideas which are designed to preserve male power and to control female power, and, implicitly at least, have become embedded in the Qurʾān and the *sunna*. Interestingly, the Islamic view of society according to this vision of complementarity is based upon a strong notion of women's power which must be restrained. It is, therefore, a part of the double notion that pervades gender construction in Islamic society (and perhaps generally): woman as powerful along with woman as needing to be dominated. There is a further irony and a contradiction involved in this. Women achieve a secure sense of gender identity through restrictive and oppressive controls over their being (and especially their sexuality); the very controls which are imposed have the result of identifying women strongly as women.

Islamic answers

Most writings by Muslim women on Islam and the "problem" of women emphasize that the problem is, in fact, not a religious one; religion is the answer, not the problem or the source, according to these authors. Religion, as found in the Qurʾān and the *sunna*, provides a definition of the "natural order" of things and the proper implementation of this will lead to the satisfaction of all people—men and women—in society.

One very popular expression of this, a traditional one in Christianity also, is to see the husband in relationship to his family as a mirror of the relationship between God and humanity. This is a cosmic reflection, then, of the natural order of things, which is also echoed in the biological differences between men and women: woman as nurturer, man as aggressor. The basis for this is, of course, to be found in the divine affirmation that two genders have been created—not one, but two. If God had intended each human being to have been capable of all dimensions of life, he would have created only one gender. Furthermore, Muslim apologists point out, women are not burdened by the Biblical image of being the source of evil because in the Qurʾān the story of Adam and Eve does not reflect those ideas in its retelling. Likewise, the "gender" of God is not an issue. Arabic only has two grammatical genders and their separation is, to a large extent, arbitrary. The fact that the noun for God is grammatically masculine does not reflect, according to this view, any pre-eminence of the male.

This kind of apologetic trend dominates the discussions and there seems to be little evidence of any attempt at a feminist theological vision of Islam. The questions may well be broached at some point in the future: what would it mean, for example, for all people, male and female, to be members of a community of *Muslimāt* (that is, the feminine plural of Muslim, itself the singular masculine form) rather than the *Muslimūn*, as it is now expressed in the masculine plural form? Writers such as Riffat Hassan come the closest to raising such issues but this is generally done in academic circles and even then does not lack the apologetic tendency. It may well be, however, that women writers will emerge, writing in Arabic, Persian, or Urdu, who do not feel the same needs to challenge "Western misunderstanding" about Islam, and who will start to define a female theological vision.

The use of the past

The most frequent observation made, rarely without patronizing overtones, is that the "status of women" given in the Qur'ān is a vast improvement on that of the pre-Islamic period. Before Muḥammad, female children were subject to infanticide, women were the possessions of men without any rights, and so forth. "In the days of Ignorance, it was common among women to freely mix [in] public. They exposed any part whatsoever of their [bodies] to the public gaze. It was not considered indecent or immoral" (Alam 1990: 82). The coming of Islam empowered women, to the point that their legal rights exceeded those of European women until very recently. This view, however, is opposed by other writings which speak of the power and prestige that women had in the pre-Islamic period, which men, under the guise of a (mis)interpreted Qur'ān, have gradually removed. ʿĀʾisha, the wife of Muḥammad, who is a frequent source of authority in *ḥadīth* and famous as the leader of a revolt in early Islamic times, is the central role model of such perspectives. Even more radical approaches to the material suggest that Islam itself was responsible for the movement away from women's power (a power sometimes even linked to a matriarchal system) toward the present position of subjugation.

From the perspective of a historian, it may be pointed out that all these views are based upon selective citation of evidence. Women in pre-Islamic Arabia may be portrayed as powerful and active, or as tyrannized with no power, according to which facts are presented. What must be remarked, therefore, is that all of these approaches are attempts to remythologize society with a more productive vision. That vision will be one which embraces the ideals of the group concerned: for the Islamist, the "myth" of empowerment via Islam; for the feminist, the "myth" of women's potential gradually removed by men (either as embodied in Islam or as "misinterpretation" of Islam). The problem remains that these are myths which are easy to deconstruct.

Classical Islam itself provides a mythological picture of pre-Islamic society, as was pointed out in Chapter 1. By Islamic definition, *jāhiliyya*, the age of ignorance, is everything that Islam has come to remove. The picture found in classical texts, therefore, of a matriarchal society in which women played an active role is a part of the Islamic myth itself. That is how Muslim males of the ninth and tenth centuries pictured a society which was at its lowest point morally and socially: women in control! This myth stands in tension with the other aspect of the pre-Islamic mythic picture which sees Islam as providing moral growth from the pre-Islamic period—thus the picture of the improvement in women's rights—but the aspect of women in this account provides only part of the story. Rather, this myth provides a general evaluation of the overall legal accomplishment of Islam. Each element of Quranic law has become embedded in narrative detail as evidence of this transformation accomplished by Islam. In a typical development of structural myths, both aspects exist side by side, acting to control society and justify present practice; each probably has its origin in a specific historical situation and reflects aspirations or frustrations of a certain period. Their continued existence together poses problems only for modern historians who tend to isolate one element from the narrative structure in the desire to create coherence out of the historical records, and for those who wish to remythologize.

Ḥijāb in the modern context

The preservation of the home as an Islamic focal point of life has become a central defense of much of Muslim life in the modern world, especially in geographical areas which are not predominantly Islamic. With secular society encroaching from all sides, the home becomes the representation of an Islamic paradise, an oasis of divinely structured society located in a context fully awash with everything Islam rejects. *Ḥijāb*, in this mode of behavior, becomes a home-oriented activity. Once again, this personalization of religion may be suggested to be both the result and the cause of this particular interpretation and way of being Muslim. One's own religious behavior becomes the most important aspect of the exercise of Islam, rather than in its communal manifestation, and seeing its implementation as limited to one's own home (at least in the religion's social implications) seems to act as a line of defense. The possibility exists of taking the personalization of Islam to its fullest extent and, in the specific case of the Islamic notion of the seclusion of women, speaking of the necessity of the *ḥijāb* of the heart as the only requirement. While such interpretations certainly have a heritage in Islamic mysticism, their role in legitimating personal behavior in secularized society should not be underestimated.

Inevitably such matters have become highly politicized in contemporary times and it becomes difficult to extract a clear sense of the meaning of such symbols from their overall context. Nowhere is this more obvious than in discussions in France in early 2004 and the subsequent more general legislation against hiding one's face (as occurs with the forms of veiling known as *niqāb* and *burka*), such that the banning of symbols of religion from state schools (including thus the wearing of *ḥijāb* by young girls) has resulted in an additional level of complexity for Muslim identity and for the interpretation of modern Islam. Some have argued that the act by those outside Islam of identifying the *ḥijāb* as objectionable under the guise of separation of religion and the state has reinforced a notion among Muslims that secularism is anti-Islamic. Those Muslims to whom the *ḥijāb* was not an important issue now see, as a result of pressure from outside, that it is

Figure 16.1 Muslim women, displaying different traditions of body-covering, talk during a meeting with Imam Ali El Moujahed in Montreuil, outside Paris. At the same time (May 2010), the French parliament unanimously banned the wearing of face-coverings in public spaces. Source: AFP/Getty Images.

significant. Wearing *ḥijāb* becomes a mark of valuing Islam rather than secularism in a situation in which that binary opposition is presented by those outside the religion as the only possibility. The message seems to be that either one is a dangerous fundamentalist in *ḥijāb* or one is a lover of all things French; such is the nature of French *laïcité* that it sees a religion unregulated by the state as a threat to secularism. For Muslims in such a situation *ḥijāb* is certainly not (necessarily) a symbol of "the tyranny of fundamentalism," as those outside have tried to portray it, but the only possible response that is available in order to assert one's Muslim identity in a society which wishes to see no external differences between people and views religion as a private matter. For women the situation has aggravated an already difficult one by removing the element of choice in the wearing of a headscarf. Where previously this could be a matter for debate, French law now subtly suggests that the wearing of *ḥijāb* is mandatory for Muslim women except that now it is to be frowned upon or even illegal.

Women in the Muslim *umma*

An oft-quoted statement by the Egyptian feminist Nawāl al-Saʿdāwī is worth repeating; she is arguing against Islamist suggestions that the natural place for women is in the home and that corruption will occur if women are encouraged to seek employment outside the home:

> These men [who make this argument] ignore the fact that the majority of women in Egypt (80 per cent or more) are peasants and have never worn the veil. They leave their houses every morning to work with a hoe in the fields or to carry loads of dung or pails of water on their heads. Does this mean that these men think these millions of Egyptian women have abandoned their femininity which nature has given them, and are exposed to moral corruption or lack of protection for their religion and honor? If so, why have these men kept quiet? . . . Why have they not demanded that the peasant women be protected inside the homes and not be made to go to work in the fields?
>
> Since we have not heard of any of them making such a demand, does that mean that they consider these millions of Egyptian women corrupt in their morals or lacking in femininity or having little honor and religion? Or do they believe that femininity and honor are qualities enjoyed only by a small minority of Egyptian women?
>
> (Saʿdāwī, as quoted in Hoffman-Ladd 1987: 35)

Saʿdāwī's argument brings two points to the fore. One, powerful feminist voices do have a presence in the Islamic world, despite the opposite sense one might receive through media presentations. Two, and more salutary, Saʿdāwī reminds us that, in fact, for the vast proportion of Muslim women, the "crisis" of modernity has brought a negligible effect. Islamist arguments are, to a large extent, phenomena of the urban centers, where social and economic factors loom as the stimulus behind the rejection of feminist argumentation regarding the place of women in society. For women in rural areas, the Islamic social system remains intact and coherent, rendering men and women significant social actors within their own particular fields of control. Those fields of control, it is to be remembered, regulate relations not only within each gender but also between them: men and women establish power structures both over each other and among their own same-gender groupings.

The reality of the situation in the urban context cannot be denied, however. The (re)-assertion of male authority over women, characteristic of Islamism, and in many cases the assertion of the state's power to control women's activities are symptoms of economic and social pressures resulting from the radical restructuring of society taking place in so many areas of the Muslim world. The economic roles of women in society have changed substantially and the declaration of Islamists that women belong in the home is a cry of sorrow to return to the safe values of the past as elaborated in the Qur'ān and the *sunna*, where men's economic and social roles were firmly established. This attitude is well illustrated by the recent move in Morocco to eradicate polygamy and raise the age of legal marriage to 18 from 15. One Islamist is quoted (as reported in *The* [Toronto] *Globe and Mail*, January 21, 2004, p. A12) as having said in reaction, "There are men who, for physical reasons, cannot satisfy themselves with only one wife." A government official retorted, "In that case they should seek treatment." Overall, this is a phenomenon not unique to the Muslim world, of course. Nor is it only a matter of male concern. When there are few, if any, roles for women to play in society outside the (traditionally) prescribed ones, the (re)adoption of things such as Islamic dress or the rejection of feminist ideology may be taken as an expression of women's own frustration at social and economic conditions. It is out of this frustration and rethinking that may yet emerge a new vision of Islam.

The move outside Islam

Feminism presents one route for a reorientation of Islam, However, it is also a common phenomenon in religion that if the questioning of the authority of the past is taken far enough in the desire to be able to accommodate or compensate for the changes of the modern period, there is a need for a new source of authority. This may even account for the rise of each religion in its formative period. Modernity, as such, may not be the root cause of the emergence of such movements, therefore, but they may stem from a very basic dislocation in human existence. Such an understanding can be used to characterize various offshoots of Islam in the modern period which clearly have a Modernist stance and a renewed sense of authority.

The Aḥmadiyya is one such group, founded by Mīrzā Ghulām Aḥmad (1835–1908) and now comprising some four million members. Ghulām Aḥmad was educated with law or government service under the British in mind, but in 1877 he started devoting himself to the cause of Islam. His earliest writings aim towards a revitalization of Islam within the modernizing platform. As early as 1882, he claimed to be the *mujaddid*, "renewer," of Islam and, by 1891, had put forth the proclamation that he was the promised Messiah of the Muslim community. Later, he suggested he was also an avatar of Krishna, Jesus returned to earth, and the manifestation of Muḥammad. He claimed to be a prophet in receipt of revelation, but one who was sent without a book of scripture or a new religion (and thus he always asserted that he was subordinate to Muḥammad). His function was to return Islam to its proper formulation, by means of a prophetic-revelatory authority within a messianic-eschatological context. Debate has followed Ghulām Aḥmad, dividing both his followers and the Muslim community as a whole, concerning both the extent of and the validity of his claims, and the status of the finality of Muḥammad's prophethood and revelation, doctrines which are considered central to Islam as it had been classically defined. For our purposes here, however, it is sufficient to note that the Aḥmadiyya vests authority in Ghulām Aḥmad beyond that normally associated even with a *mujaddid*. This was done in support of a Modernist stance, embracing modern science and many moral ideals associated with the Enlightenment, in combination with a return to the essence of Islam as it is revealed in the Qurʾān and through the guidance of the person of Mīrzā Ghulām Aḥmad. For the Aḥmadiyya, the correct interpretation of Islam has been vested with the authority of revelation.

The members of the Aḥmadiyya proclaim themselves to be Muslims, although in countries such as Pakistan they have been declared outside the Islamic community and in many places severe concerns have been raised concerning their missionary activity, which remains a very strong emphasis of the movement, reflecting an effort from the very beginning to counter Christian missionary activity in India; the missionary activity is also associated with an active Qurʾān translation program, something generally not encouraged within more traditional circles. The situation is quite different for the Baháʾís, who do not wish to consider themselves Islamic but rather proclaim themselves to be members of a new "World Faith" which supersedes Islam.

The Baháʾís trace their origins to ʿAlī Muḥammad Shīrāzī (1819–50) of Iran, who referred to himself as the Bāb, the "Gate," and proclaimed himself to be the returned Hidden Imām, longed for by the Shīʿa, and a prophet of God. His appearance is taken to imply the abrogation of Islam and the initiation of a new religious dispensation. After the Bāb's death, Mīrzā Ḥusayn ʿAlī Nūrī (1817–92), who took the name Bahá'u'lláh, proclaimed himself the Messiah who had been promised by the Bāb in the words "He whom God shall make manifest." Baháʾuʾlláh's platform was strongly Modernist from the Muslim perspective within which it arose, and the Baháʾí faith remains that way. Legal reforms on matters such as women and family rights were implemented; disarmament, world government, and interreligious harmony became central proclamations, much in keeping with certain nineteenth-century European ideals (parallel to Christian and Jewish movements at the time). From the perspective of the history of religions, this was an attempt to re-universalize Islam (even religion in general) by taking it out of its culturally bound forms and into the modern context.

As with the Aḥmadiyya, the Baháʾís support a program of modernization emerging from the context of Islam, but, in this case, not by a return to the sources and a renewal of the past; rather, this takes place through a replacement of the sources of authority (even though the Bahá'ís do revere the Qurʾān, as they do all other scriptures, as the "word of God"). This sort of radical rupture with the past is, of course, precisely what more conservative elements of society fear Modernists of all types are actually aiming towards.

The role of Muslim intellectualism

Many of the Modernist voices that are being heard coming from within, rather than from outside, the Muslim context have at least one common element among them: they speak from an intellectual context. This is an often neglected source of Islamic thinking in surveys (and categories) of modern Islamic trends. This neglect may come as something of a surprise to students of other religions, since it would not seem possible to study modern Christianity without taking into account Hans Küng, for example; nor could we consider modern Judaism without Emil Fackenheim. None of these people can claim to represent a very substantial portion of the believers within the religion as their followers, it might be argued, yet it would seem that a picture of those religions within the modern world would just be incomplete without them.

In fact, in the cases of Judaism and Christianity, I do not perceive that there is much difficulty in including such figures in a survey of modern thought; it is more likely, in fact, that the conservative sides of those two religions are going to be dismissed as having no significantly enunciated platform to be discussed. When we come to the study of the future of modern Islam, however, the case seems to be different. Attention to the intellectual side sometimes seems to be sadly lacking. Many reasons for this can be suggested. Often the excuse is made that the intellectual trend does not seem significant numerically within Islam (especially as compared to modern Judaism and Christianity). Where are we supposed to turn to find the impact of such people? But yet, it would seem overly paranoid to suggest, in this era of the ramifications of attacks on Orientalism by people such as Edward Said, that the suspicion is that this ignoring of the intellectual trend is a part of the necessary degradation of Islam itself by Orientalists. To credit Islam with the possibility of such persons existing would seem to be counter to the basic Orientalist stance of picturing Islam as a constraining and reactionary force.

Mohammed Arkoun (1928–2010), an Algerian who lived and worked in Paris and wrote primarily in French, is one of those intellectuals who is often ignored, not being considered representative of anything to do with modern Islam itself. The first impression some people receive of a figure such as Arkoun is one of a person who has "sold out" to the West, a person who has adopted so much of the European intellectual tradition that there is no Islamic root left in any meaningful sense. Of course, it is a fact that, in general, many of the intellectuals found in modern religions do live and work in the university context and conduct themselves as academics, with all that requires—learned papers, prolific production of books and articles—and this seems to give some credence to the stance that such people do not need to be considered part of the intellectual construct of the given religion as such. This may account for some of the reality behind the idea that there do not seem to be many people like Arkoun in Islam. Many perhaps are lurking within universities without ever identifying themselves in a particularly overt way.

Arkoun himself wishes to use the term "the critical tendency in current Islamic thought" when speaking of the "intellectual and scientific directions" in modern Muslim thinking. Significantly, in terms of understanding how his position fits into the overall picture, he has clearly attempted to embrace what he would term a *contemporary* theoretical stance (as opposed to simply modern, that being equated to a historicist perspective), and this he sees as the basis of his work. Arkoun poses the question in an essay written as an introduction to a translation of the Qurʾān and then reprinted in his *Lectures du Coran*: "How should the Qurʾān be read?" with an emphasis on the idea of "How should it be read today?" This is not a question commonly posed in the Muslim framework and reveals immediately Arkoun's concerns. The point is not really one of simply how to read it, but how to understand the book in light of modern intellectual thought. The problem is, as the Christian post-modernist theologian Mark C. Taylor expresses it:

> [T]he "texts" that have guided and grounded previous generations often appear illegible in the modern and postmodern worlds. Instead of expressing a single story or coherent plot, human lives tend to be inscribed in multiple and often contradictory texts. What makes sense and is meaningful in one situation frequently seems senseless and meaningless in another setting. The resulting conflict creates confusion that extends far beyond the pages of the book.
>
> (Taylor 1984: 3)

How, then, is one to retrieve the Qurʾān both from the mountains of learned philological knowledge and from the literalist tendencies of many modern Islamic movements, and to discover something which speaks to the modern, intelligent individual? As Arkoun suggests, the task is one that is already underway in Judaism and Christianity but is still to be confronted in the Islamic context. It means coming to an understanding of the social and historical conditioning of all human existence, including language, leading to a liberation from the categories of thought imposed by past places and eras. This is not simply a study of history, because that discipline, in much of its Orientalist manifestation, is still deeply entrenched in the nineteenth-century notion of a search for absolutes and essentials. Rather, the historicity of knowledge will be discovered by the totality of the methods of the social sciences, according to Arkoun, asking questions not of "what really happened" (in the formulation of the discipline of history) but how it is that certain ideas came to be a part of the social imagination and what the role is that those ideas play in construction of reality for society.

Mohammed Arkoun passionately believes that what he has to say is of relevance not only to the university academic tradition, but also to the Muslim faith. The claim is that what he says should have some bearing on the basic understanding of faith in the modern world and how that faith should be expressed and understood, not only in the academic framework but also from within the faith perspective. His position may represent a thread of Islamic Modernism in the intellectual, theological sense, but it is one which is very attuned to the beginning of the twenty-first century. Other Modernists from a lay background (as is the case with Arkoun) have pursued scholarship but have frequently found theological liberalism too dangerous a course to follow. Whether that will change in the future we must wait to see.

In the posing of these questions Arkoun is marked as "post" the Modernists of Islam, as one who ventures into post-modernism, or even a "post-Islamic" position, if that be understood in the same manner that post-modernism is intimately linked with Modernism. However, the adverse reaction which such positions evoke amongst other enunciators of modern visions of Islam cannot be overestimated. The historicity of Islam is seen as being rejected in the attempt by Arkoun and others like him to escape from the dualisms of religion and society; as in similar suggestions in contemporary Christian thought, such views are often termed destructive of everything which people hold dear in their religion.

New voices in a Traditionalist framework

An example of theological reflection within Islam that presents a more conservative framework for discussion is to be seen in the works of Shabbir Akhtar, who has been cited a number of times in this book already. Akhtar became famous during the uproar over Salman Rushdie's *The Satanic Verses*; he was an extremely eloquent spokesman for the Muslim community, especially in Bradford, England, where much of the controversy was centered. Akhtar has a Doctorate in Philosophy of Religion and currently teaches Philosophy in an American university. He brings to the modern expression of Islam precisely that which is said to be missing: a theological re-evaluation of Islam, expressed in modern philosophical terms. Consider the following:

> The silence of God in this increasingly religionless age is certainly damaging to the faithful outlook. It does seem to open up the possibility of supplying impressively plausible cases for the atheistic stance. Indeed it creates a serious doubt about God's alleged miraculous activities even in the past. Is it not an arguably superior assumption that the different human claims about the miraculous are better explicable in terms of a cultural shift in our thinking rather than in terms of God's decision to introduce in recent years a basic alteration in his ways? Given the credulity and gullibility of early

> man, his ignorance of the moods of Nature—an ignorance poorly compensated by the pagan appeal to magic and its illusory technique—the atheist's suggestion is surely not altogether implausible.
>
> The current silence of Allah could spell a crisis for Muslim faith. Nature is as revealing as it is ambiguous, hence of course the need for a revelation in a sacred language in the first place. The God of Islam seems to have retreated from Nature and community, the two matrices in which, according to religious believers, he typically used to reveal himself.
>
> (Akhtar 1990: 84)

Akhtar's point is that the challenges of contemporary philosophy to the tenability of religious faith as a whole have been ignored by Muslims but they can only continue to be ignored at the peril of the survival of the faith itself. Christianity, for Akhtar, has virtually self-destructed through the efforts of (Protestant) theologians bending over backwards to assimilate the latest theories of secularism to their faith. This too will happen to Islam if the example of Christianity is not studied carefully and profit taken from the mistakes made in that arena.

Akhtar's theological position tends to support the moderate side of Islamism. Most significant in this is the all-encompassing nature of Islam (Christianity's "render unto Caesar what is Caesar's" has, it would appear for Akhtar, been misused in recent centuries to support the separation of church and state). But it is in the reformulation of philosophically supported arguments in favor of traditional Islamic doctrine—the inerrancy of the Qur'ān, the eternal message of scripture, the concept of the one God—that Akhtar, as he says of himself, breaks new ground. Just what the future might hold for this development is certainly unclear. For many Muslims, it would seem that even the opening of such questions for debate is going too far. For Akhtar, however, the failure to treat such questions openly and honestly could spell the end of Islam as a viable religion in the modern, secular context. Akhtar's future inquiries could well move him out of the Islamist camp, which he has defended "out of a desire to empathize with members of his own community, to avoid taking the road that enticed the intellectually gifted sons of Islam into the enemy camp, so to speak" (Ruthven 1990: 129). In other words, Akhtar has not yet created for himself (and those like him) a philosophically integrated and consistent stance within Islam; further work in the area and, as Malise Ruthven has pointed out, greater exposure to the classics of Muslim philosophy, theology, and history, may well yet produce that new vision. Indeed, as time goes by, Akhtar himself seemed to be discouraged by the possibilities; in 1997, after three years of university lecturing on philosophy and comparative religion in Malaysia, he resigned his position. He found his fellow Muslim intellectuals totally lacking "a sense of history" and was appalled when told "Believers . . . [have] nothing new to learn. Western-style free inquiry is aimless.

Besides what is the point of free inquiry if God has already revealed to us the whole truth?" He was totally dismayed at the lack of intellectual freedom: "Freedom is a precondition of profundity: no wonder philosophy has no place in the cultural life of Muslims" (Akhtar 1997: 15). Akhtar's line of thought is full of possibility for a "re-visioning" of Islam, but the likelihood of it being taken up by a new generation of Muslim intellectuals is uncertain.

Challenges to Akhtar's position exist also, precisely in the way in which he, himself, sees them as coming. Ibn Warraq is one of those writers who sees the failure of freedom of thought in Islam, along with what he describes as a dismal track record of concern with basic human rights, as reason enough to abandon Islam (and all religion). For Ibn Warraq, "Muslims cannot hide forever from the philosophical insights of Nietzsche, Freud, Marx, Feuerbach, Hennell, Strauss, Bauer, Wrede, Wells, and Renan" (Ibn Warraq 1995: 33). For him, however, religion becomes impossible when viewed in light of modern thought, and he willingly declares himself an apostate and a "secular humanist." Islam cannot be redeemed in any way because it is fundamentally flawed: "Perhaps the worst legacy of Muhammad was his insistence that the Koran was the literal word of God, and true once and for all, thereby closing the possibility of new intellectual ideas and freedom of thought that are the only way the Islamic world is going to progress into the twenty-first century" (Ibn Warraq 1995: 350). On the evidence of the people discussed in this book, by no means do all Muslims find Ibn Warraq's conclusions compelling. Some certainly recognize more than others the need for carefully considered contemplation of the future role and structure of Islam. But the value of Islam as a source of identity, as a grounding in life, as a way to understand existence, and as a way to relate to God is far too strong for the challenges of today not to be faced up to.

Putting matters in perspective

The challenges to Islam and the future directions it could take are apparent, especially when the issues are taken out of the newspaper headlines and placed within the lives of individuals. Underlying all such discussions are the topics related to the status and interpretation of the fundamental religious sources of authority. It is important, however, to reflect just briefly upon what all this might mean in terms of Muslim religiosity, although that is a question which is not easy to approach. Richard Antoun puts it well:

> How are we to determine, for instance, whether the building of new mosques, the establishment of government-sponsored religious publishing houses, the setting aside of special places in parliament for prayer, the establishment of religious political parties, or the establishment of bureaus to safeguard the Holy Quran are indications

> of religious-mindedness, indications of a shift in the attitudes of elites only, or simply an increase in political action in the name of Islam? Is an increasing use of Arabic, an increase in veiling, an increase in attendance at the Friday congregational prayer, or an increase in pilgrimage to be taken as an increase in piety, religious-mindedness, or hypocrisy?
>
> (Antoun 1989: 248)

The fact is that the range of contemporary Muslim religiosity varies tremendously. One of the reasons for this is that people understand and "use" religion in a variety of ways; that is true whether we are dealing with Islam or Christianity or any other religion. The following summary within a contemporary anthropological study provides an interesting perception of the ways in which Islam manifests itself:

> In this village, Islam can take the form of a bland legalism or a consuming devotion to the good of others; an ideology legitimizing established status and power or a critical theology challenging this very status and power; a devotive quietism or fervent zealotism; a dynamic political activism or self-absorbed mysticism; a virtuoso religiosity or humble trust in God's compassion; a rigid fundamentalism or reformist modernism; a ritualism steeped in folklore and magic or a scriptural purism.
>
> (Loeffler 1988: 246)

The basis for these variations appears to depend on a wide variety of factors: childhood experiences, individual personality, education, general social context, and so forth. All the variations, however, emphasize the independence of thought which is possible even within a society frequently characterized by its apparent uniformity. Plainly, Islam is a multifaceted phenomenon which is able to encompass within its fold many different views of the world and of religion in general.

The diversity of Muslim voices will remain. The intellectual evolution of the community will continue. Powerful voices of different stripes will continue to push the community to self-examination and healthy debate. Clearly, however, the contemporary situation is often viewed (out of necessity) as a crisis rather an opportunity. Groups such al-Qaeda, who proclaim that any Muslim who does not struggle in a *jihād* against the Saudi government, American interests, and the Israelis, is an unbeliever or an infidel, function to create deeper fractures within the community rather than solve the problems being faced. A response to such groups and platforms which simply then declares these "radicals" not to be a part of the true, peace-loving Islam likewise results in a confusion of identity for Muslims themselves: how to respond to those who proclaim their Muslim status but act in a manner which is unbecoming to Islam? It hardly needs to be reiterated that such a problem has faced Islam and Muslims from the very beginning.

Al-Qaeda does proclaim that its actions are the legitimate expression of Islam. Underneath its position is a fundamental principle which asserts that there exists such a thing as a single and pure Islam which was practiced by Muḥammad and his closest followers, known as the *salaf* (and thus adherents to this position are often termed Salafis). The use of violence toward the goal of spreading Islam is believed to be an Islamic duty. To argue this position, a number of dogmatic and rhetorical points are made. To begin with, they reject those who disagree with their stance by declaring them corrupt (a frequent charge against governments), ignorant (of religious law), and hypocritical (usually because of their actions which support the United States). Next, they declare that a defensive *jihād* is needed against the United States and its interests because the West has declared war on Islam. Finally, the highly contentious point is made that the killing of civilians purposely is allowable under certain conditions in Islamic law. It is declared that those conditions are being met because, for example, such acts against civilians are reciprocal, the civilians cannot be distinguished from combatants, and civilians are—by the process of democratic elections and public opinion—supporting the corrupt forces.

The success—or at least the influence—of groups such as al-Qaeda in attracting followers reflects the reality that discourse about Islam in the public sphere which emphasizes basic issues of the rights of individuals and the like (what is often referred to as "political Islam") is dominant among all Muslims. Islam has become the only vehicle for enunciating the concerns of people in the Muslim world. Political Islam serves as the critique of authoritarian regimes, of foreign powers, and of oppression in a culturally "safe" manner, precisely because Islam itself remains a largely unquestioned ideology. The widespread success of political Islam is very much a function of modernity in both its technology and its appeals. Mass communications through every possible means result in knowledge of contemporary events and debates spreading among Muslims instantaneously. The championing of the rights of peoples, whether they be Palestinians, Kurds, or Afghans, is a discourse born of an age of charters of human rights. The rhetoric against authoritarian government capitalizes upon notions of democracy and rightful distribution of political, economic, and social power. It is notable that these pressures can also create a counter-effect, as was seen with the Taliban in Afghanistan, whose highly conservative approach to Islam displayed a response to these very same pressures but was characterized by a rejection of all external critiques and a redefinition of its own notions of "rights." Such could be true of other groups such as al-Qaeda as well, but their practical socio-economic platforms generally remain very ill defined, and only if or when they achieve political power would the character of their stance become fully apparent. Given the general instability of the political context in the Middle East at least, making predictions at what would happen should political Islam truly come into ascendancy is hazardous in the extreme. The situation in the aftermath of the war in Iraq, with the struggles between factions of Islam, both within Sunnī and Shīʿī camps and between them, illustrates the incredible fluidity of political alignment, often leaving the less-Islamically defined powers managing to walk a narrow and dangerous path, at least temporarily, to hold the balance of power.

Parvez Manzoor has described the situation as one in which "Islam itself has been devoured by the nihilism of modernity":

> The ransoming of Islam's universality for parochial causes, the sacrifice of its humanity for primal passions, the repudiation of its legal reason for self-endorsing piety, the relinquishing of Divine justice for messianic terror, all of which were the distinguishing marks of these terrorist deeds, have still not entered the public debate. Islam, there's no mistaking, is as much a victim in this tragedy as any other.
>
> (Manzoor 2002: 5)

Manzoor's response is to push for a re-enunciation of an Islamic "moral vision" that will address the universal issues which humanity faces. That Islam remains in the parochial and specific situation of those who try to enunciate its position is its failing, for Manzoor. Muslims, he says, must confront the issues of "faith and violence, transcendence and existence, politics and morality"; a theological rethinking is required in order to reaffirm Islam in the face of modernity.

Other thinkers would express matters differently but all agree that answers must come through Islamic principles. The strengthening of what some people are calling "civil society" within the Muslim world is seen in the increasing emphasis on education, freedom of speech, and freedom of the press in the countries of the Muslim world. Replacing in some contexts the word "democracy" as the key goal for which Muslims should strive, civil society is understood as that which lies underneath contemporary democratic principles. It suggests that there are parallel social institutions within society that act alongside the state in the public sphere and serve to promote and safeguard the interests and concerns of citizens. This, it is argued, has a strong basis in Islamic history, as is perhaps illustrated by the tension between scholarly and caliphal power in classical times. Today, we may be seeing this emerge in the "digital *umma*" as the Muslim community asserts its existence online. The concept of civil society itself may be more of a critical tool for scholars and a motivating slogan for activists than a concept easily identified and developed, but the very fact that the notion is being grappled with and considered once again demonstrates the range and the depth of Muslim commitment to having Islam continue to be relevant to day-to-day life.

Muslim faith is a complex phenomenon, just as is any other religion. It may be tempting to suggest that there are two different faces to Muslim religiosity: the intellectual debate over principles of the faith confronting the personal practice of individual Muslims. The danger here is that we may exaggerate a dichotomy which, while it may have a certain analytical convenience, may lead to a distortion of the presentation of Muslim faith. Better would be a conception which sees faith on a continuum, attempting self-conscious definition at times and reaching into the experiential dimension of religion in order to refresh those definitions at other times. This would seem to be the genius of religion, and of Islam especially.

The Gülen movement

Fethullah Gülen (b. 1941) is the leading contemporary inheritor of the Turkish Modernist tradition of Bediüzzaman Said Nursi (1876–1960) and the Nurçuluk movement. Spread across the world largely through Nursi's writings, the movement stresses inter-faith dialogue within the context of a common, popular religion, rural in character, and deeply influenced by Sufism. The emphasis of this faith falls on core ethical and religious values rationally understood, with little attention to political action (Said Nursi famously exclaimed, "I take refuge in God from Satan and politics"), although clearly situated within Nursi's native Turkish context. Religion and science, and tradition and modernity, are reconciled with Islam as well as Turkish nationalism, education, and economics. Personal spiritual growth is emphasized, integrated within a thoroughly modern political-social and economic system.

Fethullah Gülen stresses his own traditional upbringing and his solid religious training, having worked as a state *imām* from 1959 to 1981. He thus wishes to distinguish himself from the typical Islamist who comes from a secular background. A prolific author, Gülen has been deeply involved in setting up a network of schools throughout the Balkans and Central Asia. The schools feature a secular and modern curriculum but are taught by members of his religious organization, which then facilitates religious education as a complementary activity. The goal of this approach is to educate the new generation of leaders in Turkey and elsewhere, who will then be motivated to maintain a secure place for Islam within the modern secular Turkish state. This, some commentators suggest, represents a push against the privatization of religion that was the key to Atatürk's secular Turkey and a return of Islam to the public sphere. Such is the meaning that can be derived from a statement by Gülen such as:

> Islam does not propose a certain unchangeable form of government or attempt to shape it. Instead, Islam established fundamental principles that orient a government's general character, leaving it to the people to choose the type and form of government according to time and circumstances.
>
> (Gülen 2001)

In religious terms, the Gülen movement is conservative but, because of its political stance, is not accurately described as fundamentalist or Islamist. The outward performance of religion is not stressed so much as the inward intention and attitude of the "heart." The development of the Muslim individual is the goal. Gülen speaks of asceticism, piety, kindness, and sincerity as the key to Islam, in keeping with a Ṣūfī frame of mind. (This connection to Sufism is politically charged in Turkey because it is illegal to create a new Ṣūfī order within the country.) A Muslim motivated in this way will naturally perform the required religious legal duties as derived from the Qur'ān and the *sunna*.

Good overviews of the Gülen movement are found in the essays contained in M. Hakan Yavuz and John L. Esposito (eds.), *Turkish Islam and the Secular State: The Gülen Movement*, Syracuse: Syracuse University Press, 2003, and in the special issue of the journal *The Muslim World*, 95/3 (1995), called "Islam in Contemporary Turkey: The Contribution of Fethullah Gülen."

Suggested further reading

Mohammed Arkoun, *The Unthought in Contemporary Islamic Thought*, London: Saqi Books, 2002.

Khaled M. Abou El-Fadl, *And God Knows the Soldiers: The Authoritative and the Authoritarian in Islamic Discourse*, Lanham, MD: University Press of America, 2002.

Robert D. Lee, *Overcoming Tradition and Modernity: The Search for Islamic Authenticity*, Boulder, CO: Westview Press, 1997. (An examination of the ideas of Iqbāl, Quṭb, Sharī'atī, and Arkoun.)

Ann Elizabeth Meyer, *Islam and Human Rights: Tradition and Politics*, 4th edition, Boulder, CO: Westview Press, 2007.

Anne K. Rasmussen, *Women, the Recited Qur'an, and Islamic Music in Indonesia*, Berkeley: University of California Press, 2010.

17 *Perceptions of Muslims in the twenty-first century*

Muslims have wrangled amongst themselves since the dawn of Islamic history over their identity as Muslims, what that means, and how it should be manifested in the world. The previous chapters of this book have detailed many of those struggles. External pressures during those past time periods have occasionally created crisis points which have stimulated an inward search for security in the Muslim religious heritage. Those events tended to be localized, with each geographical area experiencing its own pressures and responses. The twenty-first century presents a world of a different character. The reality of globalization, with its components of mass and instantaneous communications and economic interdependencies, results in localized actions in the name of Islam having an impact well beyond national borders. It has also created a situation in which those actions have an impact (sometimes physical, sometimes purely emotional) on non-Muslim populations around the world. The resonances of that impact have a correlating impact on the sense of identity for Muslims themselves as they grapple with what other people think of their religion and, in some cases, how they act upon those impressions and, often, prejudices. Certainly the attention of others has its positive side too, as more interest in understanding the nature and features of Islam manifests itself. This occurs even in the face of overwhelmingly negative portraits that are encountered so frequently in the media with the "war or terror" and the repetition of the litany of events—9/11, 7/7, Madrid, the shoe bomber, the underwear bomber—that mark the era of violence in the name of Islam.

Islamophobia

The reality of what Muslims sometimes face in the contemporary world is often encapsulated in the word "Islamophobia." The term itself may well be misleading because its literal meaning, "fear of Islam," is not really an accurate representation of Muslim experience. What the term does refer to, as definitions which expand upon the literal sense of the word make clear, is a fear—and resulting action based upon that fear—of an imaginary Islam. The imaginary Islam that provokes this fear derives from perceptions based upon misleading generalizations that are not subject to nuanced analysis. This creates a fear that then leads those who conceive the world in this fashion to treat Muslims in a prejudiced way, parallel to what is often described as racism. Lying behind this fear of Islam (when Islam is understood in this fashion) are political orientations that are deeply conservative and attitudes that frequently have little to do with Islam or Muslims as such; they do, however, reflect the insecurities of those who see the world changing around them and who sense (or fear, even) a loss of their own power and influence, and of the security of the established order.

This clarification of the sense of Islamophobia is important because the word and concept have been subject to extensive critique. Some people have argued that the entire concept has a chilling effect on any form of critical discussion and that it encourages "political correctness." To say anything critical of Islam or even of Muslims is, some have felt as a result, a dangerous thing to do. However, if one understands the concept of Islamophobia not as speaking about Islam or Muslims as such, but rather as about how Islam is conceived by those outside the faith, then the concept conveys not criticism of Islam but criticism of the way in which people conceive Islam. Of course, this can be confusing because the word "Islamophobia" itself seems to suggest that some sort of singular "Islam" does exist of which one can be fearful. But this would be a mistaken interpretation of what is intended by this complex, but useful, word.

A simple example may well help. I had been quoted in a local newspaper as explaining that Muslims were in a constant process of engaging with and interpreting the Qurʾān, explaining briefly what has been treated in earlier chapters of this book. A local reader wrote to the editor the following week to tell me that I was wrong: the Qurʾān was binding on all Muslims for all time and not subject to interpretation (beyond the differences between the law schools, a concession by which the letter's author intended to display his knowledge of the subject). For this writer, if the Qurʾān says something (such as "Slay the unbelievers wherever you find them," Qurʾān 9/5), then Muslims are (deep down, at least) compelled to do such a thing in every given situation, regardless of how Muslims understand the context of that verse and how such a ruling might be applied in legal thinking. This is a position typical of Islamophobia in that the author treats all Muslims as unchanging automatons and slaves to their religion. The parallel in the Christian case does not appear to resonate with such people: that some militants may justify bombing abortion clinics in the name of Christianity does not lead to generalizations about violence being inherent in that faith, it seems.

In 1996, the Runnymede Trust in England, an organization with the tag line "Intelligence for a Multi-ethnic Britain," established a Commission on British Muslims and Islamophobia. This was a follow-up to their earlier study on anti-Semitism in England published in 1994. Their report, *Islamophobia: A Challenge for Us All*, was published in November, 1997, notably well before the attention-grabbing violence of the destruction of the twin towers in New York or the bombing of buses in London. In the report, Islamophobia was defined as "an outlook or world-view involving an unfounded dread and dislike of Muslims, which results in practices of exclusion and discrimination." The report did recognize the problematic nature of the word Islamophobia itself but felt it was best to continue with its usage, even though the word did appear to be a relatively recent coinage and thus potentially could have been replaced. The report has had a continued influence on all discussions of Islamophobia since that time, especially for what it enumerates as the eight characteristics of a "closed" concept of Islam which is at the core of Islamophobic attitudes, compared to the "open" views which more accurately describe the life and faith of Muslims:

1 Islam is seen as a single, monolithic bloc, static and unresponsive to new realities, as opposed to being seen as diverse and progressive, with internal differences, debates, and disagreements.
2 Islam is seen as separate and "other" in the sense that it does not share aims or values in common with other cultures and is not affected by nor has any influence on those other cultures, as opposed to emphasizing its interdependent characteristics in sharing values and aims.
3 Islam is seen as inferior to the West, being barbaric, irrational, primitive, and sexist, as opposed to be being seen as distinctly different but not deficient and equally worthy of respect.
4 Islam is seen as violent, aggressive, threatening, supportive of terrorism, and engaged in a clash of civilizations, as opposed to being an actual or potential partner in joint cooperative enterprises and in the solution of shared problems.
5 Islam is seen as a political ideology, used for political or military advantage, as opposed to being seen as a genuine religious faith, practiced sincerely by its followers.
6 Criticisms made of "the West" by Muslims are rejected out of hand, as opposed to subjecting those criticisms to consideration and debate.
7 Hostility towards Islam is used to justify discriminatory practices towards Muslims and the exclusion of Muslims from mainstream society, as opposed to debates and disagreements with Islam not diminishing efforts to combat discrimination and exclusion.
8 Anti-Muslim hostility is accepted as natural and normal, as opposed to critical views of Islam themselves being subject to critique for accuracy and fairness.

There is no doubt that questioning of this description has taken place on many levels. One may well wonder if all these characteristics have to be demonstrably present (and in what proportions) for something to be declared "Islamophobic." Part of the critique of this sort of inventory is that it does not highlight the very real discrimination that some Muslims experience as a result of attitudes which pervade society, especially in Europe and North America. The target of such attitudes, it has been argued, is the person of the

Muslim and not Islam itself, and thus any proposed definition really needs to revolve around the people and not an abstract concept. Fred Halliday (1999: 898) has suggested the term "anti-Muslimism." Further, Halliday has gone on to point out that the term, if used unreflectively, seems to continue the distortion that lies at the heart of Islamophobia itself, the idea that there is one Islam against which the phobia can be directed. This distortion obscures the reality of Muslim diversity but also fuels the discourse of those Muslims who wish to assert a definition of Islam that is itself singular and absolute. Other writers have suggested that more refined definitions would allow the term Islamophobia to continue to be used meaningfully, given the reality of the phenomenon. Chris Allen, at the end of a book-long study of the matter, defines the concept this way:

> Islamophobia is an ideology, similar in theory, function and purpose to racism and other similar phenomena, that sustains and perpetuates negatively evaluated meaning about Muslims and Islam in the contemporary setting . . . subsequently pertaining, influencing and determining understanding, perceptions and attitudes in the social consensus . . . that inform and construct thinking about Muslims and Islam as Other. . . . As a consequence of this, exclusionary practices—practices that disadvantage, prejudice or discriminate against Muslims and Islam in social, economic and political spheres . . . including the subjugation to violence—are in evidence. For such to be Islamophobia however, an acknowledged "Muslim" or "Islamic" element . . . must be present.
>
> (Allen 2010: 190)

Such critiques and refinements of the way in which the concept is formulated and employed are important and demonstrate the need to interrogate the topic carefully. This significant level of discussion concerning the term does not displace the reality of the phenomenon. However, there are others who, in their reaction to the term, demonstrate the reality of Islamophobia itself:

> Muslims should dispense with this discredited term [of Islamophobia] and instead engage in some earnest introspection. Rather than blame the potential victim for fearing his would-be executioner, they would do better to ponder how Islamists have transformed their faith into an ideology celebrating murder (Al-Qaeda: "You love life, we love death") and develop strategies to redeem their religion by combating this morbid totalitarianism.
>
> (Pipes 2005)

The intense reaction to Islam and Muslims in recent years that characterizes the tangible outcome of what we term Islamophobia comprises a lengthy list of incidents that have drawn media attention and, in the process, fueled an exaggerated Islamophobic reaction: Geert Wilders' film *Fitna*, the Danish cartoons, the Swiss minaret debate, the threat of the Qurʾān burning in Florida, the continued belief that Barack Obama is a Muslim, and the French headscarf and *niqāb* decisions, among many others.

These provocative reactions to Islam and Muslims need to be understood in a variety of ways. Olivier Roy suggests that,

> At a time when the territorial borders between the great civilizations are fading away, mental borders are being reinvented to give a second life to the ghost of lost civilizations. . . . Ethnicity and religion are called to draw new borders between groups whose identity relies on a performative definition: we are what we say we are, or what others say we are. These new ethnic and religious borders do not correspond to any geographical territory or area. They work in minds, attitudes, and discourses.
>
> (Roy 2005: 7)

The contemporary focus on religious identity manifested in Islamophobia is reinforced by every action and reaction in the global context that is framed, for whatever reason, in religious terms. When Islam is used as the ideology behind violence, some members of the group attacked perceive their own religious identity as being under siege and thus they portray the battle as one between religions. However, underneath this superficial expression of anxiety is a far deeper concern that has left some people fundamentally confused, disoriented, and adrift. No longer is it clear what is meant by the culture of a geographical place; yet, that sense of place—most obviously in the notion of the nation state—has been the rallying point of recent history and the creator of identity. This is experienced on all sides. Considering the case of Muslims in Europe, that sense of how to locate themselves as people who are thoroughly "European" in language, education, and attitude (as, for example, is manifested in the individualization of faith) within a culture that has lost a firm sense of national boundaries with the emergence of the European Union is matched by national uncertainty over where values reside. The reaction of dissatisfied Muslims and nervous other groups is one of longing to reclaim an imagined past in order to create a sense of belonging and of control over the destiny of the individual. The outcome—and the impact—of such thinking is clear in both the attraction of Islamism among Muslims and the fear-mongering associated with the invention of the term "Eurabia" as a warning flag for an imagined future. Europe has become foregrounded in these debates, although to a great extent it is American voices who are raising the loudest alarm bells, Europe being seen as being on the front lines of the "clash of civilizations" that characterizes a part of the post-September 11, 2001, world view of many Americans. One commentator on this American concern points out that this is "a variation on the conservative Cold War vision of Europe as vulnerable to the spread of communism—only now, Muslims have replaced Soviets and Euro-communists as the enemies" (Vaïsse 2010: 86). Any discontent that the Muslim populations of Europe may express—discrimination, unemployment, urban alienation—is explained in this view by religion and culture rather than politics and economics. This is underpinned by the Islamophobic view that Muslims are different and their identity is incompatible with whatever Europe and North Americans may conceive Euro-American identity to be.

Islamophobia and hate speech

The manifestation of Islamophobia has been the subject of some complex legal discussions in many places in the world. In Canada, some of the work of Mark Steyn, a prominent promulgator of fear concerning the spread of Islam and the influence of Muslims on Europe and North American society, was subject to legal complaints by some Muslim groups. The complainants suggested that the printing of "The Future Belongs to Islam," an extract from Steyn's *America Alone: The End of the World as We Know It* (first published in 2006), in a Canadian magazine was "hate speech" within the definition of that activity under Canadian human rights legislation. Their reasoning was that the article made a particular group of people a target for potentially discriminatory action. The complainants argued that Steyn suggested that there is an ongoing war between Muslims and non-Muslims, that Muslims are part of a global conspiracy to take over Western societies, and that Muslims living in the West need to be viewed through this lens as the enemy. As such, the material suggested that religious identity and beliefs were being used to target an identifiable group in a dangerous and defaming way, in contravention of human rights legislation. The complaints were, in the end, unsuccessful according to the final tribunal decision in 2008, primarily because the complainants did not demonstrate any actual impact of this particular publication such that it could be shown that the article rose to the levels of hatred and contempt required by the law. The complaints did, however, provoke a good deal of discussion of both the fallacies of Islamophobic views and the appropriate limits on free speech.

Steyn's argument in his book and the magazine extract is based on a (mis)perception about the nature of Islam (and religion in general). He states, "Islam, however, has serious global ambitions, and it forms the primal core identity of most of its adherents—in the Middle East, South Asia and elsewhere" (Steyn 2008: xxxv). This notion of "primal" characteristics recurs on the next page of the book (p. xxxvi) when he invokes "humanity's primal instincts, not least the survival instinct." The implication appears to be that, for Muslims, Islam takes its place alongside basic instincts; from the point of view of the discussion here, this must be recognized as one of the characteristics of Islamophobia in that it conceives Muslims as unable to act outside this imagined notion of authoritarian Islam.

This approach to Islam is grounded in a projection of ideas onto Muslims as a whole. In such a view, as the sentences just quoted show, Islam is portrayed as an unchanging, instinctual matter, whereas, on the level of human behavior in reality, Muslim beliefs and actions are always changing in response to the political, economic, and social situation. Underneath the assertion of Islam as a "primal core identity" is an idea that Muslims are controlled by an unchanging text of the Qurʾān and are unable to act outside of a fixed meaning. Within this kind of understanding and with polemical ends in mind, texts can be extracted from the Qurʾān regardless of their original context and the history of their interpretation because the scripture is viewed as "primal" and "core" for those who identify with it. People such as Steyn who make these claims seem to demand that Muslims must behave in certain ways because their scriptural text "says" certain things and "obviously" Muslims "must" follow those things. However, the history of Islamic culture demonstrates the obvious falsity of this view through the ever-changing nature of how the text of the Qurʾān has functioned in Islamic society, how it has been interpreted, and how its provisions have been enacted. Polemicists such as Steyn are more demanding of religious adherents than the most rabid fundamentalist!

One simple illustration of how accusations against Islam and Muslims become structured in Steyn's writing is useful because his approach is typical of many anti-Islamic writers. He takes a simple historical fact which one would have to agree was "true" and then he constructs that into a theory that fits his particular anti-Islamic stance. For example, he speaks of *jizya*, the Muslim poll tax on non-Muslims (Steyn 2008: 164), in order to suggest that the main funding burden in classical Islamic society ever since the time of Muḥammad fell on non-Muslims. Certainly, the poll tax was an important source of revenue for governments at particular points in history (especially when expenditures were high) and as a result there do seem to have been periods of active discouragement of conversion to Islam during Islamic history—although the reasons for this are far more complex than a simple financial issue. Sometimes the conversion of an individual did not, in fact, change the level of overall taxation at all, because taxes were levied at the communal level and not the individual level. More often, it was the populace's move away from rural lands to urban settings that was discouraged, because this is what reduced taxation revenues significantly. But there were other sources of revenue (*zakāt* was very specific about what it could be used for and was not always under government control), such as land tax (especially), market taxes, customs duties, and government services, that provided greater sources of revenue (and certainly demonstrate the "economic innovation" that Steyn would like to see but feels Islamic society did not manifest) than the *jizya* would have provided. Of course, linking all of this to Muḥammad, as Steyn does, is historically quite anachronistic since the structures of government bureaucracy did not exist in Muḥammad's time at all; rather, the taxation systems developed according to pre-Islamic local practice (in the pragmatic ways the Arab rulers developed state bureaucracy). Regardless of all these facts, which need to nuance a view of the relationship between the poll tax and conversion, setting the scenario up in this way allows Steyn to accomplish his goal of portraying Islam as "bad" to its core ever since its foundation. His conclusion to this section is the most revealing aspect of this attack because there the point behind his raising the topic becomes clear and his anti-Islamic position becomes enunciated, despite the fact that he has no clear understanding of Islamic history and lacks the facts to back up his assertions. All the claims simply arise from the notion of the existence of a poll tax on non-Muslims:

> When admirers talk up Islam and the great innovations and rich culture of its heyday, they forget that even at its height Muslims were never more than a minority in the Muslim world, and they were in large part living off the energy of others. That's still a useful rule of thumb: if you take the least worst Muslim societies, the reason for their dynamism often lies with whichever group they share the turf with—the Chinese in Malaysia for example.
>
> (Steyn 2008: 164)

Lying underneath all of polemic against Islam, however, is Steyn's view of the kind of society he wishes to live in, which is really the point of his rhetoric. Says Steyn, "The Muslim critique of the West—that we are decadent vulgar narcissist fornicating sodomites—is not without more than a grain of truth" (Steyn 2008: 16). In order to achieve certain moral, social, and political goals that Steyn has in mind, the "other" is tyrannized in a form of self-critique. In the process of doing that, of course, group membership is defined in such a way as to exclude and include people in clearly prejudicial ways. Steyn characterizes the society in which he currently lives as a "wobbling blancmange of cultural relativism" (Steyn 2008: xxi), with its "slatternly image of post-feminist Western womanhood" (Steyn 2008: 67–8). Big government is ultimately Steyn's target when he argues that the "big brother" nature of modern "socialist" governments have removed any independence, resilience, and will of individuals. For him "freedom" means limited government, personal responsibility, and free enterprise:

> There is a correlation between the structural weaknesses of the social democratic state and the rise of a globalized Islam. The state has gradually annexed all the responsibilities of adulthood—health care, child care, care of the elderly—to the point where it's effectively severed its citizens from humanity's primal instincts, not least the survival instinct. . . . Big government is a national security threat: it increases your vulnerability to threats like Islamism, and makes it less likely you'll be able to summon the will to rebuff it.
>
> (Steyn 2008: xxxvi)

So, in a typical "scapegoat" exercise, the emergence of Muslims as a significant (although still demographically tiny) minority within Euro-American society becomes the threat to be held out in the call for the neo-conservative political agenda. Steyn's summons is for a "return" to the libertarian ethos, and, he suggests, if we do not do that, just look what will happen! We will all become Muslim, living under the *sharīʿa*! The immediate danger of Steyn's platform is seen when one wonders how many of his readers will bother to think about what he is saying in terms of the critique of contemporary American and European society, but rather will simply stay with the anti-Islamic surface reading and see the solution as just hating Muslims.

The fear of *sharīʿa*

In many discussions of the impact of Muslims on the modern Euro-American state, *sharīʿa* is the key term that is raised. In those contexts, *sharīʿa* has become a "code word" by which non-Muslims especially (but many Muslims too) speak of the imposition of laws that infringe on contemporary values, especially those encapsulated under the catchphrase "human rights" as related to women and religious minorities. One typical Islamophobic aspect of this concern is seen when this attitude is compared to the way that the *sharīʿa* is conceived within the reality of the Muslim modern world. The compromises that have taken place over the past century with the emergence of the modern nation-state in countries dominated by Muslims show that *sharīʿa* is not a single entity but a negotiated range of power-sharing in which political allegiances are incorporated into the *sharīʿa*, with religious authorities being given power over what are mutually acceptable domains, usually focusing on aspects of family law and public morality as reflections of private moral codes. Regardless of this reality, *sharīʿa* is spoken of as a "totalitarian" system totally contrary to the Western style (and especially the American) of government. Often, and especially among the most vocal of anti-Muslim spokespeople such as David Horowitz and Pamela Geller, the invocation of a compulsory sense of *jihād* among Muslims is used as a gloss of what it would mean to have the *sharīʿa* enforced in Europe or the United States. Such charges bring about a fear of American distrust and animosity towards Islam that hangs over the heads of Muslims as they grapple with the claim that *sharīʿa* could, or even should, be introduced.

In the context of reasonable discussions of the *sharīʿa* in, for example, Britain and Canada, the emphasis always falls on how to balance group rights and ethno-cultural differences with the general legal principles held to apply to all citizen of the nation-state. Can certain aspects of an identifiable community's self-regulation enhance the group's position and integration within society as a whole? Does such acceptance of the validity of *sharīʿa* regulation enhance the sense that Muslims are respected for who they are in their country of residence and that a Muslim sense of identity can find its place, integrated within the whole? Or will that acceptance of the applicability of areas of the *sharīʿa* result in the imposition of the will of a certain portion of the group on others in a way that is found by some members of the group to be undesirable and in tension with the principles of society as a whole? Women's rights are the most frequent target of such concerns. In Ontario, Canada, during the period 2003–2006, there was discussion of a proposal that Muslim *sharīʿa* courts could function under the province's Arbitration Act and thereby deal with disputes involving contracts, inheritance, and divorce in situations where the parties were willing to have the matter settled in such a manner. Reaction was extremely mixed and often heated. Some argued that integrating Islamic law under the principles of state law might mean that Muslims would see the overall integrationist point that Islamic law could coexist within the Canadian law and be subject to it. Others argued that the protections offered by provincial law would be lost for the less powerful in the Muslim community, especially women, who would feel compelled to submit to Islamic arbitration even in situations where it might not be in their best interests in order to maintain their place within their own community. The pressure, it was argued, would be immense. While these sorts of discussions, when conducted reasonably and soberly, have helped to define the place of Muslims in multicultural situations, they have, in some instances, added fuel to the fire of Islamophobia. The inference that some people take from such discussions is that Islam and Muslims are "other" and do not share common values even in the most basic of aspects.

Fear and suspicion

Even among those who do not necessarily share a view that may be described as fully Islamophobic, there often seems to be a lingering suspicion about the genuineness and honesty of Muslims in their self-presentation. Part of this goes back to the attitudes of people like Mark Steyn. Muslims simply *must* be a certain way, for Steyn (anti-democratic, for example), because the Qurʾān demands that they be so. One cannot really be a "moderate Muslim" in this view because such a position must necessarily be a deception to trick the innocent and unwary. However, this sense of suspicion about Muslims goes much further. Recent polls in the United States have suggested that almost one in five Americans thinks that Barack Obama is really a Muslim. The close connection between this idea and a disapproval of Obama's actions is also there: a good proportion of those who think Obama is a Muslim disapprove of his actions as President and, further, a good number think that his actions are influenced by his religious beliefs. One obvious, but rarely enunciated, riposte to such sentiments was provided by the American former Secretary of State under George W. Bush, General Colin Powell, who said in an interview:

> I'm troubled by . . . what members of the [Republican] party say. And it is permitted to be said such things as "Well, you know that Mr. Obama is a Muslim." Well, the correct answer is, he is not a Muslim, he's a Christian. He's always been a Christian. But the really right answer is, what if he is? Is there something wrong with being a Muslim in this country? The answer's no, that's not America. Is there something wrong with some seven-year-old Muslim-American kid believing that he or she could be president? Yes, I have heard senior members of my own party drop the suggestion, "He's a Muslim and he might be associated [with] terrorists." This is not the way we should be doing it in America.
>
> (Powell 2008)

However, that sort of reasoned response is no match for prejudice. The motif of "hiding one's religion" resounds strongly and links to a sense that Muslims cannot be trusted. It is doubtful that the general public has any knowledge of the formative Shīʿī concept of *taqiyya*, "dissimulation," that allows for one's status as a Shīʿī to be denied in the face of dangers posed by the Sunnī majority to Shiʿites. That word is sometimes invoked, however, especially on some polemical websites when they wish to convey the idea that underneath all Muslim beliefs is a secretly held doctrine which must manifest itself at some point: *jihād*.

In no instance has this accusation of treachery been more pronounced than in the case of Tariq Ramadan. A Swiss citizen, Muslim academic, and champion of moderate Islam, Ramadan is often associated in a negative way with his grandfather, Ḥasan al-Bannāʾ (1906–49), the founding figurehead of the Muslim Brotherhood in Egypt. This ancestry has brought the accusation upon Ramadan that he shares the supposed goals of the Brotherhood and wishes to establish a community of Muslims in Europe so that he may then champion the return of the caliphate and the imposition of Islamic law. These charges are all couched in the underlying theme of deception. The suggestion is made that apparently "moderate" Muslims such as Ramadan are the greatest threat to the values of Europe and North America (and increasingly places such as Australia and New Zealand) because of the way they have lured "liberals" to support their Muslim aspirations. Such rhetoric usually does become mired in the right-wing/left-wing dichotomy. What such accusations miss is the sense of Ramadan as a pragmatist whose audience consists of the Muslims of Europe and elsewhere, for whom he is struggling to assure a positive future which will see them reap the benefits of European citizenship while maintaining their religious identity. Ramadan knows that the greatest threats facing Muslims are twin: the forces of secularism—which he feels leave people adrift and valueless—and the forces of puritanical religion that wish to reject any participation in civil society. To maintain his credibility, Ramadan takes a pragmatic approach that sees Islam in Europe evolving over time to arrive at a new enunciation that will allow full participation in liberal, democratic societies; he cannot simply announce a radical platform and expect people to follow along, not with such strong forces opposing him. In one of the most contentious of issues, despite Ramadan's focus on justice (along with the individual's dignity, integrity, autonomy, development, education, intelligence, welfare, health, and inner balance) as the driving principle of Islam, he did condemn the Quranically prescribed punishments for crimes (*ḥudūd*) that grab the attention of those who express anti-Islamic sentiment. For Ramadan to say absolutely that such laws did not apply anymore, when they are clearly stated in the Qurʾān, would result in his marginalization as a reformist figure in the eyes of many Muslims. Rather, his call for a moratorium on the implementation of such laws was based on a notion of the gradually evolving nature of Muslim society (as witnessed by the changes that Islamic law has undergone in the past in elements such as the abolition of slavery and the domination of monogamy) that will allow for integration into civil society as a whole. According to Ramadan, Muslims should hold to the ultimate value of Islam—that being justice—rather than take a literal approach to the Qurʾān, thinking that such an approach is the best way to manifest their faith, yet, in doing so, creating more injustices in the world. "This is plain injustice," he said in an interview. "Yes, we have texts dealing with capital punishment, corporal punishment and stoning. But what are the conditions and the context? It is so important now that we have these discussions about the injustices done in our name. In the name of Islam we have to stop" (Ramadan 2007). Overall the approach of Ramadan needs to be recognized as a challenge to the truly conservative and radical elements in Muslim society, even though his position may not mesh fully with the current values of liberal society. What Ramadan stands for, in the words of one commentator, is the best solution for finding a way to stop the growth of extremism:

> The most helpful strategic victory in the struggle against Islamic radicalism would be to undermine the narrative that the West is at war with Islam. . . . Muslim communities are more likely to reject such extremists when they do not feel that their faith is being attacked as fascist [or deceitful, one might add] or that they can only be accepted if they embrace Israel and the policy preferences of American conservatives.
>
> (Lynch 2010: 147)

Ramadan's message, however, is often critiqued not for its substance but for what commentators believe he "must" believe "deep down." The insidious nature of such accusations is found in the fact that there is no way to argue against them except from the comfort of historical reflection based upon the record of performance.

The Muslim conception of Islam

The question which must be brought to the forefront at this point is one of the impact this context of outside perceptions of Islam has on Muslims and their own conceptions of Islam. There is no doubt that many Muslims in Europe and North America have found the beginning of the twenty-first century a difficult time to manifest their faith in public. Yet, at the same time, there has been an increased emphasis upon visible manifestations of the faith in ways that have become stereotypical, such as beards and veiling. Notably, surveys in the United States in the mid–1980s revealed that few young Muslim women wore the *ḥijāb*; however, since the early 1990s, veiling has become a much more visual marker among Muslims. Many factors have been isolated as to why this has happened. The success of multiculturalism has made it possible for individuals to manifest their own identity; there has been an increased awareness of that fact among Muslims themselves, and this has allowed for a political attitude that allows and even encourages assertion of identity. But most insightful of all, especially in the context of this chapter, is the following as conveyed by the analysis of Syed Ali, who speaks of the situation in today's United States post-September 11, 2001:

> One result of these events has been self-evaluation on the part of Muslims in America. They ask themselves what it means to be Muslim, and if, indeed, they are Muslims in any meaningful way. A suburban New York City imam whom I interviewed in 1999 put it this way: "In times of crisis, you need to define yourself. In times of dormancy, you can be complacent." The first Gulf War, in his estimation, while having a negative impact initially for Muslims in the U.S., was overall not a bad thing for Islam in the U.S. He said, "The Gulf War exposed Americans to Islam. People started asking about Islam, and Muslims attempted to define Islam themselves."
>
> (Ali 2005: 524)

One further conclusion may be drawn from these observations. As sociologists have frequently commented, the increased ostracism faced, and antagonism felt, by a group often favors the increased sense of communal identity among those people. The further such antagonism goes, the deeper the sense of the need to find a solid identity within

Figure 17.1 Local and national leaders of Muslim organizations hold a press conference in September 2010 in front of the proposed site of the Park51 community centre (which would incorporate a mosque within it) in downtown New York City, near the site of the September 11, 2001, destruction. The group expressed its support for the building project and stated, "We stand for the constitutional right of Muslims and Americans of all faiths to build houses of worship anywhere in our nation as allowed by local laws and regulations." Source: Getty Images.

one's own social grouping. For some of those people, this goes so deep as to push them into extremism. For others, the vast majority, it leads to a renewed expression of faith, although finding the mode and manner for the expression of that faith continues to be a vital topic of Muslim debate.

The *ḥalāl* foods controversy

In September of 2010, the *Daily Mail* of London ran a story which exposed the serving of meat at "some of Britain's most popular sporting venues, pubs, schools and hospitals" that had been slaughtered according to Muslim ritual practices. The objection was raised that this was being done "without the public's knowledge." Follow-up stories also indicated that supermarkets were selling such meat without indicating the slaughtering background. This was presented as an issue because of lingering doubts about the humaneness of such ritual practices, a longstanding debate in the United Kingdom, where pre-stunning of animals is required by law in abattoirs unless there are religious reasons for following other butchering practices (and thus allowing for kosher and *ḥalāl* procedures). This concern is an inconsistent one on the part of consumers, just as is the concern for animal welfare in general. The condition in which the animals intended for human consumption are raised is far less frequently commented on as a matter of concern. The slaughtering procedure, when seen in this overall context, is just the final stage of a long and cruel process of factory farming.

On the surface, the issue seems to be related to an Islamophobic concern over the creeping "Islamicization" of Europe. Some have suggested, however, that this concern should also be viewed within the context of more generalized concerns regarding knowledge of the source of one's food. The "mad cow disease" scares of 1996 and onwards make the ambiguity over the source of one's food a very real worry for many.

The fact that much available meat is slaughtered according to Muslim ritual practice is a reflection of the globalized food market of today. It is reported that 70 percent of New Zealand lamb imported into Britain and 20 percent of the overall exports of Canadian beef are slaughtered in this way, because a major export market for meat in general is the Muslim world. It thus becomes primarily a matter of economics that drives the facts: given the quantity of meat that is produced this way, it simply becomes cheaper.

This "exposé" of slaughtering practices is just one element in the ongoing public debate concerning the presence of Muslims in Europe and North America. French controversies concerning some branches of the popular hamburger chain Quick using *ḥalāl* beef and turkey meat arose in 2009. The mayor of Roubaix was reported to have launched a legal complaint about "prejudicial religious catering," calling the offering discrimination against non-Muslim customers. In England, also during 2009, some outlets of KFC declared themselves to be serving only *ḥalāl* products (catering to local market demands). A media story that emerged in March 2010 (again in the *Daily Mail*) spoke of a man who was "left fuming" that he could not get bacon on his chicken burger; he found this "extremely unfair" because he did not want to have certain eating preferences forced upon him.

The concern about the spread of Islamic food practices has also been felt in the United States. Robert Spencer, an avid writer of anti-Muslim works, used his jihadwatch.org website to alert his readers to the news that Campbell Soups in Canada was going to be producing *ḥalāl* soups. Spencer focused on the *ḥalāl* certification being provided by the Islamic Society of North America, which he accused of having ties to Hamas and the Muslim Brotherhood (that being a frequent polemical motif in the United States). This resulted in a Facebook group calling for a boycott of Campbell Soups. Three thousand people signed up within two weeks.

Food—like the *ḥijāb*—provides both a symbol of Muslim identity and a target for those who express their fear of Islam in terms of the imposition of *sharīʿa* law on the non-Muslim world.

The section "Animal Rights and Ritual Slaughter" (pp. 117–22), in Jytte Klausen, *The Islamic Challenge: Politics and Religion in Western Europe*, Oxford: Oxford University Press, 2005, provides some helpful background to this overall issue. For a broad view of the economic and political issues, see Florence Bergeaud-Blackler, "New Challenges for Islamic Ritual Slaughter: A European Perspective," *Journal of Ethnic & Migration Studies*, 33 (2007): 965–80.

Selected further reading

Chris Allen, *Islamophobia*, Farnham: Ashgate Publishing, 2010.

John L. Esposito and Ibrahim Kalim (eds.), *Islamophobia: The Challenge of Pluralism in the 21st Century*, Oxford, New York, Oxford University Press, 2011.

Ron Geaves, Theodore Gabriel, Yvonne Haddad, and Jane Idleman Smith (eds.), *Islam & the West Post 9/11*, Aldershot: Ashgate, 2004.

Jytte Klausen, *The Islamic Challenge: Politics and Religion in Western Europe*, Oxford, Oxford University Press, 2005.

Tariq Ramadan, *Western Muslims and the Future of Islam*, Oxford, Oxford University Press, 2004.

Glossary

ʿAbbāsids dynasty of caliphs ruling from 750, through the era of the flowering of Islam, and coming to a final end in 1258, although it had lost any meaningful power several centuries earlier with the rise of the Buwayhids.

adab "morals" or "courtesy"; the habitual way of acting in accordance with social standards.

adhān the call to prayer.

Allāh Arabic for God.

amīr commander or prince, frequently used in reference to the person who leads the community.

āya verse of the Qurʾān; also used in a general meaning of "sign" from God.

baqāʾ Ṣūfī term for the mystic's "continuance" of existence with God.

basmala the statement at the beginning of each *sūra* of the Qur'an (except *sūra* 9), "In the name of God, the Merciful, the Compassionate," also used by Muslims as an invocation.

Burāq the winged creature which carried Muḥammad on his "night journey" (*isrāʾ*) from Mecca to Jerusalem.

Buwayhids dynasty of Shīʿī Persian military rulers who took over rule in 945 and which lasted until the takeover by the Sunnī Seljuq rulers in 1055 (also spelled Būyids).

dhikr "mentioning" or "remembrance"; term used for the chant in Ṣūfī meditations.

dhimmī a member of a protected community, especially referring to the Jews and Christians who live under Muslim rule. The right to practise their own religion was guaranteed by their payment of a special poll tax, the *jizya*.

dīn religion; the word is used in the Qurʾān to refer to the specific beliefs and practices of people.

duʿāʾ "calling" upon God, used for informal prayer and supplication, as compared to *ṣalāt*.

fanāʾ Ṣūfī term for the "passing away" or absorption of the individual into God.

fātiḥa "opening," the first *sūra* of the Qurʾān, used especially in prayer.

fatwā a legal decision rendered by a *muftī*, who is a jurist qualified to make decisions of a general religious nature.

fiqh jurisprudence, the science of religious law, as described by the jurists known as the *fuqahā*ʾ (of which the singular is *faqīh*).

ghayba "occultation" of the last Imām in the Shīʿī tradition.

ghusl major ablution, requiring a full washing.

ḥadd the restrictive ordinances of God as stated in the Qurʾān, all of which have a specific penalty involved for their violation.

ḥadīth a tradition or written report, being the source material for the *sunna* of Muḥ ammad, gathered together in the six books of authoritative traditions in Sunnī Islam.

ḥajj pilgrimage to Mecca performed in the month of Dhū ʾl-ḥijja, one of the "Five Pillars" of Islam; a requirement for all Muslims, if they are able, once in a lifetime.

Ḥanābila the Sunnī school of law (the "Ḥanbalī school") named after Aḥmad ibn Ḥanbal (d. 855).

Ḥanafiyya the Sunnī school of law named after Abū Ḥanīfa (d. 767), the "Ḥanafī school."

ḥanīf the attribute, especially ascribed to Abraham in the Qurʾān, of being a sincere believer in God.

ḥijāb the veil or partition which prevents men from gazing at the "charms of women." A variety of styles exist but most emphasize covering the hair and hiding the shape of the body.

Ḥijāz region in the west of Central Arabia, the birthplace of Muḥammad.

hijra Muḥammad's emigration from Mecca to Medina in the year 622 CE, understood as the date for the beginning of the Muslim *hijrī* calendar.

iḥrām the state of consecration into which the pilgrim enters (thus becoming a *muḥ rim*) in order to perform the *ḥajj* or the ʿ*umra*.

iʿjāz doctrine which states that the Qurʾān cannot be imitated; the "inimitability" of the Qurʾān.

ijmāʿ "consensus," one of the four sources of law in Sunnī Islam, the others being Qurʾān, *sunna*, and *qiyās*.

ijtihād the use of one's "personal effort" in order to make a decision on a point of law not explicitly covered by the Qurʾān or the *sunna*; the person with the authority to do this is called a *mujtahid*.

imām literally, the "model," here generally referring to the prayer leader in the *ṣalāt* who stands in front of the rows of worshippers, keeping their actions in unison during the prayer. The word is also used in other contexts. It is a title of the revered early leaders of the Shīʿa who are the source of authority in that community; these Imāms are ʿAlī ibn abī Ṭālib and certain of his descendants who were designated as holding the position. The word is also commonly used as a title of the founders of the Sunnī schools of law—Abū Ḥanīfa, Mālik ibn Anas, al-Shāfiʿī, and Ibn Ḥanbal—and similarly for other significant religious figures.

Imāmī generic name given to the largest group of the Shīʿa, the Ithnā ʿAshariyya.

īmān faith; one who has faith is a *muʾmin*.

iṣlāḥ "reformism," especially in the nineteenth-century Arab world as proposed by people such as Muḥammad ʿAbduh.

Islam the name of the religion preached by Muḥammad, so named in the Qurʾān, literally meaning "submission"; those who adhere to Islam are called Muslims.

Islamist a contemporary movement among Muslims which emphasizes a "return" to the Qurʾān and *sunna* as the basis of a revival of Islam, with an emphasis on Islam as the political basis of society; often called "fundamentalist."

ʿiṣma a doctrine which states that the prophets, and especially Muḥammad, were protected from sin (*maʿṣūm*) during their lifetimes. It is also applied to the Shīʿī Imāms.

isnād the chain of authorities through whom a *ḥadīth* report has passed; the list of these people forms the first part of the *ḥadīth* report, the text which comes after it being called the *matn*.

isrāʾ Muḥammad's "night journey" to Jerusalem, connected to the heavenly ascension, *miʿrāj*.

jāhiliyya the "Age of Ignorance," historically seen to be before Muḥammad but in a general religious sense referring to ignoring, or ignorance of, Islam; especially used with moral overtones.

jihād "striving for the faith" or "holy war," sometimes seen as a "sixth pillar" of Islam.

jinn genies, another dimension of animate creation on earth.

jumʿa in reference to prayer, *ṣalāt*; it is the Friday noon gathering of the community which is enjoined in the Qurʾān and which takes place in the *jāmiʿ* or congregational mosque.

Kaʿba the sacred black cube building in the middle of the mosque in Mecca; Muslims face in the direction of the Kaʿba when they perform the ritual prayer (*ṣalāt*) and circumambulate it when they perform the pilgrimage (*ḥajj* or *ʿumra*).

kalām literally, "speech"; refers to a mode of theological discussion framed in terms of an argument and thence to speculative theology as a whole.

khalīfa Caliph, the leader of the Sunnī community, the "successor" to Muḥammad.

khaṭīb the person at the Friday noon prayer who delivers the address, the *khuṭba*.

Khawārij group in early Islam who believed in absolute devotion as the mark of a true Muslim, all others being unbelievers (singular: Khārijī; also known as the Kharijites)

khuṭba the address given at the Friday noon prayer by the *khaṭīb*.

madhhab a school of law formed around one of the four early figures significant in juristic discussions (Abū Ḥanīfa, Mālik ibn Anas, al-Shāfiʿī, Ibn Ḥanbal) (plural: *madhāhib*).

Mālikiyya followers of the legal school named after Mālik ibn Anas (d. 795).

maʿrifa mystical knowledge.

maṣlaḥa "general good" and "public interest," used as a basis for legal decisions.

matn the text of a *ḥadīth* report, as compared to the *isnād*, the chain of transmission.

mawlid birthday; specifically the celebration of the birthday of Muḥammad.

miḥna the "inquisition," primarily under the ʿAbbāsid caliph al-Maʾmūn (ruled 813–33), which demanded that government officials and religious leaders adhere to the doctrine of the "created Qurʾān."

miḥrāb the niche in the wall of a mosque marking the *qibla*, or direction of prayer towards Mecca.

minbar the "pulpit" on which the *khaṭīb* gives the address (*khuṭba*).

miʿrāj the "heavenly ascension" of Muḥammad, reported to have taken place around the year 6 of the *hijra*, in which he met with the prophets of the past, was given visions of heaven and hell, gazed upon God, and was given the command of five prayers a day for all Muslims.

Modernist a contemporary movement among Muslims which emphasizes the need to reform Islam in keeping with modern times; they frequently emphasize the personal and rational nature of religion as a way of accommodating change.

muftī a jurist who is authorized to give a *fatwā* or legal decision on a religious matter.

mujaddid a renewer of the faith, stated in a *ḥadīth* report to appear in the Muslim community every 100 years, in order to revive the true spirit of Islam through the process of *tajdīd*, "renewal."

mujtahid a jurist who is qualified to exercise *ijtihād* or personal effort in making legal decisions on matters where there is no explicit text of the Qurʾān or the *sunna* to be followed.

Murjiʾa group in early Islam who held the *status quo* position in the debates over faith, of generally connected to Abū Ḥanīfa (d. 767).

Muslim a person who follows the Islamic religion.

Muʿtazila a theological school of thought which blossomed in the eighth and ninth centuries; it stressed human free will and the unity and justice of God, and embraced Greek rationalist modes of argumentation. In modern times, certain thinkers (e.g. Muḥammad ʿAbduh) are sometimes considered "neo-Muʿtazilī" because of their reintroduction of some of these ideas.

nahḍa the renaissance of the Muslim world in general that was pictured by reformers as resulting from the cultural renewal which would take place in modern times.

Orientalist basically those who study the Orient, specifically meaning Europeans (and in more recent time North Americans) who have studied Islam. The connection of such people to Christian missionizing and to colonial ruling powers has led to the term having negative connotations, especially in the wake of the analysis of Edward Said,

Orientalism (New York: Pantheon Books, 1978), which argued that the Orientalist's perception of Islam was structured by the fundamental power relationship between the Islamic world and the colonial rulers.

purdah a term from India referring to seclusion and veiling of women; the same as *ḥijāb*.

qadar preordination of events by God.

Qadariyya group in early Islam who argued for free will in the theological debates, precursors of the Muʿtazila.

qāḍī a judge who makes decisions on the basis of the religious law.

qibla the direction in which one faces in prayer (Mecca), marked by the *miḥrāb* in the mosque.

qiyās "analogy," one of the four sources of law in Sunnī Islam, the others being Qurʾān, *sunna*, and *ijmāʿ*.

rakʿa cycle of postures through which a person goes in performing the *ṣalāt*: standing, bowing, prostrating, sitting.

ṣadaqa charity, often used interchangeably with *zakāt*, but also with the sense of free-will offering rather than a required donation.

salaf the "pious ancestors," the first three generations of Muslims, who some modern Islamists (also known as Salafis) hold up as embodying the ideal manifestation of Islam.

ṣalāt the prescribed five prayers a day, one the "Five Pillars" required of all Muslims.

ṣawm fasting performed in the month of Ramaḍān, one of the "Five Pillars" required of all Muslims (also called *ṣiyām*).

Shāfiʿiyya followers of the school of law named after al-Shāfiʿī (d. 820).

shahāda "witness to faith"; saying (in Arabic), "There is no god but God and Muḥammad is His messenger"; one of the "Five Pillars" required of all Muslims, indicating conversion to Islam but also a part of the ritual prayer (*ṣalāt*).

sharīʿa the religious law derived from the four sources of law in Sunnī Islam (Qurʾān, *sunna*, *qiyās*, and *ijmāʿ*).

shaykh literally, "an old man" and used as a term of respect for a religious teacher; used especially of a Ṣūfī master.

Shīʿa the religio-political party championing the claims of ʿAlī ibn abī Ṭālib and his heirs to the rightful leadership of the community and to their status as Imāms; since the beginning of the sixteenth century, the Shīʿī position has been the official state religion of Iran and most of its followers live there. They comprise about 10 percent of the world population of Muslims.

shūrā "consultation," a concept to which Islamists frequently appeal when speaking of Islamic ways of structuring governments.

silsila the Ṣūfī "chain" of authority which traces spiritual lineage.

Sīra the biography of Muḥammad as found in written form.

Ṣūfī an adherent to the mystical way of Islam, Sufism, *taṣawwuf*.

sunna "custom"; the way Muḥammad acted, which is then emulated by Muslims. The source material for the *sunna* is found in the *ḥadīth* reports. The *sunna* is one of the four sources of law for Sunnī Islam, along with Qurʾān, *qiyās*, and *ijmāʿ*.

Sunnīs the majority form of Islam, those who follow the *sunna* (thus being called the *ahl al-sunna*), who do not recognize the authority of the Shīʿī Imāms.

sūra a chapter of the Qurʾān.

tafsīr interpretation of the Qurʾān, especially as found in written form. Such books generally follow the order of the Quranic text and pay attention to the meaning of each word or sentence.

taqiyya doctrine in Shiʿism that allows "dissimulation," that is, denying one's Shīʿī allegiances and not performing outward manifestations of one's faith in order to protect one's life.

taqlīd the reliance upon decisions made in the past in matters of religious law; the word is set in opposition to *ijtihād*, "personal effort," and frequently has a negative sense in the modern context.

ṭarīqa "the way" of Sufism; a Ṣūfī order or brotherhood.

taṣawwuf Sufism, the mystical way in Islam.

ṭawāf the ritual of the circumambulation of the Kaʿba during the pilgrimage.

tawakkul "trust" in God, especially among the Ṣūfīs.

tawḥīd doctrine holding to the proclamation of the unity of God.

Traditionalists term used primarily for the followers of Ibn Ḥanbal (d. 855), who rejected the claims of rationalism especially in early theological discussions. The inheritors of that position in modern times may follow any legal school but maintain an attitude of adherence to the legal (and religious) decisions of the past.

ʿulamāʾ the learned class, especially those learned in religious matters (singular: *ʿālim*).

Umayyads the first dynasty of caliphs, ruling from 661 until the takeover of the ʿAbbāsids in 750.

umma the community; the body of Muslims.

ʿumra the "visitation" of the holy places in Mecca, the lesser pilgrimage; it can be performed at any time of the year but is also joined with the *ḥajj*.

Wahhābiyya the followers of Ibn ʿAbd al-Wahhāb (d. 1787); a revivalist-purificatory movement in Arabia which became (and continues to be) the official religious policy of Saudi Arabia, now often called the Salafiyya.

wilāya position of ʿAlī as the "friend" (*walī*) of God.

wuḍūʾ minor ablution required prior to some ritual performances.

zakāt alms tax, one of the "Five Pillars" required of all Muslims.

References

Abdel-Kader, Ali Hassan (1976) *The Life, Personality and Writings of al-Junayd*, London: Luzac.

Adams, Charles J. (1976) "The Authority of the Prophetic Ḥadīth in the Eyes of Some Modern Muslims," in Donald P. Little (ed.), *Essays on Islamic Civilization presented to Niyazi Berkes*, Leiden: Brill, pp. 25–47.

Ahmad, Aziz (1967) *Islamic Modernism in India and Pakistan 1857–1964*, London: Oxford University Press.

Akhtar, Shabbir (1990) *A Faith for All Seasons. Islam and Western Modernity*, London: Bellew.

— (1997) "Ex-defender of the Faith," *Times Higher Education Supplement*, August 22: 15.

Alam, Miss Shaista Aziz (1990) "Purdah and the Qur'ān," *Hamdard Islamicus*, 13: 77–90.

ʿAlī, Maulānā Muḥammad (1950) *The Religion of Islām: A Comprehensive Discussion of the Sources, Principles and Practices of Islām*, 2nd edition, Lahore: Aḥmadiyya Anjuman Ishāʿat Islām (first published 1935).

Ali, Syed (2005) "Why Here, Why Now? Young Muslim Women Wearing *Ḥijab*," *The Muslim World*, 95: 515–30.

Allen, Chris (2010) *Islamophobia*, Farnham: Ashgate Publishing.

Antoun, Richard (1989) *Muslim Preacher in the Modern World. A Jordanian Case Study in Comparative Perspective*, Princeton: Princeton University Press.

Arkoun, Mohammed (1979) "The Death Penalty and Torture in Islamic Thought," *Concilium*, 120: 75–82.

Ashʿarī, Abū ʾl-Ḥasan ʿAlī ibn Ismāʿīl al- (1940) *Abu ʾl-Ḥasan ʿAlī ibn Ismāʿīl al-Aśʿarī's al-Ibānah ʿan Uṣūl ad-Diyānah (The Elucidation of Islām's Foundation)*, Walter C. Klein (trans.), New Haven, CT: American Oriental Society.

— (1953) *The Theology of al-Ashʿarī* (al-Ashʿarī's *Kitāb al-Lumaʿ*), Richard J. McCarthy (trans.), Beirut: Imprimerie Catholique.

Azzām, ʿAbd al-Raḥmān (1965) *The Eternal Message of Muḥammad*, New York: Mentor Books.

Badawi, Zaki (1999) "Zakat: A New Source of Development Finance?" *Q News: A Muslim Magazine*, 310 (August): 32.

Baghdādī, ʿAbd al-Qāhir al- (1928) *Kitāb Uṣūl al-Din*, Istanbul: Dār al-Funūn al-Tūrkiyya.

— (1987) *Kitāb al-Nāsikh wa'l-Mansūkh*, Ḥilmī Kāmil Asʿad ʿAbd al-Hādī (ed.), Amman: Dār al-ʿAdawī.

Baljon, J. M. S. (1958) "Pakistani Views of Ḥadīth," *Die Welt des Islams*, NS 5: 219–27.

Berger, Morroe (1970) *Islam in Egypt Today: Social and Political Aspects of Popular Religion*, Cambridge: Cambridge University Press.

Berger, Peter (1977) *Facing Up to Modernity: Excursions in Society, Politics, and Religion*, New York: Basic Books.

Brown, Daniel (1999) "Islamic Ethics in Comparative Perspective," *The Muslim World*, 89: 181–92.

Bukhārī, al- (1984) *al-Ṣaḥīḥ, Kitāb Faḍā'il al-Qur'ān*, Muḥammad Muḥsin Khān (ed. and trans.), 5th edition, New Delhi: Kitab Bhavan.

Burton, John (1987) *Abū ʿUbaid al-Qāsim b. Sallām's K. al-Nāsikh wa-l-Mansūkh, Edited with a Commentary*, Cambridge: E. J. W. Gibb Memorial Trust.

Calder, Norman (1993) "Tafsīr from Ṭabarī to Ibn Kathīr. Problems in the Description of a Genre Illustrated with Reference to the Story of Abraham," in G. R. Hawting and A.-K. A. Shareef, *Approaches to the Qur'ān*, London: Routledge, pp. 101–40; reprinted in his *Interpretation and Jurisprudence in Medieval Islam*, Aldershot: Ashgate/Variorum, 2006, chapter IV.

Christmann, Andreas (2009) *The Qur'an, Morality and Critical Reason: The Essential Muhammad Shahrur*, Leiden: Brill.

Conrad, Lawrence I. (1995) "The Arab-Islamic Medical Tradition," in L. I. Conrad et al., *The Western Medical Tradition, 800 BC to AD 1800*, Cambridge: Cambridge University Press, pp. 93–138.

Coulson, N. J. (1964) *A History of Islamic Law*, Edinburgh: Edinburgh University Press.

Cox, Harvey (1984) *Religion in the Secular City: Toward a Postmodern Theology*, New York: Simon and Schuster.

Cragg, Kenneth (1985) *The Pen and the Faith: Eight Modern Muslim Writers and the Qur'ān*, London: George Allen and Unwin.

Cragg, Kenneth, and Speight, Marston (1980) *Islam from Within: Anthology of a Religion*, Belmont, CA: Wadsworth Publishing.

Dashti, Ali (1985) *Twenty Three Years: A Study of the Prophetic Career of Mohammad*, F. R. C. Bagley (trans.), London: George Allen and Unwin.

Dols, Michael (1977) *The Black Death in the Middle East*, Princeton: Princeton University Press.

Fakhry, Majid (1997) *A Short Introduction to Islamic Philosophy, Theology and Mysticism*, Oxford: Oneworld.

Faruqi, I. H. Azad (1982) *The Tarjuman al-Qur'an: A Critical Analysis of Mawlana Abu'l-Kalam Azad's Approach to the Understanding of the Qur'an*, New Delhi: Vikas Publishing.

Fischer, Michael M. J., and Abedi, Mehdi (1990) *Debating Muslims: Cultural Dialogues in Postmodernity and Tradition*, Madison: University of Wisconsin Press.

Fisher, Mary Pat, and Luyster, Robert (1991) *Living Religions*, Englewood Cliffs, NJ: Prentice Hall.

Gätje, Helmut (1976) *The Qur'ān and Its Exegesis: Selected Texts with Classical and Modern Muslim Interpretations*, Berkeley: University of California Press.

Geertz, Clifford (1968) *Islam Observed: Religious Development in Morocco and Indonesia*, New Haven, CT: Yale University Press.

Ghazālī, Abū Ḥamīd al- (1965) *Iḥyā' 'Ulūm al-Dīn*, Cairo: al-Maktaba al-Tijāra al-Kubrā.

Graham, William (1983) "Islam in the Mirror of Ritual," in Richard G. Hovannisian and Speros Vryonis Jr. (eds.), *Islam's Understanding of Itself*, Malibu, CA: Undena Publications, pp. 53–71.

Gülen, Fethullah (2001) "A Comparative Approach to Islam and Democracy" (available online at http://www.fgulen.org/recent-articles/1027-a-comparative-approach-to-islam-and-democracy.html).

Gutas, Dimitri (1998) *Greek Thought, Arabic Culture: The Graeco-Arabic Translation Movement in Baghdad and Early 'Abbāsid Society (2nd–4th/8th–10th Centuries)*, London: Routledge.

Haddad, Yvonne Y. (1982) *Contemporary Islam and the Challenge of History*, Albany: State University of New York Press.

Halliday, Fred (1999) " 'Islamophobia' Reconsidered," *Ethnic and Racial Studies*, 22/5: 892–902.

Haykal, Muḥammad Ḥusayn (1976) *The Life of Muḥammad*, Isma'il Ragi A. al Faruqi (trans.), Indianapolis, IN: North American Trust Publications.

Hodgson, M. G. S. (1974) *The Venture of Islam: Conscience and History in a World Civilization, vol. 3: The Gunpowder Empires and Modern Times*, Chicago: University of Chicago Press.

Hoffman-Ladd, Valerie J. (1987) "Polemics on the Modesty and Segregation of Women in Contemporary Egypt," *International Journal of Middle East Studies*, 19: 23–50.

Hong Kong Muslim Herald (1991) "The True Religious Value of Daily Prayers," *Hong Kong Muslim Herald*, 14(5) (Rabi-Thani 1412 AH [October]): 2–2 [*sic*].

Hourani, Albert (1983) *Arabic Thought in the Liberal Age 1798–1939*, 2nd edition, Cambridge: Cambridge University Press.

Husain, Ashfaque (1960) *The Quintessence of Islam: A Summary of the Commentary of Maulana Abul Kalam Azad on al-Fateha, the First Chapter of the Quran*, Bombay: Asia Publishing House.

Ibn ʿAbd al-Wahhāb (1977) *Muʾallafāt al-Shaykh al-Imām Muḥammad ibn ʿAbd al-Wahhāb*, Riyadh: Jāmiʿat al-Imām Muḥammad ibn Saʿūd al-Islāmiyya.

Ibn Bābawayh (1942) *A Shīʿī Creed. A Translation of Risālatu ʾl-Iʿtiqadāt*, A. A. A. Fyzee (trans.), Oxford: Oxford University Press.

Ibn Ḥanbal (1976) *Kitāb al-zuhd*, Beirut: Dar al-kutub al-ʿilmiyya.

Ibn Hishām (1955) *al-Sīra al-Nabawiyya*, Muṣṭafā al-Saqā *et al.* (eds.), Cairo: Ḥalabī.

Ibn al-Kalbī (1941) *Kitāb al-Aṣnām*, R. Klinke-Rosenberger (ed.), Leipzig: Otto Harrassowitz.

Ibn Taymiyya (1978) *Muqaddima fī Uṣūl al-Tafsīr*, in his *Daqāʾiq al-Tafsīr*, Muḥammad Jalaynad (ed.), Cairo: Dār al-Anṣār.

Ibn Warraq (pseudo.) (1995) *Why I Am Not a Muslim*, Amherst, NY: Prometheus Books.

Johns, A. H. (1990) "Let My People Go! Sayyid Qutb and the Vocation of Moses," *Islam and Christian–Muslim Relations*, 1: 143–70.

Khayyāṭ, Abū ʾl-Ḥusayn b. ʿUthmān al- (1957) *Kitāb al-intiṣār: Le Livre du triomphe et de la refutation d'Ibn Rawandī l'hérétique par Abū al-Ḥusayn b. ʿOthmān al-Khayyāṭ le Muʿtazil*, A. N. Nader (ed. and trans.), Beirut: Editions les Lettres Orientales.

Khomeini, Ayatollah (1985) "Hajj and the Ummah's Modern International Relations," in Kalim Siddiqui (ed.), *Issues in the Islamic Movement 1983–84*, London, Open Press, pp. 98–9.

Kindī (1887) *The Apology of al-Kindy, Written at the Court of al-Mâmûn (Circa A. H. 215; A. D. 830) in Defence of Christianity against Islam*, William Muir (ed. and trans.), 2nd edition, London: Society for Promoting Christian Knowledge.

Krentz, Edgar (1975) *The Historical-Critical Method*, Philadelphia: Fortress Press.

Lazarus-Yafeh, Hava (1981) *Some Religious Aspects of Islam: A Collection of Articles*, Leiden: Brill.

Loeffler, Reinhold (1988) *Islam in Practice: Religious Beliefs in a Persian Village*, Albany: State University of New York Press.

Lynch, Mark (2010) "Veiled Truths: The Rise of Political Islam in the West," *Foreign Affairs*, 89(4): 138–47.

McDermott, Martin J. (1978) *The Theology of al-Shaykh al-Mufīd (d. 413/1022)*, Beirut: Dar el-Machreq.

McDonough, Sheila (1970) *The Authority of the Past: A Study of Three Muslim Modernists*, Chambersburg, PA: American Academy of Religion.

Manzoor, Parvez (2002) "Against the Nihilism of Terror: Jihad as Testimony to Transcendence," *Muslim World Book Review*, 22/3 (April–June): 5–14 (available online at http://www.algonet.se/~pmanzoor/jihad-mwbr.htm).

Marghinānī, al- (1975) *al-Hidāya: Sharḥ Bidāyat al-Mubtadi'*, vol. 1, Cairo: Ḥalabī.

Mawdudi, Sayyid Abul A'la (1985) *Let Us Be Muslims*, Khurram Murad (ed. and trans.), Leicester: The Islamic Foundation.

Merad, Ali (1977) "Reformism in Modern Islam," *Cultures*, 4: 108–27.

Mernissi, Fatima (1987) *Beyond the Veil: Male–Female Dynamics in Modern Muslim Society*, revised edition, Bloomington: Indiana University Press.

— (1991) *Women and Islam: An Historical and Theological Enquiry*, Oxford: Basil Blackwell.

Momen, Moojan (1985) *An Introduction to Shi'i Islam*, New Haven, CT: Yale University Press.

Murad, Abdal Hakim (2003) "The Clash of Caricatures," *Islamica Magazine*, 10 (Winter): 6–10.

Muslim ibn al-Ḥajjāj (1955–6) *Ṣaḥīḥ Muslim*, Muḥammad Fu'ād 'Abd al-Bāqī (ed.), Cairo: Dār Iḥyā' al-Kutub al-'Arabiyya.

Nurbaki, Haluk (1986) *Verses from the Glorious Koran and the Facts of Science (V)*, Metin Beynam (trans.), Ankara: Turkish Foundation for Religious Publications.

Pipes, Daniel (2005) "Islamophobia?" *New York Sun*, October 25 (available online at http://www.danielpipes.org/3075/islamophobia).

Powell, Colin (2008) Interview on "Meet the Press," October 19 (available online at http://www.msnbc.msn.com/id/27266223/).

Qurṭubī, al- (1967) *al-Jāmi' li-Aḥkām al-Qur'ān*, Beirut: Dār Iḥyā' al-Turāth al-'Arabī.

Quṭb, Sayyid (1979) *In the Shade of the Qur'ān (Fī Ẓilāl al-Qur'ān)*, vol. 30, M. Adil Saladi and Ashur A. Shamis (trans.), London, MWH London Publishers.

Rahman, Fazlur (1955) "Internal Religious Developments in the Present Century Islam," *Cahiers d'histoire mondiale/Journal of World History*, 2: 862–79.

— (1979a) "Islam: Challenges and Opportunities," in Alford T. Welch and Pierre Cachia (eds.), *Islam: Past Influences and Future Challenges*, Edinburgh: Edinburgh University Press, pp. 315–30.

— (1979b) *Islam*, 2nd edition, Chicago: University of Chicago Press.

— (1980) *Major Themes of the Qur'ān*, Minneapolis: Bibliotheca Islamica.

— (1982) *Islam and Modernity: Transformation of an Intellectual Tradition*, Chicago: University of Chicago Press.

Ramadan, Tariq (2007) "Tariq Ramadan: Do You Trust This Man," interview with Deborah Orr, *Independent*, March 11 (available online at http://www.independent.co.uk/news/people/profiles/tariq-ramadan--do-you-trust-this-man-439564.html).

Rāzī, al- (1848) *A Treatise on the Small-pox and Measles, by Abú Becr Mohammed ibn Zacaríyá ar-Rází (Commonly Called Rhazes)*, William Alexander Greenhill (trans.), London: Sydenham Society.

Reichert, Rolf (1981) "Muslims in the Guyanas: A Socio-economic Overview," *Journal: Institute of Muslim Minority Affairs*, 3(ii): 120–6.

Rifaat, Alifa (1985) *Distant View of a Minaret and Other Stories*, Denys Johnston-Davies (trans.), London: Heinemann.

Rosenthal, Franz (1969) "The Defense of Medicine in the Medieval Muslim World," *Bulletin of the History of Medicine*, 43: 519–32; reprinted in his *Science and Medicine in Islam: A Collection of Essays*, Aldershot: Variorum, 1990, chapter VIII.

Roy, Olivier (2005) "A Clash of Cultures or a Debate on Europe's Values?" *International Institute for the Study of Islam in the Modern World (ISIM) Review*, 15 (Spring): 6–7.

Ruthven, Malise (1990) *A Satanic Affair: Salman Rushdie and the Rage of Islam*, London: Chatto and Windus.

Schacht, Joseph (1950) *The Origins of Muhammadan Jurisprudence*, Oxford: Oxford University Press.

Shāfiʿī, al- (1983) *al-Risāla fī Uṣūl al-Fiqh*, Muḥammad Sayyid Kilānī (ed.), Cairo: Ḥalabī.

Shams al-Dīn, Shaykh Muḥammad Mahdī (1985) *The Rising of al-Ḥusayn: Its Impact on the Consciousness of Muslim Society*, I. K. A. Howard (trans.), London: Muhammadi Trust.

Shepard, William E. (1987) "Islam and Ideology: Towards a Typology," *International, Journal of Middle East Studies*, 19: 307–36.

Sivan, Emmanuel (1985) *Radical Islam: Medieval Theology and Modern Politics*, New Haven, CT: Yale University Press.

Smith, Jane Idleman (ed.) (1979) *The Precious Pearl: A Translation from the Arabic*, Missoula, MT: Scholars Press.

Smith, Margaret (ed. and trans.) (1950) *Readings from the Mystics of Islam*, London: Luzac.

Steyn, Mark (2008) *America Alone: The End of the World as We Know It*, reprint edition, Washington: Regnery Press.

Ṭabarī, al- (1971) *Jāmiʿ al-Bayān ʿan Taʾwīl Āy al-Qurʾān*, Aḥmad and Maḥmūd Shākir (eds.), Cairo: Dār al-Maʿārif.

Tādifī, Muḥammad ibn Yaḥyā al-Ḥanbalī al- (1998) *Necklaces of Gems (Qalāʾid al-Jawāhir) A Biography of the Crown of the Saints Shaikh ʿAbd al-Qadir al-Jilani*, Muhtar Holland (trans.), Hollywood, FL: al-Baz Publishing (available online at http://shaikhsohail.wordpress.com/2009/09/01/necklaces-of-gems-part-8/).

Taylor, Mark C. (1984) *Erring: A Postmodern A/theology*, Chicago: University of Chicago Press.

Tirmidhī, al- (1987) *al-Jāmiʿ al-Ṣaḥīḥ*, Aḥmad Shākir (ed.), Beirut: Dār al-Kutub al-ʿIlmiyya.
Vaïsse, Justin (2010) "Eurabian Follies: The Shoddy and Just Plain Wrong Genre that Refuses to Die," *Foreign Policy*, 177: 86–8.
Wāḥidī, al- (1969) *Kitāb Asbāb al-Nuzūl*, Aḥmad Ṣaqr (ed.), Cairo: Dār al-Kitāb al-Jadīd.
Wansbrough, John (1978) *The Sectarian Milieu: Content and Composition of Islamic Salvation History*, Oxford: Oxford University Press.
Watt, W. Montgomery (trans.) (1963) *The Faith and Practice of al-Ghazali*, Lahore: Sh. Muḥammad Ashraf. (Includes a translation of al-Ghazālī, *Bidāyat al-Hidāya*.)
Waugh, Earle H. (1989) *The Munshidīn of Egypt: Their World and Their Song*, Columbia: University of South Carolina Press.
Wensinck, A. J. (1932) *The Muslim Creed: Its Genesis and Historical Development*, Cambridge: Cambridge University Press.
Williams, John Alden (ed. and trans.) (1963) *Islam*, New York: Washington Square Press.
Yusuf, Hajji Shaykh (1943) "In Defense of the Veil (Charles R. Pittman, trans.)," *The Muslim World*, 33: 203–12.

General index

Note: "al-" is ignored in alphabetizing; all Arabic characters are ordered by English representation.

Index of Qurʾān citations